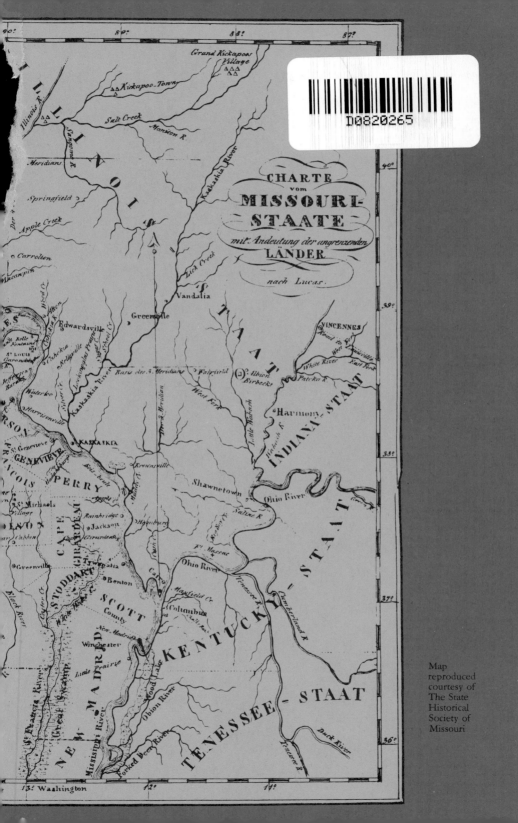

CHARTE vom MISSOURI-STAATE

mit Andeutung der angrenzenden LÄNDER

nach Lucas.

ILLINOIS-STAAT

INDIANA-STAAT

KENTUCKY-STAAT

TENESSEE-STAAT

Grand Kickapoo Village
Kickapoo-Town
Salt Creek
Mamion R.
Kaskaskia River
Meridians
Springfield
Apple Creek
Carrolton
Vandalia
Greenville
Edwardsville
VINCENNES
Fairfield
Albion Birbecks
Basis des 3. Meridians
West Fork
Harmony
St. Genevieve
GENEVIEVE
PERRY
KASKASKIA
Brownsville
Shawnetown
Ohio River
Saline R.
Ft. Massac
Ohio River
Caro
St. Michaels Village
Rainbridge
Jackson
Girardeau
Hamburg
CAPE GIRARDEAU
Greenville
Benton
SCOTT County
STODDART
Columbus
Mansfield Cr.
New Madrid
Winchester
Little Prairie
NEW MADRID
Wood Lake
Mississippi River
Obion River
Forked Deer River
Duck River
Cumberland R.
White River
Patoka R.
East Fork
Little Wabash
Washington

40°
39°
38°
37°
36°
90°
89°
88°
87°
13°
12°
11°

Map reproduced courtesy of The State Historical Society of Missouri

D0820265

6332

35.00
1st

Report on a Journey to the
Western States of North America

Gottfried Duden

Report on a Journey to the Western States of North America

and a Stay of Several Years Along the Missouri (During the Years 1824, '25, '26, and 1827)

Gottfried Duden

An English Translation

James W. Goodrich, General Editor

George H. Kellner, Elsa Nagel, Adolf E. Schroeder, and W. M. Senner Editors and Translators

The State Historical Society of Missouri
and
University of Missouri Press
Columbia & London, 1980

Copyright © 1980 by
The Curators of the University of Missouri
Library of Congress Catalog Card Number 79–3335
Printed and bound in the United States of America
University of Missouri Press, Columbia, Missouri 65211
All rights reserved

Library of Congress Cataloging in Publication Data

Duden, Gottfried.
    Report on a Journey to the Western States of North
America and a stay of several years along the Missouri
(during the years 1824, '25, '26, and 1827).

Translation of Berich über eine Reise nach den
westlichen Staaten Nordamerika's . . .

Includes index.
    1. United States—Description and travel—1783– 1848.
2. Missouri—Description and travel—1783– 1848.
3. Duden, Gottfried. I. Goodrich, James W.
II. Title.
E165.D8413   977.8'03   79– 3335
ISBN 0– 8262– 0295– 0

Foreword

For more than sixty years The State Historical Society of Missouri has had an interest in publishing an edited English translation of Gottfried Duden's *Report On a Journey to the Western States of North America,* a work of great historical significance to Missouri. In 1917–1918, a rather inauspicious time, *The Missouri Historical Review* published part of Duden's famous book translated by Prof. William G. Bek. This unedited portion renewed interest in Duden's observations of Missouri and its society in the 1820s and 1830s, but further investigation was delayed.

In 1964, Elmer Ellis, President of the University of Missouri, Trustee of the Society, and a member of its Finance Committee, proposed that the Society translate, edit, and publish Duden's complete *Report.* As a distinguished western historian and a student and friend of Professor Bek at the University of North Dakota, President Ellis believed in the value of making such an edition available to the public. The Finance Committee of the Society accepted his proposal.

Between 1964 and the fall of 1979, when the University of Missouri Press agreed to publish the book for the Society, many persons have engaged in translating and editing *Report On a Journey to the Western States of North America.* Professor George Kellner of the University of Rhode Island has written portions of the introduction and assisted with the editing and annotation of the first nineteen letters of this volume. Other generous contributors are identified in the Acknowledgments and on the title page. The Society is indebted to each of these persons whose work has made possible this edition of a book indispensable to an understanding of early Missouri and its pioneer settlers.

Richard S. Brownlee
Director and Secretary
The State Historical Society of Missouri
Columbia, Missouri
14 January 1980

Editors' Introduction

I

Many of the nineteenth-century European notions of the promises of American life owed their origin and longevity to a host of American promoters.[1] Agents representing land companies, steamship lines, railroads, state governments, and manufacturing interests flooded Europe, distributed enticing literature, and influenced many Europeans to emigrate to the New World. However, even though Americans served as their country's best promoters, foreigners contributed immeasurably to the prevailing image of America as a land of opportunity.

A decade before the rise of mass immigration in the 1830s, a succession of travelers crossed the Atlantic, made their observations, and wrote of their experiences. For the most part these foreigners came from England and France, but it was the German people who seemed most susceptible to promotional literature. For this reason German accounts attracted a larger readership and exerted a greater influence upon their writers' countrymen.[2] Between 1827 and 1856 over a hundred and fifty titles that could be considered emigration literature were published in Germany. Although some of these volumes presented the attractions of Eastern Europe and South America, the majority dealt with the United States.[3] Evidence strongly suggests that the concentration of German settlement in midwestern states in the first half of the nineteenth century tended to follow and was partly a response to promotional literature relating to this region.[4]

Although some of these German authors wrote excellent accounts, many emulated and all were overshadowed by the promotional activities of a Rhinelander named Gottfried Duden. From 1829 to 1840 Duden wrote and published several editions of *Bericht über eine Reise nach den westlichen Staaten Nordamerikas (Report on a Journey to the Western States of North America)*, two editions of *Ueber die wesentlichen Verschiedenheiten der Staaten und die Strebungen der menschlichen Natur (Concerning the Significant Differences of the States and the Ambitions of Human Nature)*, a two-volume work on *Europa und Deutschland von Nordamerika aus betrachtet (Europe and Germany as Viewed from North America)*, an analysis of *Die nordamerikanische Demokratie und das v. Tocqueville'sche Werk (The North American Democracy and de Tocqueville's Work)*, and several additional articles and pamphlets on both emigration and jurisprudence.[5] Together, these works significantly influenced German emigration before 1860 and represented an outstanding example of one German's attempt to heighten his countrymen's awareness of American opportunities.

Despite the importance of Duden's collective works, his *Report on a Journey to the Western States of North America* most attracted the attention of the German public and pulled Duden into the center of German emigration circles. The book's timing, format, comprehensiveness, literary qualities, and idyllic descriptions of pioneer farming in Missouri all combined to make it an instant success. Discontented individuals in Germany and Switzerland enthusiastically read it, organized emigration societies in accordance with Duden's advice, and began their preparations for an Atlantic crossing. After they settled in the United States, these people's letters and reports mailed home to relatives and friends, though not always supportive of Duden's findings, contributed to the popularity of his book and helped broaden its circulation.

When the first wave of the mass immigration of the nineteenth century reached the shores of America in the early 1830s, thousands of uprooted Germans headed for the Midwest. The arrival of these Germans in Missouri marked the origin and created the nucleus of that state's German element. By 1860, Missouri's population totaled 1,182,012. The steady influx of German settlers had pushed Missouri to sixth position among the states in the size of its foreign-born German population with 88,487. The city of St. Louis had attracted 50,510 of the German immigrants, and the rest had scattered along the Missouri River and it tributaries.[6]

The success of Duden's book and the resulting concentration of Germans in Missouri have brought Gottfried Duden to the attention of historians of American immigration. Echoing the sentiments of other historians, O. G. Libby noted that Duden's account had an "enormous impetus" to German emigration, and Marcus L. Hansen, in his classic study *The Atlantic Migration, 1607–1860,* called it the "most important piece of literature in the history of German emigration."[7]

Unfortunately for historians and for other persons interested in Missouri's German heritage, an in-depth biography of Duden does not exist. Likewise, none of his works has ever been translated and published in English. Alice H. Finckh has translated a small segment of Duden's two-volume work *Europe and Germany as Viewed from North America,* publishing it as "Gottfried Duden Views Missouri, 1824–1827."[8] William Bek, the historian most active in the study of Missouri Germans, has translated and edited portions of Duden's *Report on a Journey to the Western States of North America* as "Gottfried Duden's 'Report', 1824–1827."[9] Although both authors have recognized Duden's importance, their accounts fail to cast Duden into a proper historical perspective, omit much of his advice to prospective emigrants, and are necessarily limited in scope. The present volume is the first complete English translation of Duden's original work. As such, it fills a historical void and provides both the professional historian and the public with a significant document on the origins of Missouri's rich German heritage.

II

Gottfried Duden was born in 1785 in the town of Remscheid, Duchy of Berg, in what is now Germany.[10] His parents belonged to Remscheid's professional class and thus enjoyed an assured status and social prestige. His father, Leonhard, owned the town's government-sanctioned apothecary business. Leonhard Duden's second marriage to Maria Katherina Hartcop, daughter of a wealthy iron foundry owner, further enhanced the family's economic and social position.[11] If children born into such a social environment declined to follow their father's calling, they either entered a related profession or sought employment in government. Gottfried Duden preferred the latter and, as was customary, received the traditional classical education and the necessary preparation for government service. Although Duden gained knowledge in several professional disciplines, including medicine, during his university studies, he concentrated on jurisprudence. At the age of twenty-one he began his legal studies at Düsseldorf, and after a short stay in Heidelberg he transferred to Göttingen, where he received his law degree in 1810.[12]

In 1811 Duden obtained a royal appointment as an attorney in the Prussian civil service. As a bureaucrat he seems to have been mobile in his profession, serving in several important positions in town governments; all, however, were located only a few miles from his place of birth. His first appointment was as auditor for the courts of Düsseldorf. Duden interrupted his judicial career from 1813 to 1814 and enlisted as a lieutenant in the First Battalion of the Second Bergian Infantry Regiment, which later became the Twenty-eighth Prussian Infantry Regiment. With the end of the Napoleonic War, Duden returned to civil service. He served as a justice of the peace for Mülheim and Richrath (Langenfeld) for three years and then resumed his duties as a jurist in Cologne. In the fall of 1823, ill health and his decision to visit America to investigate the prospects for German settlement there prompted Duden to seek royal release from his civil service duties.[13]

III

Duden's decision to visit America and to attempt to locate a favorable area for German emigrants was influenced by three main factors: his native region's social and economic problems following the Napoleonic Wars, the reaction of certain Rhineland states to these problems, and Duden's official and personal activities prior to 1823.

In Duden's youth the region of his birth was a mosaic of duchies and princely domains. Remscheid itself had been a quiet town nestled in the forests along the western hills of the Bergian Land. A few miles to the west flowed the Rhine, Germany's main north-south artery of trade and communication. To the north, sandwiched between the Ruhr and Lippe rivers, were the cities of Essen, Bochum, and Dortmund. To the south, the towns of Solingen, Bonn, and Cologne, and to the west Düsseldorf and occasional villages marked Remscheid's surroundings. Even though the area had not yet displayed signs of the economic boom that would later transform it into the heart of Germany's industrial region, its central location on the trade arteries of Germany gave it and would continue to give it military importance and would offer its residents opportunities for travel, plus provide an awareness of distant places.

In the first half of the nineteenth century the area was severely affected by the rapid changes brought about by the Napoleonic Wars, Napoleonic codes, Prussian rule, an unprecedented population growth, and a corresponding decline in economic opportunities.[14] Distressed by their immediate lot and fearful of the future, thousands of Germans fled to the Netherlands to board ships for distant lands. Thousands more flocked to towns and cities along the Rhine in search of employment in an economy plagued by a postwar depression and crop failures in 1816 and 1817. Forced into already overcrowded housing, unemployed Germans swelled the ranks of those already in poverty and overburdened existing relief agencies. As a consequence, robberies and other crimes increased significantly.[15]

This exodus of Germans to other nations, their emigration to the towns and cities, and the social disorders in the Rhineland influenced many states to investigate the causes of such problems and to seek potential solutions to them. Hampered by a rigid delineation of authority among the Prussian, state, and local governments, some states simply issued decrees prohibiting people without visas and adequate financial resources from emigrating. A few states created courts of inquest and took depositions from emigrants as to the reasons for their departure. Other states, such as Württemberg, took a more imaginative and resourceful approach and established bureaus of emigration.[16]

Despite these efforts only a handful of Germans gave serious attention to the emigration movement. Friedrich List, head of Württemberg's bureau of emigration affairs, did investigate the subject and concluded that the German people's deep discontent, oppression, and lack of political freedom as "citizens of state and community" caused them to migrate.[17] Hans C. von Gagern, liberal nationalist and friend of Prussia's reform architect Baron Karl vom Stein, acquired firsthand knowledge of the emigration as a Bundestag representative to the Netherlands in 1816–1817. Influenced by Thomas Malthus and William Godwin, Gagern thought that overpopulation and the rapidly changing economic order of the Rhineland constituted the chief reason for the emigration and the spread of social discontent. Gagern's solution to the problem was simple: Germans should learn from history, especially from that of Greece and Rome, and seriously entertain the concept of planned colonization.[18]

Even when the exodus of 1816–1817 ground to a virtual halt, Gagern continued to publicize the emigration issue. He persuaded his cousin, Moritz von Fürstenwärther, to travel to America and report to him on the conditions of Germans there.[19] By 1826 Gagern had become convinced that emigration was morally good because it would remove the poor and dissatisfied, to the advantage of both the emigrants and Germany. When Gagern took his seat in the upper chamber of the Hesse-Darmstadt Diet three years later, his friend Baron Karl vom Stein recommended that he read Duden's book on America.[20]

Just as List, Gagern, and others had formed their opinions on emigration and Germany's problems on the basis of their civil duties and observations, so too had Gottfried Duden. Since his youth Duden had witnessed and had appeared troubled by the social transformation of his native region and its seemingly confused political situation. His duties as a jurist had brought him into frequent contact with Germany's discontented masses, and his service with the Mülheim court of inquest had afforded him the opportunity to study the emigration. Deeply moved by the emigrants' stories of hardships and paternalistically concerned about the present and the future of the German people, Duden could not remain idle. Consequently, he launched a personal investigation into their problems.[21]

Duden's initial response to the crisis, again like that of Gagern and others, was to accept the theories of Malthus and Godwin and to claim that overpopulation constituted the source of the German people's problems. But Duden thought such an explanation too simple because it failed to account for a variety of social forces then operative within Germany. His concern with Germany's reactionary politics following the Napoleonic Wars led him to investigate the political nature of the German state and its relation to the individual. Duden concluded this eight-year study in 1822 and published it as *Concerning the Significant Differences of the States and the Ambitions of Human Nature.*[22]

The book's arguments, unquestionably based on Duden's observations as a civil servant and on his thoughtful examination of a variety of political treatises, clearly marked Duden's entry into the camp of those liberal nationalists who stressed the German people rather than the German state. Duden wrote that a state experiencing many rapid and confusing changes would fail to function effectively. Political authorities in such situations, he added, would be prone to act hastily and often harshly in order to maintain power and to preserve a degree of societal stability. Consequently, he reasoned, governments so affected must either launch sweeping reform movements, which he deplored, or deny the masses their natural rights and freedoms. In his opinion, oppressive economic and political measures would compel people to adopt one of three basic human tactics for survival: blind obedience to authority; opposition to laws designed to protect members of society; or emigration to other lands. Obedience and opposition, Duden concluded, tended to obscure the basic purposes for which a state had originally been organized, thereby denying it and its citizens an important means for achieving a higher level of civilization. Planned emigration, undertaken by men of sound ethics and directed toward countries with sufficient economic opportunities and assured freedoms, could restore to emigrants a renewed sense of vigor for personal growth and cultural improvement.[23]

Thus, by 1822, Duden had concluded that the major problems of the German people in his region stemmed from the political, social, and economic consequences of overpopulation. He had also reached a stage in his promotional thinking where emigration to another country seemed one viable solution to the predicament of his countrymen. Although only a handful of Germans were leaving their native states for America in the 1820s, their departure further encouraged Duden. Partially familiar with the American political process, Duden now began to acquaint himself with American conditions and with the prospects for German settlement. He avidly read the literature on America, hoping to obtain detailed information from which to judge which American area was best suited for Germans in regard to climate, soil fertility, cost of land, and arteries of transportation; how an actual settlement could be made in either a plains or forest environment; and what expenses, inconveniences, and dangers awaited prospective settlers. Duden found the works that he consulted deficient in a variety of ways. None of them suited his desire for thoroughness and detail. None could be used as a manual instructing Germans on emigration.

Despite these disappointments and a scarcity of specific information, Duden concluded that German emigrants headed for America ought to join Americans in their westward movement and try to locate in areas with a low man-to-land ratio that nevertheless offered an abundance of economic opportunities. He theorized that settlement west of the Allegheny Mountains would be acceptable but that the Mississippi valley would be especially ideal. Since no literature dealt comprehensively with the region, Duden could not honestly suggest that Germans settle there without first making a personal appraisal of the area.

Consequently, in 1824 Gottfried Duden embarked for America with Ludwig Eversmann, son of a Berlin mine surveyor.[24] True to his conviction that emigrants should follow America's westward march, he arrived in St. Louis in October. During his brief stay there he investigated Illinois and thoroughly scouted the land on both sides of the Missouri River. Duden was delighted with the region and purchased over 270 acres of land, both public and private, in Montgomery (now Warren)

County, Missouri.[25] For the next three years Duden went through the motions but performed few of the difficult tasks required in pioneer farming. Convinced that the area was well suited for German settlement, he then returned to Germany and in 1829 published fifteen hundred copies of his observations. *Report on a Journey to the Western States of North America* supplied Germans with their most comprehensive study of Missouri in the first half of the nineteenth century and its publication marked the beginning of Duden's efforts to "stimulate Germans for colonization."[26]

IV

The *Report on a Journey to the Western States of North America* was a masterpiece of promotional literature. Duden's adroit pen wove reality with poetry, experience with dreams, and contrasted the freedom of the forests and democratic political institutions in America with the social narrowness and political confusion in Germany. He glorified the routine of pioneer existence, praised Missouri's favorable geographical location, and emphasized its mild and healthy climate. He dwelt on the benevolence of its nature and the abundance of its fish and wildlife, and contrasted Germany's poverty and hunger with America's plenty. So overwhelmed with what he saw and experienced, Duden feared Germans would not believe him: "It appears," he wrote, "too strange, too fabulous."[27]

By the 1820s America had lost much of its earlier attraction for Germans contemplating emigration. Bitter reports of disenchanted Germans returning to their native land after trying life in America circulated widely and dampened the enthusiasm of others. Although a few Germans still sailed for the New World, most now headed for the heavily promoted countries of Brazil, Poland, or the Transcaucasian lands of the Russian Empire. German emigration to these areas, however, began to lessen toward the end of the decade when fraudulent promotional schemes had been exposed and dissatisfied emigrants had returned. In an atmosphere of distrust, Germans once again cautiously looked toward the New World.[28]

Though the idea of emigration to America began to revive, accurate and reliable information about the country still remained scant. Earlier negative testimonials on American conditions reported by returning emigrants tended to corroborate the pessimistic descriptions found in the works in Fürstenwärther and Gall. These authors had done little to dispel inaccurate notions about the trans-Mississippi West. Many Germans and other Europeans, and even Americans, accepted reports that described the interior of America as largely uninhabitable, arid, and harsh in climate, deserving the label *Great American Desert*.[29]

Gottfried Duden's account not only met the needs of those Germans entertaining thoughts of emigration to America, it also helped appreciably to create a favorable climate of public opinion concerning the interior of America, particularly Missouri. His use of the personal-letter format and his recording of almost daily personal experiences from throughout the entire process of setting up a pioneer farm also combined to make the account believable, personable, and informative.

Duden pictured Missouri and its environs as being quite the opposite from desolate, as having a gratifying environment for farming and as being ideally located for mercantile development. Missouri's location, topography, climate, and natural resources all reminded him of his native Rhineland. Like the Rhine and its tributaries, the Mississippi and Missouri rivers served the interior as main avenues of trade and communication, provided cheap water transportation, and offered fertile bottomlands. At the rivers' confluence, St. Louis bustled with commercial activity, while southwest of her lay rich deposits of coal, iron ore, and lead. In the nearby countryside an abundance of fertile and relatively cheap government land awaited cultivators. Then, too, forests abounding in wildlife of every imaginable kind covered hills and broke the monotony of level prairies. Missouri was described as a veritable paradise awaiting the arrival of Germany's Adam and Eve.

In addition to Missouri's choice location and good lands, nature's benevolence supplied the prospective settler with a substantial amount of his food. So abundant were turkey, deer, rabbit, and other game that Duden saw no need for a farmer to slaughter more than an occasional hog of his own for meat. Wild fruit trees produced the most succulent apples, pears, and cherries; and grapevines growing a hundred feet high on trees covered the picturesque hills along the Missouri River valley. Admittedly, Duden declared, much of this land belonged to the government; but unlike Germany, in the United States foresters and government officials seldom restrained people from using the wooded lands. And because of such plenty, Duden was fond of repeating, thieves simply did not exist. Property and life were safe in Missouri.

To assure his readers that Germans could readily tame Missouri's wilderness and that it could provide them with all the comforts of civilization, Duden meticulously described the clearing, fencing, cultivating, and harvesting of his lands and crops. Because Duden hired help for these tasks, he turned pioneer farming into a gentleman's occupation and demonstrated it with an idyllic portrayal of his daily routine. After a magnificent sunrise he walked or rode in the countryside in quest of breakfast, which sometimes consisted of squirrel, pigeon, or wild turkey. He often spent the remaining morning hours meditating or reading. Afternoons he devoted to riding, to visiting nearby friends, or to recording his observations and experiences.

Although Duden gave free play to his imagination in his assessment of the benevolence of Missouri's nature and economic potential, he treated American institutions in a more structured and restrained manner. Believing that many Germans were familiar with American political machinery, election procedures, and constitutional rights, he saw no need to repeat such basic information. Consequently, he focused on the stability of American democracy and appended his philosophical analysis of the subject to the main body of the book. This stability, Duden told his readers, did not rest on the imposing stature of the founding fathers, or on the subsequent political leaders, or on the history of excellent legislation. It rested entirely upon the abundance of America's economic opportunites, which were derived from the physical environment. America's plenty satisfied every person's physical, emotional, and ethical needs; it created a congenial social environment that offered all settlers an "abundance of innocent pleasures in rural surroundings, and at the same time keeps them away from the spheres of vanity, ambition, and desires for power." Since the majority of American citizens engaged in farming, consensus about beneficial national policies and legislation seemed assured, and any drastic or unforeseen changes in the structure of American democracy seemed almost absurd. Consequently, Duden reasoned, Americans would continue to retain their democracy, their rights, and their freedoms.

These arguments, delivered with force and commitment after Duden's American experience, were logical conclusions based upon his 1822 study of the political and social consequences of overpopulation in Germany. Later they became the thesis for his two-volume work *Europe and Germany* and the basis for his main criticisms of Alexis de Tocqueville's *Democracy in America,* which pointed out the Frenchman's superficiality and many contradictions.

With abundant virgin land and democracy as his main arguments for emigration, Duden hoped to blunt any adverse German reaction to the repressive aspects of Negro slavery. His discussion of the institution centered on three main topics: recognition of the slavery problem, minimization of its undesirable ramifications, and emphasis on its potential benefits for German emigrants. He admitted that slavery existed in Missouri, called it a moral evil, and thought that it might constitute a problem for Germans. Yet Duden never visualized it as a major problem because slaves were few in Missouri and unlikely to increase due to the state's diversified economy. He also reminded his readers that Persia, Egypt, and Rome had managed to thrive under the burden of slavery and that slavery's presence in Missouri did not automatically impede progress. Furthermore, Duden asserted, Missouri's slaves behaved well, would not be emancipated suddenly, and would never be allowed to intermarry with whites. Economically, he saw the black's condition in America as at least equal to that of the oppressed German day laborer and as even better than that of the European servant. He also hinted that German settlers who could afford two slaves should consider buying them, because they would perform all necessary labor on a farm.

Duden's treatment of American institutions was always permeated with his firm belief in the agrarian way of life and by his growing pessimism regarding worsening social conditions in Germany. During his American experience Duden became convinced that Missouri possessed regenerative qualities superior to those Tacitus had described in his *Germania*. For Duden the simple and tranquil communal life of former centuries had disappeared in the Germany of the 1820s, leaving the people without vitality and solidarity. Each component of German society, Duden believed, followed its separate way: the farmer's concern was with his land; the artisan saw meaning only in his trade; the merchant wanted only money; the educated hid behind the mask of their knowledge; the official was preoccupied with his office; and the soldier found refuge behind his weapons. Few Germans cared about or concerned themselves with the plight of their fellowmen.[30] Thus, Duden felt that his country was headed for self-destruction as though this, too, were part of an orderly process of nature.

Emigration to Missouri or to some other part of America where an abundance of natural resources existed offered a solution and provided a means of preserving the vitality of the German people. No matter, argued Duden, that Missouri was isolated from the cultural currents of Europe and that Americans emphasized the materialistic life. In America culture was predicated on the practical and utilitarian and not on institutional learning, and Americans were better for it because they tilled the soil and were as one with nature. With the eighteenth-century essayist J. Hector St. John de Crèvecoeur, Duden saw the American as a new man, a culturally regenerated European interacting with a benevolent new environment.[31]

Duden's advice to prospective German emigrants reflected both his admiration for this new America and his obsession with rescuing some elements of German civilization. Thus, he urged Germans to emigrate to America in groups and establish farming communities. "No plan in this age," wrote Duden, "can promise more for the individual or group." Once established, such communities would become centers of German culture and the mainstays of a transplanted Germania, a second *Vaterland* for all emigrated Germans. The people of these communities would have ready access to the bountiful forests and fertile lands; live in peace, harmony, and freedom; and above all, be cleansed of their undesirable characteristics. Duden even suggested that if enough Germans came they might be able to establish an all-German state.

Duden knew that success for his planned farming communities depended on proper preparation, sufficient capital, and selective emigration. Accordingly, Duden encouraged prospectve emigrants to organize emigration societies, dispatch advance agents to inspect settlement locations and arrange transportation, and pool their financial resources. Organization also would contribute to the selection of persons with diversified talents and sufficient capital. Once organized, these societies would facilitate easier emigration and supply a sufficient number of settlers to establish economically self-sufficient and socially cohesive communities.

Duden's advice allowed scant room for the unfortunate poor. Since he hoped for emigration of some monied and cultured Germans, he naturally stressed monetary requirements. Duden estimated that a family of five would need at least 800 to 1,000 Prussian thalers, roughly 775 to 900 dollars, to emigrate to the New World and there establish a new home. With this sum, each family could purchase eighty acres of land, several farm animals, a log cabin, and some basic home furnishings. There would be enough remaining so that American labor could be hired to clear and fence from five to seven acres, thereby avoiding the danger of illness from overexertion during the first summer. In addition to money, each family should expect to bring a sizable supply of tools and implements.

None of Germany's poverty-stricken artisans and peasants possessed sufficient money or tools to qualify for emigration under the requirements outlined by Duden. Although their misery had been partially responsible for his interest in German colonization, he allotted them no clearly defined place in his new *Vaterland.* He noted briefly that skilled artisans and laborers were desperately needed in St. Louis and that the city hungered for the services of brewers, tanners, cabinetmakers, shoemakers, saddlers, and blacksmiths. And since St. Louis imported most of her pottery, glass, iron, chemical, and pharmaceutical products from other areas, Germans familiar with their production could easily establish enterprises there, Duden thought.

The availability of steady employment and other economic opportunities in St. Louis failed to deter Duden from emphasizing rural settlement and the establishment of German farming communities. Ironically, in the three decades before the Civil War, St. Louis became a safety valve for many disenchanted Germans who had tried and failed at pioneer farming in Missouri and the chief attraction for newly arriving Germans. This reversal of Duden's original hopes reflected the extent to which he had exaggerated the benevolence of Missouri's wilderness, his overly optimistic appraisal of the ease with which cultured Germans could make the transition to pioneer farming, and his unrealistic suggestion that only skilled and monied Germans emigrate. These weaknesses were apparent in the failure of organized emigration societies and resulted in the growth of literature critical of Duden's findings.

V

In the 1830s Germans thinking of emigrating to Missouri usually planned to do so as members of colonization societies. Almost immediately after the publication of Duden's account of his stay in Missouri, such societies rose in popularity throughout western Germany and Switzerland. Particularly significant were the societies located in Hesse-Darmstadt, where a wide range of emigration literature and heightened emigration fever developed that state into the center of German emigration activities.[32]

The best known of the colonization societies destined for Missouri in response to Duden's work were the Giessen Emigration Society led by Friedrich Münch and Paul Follenius, the Mühlhausen Colonization Society organized by E. K. Angelrodt, the Osnabrück Colonization Society of Heinrich von Martels, the Swiss Colonization Society, Sursee, directed by Joseph Suppiger and Kaspar Köpfli, and a group of Berlin settlers under the leadership of Philipp Barez. Later, several other groups joined those already in Missouri, including several hundred old order Lutherans from Saxony under the leadership of Martin Stephan, who had been familiar with Duden's account since 1833.[33]

For many emigration societies Duden's book constituted the sole guide for their emigration; for others it became daily reading material.[34] Organizers quickly realized the merits of Duden's work and submitted their plans to him for approval or corresponded with him regarding additional information for their prospective ventures. Paul Follenius, while a student at Giessen in 1819, proposed that German liberals repressed by the Karlsbad Decrees relocate in the New World and there spread their ideas. The government, however, acted against the leaders and the project collapsed.[35] Duden's book rekindled Follenius's plans. As one of the leaders of the Giessen Emigration Society of 1834, Follenius submitted that organization's plans to Duden long before their departure. Duden approved of the plans "most heartily."[36] Heinrich von Martels, according to Duden, also consulted him before von Martels's group sailed for America, and Duden wrote in his 1834 edition that von Martels asked him to comment upon the latter's book entitled *Letters Concerning the Western Part of the United States of North America.* The leaders of the Swiss Emigration Society, Duden implied, also carried on a detailed correspondence with him shortly before their plans for emigration crystallized.[37] Individuals such as Theodor Hilgard first read and reread Duden and then consulted him on the finer points of emigration. Hilgard was deeply impressed with Duden's account and defended all aspects of his advice on emigration.[38]

In keeping with Duden's advice, some emigration societies dispatched advance agents to Missouri to substantiate the promoter's findings, to locate suitable land, and to make transportation arrangements.[39] The Suppiger-Köpfli party and the Philipp Barez group employed agents to check on Duden's reliability. One such agent reported that he saw everything "letter for letter" as Duden had written.[40] Not all, however, wrote such glowing reports. Joseph Suppiger's caution was evident when he reported, "What I saw was good and beautiful, but I saw it only in passing. l saw the flower and the bud, but I have yet to feel the thorn."[41]

Duden's book had an immense appeal to the foes of German reactionism of the 1830s, who had long admired the government of the United States. Some of them had demonstrated a deep interest in the future of the German people and, like Duden, had predicted the ruin of German civilization. Duden's proposals for planned colonization and the establishment of rural farming communities attracted their attention. Consequently, when the early settlement societies such as the Giessen Emigration Society drafted their organization plans in 1833 they thought in terms of establishing a rejuvenated Germany in North America.[42]

Ironically, the well-educated Germans of the early emigration experienced a host of difficulties establishing their settlements and within a few years abandoned most of their original intentions. Those Germans who remained on the land and struggled with pioneer farming soon became known as "Latin Farmers." Their education, their leadership, and their achievement made them a small but significant group of the German-American population and the vanguard of Missouri's sizable German element.[43] Although the Duden-implanted and the Follenius-Münch-Bromme-projected idea of a New Germany in Missouri's wilderness failed to materialize, it strongly influenced the German Philadelphia Settlement Society to locate in Missouri. While Hermann, Missouri, never became a new Germany, it did become known as "Little Germany" and proudly continued German culture well into the twentieth century.[44]

VI

The German romantic movement exerted an important influence on Duden, and he in turn served as an inspiration to one of its schools. Romanticism in Germany, as in no other country, influenced the nation's social and political thought. While most German romantics believed that the German people had strayed from the true course of their cultural development, not all of them agreed on how best to restore a proper sense of direction. One school drifted from admiration of the liberal West into the camp of political nationalism where they advocated greater national power through unification. A second group, preoccupied with the German people's common history, descent, and language, sought to glorify the past, especially the spirit of the Teutonic forests and the legends of the epic poem *Nibelungenlied.* A third group, inspired by a prevailing belief in nature's revitalizing qualities, called for a return to the agrarian, simpler way of life. The latter group read Duden, quoted his descriptions of Missouri, and even in some cases traveled to America in search of his paradise.[45]

Two German poets, Nicolaus Lenau and Ferdinand Freiligrath, became influential agrarian romantics. Both were under the spell of Duden's book, and both had committed themselves to the idea of a transatlantic, agrarian-based *Vaterland.* They, and others like them, popularized Duden's findings in imaginative German literature that proved especially attractive to Germans dissatisifed with their homeland's cultural and economic conditions.[46] After reading Duden, Lenau became obsessed with the idea of visiting Missouri, and his literary production showed signs of his newfound captivation. "My poetry lives and thrives on nature," he wrote, "and in America nature is more beautiful and powerful than in Europe." His utterly romantic view of life and nature seems to have eluded him in actuality. His visit to America, undertaken with great expectations, ended in loneliness and disillusionment, and he returned to Germany without ever reaching Missouri.[47] Freiligrath, on the other hand, was in political exile in England when he first read Duden and the novels of Friedrich Gerstäcker. He borrowed much from Duden in his early writings and later continued to celebrate nature in America and the saga of German emigrants. His poem "Die Auswanderer" ("The Emigrant"), first published in 1832, evoked in romantic terms the new life in Missouri, but it also anticipated the homesickness many emigrants would experience.[48]

The enthusiastic reception of Duden's work by some of the German romantics only increased the already too optimistic expectations of emigrants. Before departing from their native land many emigrants had imagined themselves worthy inheritors of the land of promise and ultimate beneficiaries of its revitalizing qualities.[49] Instead of a dreamed-about Eden, however, they discovered a dense forest; instead of an idyllic life, they found themselves involved in exhaustive work. Frustrated and discontented, they focused on Gottfried Duden, making him their scapegoat. Some unhappy German immigrants now called his book "Duden's Eden," and others referred to his Missouri farm as the "castle in the sky."[50] These and other derogatory accounts circulated widely throughout Germany.

The failure of the early emigration societies coupled with such negative reports moved Germans to sympathy for their departed countrymen and led to denunciation of Duden's ideas as unrealistic. In 1833, *Das Hannoverische Magazin (The Magazine of Hanover)* carried an anonymous attorney's caustic account of the German emigration to Missouri in which the author blamed Duden directly for the misfortunes of so many innocent people.[51] The following year the

Jenaische Literatur-Zeitung (Literary Journal of Jena) published a series of articles condemning Duden and his book. One of these articles castigated the *Report* as "shallow, fantastic, and exaggerated."[52] The respected magazine *Didaskalia* also focused on the debates and criticisms throughout 1836.[53]

A few critics denounced the influence of Duden's book but still recognized its achievements in certain ways. H. Leo, a professor of history at the University of Halle, thought that Duden stood on solid ground when he confined himself to a narrative of his personal experience and descriptions of terrain. But when he passed moral judgment on his own country and philosophized about the people's need for closer contact with nature, his conclusions were irrational and damaging to Germany.[54] J. H. Rausse visited America and after his return to Germany in 1836 published his personal observations. Rausse agreed with Duden as to Missouri's abundance of fertile land and its potential for economic prosperity. However, he severely criticized Duden for his colonization scheme. Rausse saw colonization in terms of human losses rather than as a revitalization of man. "Every creature loses there [in America]," he wrote, "its most becoming aspects . . . the woman her shame and beauty, the man his courage."[55]

At first Duden consoled himself by believing that such attacks were harmless and too ridiculous to deserve an answer.[56] As the number of critics grew, however, he felt compelled to refute them. He was too deeply involved in the entire German exodus and too desperately committed to his dream of German colonization to stand accused without a defense. Consequently, from 1832 to the end of the decade, Duden immersed himself in the problems of German emigration, the state of the German people, and changes in American conditions affecting settlement. He skillfully answered his critics in the 1834 edition of his *Report* (see Appendix I), in his *Tocqueville's Work,* and more generally in his two-volume study *Europe and Germany.*[57]

Duden's rebuttals were clearly designed to retain his credibility and, as such, had a twofold purpose: to silence increasingly vocal critics and to clarify some frequently misinterpreted portions of his work. He replied to one anonymous critic who had castigated his colonization scheme: "I do not feel like playing the philanthropist with such a sneerer and cannot force myself to overlook compassionately the faults which he reveals in his ridiculous insolence."[58] Duden characterized a lawyer critic in an equally harsh manner, stating the man was "without talent and practice" and had criticized his work without having read it. He showed even less tolerance for H. Leo and others whom he summarily dismissed as "nincompoops."[59] J. H. Rausse, who had the audacity to liken himself to Duden, was rebuffed as "insane," and his account of emigration was passed off as "idiotic."[60]

In his assessment of why some emigrants had become disillusioned

Duden was hesitant to fault his own overly optimistic attitude. "Truthfully, I confess my guilt," wrote Duden, but he added that the emigrants' refusal to heed his advice was the main cause for their troubled condition. He repeated his earlier statements in which he had cautioned his readers that successful emigration required preparation, money, and a select group of people. Unfortunately, concluded Duden, only the "incapable of incapables" seemed to have emigrated to Missouri. Duden also believed that many of the early emigrants had lacked common sense, and even if they had realized their limitations, "who would admit to such a failure?"[61] These and other personal failings made many unfit for emigration and even less fit to cope with a new and raw environment. Unfortunately, according to Duden, those who settled in Missouri unprepared were forever destined to become "offerings of misunderstanding."[62]

Although Duden unquestionably felt insulted and deeply hurt by the mounting criticism, he still continued to believe that a "Garden of Eden" endowed with unlimited opportunities existed in Missouri. Part of Duden's continued optimism stemmed from his commitment to German colonization, but a major portion of it came from reports of German immigrants who substantiated his earlier findings and from his own obsessive reading of all the new literature on American conditions. His writings also exhibited a wide range of knowledge on a number of subjects directly or indirectly related to his experience in the state. For example, Duden's comments concerning the climate illustrated his awareness of some of the more sophisticated thinking on the subject at that time. Similarly, he wrote on archaeology, and he demonstrated that he had examined the works of the leading contemporary authorities such as Caleb Atwater and John Heckewelder. His comments about overpopulation were enlightened for the period and even for later. Granted, on occasion he exaggerated Missouri's potential. And some of his discussions, in particular those about slavery, are jumbled, confused, and difficult to comprehend. Nevertheless his writings suggest that he possessed an enormous range of interests and that he had explored these by consulting some of the best authorities.

The thrust of anti-Duden literature cut deeply into Duden's effectiveness as an objective promoter of German emigration. He did manage to regain some of his former status through his defense and through the favorable reports of others. In 1837, Duden prepared his last known written defense,[63] which one scholar characterized as a "bitter, disillusioned statement," in which he blamed himself for assuming that his countrymen would follow his advice.[64] Duden abandoned his original idea of converting Germans to colonization in the 1840s and returned to the study of jurisprudence.[65] In 1855 he died in retirement at Remscheid, his place of birth.[66]

Even though Duden's idea of a new *Vaterland* had gone awry, he had exerted a profound impact on the nature of German emigration for over a decade. The type of emigrants, their expectations, their routes of travel, and their choice of location for settlement all reflected Duden's influence. And some of the most articulate Germans who had followed Duden's call, such as Friedrich Münch and Gert Göbels, later took up the pen to promote emigration to Missouri. The large number of Germans who settled in the Midwest in response to Duden's *Report* and their significant contributions to the economic, political, social, and cultural development of the state confirm that it was the most important piece of literature in the history of German emigration.

Editorial Policy

Due to the many inconsistencies and inaccuracies in Duden's work, it is necessary to explain the stylistic and factual changes incorporated in this translation. First of all, some consistency has been attempted regarding the use of abbreviations, capitalization, and numbers. To facilitate easier reading, lengthy and awkward German sentences have occasionally been translated into more than one complete thought. In addition, standard American punctuation has been used throughout.

The scientific or Linnaean names are those used by Duden. In many cases his use of scientific terms was mistaken or does not correspond with present-day usage. These terms have been consistently capitalized, but no attempt has been made in the text to indicate the proper terminology. The annotations, however, do refer to sources that can be valuable in comparing Duden's usage with that current today.

The translation that follows is of the 1829, or first, edition of the *Report*. There were in addition three other editions. In 1832 and again in 1835 a special edition was printed in St. Gallen, Switzerland, under the sponsorship of the Swiss Emigration Society. Except for typographical corrections, the text remained unchanged.

The 1834 edition, printed in Bonn, was revised at length by Duden. The revisions made by Duden were primarily to rebut his critics and to expand or correct certain passages, statements, or phrases. In addition, Duden altered the sentence structure, often making two complete thoughts out of originally lengthier statements. From a historical context, Duden's changes represent his rethinking of his original work, particularly in response to the critics. The editors recognize the importance of these revisions, consequently all the changes Duden made in the 1834 edition, except sentence structure, are included in an appendix to this translation. At every point in the text where a revision was made by Duden, a number appears in brackets. These numbers refer to the listings in Appendix I, which will indicate the nature of the change made by Duden.

In addition, there are two other sets of notes that appear in this volume. The notes that appear at the bottoms of the pages, indicated by asterisks in the text, are Duden's as they appeared in the first edition of his *Report*. The numbered footnote indicators refer to the editors' explanatory notes, contributed by all of the individuals mentioned on the title page and in the Acknowledgments, which appear in Appendix II. These notes provide annotations for works and men mentioned by Duden, cite resources for a reader interested in finding more information on a subject discussed by Duden, and indicate when information given by Duden is mistaken. An effort has been made, however, to keep these notes to a minimum; they are meant to guide the reader to other sources and to indicate points of interest rather than to elucidate every detail mentioned by Duden in his letters.

Acknowledgments

Since 1975 a number of people have offered assistance to the general editor. Without their advice and comment this annotated translation would not have been possible. Portions of the manuscript were read and commented upon by Richard S. Brownlee, Director and Secretary of The State Historical Society of Missouri; Lewis E. Atherton, Professor Emeritus of History; Noble E. Cunningham, Professor of History; William M. Wiecek, Professor of History; Robert J. Rowland, Professor of History; James D. McQuigg, Professor of Atmospheric Sciences; Grant L. Darkow, Professor of Atmospheric Sciences; Richard C. Smith, Assistant Director of Fisheries/Wildlife; William H. Elder, Professor of Fisheries/Wildlife; and Walter A. Schroeder, Instructor of Geography; all members of the faculty and staff of the University of Missouri– Columbia. Charles Dew, Professor of History, William College, and James M. Cope, M.D., also offered advice and suggestions concerning specific portions of this book. The staff of a number of state historical societies and public libraries sent valuable information needed for the completion of the book. They have been thanked personally for their efforts. Staff members of The State Historical Society of Missouri who assisted on more than one occasion are Carol Van Tine, Karen Duree, and Priscilla Evans. Rebecca Schroeder assisted Adolf Schroeder, Professor of German at the University of Missouri– Columbia, with the refinement of the translation. W. M. Senner, Professor of German at Arizona State University, Tempe, also provided valuable suggestions pertaining to the clarity of the translation. Hiroko Somers graciously typed the translation and annotations.

Any errors or omissions are solely the responsibility of the general editor.

J. W. G.
Columbia, Missouri
25 February 1980

Contents

Report on a Journey to the
Western States of North America

Gottfried Duden

and because the excited state of mind of the writers was revealed all to clearly to the critical reader.

In one work I discovered a very exalted state of mind, which was constantly overflowing with poetic embellishments and extravagant praise; in another, a pessimistic attitude, which gave a depressing character to all descriptions. The attitude expressed in the first type was due mostly to an enthusiastic partiality for the political institutions of the North Americans. The pessimistic frame of mind was, on the other hand, usually the result of the writers' disappointed hopes. America was supposed to offer them treasures that Europe had unjustly denied them. In America, intellectual powers that were not appreciated in the home country were to find brilliant recognition. What is more natural than to pour out one's grief over the failure of such plans in complaints about the land and its inhabitants; just as it is, on the other hand, to view everything concerning the new home as surrounded, as it were, with a blissful charm when chance has led one to the lap of abundance and joy after one's arrival. We experience it daily when the same surroundings sometimes seem cheerful and attractive, sometimes dreary and repelling, according to whether our inner mirror is clear or dimmed. And yet only [P-2] a few people are capable of judging the pleasant and the unpleasant according to its dependence on a change in their own natures. Therefore, many emigrants were astonished to find evils in the distant country that they had long been familiar with and had thought to escape. They did not sense that they had brought these evils with them in their own personalities.[9]

Individuals who describe objects as they are reflected in their own state of mind cannot be accused of any evil intentions, however much their descriptions may deviate from the truth. The reporter acts entirely in accordance with his own nature when he describes his impressions as he has experienced them. His judgment is therefore no less subject to doubt. This is especially true of all the emigrants who return quickly from a very large country to their homeland. Who can expect an accurate account from someone who is overcome by bitter regret as soon as he enters the new environment? Aside from all the unfamiliar, unpleasant details, the glorified memories of the past restrict his receptiveness so strongly that for him only a dreary picture of the present is possible. Even the most charming aspects of the New World must appear as if seen through a gloomy mist. The less the sacrifice of the whole undertaking is for an emigrant, the more freely he will move in a foreign country. However, if the long duration of his voluntary residence does not counteract the yearning for his homeland, he is nevertheless not to be confused with the mere spectator, who, without giving up his country, undertakes an exploratory journey.

A second type of publication about North America, however, can be accused of intentional distortion of the truth. To this class belong the colorful advertisements of certain regions and conditions that were circulated because of greed and have only too often led the gullible to their destruction.[10] Most frequently one finds deliberate misrepresentations in books, written in a passionate struggle against political opinions. At the time of the French freedom vertigo, the admiration for North America was boundless. Now usually the other extreme prevails. What in the beginning was honest enthusiasm soon became influenced by intentional exaggeration and false praise of everything connected with the name of the United States. Absolute arbitrariness is today the idol around which nebulous spirits swarm. They see the opposite in the transatlantic states and consequently declare it point-blank to be the realm of evil.

Finally, the enemies of all emigration, the friends of overpopulation, must be mentioned.[11]

But even the better publications were by no means exhaustive for my purpose. I found travel adventures, pictures of cities and landscapes, peculiarities in the animal world and in the plant world. I found descriptions of customs and their usages, of the virtues and vices of the republicans, tales about Indians, and several other things, all of which have value [P-3] and can be read with pleasure. These publications provide little additional information regarding things a cautious emigrant must inquire about, other than what can be learned from whole volumes of statistical tables.

This much, however, became known to me, that the country was least to blame for the serious misfortunes that befell so many emigrants; that the blame was to be placed rather on something else than desolate steppes, bare rocks, and scanty forests, or swamps with pestilent odors (about which Friedrich Schmidt writes*).[12]

The unfortunate results of later attempts at emigration challenged me all the more to investigate what the land itself actually offered to the stranger, and this curiosity could not be appeased by the sneering and fainthearted verdict that the land was nowhere suitable. In a certain struggle with the adherents of this inert theory, I often pondered on how infinitely more valuable to humanity the distant river areas had now become because of the invention of the steamboat. Furthermore, I was more and more inclined to think that the success of emigration depended almost entirely on the way in which it was carried out. I was especially of the opinion that emigration from Europe had to be directed to the same regions where most of the natives were also looking for new homes, just as Europeans in their initial adjustment looked

---

*"Essay on the Political Conditions of the United States of North America." Stuttgart and Tübingen, 1822.

upon the natives as models. Therefore, I considered it a serious mistake to make the final goal of the journey the lands on this side of the Alleghenies, where good places would be as expensive as here.

It was in the midst of such thoughts and feelings that I arrived at the decision to inform myself firsthand about everything I had looked for in vain in the publications.

Finally, I shall mention that several years previous to this I had occupied myself consistently with the study of medicine and thought I was sufficiently informed to provide medical care for my own body.[13]

The reader may therefore judge the historical value of what I have written according to the manner in which I pursued my purpose in detail.

I am beginning the report with a series of letters which in their original format were dedicated only to friendly correspondence. They will be considered as an informal preparation for the main portion. I consider the few pages concerning the nature of the United States of North America to be of primary importance. In them I have emphasized those characteristics of the foreign country and its inhabitants that are the most essential for the ethical world and that are most deserving of the interest of Germany. And this is perhaps the place where I should sound the warning that when reading the word *overpopulation,* one should not simply think of it as an echo of earlier opinions. The statement that (western) Europe was overpopulated was made centuries ago. But its importance depends solely on evidence. If a person realizes clearly that I am talking of overpopulation only insofar as the essential foundations of the political conditions are corrupted by it, he will not confuse my remarks with those of Godwin and Malthus.[14] The real evidence that a state is overpopulated consists solely in showing that the masses of the people can be kept within the bounds of order only by force, and that this condition of the whole is due, in the final analysis, to the excessive number of people in relation to their economic circumstances. The most important and the most unfortunate result of overpopulation is the necessary oppression of the majority, which brings them very close to the lot of beasts of burden. Only insofar as this result has become evident in a country may one say that it is overpopulated. Accordingly, it is certain that a correct judgment presupposes an exact knowledge of the nature of the states and that the person who does not base his reasons on the nature of the states will never come to a conclusion that will silence all objections. For if Malthus had based his evidence of overpopulation on this, the American Everett would not have believed that he could so easily suggest the opposite.[15]

One should not expect to find in this publication any general information about the geographical location, form, or political divisions of North America, which can be found in any schoolbook. I also considered it unnecessary to include a special map since the ordinary maps of the United States are perfectly adequate. [P-4]

Contents

12

Seventeenth Letter, pages 80– 82. The lake of Lake Creek. Parrots. The carrion is removed by beasts of prey. Lead mines.

Eighteenth Letter, pages 82– 87. The author moves to his farm. His manner of life there. Description of the forests. Great abundance of fruit on the neighboring farms. Rapid growth of fruit trees. Grafting is unnecessary. The strange industry of a species of beetle.

Nineteenth Letter, pages 87– 92. Concerning the Indians.

Twentieth Letter, pages 92– 117. Protection of the cornfields against the squirrels. General description of the Americans. Conclusions drawn from the origins and the culture of the first settlers as to the culture of their descendants. The religious situation. No rank accorded to persons or to trades; no distinction between city dwellers and country dwellers; no prejudices for or against certain trades. Especial respect for agriculture. General stimulation to activity. No beggars. No thieves. Concerning the moral character of the Americans and the danger of plans against freedom. Customs and manners. The servants.—Concerning slavery in the United States with an evaluation of the morality of slavery in general.

Twenty-first Letter, pages 117– 118. The bee hunters and their methods.

Twenty-second Letter, pages 118– 121. The wild fowls; thriving of the tame fowls. The service of the dogs.

Twenty-third Letter, pages 121– 123. The mosquitoes.

Twenty-fourth Letter, pages 123– 124. Lost in the woods.

Twenty-fifth Letter, pages 125– 127. Adventure with a large rattlesnake. Success in gardening. Wild turkeys. Deer. Killing a cougar (American panther). Hunting expeditions of General Ashley over the Rocky Mountains and the discovery of a level area.

Twenty-sixth Letter, page 127. Superabundance of iron ore, table salt, Epsom salts, potassium nitrate, bituminous coal, copper. New lead mines along the Fever River.

Twenty-seventh Letter, pages 127– 130. Concerning the monuments of vanished American tribes.

Twenty-eighth Letter, pages 130– 136. Concerning health conditions and medical science.

First Letter

Rotterdam, 30 May 1824

This is probably the last letter I shall send you before my departure. On my arrival here,[1] I found an American ship prepared to sail, waiting only for a favorable wind to leave for Baltimore. [1– 1] The name of the ship is the same as that of the well-known statesman Henry Clay.

I was able to predict the opinion of N.[2] concerning my undertaking. [1– 2] If I wanted to try to change it, I should have to transform his entire way of thinking. I am glad that such a task is not a part of the preparation I must make for this trip.

I shall report to you faithfully my judgments concerning life in America. Because the judgment of every traveler is so very dependent on his expectations and on his preconceived opinions, I consider it expedient to express my expectations and opinions of America before I begin my investigations. [1– 3]

You are aware that my itinerary is directed toward the United States, and more specifically toward the regions along the Ohio River and the lower Missouri River. The regions lying in higher latitudes are, according to all reports, too cold for settlers from central Europe, and those more to the south are too hot.

I am prepared to find Europeans in the United States and am of the opinion that the political situation in that country is based more on favorable economic conditions than on the personal superiority of its inhabitants. In general, I expect no other advantage for the settler than that he can purchase fertile land at a low price and that he will be rather unrestricted in the selection of this land [1– 4] and its location with respect to trade, as well as to health and the amenities of life. Also, I expect freedom from oppressive taxation and in general independence in trade and industry such as will never be found in Europe.

Second Letter

Written 31 June 1824 [2– 1] near the Azores (called the Western Isles by the English) at 38½° North latitude and 28½° West longitude from Greenwich.

You see my friend, the heavens have not looked upon our[1] trip with special favor. On 8 June I left Helvoetsluis[2] on the ship *Henry Clay*, and

---

Asterisks refer to the notes that appear at the bottoms of the pages, which are Duden's as they appeared in the first edition of his *Report*; numbers in brackets refer to changes made in the 1834 edition, which are collected in Appendix I; superior numbers refer to the editors' annotations, which appear in Appendix II.

found myself riding the waves of the North Sea several hours later. A rather strong wind took us in two days through the entire [English] Channel (often close to the coast of England), and my hope of a rapid crossing seemed to be more and more well-founded. But suddenly the weather changed. A persistent west wind forced us—since we had no desire to sail constantly in an acutely angular zigzag (tacking) direction—to abandon the direct course[3] and brought us after twenty days to the Azores. Near these islands, which are of ill repute among sailors because of frequent [2–2] storms, we have now been completely becalmed for three days. I am writing these lines in sight of a high mountain on the island of Pico. I should like very much to feel solid ground beneath my feet for a while and to see close at hand the vineyards and the orange groves that are visible in the distance. It would be interesting, in the midst of the ocean, to wander around in an important city such as Angra, Punta de Gada [2–3], or Fayal,[4] and to watch the activities of the Portuguese, to whom these islands belong. But we must deny ourselves this pleasure. No insured vessel may, except in case of distress, enter a harbor that is not designated as on its course. The insurance companies would, in case of such action, be relieved entirely of their liability in case of accidents, or at any rate, acquire the right to demand compensation from the owner of the ship and captain.[5] So I am limited to my powers of imagination, which have sufficient material for consideration if one has read of the volcanic action at the bottom of the sea in these areas. In the sixteenth, seventeenth, and eighteenth centuries various new islands, some of considerable size, alternately appeared and disappeared here. The most recent one rose to the surface just at the time when an English man-of-war was close at hand. The captain immediately took possession of it in the name of His British Majesty. After several days it disappeared again.[6]

Up to now we have met with no special misfortunes. However, I had a severe attack of seasickness. In German medical science this illness is usually bypassed.[7] Since I have found only superficial or even incorrect statements about its nature in travel reports, I am therefore giving you more of the details based on my own experience.

It is well known that digestion depends greatly on the stimulation of the brain. Pressure on the brain, caused by thrusts or blows, often causes vomiting.[8] Bile, whose function it is to encourage activity of the digestive organs through stimulation of the intestines and to promote the disintegration of food and drink as well as the removal of the excrement through the colon, reverses its course and gets into the stomach. It is then expelled by vomiting.

Unpleasant mental stimulation has the same effect. Those whose minds are active only as a faculty of conception do not easily suffer from such stimulation; however, the effect is all the greater in the case of emotional agitation, that is, emotional disturbances.

Stimulation of the brain affects the circulation of blood, and changes in the circulation affect the brain. The degree of this dependence varies greatly. It is dependent on the excitability of the mind as well as on the bodily organs. In general it may be assumed that the brains of those persons who have never engaged in special mental activity and are healthy also show less sensitivity to merely physical influence.*

The circulation is affected by the swaying of the ship, and this disturbance produces pressure on the brain and dizziness. This is the nature of the sickness and this alone causes vomiting. The sea air, which is often mentioned in this connection, and to which all sorts of things are attributed, is completely innocent. As a rule it is purer than the air on land.

Unless there are complications, seasickness is dangerous only for those whose brains are extremely sensitive [to changes in blood pressure] and whose digestion is rather weak. Most people recover after two or three days. It seems that their organs, which at the beginning were overpowered by the foreign influence, gradually lose their sensitivity. However, this sensitivity never disappears entirely. Due to the rocking of the ship during storms, even old, hardened seamen often succumb to vomiting, and the strong appetite on sea journeys, usually attributed to better than average health, is a pathological phenomenon. It is due to the unnatural stimulation of the stomach by the products of a disturbed digestion.

Pure, cool air, good water with cream of tartar as a drink, and rice [2–4] or barley gruel as food, and the use of [2–5] sulfuric ether will protect one from developing a serious case. Nothing, however, alleviates the vomiting more than olive oil or almond oil. A tablespoonful is sufficient for one dose. One is more comfortable in fresh air than in the cabin.[10] However, at the first attack one can rarely avoid lying down, and on deck this is connected with unpleasant circumstances. Many seafarers advise against lying down because they say that one's indisposition is thereby more [2–6] prolonged. A gentle emptying of the stomach of food eaten while the patient was still well is, to be sure, beneficial. During the swaying of the ship an upright position greatly aids in vomiting. But as soon as the retching develops into a constriction of the throat it becomes absolutely necessary to lie down. Still worse advice is to follow one's usual diet. Such attempts may be suitable to those who are training to become sailors. Here, there are other considerations than those resulting merely from the nature of the illness. [2–7] The latter considerations usually permit the use of the sailor cure only in the case of healthy children. [2–8] Dried fruit (plums, apples,

---

*I need not remind you that this sentence on seasickness can be subject to exceptions, and that this cannot be carelessly reversed is proved by, among other examples, the statements of Herrn von Humboldt[9] that he always feels well at sea.

and so forth) is highly recommended. Indeed, those suffering from
seasickness show a great preference for it. Sometimes constipation
persists for ten to fourteen days without any other danger than that the
excrement becomes acid and the opening of the intestines must be
protected by oil. The generous use of cream of tartar with epsom salts
will prevent it. This remedy also eases the unpleasant stimulation that
the bile usually causes in the stomach. Good herrings or anchovies on
an empty stomach in the morning and nothing else until noon are
excellent for the traveler. Coffee probably causes head congestion.
Strenuous mental work is harmful. Continuous reading is unadvisable
in view of the weakened condition of the eyes. [2−9]

So much for the illness in its simple form. As far as complications are
concerned, one should bear in mind that not infrequently one or
another passenger brings, as the saying goes, an impure stomach with
him on board. Such a condition, especially if it has existed for some
time, is usually accompanied by some weakness of the digestive organs.
In some cases it is one of the causes of the impure matter. Therefore,
mere purgatives are often not sufficient enough to effect a cure. The
more gently they work, the less disruptive irritation they cause to the
affected organs. In the case of children, the greater vitality of continuing
development is a help. But for adults, bitter aromatic medicine and
spirituous remedies are usually required after the purging. This is the
case on land. But on sea, this course of treatment is out of the question.
The nervous system is weakened more and more by the continuous
rolling of the ship and the relation of the above-named medication to
digestion is completely changed.[11]

There are many sad examples that heat and lack of cleanliness increase the slightest danger of putrid fever and typhus. Impure air is to
be feared most. During hot weather the sea is rarely restless and
travelers can remain on deck. But in colder seasons stormy seas are
common. Then it is impossible to remain on deck, for in order to
prevent the entrance of water all vents remain closed so that the
quarters of those who are not in cabins resemble subterranean caves.
During very cold weather, which is said rarely to exceed nine degrees
(-9°) Reaumur[12] far from the coast, there may, nevertheless, be some
circulation of the outer and inner air, and those who are provided with
good covers and coats will perhaps not complain of the absence of
stoves (which are found only in the cabins). If the cold is not severe,
however, the closing of vents in a space filled with seasick persons
exposes to great danger even the European, who is accustomed to
winter huts where the greatest lack of cleanliness prevails. Arrangements preventing such a condition can be made only if the passengers
are so numerous that they exceed the sum total of the freight, which
often determines completely the consideration of other gains. If this is
not the case, the hold of the ship cannot be recommended to anyone.

Third Letter
7 August 1824

What a long journey! Nine weeks on the ocean and no land in sight. In my former letter I complained about being becalmed near the Azores. Now I could give a description of the thunderstorms and the waterspouts to which we have since been exposed. Innumerable ships glide safely back and forth, and there are persons who have sailed across the Atlantic Ocean more than a hundred times. It is only natural that those who live far from the seashore gradually believe that the dangers exist largely in the imagination. Short sea journeys can even strengthen this belief. But in general, this is far from the truth. In no situation in life is man confronted so impressively with his complete dependence on the Supreme Being as when he spends so many hours on the sea. Every captain of a ship can, without violating the truth, relate stories of occurrences in which he was threatened with destruction and in which he survived only as if by a miracle.

Of all the regions of the sea, the Gulf Stream is most productive of such occurrences. I am still close to it. We have barely succeeded in crossing it. Our first attempt was unsuccessful, for just as we were halfway across, a little below 38° latitude, the wind failed us and a complete calm placed us at the mercy of the Stream. We were driven back about four hundred nautical miles toward the great Bank of Newfoundland. This in itself was not especially fraught with danger. It is the storm clouds and the waterspouts that make a protracted delay in the region of the Gulf Stream so dangerous. Therefore, ships sailing toward Europe only rarely try to use this course. The frequent formation of these electric vapors seems to have some connection with the temperature of the water of the Stream. We always tried to avoid them as much as possible and yet twice we ran into such heavy waterspouts that we feared the deck would be shattered.[1]

The temperature of the Gulf Stream is so extraordinary that for seamen it is the surest mark of identification. The Fahrenheit thermometer indicated 87 degrees, while the temperature of the water just outside of the Stream had attained only 74 degrees.[2] In the winter the difference is still greater. The cause of this phenomenon is easily explained. Enormous masses of water, which hasten at considerable speed out of the hot Gulf of Mexico toward the north, must necessarily become noticeable in the higher latitudes because of their temperature. In regard to the origin of the mighty current, however, one should call to mind the general movement of the tropical ocean from east to west, and also the formation of the American coasts. If one considers that this movement is restricted to the torrid zone and about 8° beyond its limits, a fleeting glance at the charts will furnish a complete explanation of the origin of this greatest of all eddies in the Gulf of Mexico, as well as of its outflow along the coast of Florida. For the sea is constantly driven toward Mexico. The closer to the equator, the greater is the pressure of the water. Therefore, it is greater near the Lesser Antilles than near the Greater Antilles. Besides, the Greater Antilles, especially Cuba, present great hindrances. The current between the Lesser Antilles will then turn in the direction where it will find the least resistance. Accordingly, passing between Yucatan and Cuba it will turn toward the coast of the continent and breaking there will be forced to pass out of the basin again, between Florida and the Bahama Islands.

The Gulf Stream passes about eighty to one hundred English nautical miles off the coast of the two Carolinas and Virginia, with the exception of Cape Lookout and Cape Hatteras, which it approaches almost too closely for navigation. Its speed there is estimated at three to five nautical miles, and its width in some places is seventy to ninety nautical miles. Farther toward the north, its width increases; temperature and speed decrease. It turns more and more away from America and extends in an arch along the great Bank of Newfoundland toward the southeast, where seamen no longer take it into consideration. This bank, the main source of stockfish (dried cod), which some consider a product of the Stream, seems to break it in a manner similar to the coasts of Mexico. Probably of no small influence are the polar currents, which are very noticeable near Newfoundland, and every summer bring great masses of ice toward the south, often beyond 40° latitude.[3]

In general, life on board a ship seems very boring. I have already written you earlier that I am not able to read much. Of interest to me were only sharks, flying fish, dolphins, men-of-war, and young whales. At 38° latitude, tropical birds also appeared. Except on stormy days, we were always accompanied, however, by a species of small swallow, even in midocean, many hundred miles from land. Sometimes we threw some fat on the waves, which they ate resting on the water and twittering merrily. One can also see oceanic birds everywhere, but not in flocks like the swallows. The sailors call them "Mother carries the chicken" (the mother carries its young)[4] because of the fable that the mother hatches the eggs under her wings. Considering the swift flight of these birds, a distance of two hundred German miles is not so great, and at such a distance there is never a lack of isolated rocks. The man-of-war, of which there are several species, is an amazing animal. It belongs to the mollusks. The French call it frigate; the English man-of-war (warship).[5] It is a membranous, vesicular creature, the size of a goose egg, with its back covered by a membrane, which the animal uses exactly like a sail. The delicate creature shimmers in beautiful red, blue, and green colors. To its vesicular body are attached tentacles which one cannot touch without being burned as with fire. Dolphins (of the order Cetaceans) often passed the ship by the hundreds. We threw harpoons at then; however all that were hit tore themselves loose. When they [dolphins] arrived, flying fish rose together out of the waves in order to escape their dangerous enemies. A young shark (*Squalus carcharias,* the white shark) followed our ship for an entire day. I estimated his weight at 150 to 200 pounds. We wanted to catch him, and we even succeeded in piercing his upper jaw with a harpoon, but he tore himself loose again and disappeared. Several small fish (pilot fish), resembling a quarter-pound trout, accompanied him. The sea was calm and I saw clearly that they not only circled the jaws of the shark, but swam alternately in and out again. They [3-1] glisten in very beautiful colors and are said to have an excellent taste. The captain wanted to catch the shark because of them, for he said that he would be sure to find several of them between his jaws. We kept our distance from whales. No ship will try to approach them. With a single blow of the tail they could make a dangerous opening in the strongest walls. Most remarkable to me was the luminosity of the sea. This phenomenon is not very common. I saw it two consecutive nights in July, at approximately 30° latitude and between 56° and 60° longitude. Wherever the sea was in motion, it resembled a glowing mass. As soon as the bow of the ship cut through the waves they began to glow, and for quite some time the wake became a stream of fire. The shower of drops looked like sparks of fire. At some distance from the ship, where the sea was quiet, nothing could be seen. The water that was drawn on deck showed nothing remarkable. It could not be distinguished from ordinary seawater. This kind of luminosity is to be attributed to electricity (according to Forster).[6]

I have forgotten to remark that longitude is calculated by the distance from Greenwich [England]. You will perhaps be surprised that I even mention these degrees. However, you must not assume that astronomers can be found on merchant ships. Our ship is supplied neither with chronometers (sea clocks) nor lunar tables. At any rate, most seamen would not know how to use lunar tables. Chronometers seem to be too expensive for them. They determine the latitude by the well-known reflection octant, approximately as pupils solve the problems in their arithmetic texts without having any idea of the reasons for their work. In regard to longitude, they depend on a procedure that, even with the greatest care, produces an acceptable result only if no storms are encountered on the entire trip. From time to time the speed of the ship is measured (except in cases of sudden wind changes when the speed is measured every two hours). For this purpose a small board to which a long cord is attached is thrown overboard. As the ship progresses just so much and no more of the cord is unreeled without pulling the board and this indicates the distance covered by the ship. The experiment must, of course, be limited to a definite time, for example to a minute, which is determined by a sand clock. By the distance covered in one minute, the distance covered in the following hours is calculated, and thus the number of miles that the ship sails in an entire day. From this distance, the direction of the course, and the geographical latitude, the longitude is deduced with the aid of tables. The Gulf Stream and several storms had hindered us greatly in the use of the log, as the little board [3-2] is called. The captain hated my questions concerning the longitude, however he always willingly gave me the latitude. It is the custom of seamen who meet on the ocean to exchange their longitude calculations.[7]

At present we are between the Gulf Stream and the American coast at 39° north latitude. The sea is beginning to lose its dark (bluish green) color and is turning more nearly green, which is a sign (although not an infallible one) of lesser depth. The captain believes that a plumb line of two hundred fathoms (twelve hundred feet) would reach the bottom. Ours is only one hundred fathoms long. I hope it can be used tomorrow.

Fourth Letter
9 August 1824

The test with the plumb line has just been made, and to our great joy it struck bottom at ninety fathoms. To determine the nature of the bottom (whether it consists of rock, sand, or clay), the lower side of the plumb line [4-1] is covered with tallow. Here it indicated fine sand. My glances are often directed toward the west now in order to discover land. We are sailing at the same latitude as Cape Henlopen (opposite Cape May) and could very soon enter the Delaware River to reach Philadelphia, since the adverse south wind is exactly right for that. Perhaps we must be patient for several more days, although a favorable breeze would take us to Cape Henry before midnight.[1] But this is the lot of the sailor; sometimes he is completely becalmed, or he is even hurled back; sometimes he speeds at 12 to 14 nautical miles an hour, that is, sometimes 280– 320* nautical miles in one day. I shall try to shorten the waiting time by jotting down a few remarks about life on board ship.

On every ship (in the language of Englishmen and Americans a three-masted vessel is a ship, a two-masted one is called a brig, and a one-masted one a schooner)** there is a waiter for serving the cabin personnel, which includes the captain and two or three officers besides the passengers. In England and in North America, on ocean ships as well as on river steamers, this waiter is called a steward. He performs

---

*When the word *miles* occurs without further designation, one should interpret it as English miles. These amount to 69-3/25 per degree, the nautical (or geographical) miles only to 60. The ratio of the latter to the German miles is therefore 4 to 1; that of the former almost 4-2/3 to 1 (or 14 to 3).

**There are schooners that are larger than brigs, but the opposite is more common.

the combined services of a waiter and a valet and is probably also required to help in hoisting and lowering sails and in other work on deck that requires the cooperation of many persons.

Besides the cabin personnel, he is the only one who may enter the cabins without the express permission of the captain. No one else can even set foot on the stairs leading from the deck. I have noticed several times that new sailors who violated this rule were immediately turned back by the steward.

In general, discipline prevails on the American ships such as can scarcely be found in the regular army. No sailor may address a cabin passenger. Conversation between passengers and sailors is frowned upon by every captain. Some captains even consider a long conversation between cabin passengers and steerage passengers out of order. The laws of the Americans permit the captain to punish a sailor by beating him with a rope in the presence of the crew and, in cases of necessity, to place him in irons.

Passengers on trading vessels must provide their own bedding and liquor. The captain takes care of all other needs including medicines.*2 On packets, the captain provides both bedding and liquor and the cabin rate is adjusted accordingly. The passengers on trading vessels, however, almost always provide themselves, in addition to liquor, with mineral water, good beer, so-called Dutch (fine) zwieback, ham, lemons, oranges, honey cakes, dried apples, prunes, and so forth, not only to ward off the dreaded seasickness, but also because the ship's fare might not agree with them. The ship's hardtack will seem especially unpalatable to the traveler. On packets, cows provide fresh milk and cream. On trading vessels one must do without these things, and one should never forget a supply of mineral water and beer because not much attention is paid to the drinking water on board and, generally, several barrels of it taste unpleasantly of wood.3 My fare was eighty dollars (two hundred Dutch guilders) and my supplies, half of which went for bedding, cost me another sixty guilders. I am told the bedding can be sold on shore without loss. [4-2]

The steward on our ship is a Negro (usually they are mulattoes). He is a freeman, lives in Baltimore, and is hired for this service at a monthly rate of eighteen dollars. Ordinary sailors receive, in addition to their board, fourteen to sixteen dollars per month, the ship's carpenter eighteen to twenty, the second mate twenty, the first mate thirty.** The period of payment for these persons corresponds with the length of the trip. Only the captain is hired by the year. Some captains receive one

---

*According to American law, there must be a supply of medicine on every seagoing vessel of a definite size (I believe on every ship of more than 250 tons). To this are added brief instructions concerning its use. As a result, many captains have a tendency toward quackery.

**The two mates are officers who form a part of the cabin personnel.

hundred dollars per month and, in addition, a considerable percentage of the freight carried, so that an industrious captain can acquire a sizable fortune in a few years.[4]

In England as well as in America serious attempts have been made to improve the morals of the sailors. It is said that in a short time miracles have been performed by promoting religion among them. In this respect the Methodists have been much praised for their exertions and perseverance. As soon as the disreputable crudeness prevalent among the ship's crew has improved, good parents will be less reluctant to entrust their children to the merchantmen for practical instruction in navigation. Consequently, trade and the merchant marine will derive incalculable benefit from it.

Fifth Letter

14 August 1824

The day before yesterday we finally arrived at Cape Henry (opposite Cape Charles), at 37° north latitude, at the entrance to Chesapeake Bay. A favorable wind drove us quickly into the bay, and after more than nine weeks on the sea, we enjoyed the smooth waters. The pilot had arrived on board ship two days previously. The American pilots are in the habit of boarding the ship far enough away from the coast so that arriving ships do not have to worry about waiting for them. We sailed quickly up the bay, but only during the daytime. At night we lay at anchor to avoid shoals. Almost the entire seacoast of the United States is low. At first I saw only sand hills with scattered conifer woods. Cape Henry is a sand hill itself, topped by a lighthouse. The German word *Vorgebirge* [foothills] does not apply here. The bay is approximately three hundred [5-1] English miles long and its width varies between ten and forty [5-2] nautical miles. Everywhere one can see both shores. Its direction is almost directly from south to north. The significant streams flow from the west side. The east side is a long, narrow peninsula. The naval harbor at Norfolk, at the mouth of the James River, first attracted my attention. A better place for warships could scarcely be found. Nevertheless, it will require much money and time to complete the projected gigantic fortifications.[1] We had scarcely passed the mouth of the James River when we caught sight of that of the York. Then followed the Rappahannock, later the Potomac (on which at some distance higher up the capital, Washington, is situated), and finally the Patuxent. The shores of the bay remain low and level for a long distance. Later they rise, especially on the west, and afford beautiful views. Here everything has long been private property and the land is more expensive than along the large rivers of Germany. Along the hills surrounding the bay one sees many charming country estates whose meadows are interrupted by clusters of various kinds of trees. The smooth surface of the water was covered with large and small boats; several of them brought us fresh vegetables, fruit [5-3], melons, peaches, apples, and newspapers, all of which were heartily welcome.

Baltimore, on the Patapsco River, now lies before us. The public health officers, quickly convinced that all of us were in good health, have just departed.[2] They appeared at Fort McHenry, which efficiently guards the approach to the city.[3] In 1814 the English were defeated there, after their general had been shot to death by an inhabitant of Baltimore.[4] Because the shores of the Patapsco [5-4] rise high and steeply in terraces, and because the city is built both along [the shore] and on the heights in the form of an amphitheater, it is a beautiful sight for the traveler approaching from the southeast. There is also no lack of villas and small woods, so that the whole view, even at this season when green has disappeared from sunny places, makes a very pleasant impression. Moreover, you can easily imagine that a city of 70,000 inhabitants,[5] with its houses (built mainly of brick), warehouses, wharves, sailboats, and steamboats, covers a considerable territory. Its name is derived from Lord Baltimore, to whom these regions were granted by Charles I; the name of the state (Maryland) is derived from Henrietta Maria, the wife of the same king. The capital is not Baltimore, but the much smaller city of Annapolis.

Sixth Letter

Washington in Pennsylvania, 20 September 1824

You must not expect a description of Baltimore. I hate such a task so much that I would be tempted merely to copy the reports of others. However, I do want to mention the clean and regularly laid out streets, from which the dirt is removed by means of subterranean canals; the gas illumination in the best parts of the city; the white marble in so many dwellings; the general use of carpets, as well as the sumptuousness of furniture; all can do much to change the ideas of European arrivals that they have come to a wilderness. [6-1] Among the buildings the stock exchange and the diocesan Catholic church are especially noteworthy. One can see (at a distance from the bay) a hill in the northern part of the city with an obelisk like monument to the immortal Washington [6-2] ; in the city itself there is another monument to the citizens who fell in 1814 in the successful defense of Baltimore against the English.[1] In the museum of Mr. Peale[2] I found a complete skeleton of the mammoth (*Mammut Ohioticum*) and a complete skeleton of the megatherium (the American giant sloth) with its claw-shaped feet. In front, the mammoth was eleven feet high to the upper part of the shoulder; from the rear up to the upper part of the hip it was nine feet high and seventeen feet long. The entire desiccated skeleton is said to weigh over a thousand pounds. The megatherium almost equalled it.

At first, the great number of Negroes and mulattoes did not especially appeal to me.[3] But this feeling is very transient. Almost all the men driving rented coaches are colored people (a current expression for Negroes and mulattoes). Their coaches are of good appearance and some cannot be distinguished from a European state coach.[4] One finds them on all of the main streets, and for twenty-five cents (one franc equals five cents) they drive to any part of the city. [6-3]

The heat was rather fierce. However, because of the general custom of using umbrellas for protection against the rays of the sun one suffers less from it than on the streets of German cities. Riders with umbrellas are not an unusual sight, and for long horse rides they are considered more useful than coats, except during the short winter.

The inns in Baltimore are not more expensive than those on the lower Rhine. But if one wishes to live in private houses [6-4] ,which in North America is very common and necessary for proper rest and quiet during a longer stay, one can count on good board and room from four to five dollars per week (ten to twelve and one-half Dutch guilders). In the best inns the cost is seven and a half to nine dollars. [6-5]

Nothing about the way of life here astonishes a German so much as the frequent eating of meat. Even early in the morning the table is full of meat dishes, and in this respect there is no difference between breakfast and the noon meal. Wine is rarely served in the inns. Until now little wine has been produced in the interior, and foreign wines are subject to a high duty.* With the exception of the brandies, French brandy, peach brandy, Genevre, and whiskey (corn brandy), coffee seems to have been substituted. Coffee and tea are served not only at breakfast, but also at supper and often even at the noon meal. The spirits mentioned above are, moreover, always diluted with water, and the European who is used to wine feels quite satisfied with them. At least he is safe from the many harmful mixtures from which wine suffers in Europe. The greatest variety of dishes is served at the same time, and as soon as the food is on the table the sound of the second bell (which is preceded a quarter of an hour earlier by the ringing of a bell as a signal to be ready) calls the guests into the dining room. They often rush in hastily. As if it were a matter of very serious business and without much conversation, they appease their hunger in all haste, most often eating from one and the same plate, using their own handkerchiefs instead of napkins. In five or ten minutes they leave again. This is most disgusting in the evening. Instead of an evening meal that begins between eight and nine o'clock

---

*This duty has been lowered very recently. [6-6]

and is followed by dessert and prolonged discussion, the food is placed on the table as early as seven o'clock when the midday meal has not yet been digested. Attention is directed strictly toward filling the stomach quickly so that even a longer stay in the dining room would be considered contrary to the rules. In some inns, to be sure, tea and coffee are served around five o'clock, and then the evening meal follows at about nine. But as far as the duration of the meal and sociability are concerned, it is the same everywhere.

If you look on the map at the place where I have dated my present letter, you will notice that I am already beyond the Allegheny Mountains, and some words concerning this trip might be more welcome to you than the above descriptions relating to food and table manners.

I did not remain in Baltimore more than ten days, not longer than was necessary to make preparations for the long journey into the interior. Above all, I provided myself with excellent maps. Then I procured various letters of recommendation in order not to be entirely without support in case of accidents. Money matters I arranged by having the Bank of the United States issue me banknotes made out to me personally and redeemable in specially designated branch banks. I took with me, partly in cash and partly in banknotes, only as much as I thought I would need until I reached the next designated branch. A foreigner must be wary of accepting banknotes from strangers. [6-7] It is best to obtain them from the bank comptroller himself. Also, one must be very careful to distinguish the notes of the United States (federal) from the notes of individual states and private banks (of which there are very many). It is better to have nothing to do with the latter if one is not completely familiar with the rate of exchange.[5] [6-8]

While attending to these matters of business I and my traveling companion, a young fellow countryman who intends to settle in America as a farmer,[6] bought two draft horses and a wagon with good springs.* A part of our baggage was stored in the wagon; the rest was entrusted to freight transportation. On 25 August the journey to the Ohio began. Our first objective was the little town of Wheeling. It is 260 miles from Baltimore and connected with it by a highway (turnpike), which was constructed by funds from all the states and completed only a few years ago.[7] Baltimore is closer to the Ohio than any other seaport, and after Pittsburgh, the shortest direct route from Baltimore converges in Wheeling.

During the first days we traveled through rolling and rather extensively cultivated land. We could have imagined we were traveling in Germany had it not been for the unfamiliarity of the architecture of some of the dwellings, the general type of construction of the barns and

---

*In Baltimore there is a horse market twice a week. We found the prices low. Strong draft horses cost fifty to eighty dollars.

granaries, and the fencing of the fields. To be sure, Negro families dispelled the illusion most frequently. One soon becomes accustomed to the black faces of the adults, but groups of naked and half-naked children still arrest my attention. They all have something droll about them that one seldom notices among the whites. Aside from their color, their figures seem to be carved out of wood instead of having pleasing curves. This and their shyness in the presence of whites, as if they were considered creatures of a higher order, stimulates the interest of the European at first more strongly than can the more beautiful groups of white children.

The style of architecture mentioned above is a product of the abundance of building timber. The amount of labor involved is very insignificant. If, for example, the building is to be 30 feet long, 24 feet wide, and 18 feet high up to the roof, one fells tree trunks 24 feet long for the narrow sides, and an equal number 30 feet long for the long sides. One begins the construction at the long sides of the foundation by laying two logs on stone bases; the two logs function as base plates. The ends of these plates are tapered off on the upper surfaces for the purpose of notching the succeeding logs. Now a short log is placed on each narrow side which, after having been notched at each end, must rest firmly on the ends of the base plates. After the ends of these short logs have been tapered off, as previously the ends of the long logs, new long logs are placed on the long sides and fitted to the ends of the short ones by notching. This is repeated until the proper height is reached. Then, for the construction of the gable-shaped roof, the new logs are placed closer to each other on the long sides, which requires shorter logs than before on the narrow sides. As the new long logs are moved closer and closer together, the logs of the narrow sides become shorter and shorter until finally a single long log across the middle of the highest short logs forms the peak of the roof. Such a roof frame is then covered either with shingles and nails, or a kind of large shingle(clapboard) is placed loosely upon it and held fast by the weight of other logs. The open spaces are easily closed with clay or limestone. The logs felled for dwellings are usually squared on the outer and inner sides. According to an old custom, the structure is erected with the help of neighbors at no cost other than that of providing food.

The type of fencing is also selected with the intention of avoiding the labor of carpenters and joiners by a more generous use of wood. Split logs (rails), which are ten feet long and weigh about forty to sixty pounds, are laid in zigzag fashion over each other, thereby creating the strongest barriers (fence) [6-9], which confine horses and cattle as well as hogs. In Germany these animals are confined, but here they run around freely and the fences serve to keep them from certain areas. I shall have occasion to speak more about this later.[8]

Not less conspicuous than the buildings were the large cornfields.

Then there were interspersed plantings of cotton and the splendid miracle plant from whose seeds ricinus oil (castor oil) is gained, which is very valuable because of its gentle laxative characteristics. The soil did not seem especially fertile to us and, in general, in need of fertilizer. The woods consisted mostly of oaks and of several species of nut trees called *hickory.* Beneath them the ground was covered with a mint (penny royal) whose [6-10] fragrance became annoying in time. Among the wild birds, the beautiful colors of the woodpeckers most attracted our attention.

We drove along past Ellicott's Mill, Poplarspring, and Newmarket[9] without any diversions except the isolated brooks and small rivers winding their way through shady ravines and valleys, some to the Patapsco, some to the Patuxent.

In the broad valley of the Monocacy, a tributary of the Potomac, the landscape becomes charming. On the right shore lies the small town of Fredericktown whose surrounding region has the reputation of rare fertility. The agricultural establishments all bear the stamp of prosperity. The town itself, forty-four English miles from Baltimore, has about three thousand inhabitants. [6-11] Most of the houses are made of brick and have a pleasing architecture; the streets are wide and well paved.

Six miles beyond Fredericktown we came upon our first mountain range, which in Maryland and Virginia is called the South Range (southern mountains).

There are still many contradictions in geography books as well as in travel reports concerning the formation and the course of individual mountain ranges that go by the general name of the Alleghenies. The Americans themselves complain about it. For example, see Darby's work entitled the *Guide of the Emigrants*, which appeared in 1819 in New York.[10] Now that I have all the ranges behind me I shall attempt to communicate to you my ideas as they have developed from the combination of my own observations and the information gained from the most recent writings and maps.

For the sake of completeness, I shall begin with a few words concerning the surface of the United States in general.

From all geographic encyclopedias one can learn that the shape of North America, and especially of the United States, is determined mainly by two mountain ranges. One of these ridges is not far from the Atlantic coast and runs (except for the peninsula of Florida which juts out into the sea) almost parallel to it, from northeast to southwest. It is called the Allegheny Mountains (in a broader sense) or the Appalachian Mountains.*[11] The other, far higher and longer chain extends along the Pacific coast from northwest to southeast. It is called the Rocky Moun-

---

*The former appellation was common among the northern Indians, and is said to mean *endless mountains* in their language. The name *Appalachian* is derived from the

tains,* which can be considered a continuation of the Mexican Andes. These ranges, therefore, converge in a north-south direction, as the two seashores themselves. The coastal rivers run without any noticeable connections with one another directly to the sea; as, for example, on the Atlantic coast the Hudson, the Delaware, the Susquehanna, the Potomac, the James, the York, the Savannah, the Alabama, and others. It is peculiar to the rivers between these ranges that most of them unite in a common riverbed before they enter the sea. It looks as if, in their attempt to reach the sea, they were being gradually diverted to a middle line, to the Mississippi, which flows directly from the north to the south. The term *middle line* is all the more fitting as the most distant waters of the Mississippi have their sources in neither of the two mountain chains, but come from an expansive plateau that extends from the branches of the Alleghenies south of the large (Canadian) [Great] lakes in a northwest direction to the Rocky Mountains. It is this plateau that completely separates the Mississippi River basin from the waters that turn toward the polar sea and Hudson Bay, as well as from the tributaries of the large lakes that form the St. Lawrence River. Not far from this watershed lies the northern boundary of the United States. The waters that flow to the Mississippi from the east come partly from the plateau south of the large lakes and partly from the Alleghenies themselves. Most of them converge into the Ohio River and flow together toward the Mississippi. Others proceed directly. The important Illinois, located north of the Ohio, is one of them. Likewise, the waters coming to the Mississippi from the west have their sources partly in the northern plateau. Far greater masses, however, come from the Rocky Mountains proper. I shall mention the large Missouri, the Arkansas, and the Red rivers. To be sure, the rivers that flow into the large lakes north of the frequently mentioned plateau are rather small compared to the former, but they are extremely important for the water connection between the basin of the St. Lawrence River and that of the Mississippi since at a few places very short canals would suffice.

With this introduction, let me now tell you about the Allegheny Mountains in particular.

The mountains, beginning with the hills south of the St. Lawrence River in lower Canada and the state of New York, run at first in a southwest direction and then directly west and are known by the general name Allegheny or Appalachian. They can be divided into two main chains.[12]

Indian tribe of the same name, who lived in Georgia between the Savannah and Alatamaha rivers. It was used generally in the South.

*In the far north, the Rocky Mountains are also called the Chippewa Mountains from the great tribe of the Chippewas. There they retreat toward the northeast coast of Asia from the coast which turns due west.

The chain farther to the east is called the Alleghenies in the narrower sense. It can be traced from the hills between the Richelieu and St. Lawrence rivers in Canada to the mountains west of lakes George and Champlain, over the high plain near Utica in the state of New York, into the state of Pennsylvania to 40° 15′ north latitude, where it is cut by the Susquehanna. From that point on the range can be more accurately described as a chain. It extends through Pennsylvania and the state of Maryland where it separates the sources of the Potomac from those of the Youghiogheny. From the Potomac to the large Kanawha it divides the waters that flow into the Atlantic Ocean from those of the Ohio, extending from Maryland through the western part of Virginia between the sources of the large Kanawha and the Tennessee, then southwest toward Evansham. Its course is cut by the valley of the large Kanawha.* Then the chain (known by various local names, such as the Yellow Mountains, the Iron Mountains, the Smoky Mountains, the Unakoi Mountains) extends in the same direction along the border of Tennessee and North Carolina to 34° latitude, forming a massif between 36° and 34°. There, almost broken, it turns west and, gradually decreasing in elevation, disappears near 14° longitude (measured from Washington). Here on the west side of the Mississippi appears a branch of the Rocky Mountains, namely the Masserne Mountain Range,[14] which runs south of the Arkansas River to its confluence with the Mississippi. The space between them [Smoky and Masserne mountains] is about fifteen German miles.

The other main chain, west of the above-mentioned Alleghenies, is the Cumberland Mountains. Among the people it bears this name only in Tennessee. Among other designations, one should note in particular the Laurel Hills[15] (from the evergreen *Kalmia latifola* [6-12], called *laurel* in the vernacular). They can be traced from the region near Angelica in the state of New York, extending in a course somewhat parallel to the previously mentioned chain through Pennsylvania into the state of Virginia to the source of the Big Sandy River (the large Sand River). From here they run in a more westerly direction, about one hundred English miles, along the border of Virginia and Kentucky, and then into the state of Tennessee between the sources of the Cumberland and the Clinch rivers; then due west along the north side of 36° latitude to the sources of the Emery, a small tributary of the Clinch in Overton County; from there in a southwest direction to the sources of the small Elk River in Franklin County (at latitude 35°, 40′), where they divide into three branches that gradually become low hills. However, one can consider the northern branch, which is by far the longest, as the

---

*Whoever imagines the Allegheny Mountains (according to Volney) as a complete watershed is mistaken. Each of the main and secondary chains is cut by rivers, which is very extraordinary, to be sure.[13]

continuation of the main range. This branch continues north of the Duck River in a northwestern direction and finally, although it rises only seven to eight hundred feet above the Ohio valley, reaches the alluvial valley of the Mississippi beyond the Tennessee River. Between the Tennessee and the Cumberland rivers, accordingly, the Cumberland chain forms an arc toward the south, which cuts latitude 36° twice. Opposite the above-mentioned end of this arc, there is, on the west side of the Mississippi, the end of those hills that separate the sources of the Merrimack from the White River.[16] This end is characterized by a four hundred foot vertical limerock formation, which lies close to the Mississippi, near the city of Cape Girardeau. The interval here [between the Ozark Plateau and the southern arc of the Cumberland chain] is also about fifteen German miles.

This seems to indicate that the two main chains, or the Allegheny Mountains in a broader sense, were once connected with the Rocky Mountains and were later separated from them by the breakthrough of the Mississippi.

But the main chains described here send out many branches, some of which are so long that they deserve to be called secondary chains. These secondary chains in turn send out more or less important branches, which determine the formation of all the territory between the Mississippi, the Great Lakes, and the Atlantic Ocean. To the south, for example, branches extend to Georgia and to Alabama, and to the north through Kentucky, Ohio, and Indiana. Illinois has the fewest. There one finds great plains.

As true secondary chains, the following branches, above all, demand a special description.

First, a range of hills extends from the west side of the Cumberland Mountains, which, to be sure, is far lower than the main range, but of great importance in the formation of the western territory. This range begins near the small Elk River (a branch of the large Kanawha) and the source of the Monongahela, and extends to the north between the waters of the Monongahela and the Ohio into the state of Pennsylvania, past Waynesborough[17] and Washington, and about five miles below Pittsburgh to the Ohio River; then, on the other side, between the waters of the Allegheny River and the Big Beaver, to the southeast shores of Lake Erie.[18]

Second, just as the Cumberland Mountains have a long secondary range in the west, the Allegheny Mountains proper have two still longer ones in the east. Both emerge in North Carolina from the main chain, but diverge from it by more than fifty English miles and run in almost a parallel direction toward the northeast through Virginia, Maryland, Pennsylvania, and New York to the Hudson River where they disappear. The range closer to the Atlantic Ocean is the Southern Mountains near Fredericktown, and the other, the Northern Mountains, about fifteen English miles farther west. The names are suitable only at the point where the mountains separate from the main chain and are less suitable for their more distant parts since the direction of both runs too far toward the north. But the name *Blue Mountains* is even less suitable. It should never be used in writing, since it has no definite significance among the people. On my journey, I often asked about the Blue Mountains, and every time I noticed that the people I questioned were somewhat embarrassed. Sometimes they said that the Northern Mountains were the true Blue Mountains, sometimes they interpreted the name to refer to the Southern Mountains. Once I received the answer that this name was not generally used along the road from Baltimore to Wheeling but that it was used in Pennsylvania where the continuation of the Northern Mountains was so designated. Therefore, the confusion of terms in publications should not cause any surprise. The American Warden (in his *Account of the United States*, Edinburgh, 1819)[19] considers both ranges (the Northern and the Southern mountains) as one range, which he declares to be one of the two chains of the Alleghenies, and calls it the Blue Mountains. In the biography of Washington by John Marshall,[20] the first range (the Southern Mountains) is called the Blue Ridge. Bülow (*The Free State of North America*, Berlin, 1797)[21] gives this name to the second range (the Northern Mountains); Volney in his well-known work about the United States[22] designates the first range as such. Whoever is more interested in distinguishing between the objects themselves than in the names should keep the following in mind. The first range is cut by the Potomac about two miles below the mouth of the Shenandoah; the second range (the Northern Mountains) about eighteen miles above it (farther west). The first range runs between Fredericktown and the more western Boonsborough (Bunsberg) through Maryland, and between Lancaster and Harrisburg (which is further to the west) through Pennsylvania. Below Harrisburg it is cut by the Susquehanna. Below Reading it passes through the Schuylkill and below Easton through the Delaware into the state of New Jersey. The second range runs west of Boonsborough[23] and Hagerstown through Maryland, and west of Chambersburg, Carlisle, Harrisburg, and Easton through Pennsylvania to the Hudson River. Above Harrisburg (eight English miles) it is cut by the Susquehanna, and above Easton by the Delaware. Whoever bears this in mind will not be confused by the names of the individual sections. Thus, for instance, the Lehigh Hills, the Flying Hills, and the Oley Hills* are only parts of the first range in the state of Pennsylvania. The Kittatinny Hills belong to the second.

---

*The words *Hügel* and *Berge* (hills and mountains) are so used here that often a formation is called a hill when Germans would call it a mountain. The hills that border river valleys are called *bluffs*. All *Berge* along the Rhine would be called bluffs here.

Whoever travels from Baltimore or Philadelphia to the Ohio (below Pittsburgh) will therefore, according to the above account, run into five mountain ranges extending from north to southwest. Between these ranges are extensive valleys which are partly level and partly rolling country, and now and then one sees hills of considerable size. [6-13] The mountains are all covered from bottom to top with dense forests, and from the highway to Wheeling no summit can be seen that is higher than three thousand feet. In the southern part of Virginia they are higher, and in the north (in New Hampshire) some summits are said to attain the height of seven thousand feet.[24] But even the lower, secondary ranges, whose average height is about fifteen hundred feet, make an impressive appearance because they are very steep. Since they are not wide, they separate the various valleys like gigantic ramparts. [6-14] The valleys are well cultivated and covered with farms which, in artistic alternation with small woods and individual groups of trees, form a charming wreath around a number of blooming little towns. On the mountains, agricultural settlements are fewer. Nevertheless, no traveler will say that the highway from Baltimore to Wheeling leads through a wilderness. Along the entire way there are excellent inns at intervals of less than six English miles.

After this geographic digression I shall continue my account of the trip.

When we reached the first mountain range west of Fredericktown, the sun had already set. On this day we had planned to reach Boonsborough (Bunsberg), which lies west of the southern range. As the town was still six English miles ahead of us it did not seem advisable to keep to this plan, even though it included arrangements concerning the forwarding of our belongings. We were just on the point of stopping at the last inn before the range when our conversation was suddenly interrupted by a stranger who welcomed us in a friendly manner in the German language. He pointed behind himself, saying that his son was following with his wagon, that he was from Bunsberg and of German parentage, and that he was glad to meet immigrants from Germany, which he considered us to be. The dialect, the words themselves , and the features of the man made such a good impression on us that we accepted with pleasure his invitation to drive on with him. The ridge was covered with trees to the very top. The road seemed good and a certain amount of moonlight increased the effect of the brightly sparkling stars. For a short time we drove through open country. Not until we reached the foot of the mountains did the forests begin, and here we were soon surrounded by the glow of myriads of fireflies which made the light of moon and stars quite dispensable. At the same time, a kind of cicada (locust) buzzed so noisily that for more than an hour we could talk to one another only by raising our voices. From time to time, the general noises were drowned out by the howling of panthers, wolves, and foxes, and by the crying of many kinds of nocturnal birds. Added to these impressions were the changing views of the depths lying before and beside us which reflected the light of the moon and stars in the most manifold shadows.

Such a forest night was needed to make us realize fully that we were breathing the air of a distant continent thousands of miles away from home. Henceforth, we looked upon everything that attracted our attention during the day with a livelier interest, while every forest before our eyes again reminded us of what innumerable strange creatures we were wandering among. When we reached Bunsberg, it was almost midnight. This place is about fifty-five miles from Baltimore and has, as almost all other towns along the ranges described above, a healthful location. The heat is not so continuous there as on Chesapeake Bay. Melons, therefore, do not thrive especially well. But the immigrants from Middle Europe find it more to their liking. There are many Germans there,[25] and as we stopped there for two days in order to wait for our trunks we had the opportunity to meet several of them. To be sure, they all declared that they were born in America but they did not seem to be ashamed of their European ancestry. They were mostly Lutherans. Their pastor was obliged to preach alternately in English and in German. The town is not large but lively because of the highway to the Ohio, and everything proclaims prosperity and cheerfulness. It is surrounded by pleasant orchards and vegetable gardens which, together with the small woods between the cultivated fields, make a charming picture.

From Bunsberg we went through Hagerstown, which is comparable to Fredericktown in prosperity, through the second mountain range, the Northern Mountains, and on the third day after our departure from Bunsberg we reached the town of Hancock. It has a beautiful site on the Potomac which is famous for its picturesque banks.

Before Bunsberg, we had to stop once in the small town of Newmarket[26] in order to repair the wagon. Shortly before we arrived at Hancock the front iron axle broke. It was not the fault of the roads but the poor quality of the iron, which, because of our baggage, was put to a severe test. By means of several poles and ropes, which cooperative passersby helped us to fasten, we reached the town. We found a very good and spacious inn, but also a drunk blacksmith. However his helper, a vigorous Negro, knew enough about the trade to satisfy us in a short time.

As we continued our journey we came to large chestnut forests. The nuts were not ripe yet but had a pleasant taste. From time to time, partridges with flocks of their young crossed the highway with such calmness that we at first took them for domestic fowl.

Near the city of Cumberland we came to the Potomac for the second time, and on the following day we arrived at the third mountain range,

The vegetation on the hills as well as in the valley is very attractive and indicates far better soil than on the east side of the Allegheny Mountains.

It is said that around a hundred and forty steamers ply the Mississippi and its tributaries. Here at Wheeling the water has been too low the last few weeks, and the inns are filled with travelers who are waiting for rain. So-called keelboats, however, can always navigate. So we are not being tempted to give up our plan of reaching the Mississippi by land. Our second objective is Cincinnati in the state of Ohio. Tomorrow we shall start our journey. We must be prepared for other roads from now on. The highway has come to an end, and throughout the state of Ohio there are only such roads as are maintained by the inhabitants of individual regions.[3] [7-2] [7-3]

Eighth Letter

Tarlton, Ohio, 29 September 1824

The distance from Wheeling to Cincinnati is calculated at 260 English miles, and we have now 130 behind us.

The reputation of the state of Ohio for fertility and beauty is not undeserved. To be sure, the extreme southeastern part is very uneven, and from the shore of the Ohio at Wheeling to beyond Zanesville on the Muskingum, hills alternate with hills, some of which are so high and steep that in Germany they would be called mountains. However, they are all covered with rich humus, and stones are visible only in the channels of the brooks. There are no waste places. Where cultivation has not as yet created fields, the most luxurious forests prevail everywhere. Oaks, maples, walnut trees, cultivated chestnuts, beeches, tulip trees, sassafras trees, plane trees,[1] storax trees, ash trees, blend in colorful variety. Futhermore, one sees the bird cherry tree (*Prunus Virginiana*)[2] and the buckeye tree (*Pawia lutea*), which resembles the horse chestnut tree except for the fruit, which is considered poisonous. Innumerable springs and small rivers (branches of the Ohio) teeming with fish invite one to settle, and it is no wonder that here, so close to the old states, the population is increasing rapidly. I myself had to struggle with temptation which could be overcome only by the purpose of my trip.

All settlements have excellent orchards. Peaches are so plentiful that they are used in the production of brandy. One meets many Germans in this state. Their farmsteads and their cultivated fields are conspicuous for their excellence. Germans in America have the reputation for engaging in agricultural industry, and the descendants of Englishmen proclaim without hesitation that they like the German immigrants best, whereas complaints about the Irish are common, that they are prone to be intemperate, lazy, and quarrelsome. Several days ago we stayed overnight with a German settler, who besides caring for an extensive farm, also manages a kind of inn (called *entertainement* [*sic*]). He told us that he had come to America as a child with his father. His German home was in the neighborhood of Strassburg. He was probably about sixty years old. His farm was large and well managed. It was under the supervision of his son-in-law, who was of English descent. The latter was particularly interested in the cultivation of tobacco. He showed us leaves that bring twenty-eight to thirty cents a pound on the spot and also others that cost only four cents. The finer varieties produce far less bulk and require much greater care in cultivation and in the treatment of the harvest. This is the chief reason for the difference in price. Cotton is also grown, but only for household use; in addition, much corn and wheat, but little rye and no barley. (Therefore, beer is very expensive.) [8-1] Potatoes, sweet potatoes (*Convolvulus batates*), turnips, beans, peas, varieties of cabbage, cucumbers and melons, radishes, and so forth we saw here as everywhere else. The farmyard was full of various fowl: chickens, ducks, geese, turkeys, and guinea hens. One can imagine that nothing was lacking in the food served by our fellow countryman. Indeed, we have never had a reason to complain about that. In the inns, as well as in private establishments, much care is taken in setting a good table. The effort alone, however, must be taken into consideration. The victuals themselves are extremely cheap. In the state of Ohio we have already found more game.

The roads were poor in part. But they were passable, and the beautiful landscapes together with the sunny sky, which was clouded only occasionally by thunderstorms, compensated fully for them.

Three days ago we passed the night at Zanesville, on the east branch of the Muskingum. Here, navigation is interrupted by waterfalls, which are used for various kinds of mills, such as sawmills, oil mills, nail and cloth factories. The population of the city, including the small town of Putnam on the other side of the river, is about three thousand inhabitants. It has glass factories and two printing shops. Some of the buildings are unusually expensive looking. Along the Muskingum and its branches there is much fertile, arable land, and although the population is not sparse, it is said that very good land can still be had for five to eight dollars an acre.* The same is true of the smaller Hockhocking River,[3] which we passed the day before yesterday near New Lancaster.[4] New Lancaster has about twelve hundred inhabitants and an English and a

---

*An acre amounts to 160 square rods; a linear rod is 16½ English feet; a square rod, therefore, 272¼ square feet. To be sure there are still large areas here that can be bought at the government price. But these either have a poor location, or they are not very fertile. The most important factor [in determining price] is the distance from waterways.

German printing shop. It is not worth the effort [8-2] to collect exact statistics about every little town in the interior of the United States. Everything is too much in the process of development and changes too quickly. Near Lancaster the ground is more even and of great fertility.

Here in Tarlton we again had to have our wagon repaired. [8-3] Our rule was to stop at the inns where the mail coaches stop (stage office), because we expected better food here and proper safekeeping of the baggage. This time we made an exception and chose an inn situated at the entrance to the small town, whose owner had heard us talking and made himself known as a compatriot. Toward sundown, after we had been in the house about half an hour, our hostess came to us and with evident alarm asked whether we knew the three gentlemen who were just leaving. She then told us that these persons had just inquired whether two Germans had arrived here in a wagon. She had answered "yes" and had invited them to step into the lounge where they could find us. They had stopped at the entrance to the lounge, and peeping through the door, which was ajar, one of them had said softly to the other: "Nothing can be done here." Such behavior had seemed very strange to her, and when she had asked the strangers whether they wanted to speak with her German guests, they had left immediately. We had long been prepared for adventures with robbers; therefore, the matter did not disturb us. However, we took the precaution of loading our double-barrel guns and checking our baggage once more before going to sleep. The innkeeper, however, assured us that there was nothing to fear in his house. He was only worried that they would be lurking along the road ahead in the dense forests. On the following morning (today) we heard that these persons had been passengers in the mail coach that had arrived shortly after us, that they had spent the night in the post stage, and that they had slipped away before daybreak with the ready cash and various effects of the other passengers.

Ninth Letter

Chillicothe, 30 September [9-1]

Chillicothe[1] on the west bank of the Scioto is one of the places that one must call to the attention of those Europeans who think only of wildernesses and inhospitable wastelands when they hear the words *American interior*. The construction of this city was begun in the year 1796. It now has about six thousand inhabitants and is increasing in size every day. Most of the houses are of brick, high, and suggest wealth. The uniform layout of all American cities, which with few exceptions were developed from the free union of individual citizens, gives rather strong evidence of the maturity of Americans with regard to public affairs. Haphazard building, such as one sees almost everywhere in Europe, is an abomination to the Americans. For this city, also, a practical plan was drawn up. The streets are wide and cross at right angles. The whole makes a very pleasant impression and the life and activities of the city are in complete harmony with it. Four printing shops are constantly in action, and cotton-spinning mills, sawmills, oil mills, fulling mills, paper mills, and various kinds of factories noticeably increase the general prosperity. In addition, agriculture flourishes since near the city there is a very fertile valley of ten thousand *Morgen*.[2] On the west side of the houses rises a hill three hundred feet high, from which one has a magnificent view of the meandering Scioto, the banks of which are very picturesque. [9-2]

Not far from here, there are fortifications and mounds, which are traced back to the aborigines; the monuments along Paint Creek are said to be especially worth seeing. Among other things, there is a wall nine thousand feet long and from ten to fifteen feet high.[3] However, we must not permit ourselves to be diverted. The journey ahead of us is long, and it is rather late in the season.

Tenth Letter

Cincinnati, 7 October 1824 [10-1]

We arrived here from Chillicothe by way of Bainbridge, New Market, and Williamsbourgh.[1] The road was not very pleasant. For several days we drove through swampy forests over log dams. The constant bumping of the wheels from one log to another put our wagon to a hard test, which it fortunately survived. About ten English miles before Cincinnati we entered the beautiful valley of the Little Miami, which is well settled, and mostly by Germans.[2]

Cincinnati is called the most beautiful city of the entire West, and truly, the European, who involuntarily associates all kinds of ideas about savage life with the words *American interior*, would scarcely trust his eyes if he could suddenly be transported from his home to this city.

Before I began my journey across the ocean, I had read some articles about America. However, in spite of the most recent reports, I was nevertheless not prepared to travel [10-2] so far into the interior with the same comfort as in the hilly regions of Germany. I have met with none of the terrors with which the imagination imbues American forests. I have not even run across a rattlesnake except in the Peale Museum in Baltimore, where a young one, enjoying the best of health, was confined in a cage. To be sure, such animals do exist in the state of Ohio, but they are not so common. Neither have I seen an Indian up to the present time. So far I have spent every night in good inns, and in all of them the table was set with tame and wild fowl, with beef, pork, and the most palatable European garden products. A single man on horseback needs no more than one and one-fourth dollars per day (about three Dutch guilders) for his maintenance and the best care for his horse.

The city of Cincinnati lies on the right bank of the Ohio (465 English miles below Pittsburgh, as calculated by the course of the river; by land only three hundred miles) in the county of Hamilton, at 39° 6′ north latitude and 7° 24′ west longitude from Washington. Originally there was a fort here, which was built in 1780 and was called Washington.[3] It is no longer standing. In 1810 the population amounted to 2,500 souls, in 1815 around 6,500, in 1819 approximately 10,000 whites and 400 colored people and now about 14,000 souls. [10-3] The Ohio is fifteen hundred feet wide here. [10-4] The valley above and below the city is narrow and enclosed by the high hills. Near the city the hills retreat and leave two terraces [10-5] for buildings. The upper terrace is about eighty feet [10-6] higher than the lower one at the edge of the river. The city occupies both of them. It has over 2,400 buildings, including dwellings, warehouses, and so forth. Most of them are of brick and four stories high, and the wide streets follow a regular plan. There are twelve places for public worship: two for Presbyterians, three for Methodists, one for Baptists, one for Episcopalians, one for German Lutherans, and one for Roman Catholics. There are also five printing companies [10-7], forty doctors, and thirty lawyers.

In the so-called Museum of the West I saw a stuffed gray bear from Missouri (grizzly bear).[4] They say that this bear is so wild that as soon as hunters come upon its tracks they are compelled to hunt it in order not to be tracked and attacked by it. [10-8]

Cincinnati is a main center for the construction of steamboats. Several years ago, fifteen were built within twenty months, several of them four hundred tons.

The surrounding region is romantic and very fertile. There is probably no city in America where one can live more pleasantly and at the same time more cheaply. The large attractive market houses are provided with everything that the season offers. The best beef costs two and a half to three cents, pork one and a half to two cents, smoked ham four to five cents [a pound], a tame fat turkey cock twenty cents, a fat chicken eight cents, a dozen eggs three to four cents. There is a similar abundance of fish and game.

Opposite Cincinnati, on the left bank of the Ohio and belonging to the state of Kentucky, is the small town of Newport on the Licking River, with an arsenal; and opposite Newport is the small town of Covington. [10-9]

I must not forget to mention the excellent steam mills, several of which I have already seen in the United States, especially in Baltimore, in Washington in Pennsylvania (from where one of my letters is dated), and here in Cincinnati. The machinery is of the type that, without using manpower, the grain is drawn from the ferries up to the grinding hoppers. After the grinding, it is sent to the bolting hutch and then as purified flour lifted to the place where the barrels are filled with it. The local mill is built on a rock close to the bank of the Ohio and is a hundred and ten feet high.[5] It has seventy horsepower, and six pairs of stones produce a thousand barrels of flour per week, each weighing two hundred pounds. Moreover, I have never seen better flour in Europe than is usually on the market here.

Eleventh Letter

Louisville, 11 October 1824 [*11-1*]

We made the trip from Cincinnati to this place by steamboat. We took our horses and wagon with us on the boat. The length of the waterway is 120 English miles, which can usually be traveled in eight to ten hours. It took us fifteen hours, however, as a heavy fog forced us to stop.

The banks of the river for the entire distance are very charming. The valley plain is mostly narrow and the forest-covered hills rarely recede very far. There are no precipitous walls of rock in sight. The landscapes have a gentler character. The forests are interrupted only occasionally by farms and small towns.

On the right bank lies Lawrenceburg,[1] twenty-three English miles below Cincinnati and two miles below the mouth of the Big Miami. The town is subject to floods; therefore a New Lorenzburg has been founded on a more favorable spot six hundred paces away.

Four miles below Lawrenceburg lies Aurora. In 1818 twenty owners of fertile land in the surrounding region devised a plan for this little town and began by giving away several building sites. Soon about forty houses has been built, and then the lots were offered for sale.

Nine miles below Aurora lies Rising Sun (Sunrise) with about one hundred and thirty houses, and then, ten miles farther, Vevay follows in the Swiss district.

At present, Vevay has about two hundred houses and a printing press. In 1814 the settlement was begun on a tract of land which as early as 1804 had been granted by the Congress to about thirty Swiss families on extended credit provided they engaged in viniculture. During the next year several of these families settled where the town is now standing. I saw vineyards along the hills and it is said that the undertaking was not unsuccessful. The settlers tried several varieties; but the vines from Madeira and the Cape of Good Hope are said to flourish best, especially the latter. I tasted red wine from Vevay, which was poor enough. [11-2] Also, I can scarcely believe that vines from Madeira or from the Cape do well along the Ohio, where the winter admittedly is short, but the temperature often drops to minus 5 to 7 degrees Reaumur.[2]

Forty miles above Louisville (on the right bank of the Ohio) lies the town of Madison with about a thousand inhabitants, and ten miles farther down, New London. All these places belong to the state of Indiana. On the left bank of the Ohio, which here belongs to the state of Kentucky,* lies Petersburg, twenty-eight miles below Cincinnati. Then follow Frederickborough[3] and Ghent, all still unimportant.

Port William,[4] at the mouth of the Kentucky River, has about eighty houses, and forty-eight miles downstream at the mouth of the Little Kentucky lies Westport with about sixty houses.

The city of Louisville, on the left bank of the Ohio, where I am staying at present, has about six thousand inhabitants [11-4], beautiful buildings, and two printing shops. Immediately below the city are the falls of the Ohio, about which I wrote earlier. It is planned to provide a detour around them by means of a canal about two miles long. The joint-stock company has already been formed and the plan is about to be executed.[5]

Opposite Louisville, on the right bank of the Ohio and also above the falls, lies the small town of Jeffersonville.

Kentucky soil has long had, and still maintains, the reputation of being very fertile. However, the good land now costs on the average of twenty-five to thirty dollars (per acre), and in the vicinity of some cities even one to three hundred dollars as a result of the great increase in population and prosperity in a few years. As in most parts of the Mississippi area, limestone is prevalent, especially in Kentucky. Below the topsoil there is clay and then a layer of limestone to a depth of from two to twenty feet. It is still deeper close to the rivers. These have cut their way through it, so that within their high, steep banks they look almost like artificial canals.

Here in Louisville, also, many people are waiting for higher water in order to travel by steamboat to New Orleans and St. Louis. For some weeks the Ohio, even below the falls, has been too low, which seems very natural during the prevailing summer weather. This does not affect us. We intend to travel by land in any case in order to become acquainted with the interior of Indiana and the highly praised state of Illinois.** For now we are getting into the regions that are said to be

---

*Kentucky is an Indian word and signifies a bloody stream. The land was for a long time [11-3] the object of bloody wars among the Indians.

**The state is named for the Illinois River. This word, in the language of the Indians, is said to signify a man at the age of strength. The river was formerly called Theakiki.

especially important for European settlers. In the states we have crossed up to now, the fertile, well-situated land has long been private property, but in Illinois and Missouri such is not the case. There most of it still belongs to the Union. [11-5]

St. Louis on the Mississippi (in former Upper Louisiana) is now our objective. The route by land is calculated at three hundred miles.

Twelfth Letter

Saint Louis on the Mississippi, 26 October 1824

After an eight-week journey by land, I have finally reached the place near which I am planning to take up my temporary residence. I believe that here I can best investigate what a European can hope for in western North America and what difficulties he will face. Above all I shall observe the procedures followed by the inland settlers when they want to transform woods or savannas into arable regions, into farms and cities. I therefore intend to go into the midst of the "new settlers" to buy so-called unimproved property and, imitating them, make an attempt at transformation. If I wanted to buy a farmstead that is already established (which may often be a more advantageous plan for the person who has no purpose other than to acquire a farm) then I would probably become acquainted only partially with the many difficulties connected with the first stages of settling. I expect nothing from mere excursions from an urban residence. To carry out the main purpose of this long journey, I wish to do exactly what everyone must recognize as the most expedient procedure. Moreover, the plan has other good points, for I am freer in my choice. If I select a place on government land, I can in addition to the profitable aspects give more thought to the amenities of life, which are certainly not unimportant in similar isolation in a foreign country.

However, I must not forget that I am really writing this letter to describe the trip here from Louisville. We were on the road for twelve days. Four English miles below Louisville we left the state of Kentucky and crossed the Ohio (which is about two thousand feet wide here) to New Albany in the state of Indiana. The little town has, to be sure, a beautiful location on the charming bank of the gentle river, but it nevertheless made an unfavorable impression on me. Several houses were vacant and seemed to have been abandoned before their completion. In answer to my questions, I was told that times were hard. The Americans have been spoiled by the long wars in Europe. At that time they received exhorbitant prices for their produce, especially for wheat. Therefore they inquired often enough whether another war would not break out soon.

After leaving New Albany we drove in a northwest direction, away

from the Ohio River into the interior of the state by way of Paoli and
Washington to Vincennes. We crossed rather high hills which one
would call mountains in Germany. All were covered with dense forests.
The species of trees are the same as those in the state of Ohio. Settle-
ment in the interior of Indiana is still very backward compared to that in
Kentucky and Ohio. The towns are mostly unimportant and do not
deserve to be called towns. Often a European cannot refrain from
laughing when he is told that he is in the neighborhood of a Lisbon, a
Paris, and so forth, and he then comes upon three to six miserable huts.
The same holds for almost all the states. However, one must not be
misled to base his conclusions on this as to the general state of affairs. In
North America the planning of towns is a matter of speculation, the
success of which is very dependent on circumspection and calm investigation, which are not always practiced here.

The choicest settlements are along the Ohio, the White, and the
Wabash rivers. The state was established in 1816 and, at present, has a
population of about a hundred and fifty thousand souls.[1] Slavery is as
little permissible as in the state of Ohio and in Illinois. It is claimed that
this law is not favorable to the rapid progress of the interior. The state of
Ohio has been able to increase its population more easily through the
immigration of poor settlers from the Atlantic states. Settlements in the
more remote regions, however, require more means, which are almost
exclusively in the possession of such persons who, because of their
education and their circumstances, are relieved from spending all their
time in physical labor, and usually make use of servants or slaves in
establishing settlements. As long as the population is sparse, servants
are very expensive. I have stayed overnight in houses that were very
luxurious in their accoutrements, with costly carpets in all rooms, but
one asked in vain for a servant. The landlord was compelled, in spite of
his considerable wealth, to care personally for the horses as well as for
the guests. Furthermore, his wife and daughters had to perform the
most menial household tasks. Their only topic of conversation was that
they wished to sell their establishments in order to move to a state
where one could keep slaves.

A day's journey before Vincennes we saw in an inn a black bear
whose behavior delighted us greatly. He was about three months old
and had been caught, quite young, at the side of his mother, who had
been killed. A large bowl of milk was placed in front of him. He
embraced the bowl with his front paws as if they were arms, and as soon
as someone made an attempt to take it away from him, he tried to hold
on to it and to pull it toward him. At the same time he uttered noises of
defensive complaint not unlike those of a peevish child.

Vincennes on the Wabash is a city of about three hundred and fifty
dwellings, with two printing shops, two churches (a Presbyterian and a

Roman Catholic), a courthouse with prison cells, a seminary, a post office, and steam mills for flour and lumber. It was founded in 1735 by French emigrants who settled here far from the civilized world and in the midst of hordes of Indians. By way of the winding course of the Wabash, Vincennes is 154 English miles from the Ohio; as the crow flies, however, scarcely 60 miles.

About forty miles below Vincennes, likewise on the left bank of the Wabash and still a part of the state of Indiana, is New Harmony, a colony of Württembergers founded in 1814. The population is about eight hundred. Formerly they lived near Pittsburgh. They engaged in manufacture and wine growing. Viewing themselves as a separate religious sect, they live in strict isolation from the rest of humanity under their director and pastor, G. Rapp, whom they call Father, and in whose name all business affairs are carried on.[2]

Several miles from Vincennes, the hills and the dark forests disappeared. The landscapes now assumed a character totally different from those we had seen earlier on our journey. According to my description, the journey from the Atlantic coast up to this point had led us largely through forests that cover a rolling, mountainous, or hilly surface in charming alternation with smaller and larger river valleys. Not many miles before we reached the Wabash, we came into the region of the savannas, the natural meadows, which extend through the wide plains of Illinois to the Mississippi. The inhabitants of the United States call them *prairies*. [12-1] To be sure, we had come upon a few small meadowlands several days before, such as are found even in the state of Ohio. However, that is unimportant compared to the plains that meet the wanderer's eye in Illinois. It is assumed that two-thirds of this state, the area of which is estimated at fifty thousand square miles (about twenty-three hundred German) consists of plains.[3]

The plains in Indiana, like those in Illinois, are of two kinds: low and high. The latter are about thirty to one hundred feet higher than the others. The low ones (of which there are few) are largely wet and devoid of woods. The highland plains on the other hand are surrounded by forests, and individual groups of trees rise here and there like islands in the midst of the grassy plains. The soil is, in general, very fertile. At Vincennes the humus has been found to be twenty-two feet deep. The usual depth is two to five feet. There one can see for himself for how long any fertilizing will be superfluous because of this rich humus. The fields near that city have been under cultivation almost a hundred years and still show no signs of exhaustion. It is believed that these low plains owe their origin to water and that they were at one time, in part, the bottoms of lakes. The highland plains, however, are extended, at least visibly, by the accidental and intentional burning of the grass, which takes place almost every year and never leaves the edge of the forest undamaged. Therefore, one is probably justified, with regard to its origin, in thinking of the common practice of the Indians setting the grass cover afire for their forest hunting.

These large meadow areas did not make a pleasant impression on me. Also, for many miles between Vincennes and St. Louis the water tasted of iron vitriol and repelled me because of its sulfurous odor. This is due to a stratum of earth, which is said to be very extensive. However, the water is not considered unhealthful and the farmers as well as the livestock have become used to it. In the spring, innumerable flowers may clothe the region in beauty [12-2]; but I do not think that this attractive feature could balance the unpleasant factors. In brief my opinion on the trip through Illinois was that despite the descriptions of Mr. Birbeck [12-3][4] no one should voluntarily leave Europe to settle on these plains as a farmer. However, I am reporting this first impression to you without declaring it unchangeable. I shall remain here long enough to put it further to the test.

There was nothing that interested me here except the large prairie chickens, which weigh little less than a goose and taste rather good. What pleased me most was that we could cross the country so quickly because we were traveling during the dry season. We passed through plains six, ten, twelve, and twenty miles wide. The rapid travel by wagon found few obstacles, except those at slowly moving brooks and rivers. Near these there was a change to wooded hills now and then, which seemed more inviting. But we came to dislike these places because the wagon turned over twice. The second accident occurred at a great distance from a blacksmith, and if we had not as a precaution provided ourselves with ropes, hand drills, and screws, our vehicle would surely have left us in the lurch. This had happened to a low chaise, which lay by the wayside with a broken shaft. In traveling through Indiana and Illinois, one does not have such a choice among inns as on the highway to Wheeling. However, except in case of bad luck, one can always get by. Everywhere along the road from Louisville to St. Louis there are passable lodgings for the night at intervals of fifteen English miles at most. But one must not neglect to provide oneself in the inns of the cities with lists of good houses and also the distances between them. These are available, in part, in printed form. If the description of Friedrich Schmidt (vol. 1, p. 236)[5] ever coincided with reality, much must have changed in the last three or four years. We were never in danger of our lives. We ourselves were to blame for our wagon turning over. Neither did we have to swim across any river. We found ferries wherever they were necessary.

Moreover, except along the navigable rivers, one can buy enough good land, not only in Illinois but also in Indiana, for one and one-fourth dollars per *Morgen*. In the southern part of both states first-class land next to navigable rivers, but safe from floods, has long been private property and costs at present four to six dollars.

I take this opportunity to warn anyone against the mistake of considering the arable land in the neighborhood of American cities as cheap because such extensive areas are still available at some distance away for low prices. It is not infrequently the case that the fields near the cities are sold for two hundred to five hundred dollars per *Morgen*. This is true especially of the city of St. Louis, which I like to use as an example of one of the most remote cities.

The city of St. Louis [12-4] lies on the west bank of the Mississippi, 15 miles below the mouth of the Missouri at 38° 36′ north latitude, 982 English miles from the capital, Washington.* The width of the river here is more than one English mile. A large boat, which is propelled by wheels and two horses, furnishes the connection with the other bank. It can be compared to a steamboat, except that instead of steam, two horses are used to keep the paddle wheels in motion. It is easy to see what an advantage such an independent vessel has over the so-called flying bridges. The fare for one wagon with two horses amounts to two and one-half dollars. The east bank is low; the west one, however, beyond a low [12-5], narrow terrace, rises to a height of about seventy [12-6] feet and extends into a plain that is several miles wide. The [plain's] foundation is hard limestone, which, however, is covered by a very deep layer of fertile humus. In spite of the good soil characteristics of the entire plain, the region around the city appears rather desolate, as the woods in the vicinity were destroyed long ago and low bushes have replaced them. In the beginning (as early as the last half of the seventeenth century) St. Louis was merely a military post and was fortified as such. [12-7] Only the ruins remain. In 1764 the building of the city began.[6] The old houses built by the French** differ very noticeably

---

*When the name *Washington* is used, it generally refers to the capital of the United States. There are many cities that bear this name and, in general, many cities have the same name. For the sake of clearness, one should add not only the name of the state but also that of the county.

**As is well known, the French discovered the Mississippi territory 1670 to 1680, and also settled there first, naming it Louisiana. In the Peace of Paris, 1763, it was determined that the Mississippi River should be the eastern boundary of Louisiana. From the Atlantic Ocean to the Mississippi, all territory was placed under the rule of England. At the same time the French promised to cede the thus restricted Louisiana to Spain. This was not done, however, until 1769. In the Peace of Lunéville (1801), the French regained possession of Louisiana, but sold it in 1803, to the United States for 60 million francs. [12-8][7] The word *Mississippi*, or Messa-Chepi, is Indian and means Mother of the Rivers. The French called the river Colbert, later St. Louis; but the Indian name prevailed. The Spaniards called it la Palissada, because of the great quantity of wood that is floated down its course. According to the findings of Heckwelder [John Heckewelder][8] (pastor of the Moravian Brethren at Bethlehem in Pennsylvania, in his work

from the new houses of the Americans. What the last change in supremacy is worth to the states west of the Mississippi can be seen here also. In 1810, the city had only 1,600 inhabitants, and now there are approximately 6,000.[9] Nevertheless, considering the splendid location it is surprising that the population does not grow more rapidly. It also strikes one as strange that the fertile soil near the city is not at all utilized and that food products are almost all procured from the east bank, from the state of Illinois. The inhabitants are mostly out-of-state merchants who concern themselves with nothing except the quick sale of their wares. Few own property, and some of the married ones did not even bring their wives along because they consider their stay here so transient. In St. Louis there is the see of a Catholic bishop.

Now I am taking leave of you for a long time. My next letters will pertain mainly to the chief purpose of my journey. I hate to give [12-9] you opinions that I myself cannot yet substantiate.

You will remember that several years ago (in 1820, I believe) a Hannoverian by the name of Ernst[10] brought a company of colonists to North America. He chose the state of Illinois and settled at Vandalia, the seat of the government. The undertaking failed. Mr. Ernst, who had previously become bankrupt, died of a virulent fever. He is criticized, in regard to the prosperity of the young city, for having placed too much weight on the seat of the government. To be sure, a German can more easily make such a mistake. Furthermore, it was said that Mr. Ernst had paid the traveling expenses for many persons without making proper provisions for repayment, and so his kindness was poorly repaid. [12-10]

Thirteenth Letter

Written in Montgomery County [Missouri], 20 February 1825

I am breaking my silence so that you will at least learn where I am at present. Up to now I have been hoping in vain for letters from Europe and I am beginning to be worried about the possibilities of a regular correspondence. I probably do not need to mention that you must send your letters in duplicate. This is the general custom in regard to correspondence with countries beyond wide oceans. [13-1]

---

concerning the customs and usages of the Indian tribes), the word *Mississippi* seems to be derived from Nemaesi-Sipu, Fish River. According to old traditions, a mighty tribe of gigantic stature is said to have lived there, which was called Talligewi or Allighewi. The Allegheny Mountains are said to have derived their name from the same source. Moreover, the Missouri is the actual continuation of the stream. For, from the union of both rivers to their sources, the Missouri is almost three times longer than the Mississippi.

After I procured various charts and accounts concerning the available land from the Land Office in St. Louis (as the office dealing with the sale of public lands is called), I began the inspection of the interior of the state of Missouri.

The borders of this state are: the eastern border, the Mississippi and a part of the Des Moines River; the western, the meridian 17° 30' (from Washington, or 94° 10' from Greenwich). [13-2] The northern border is formed by the parallel 40° 30'; the southern, by the parallel 36° 30'. [13-3] The name is derived from the Missouri, an Indian tribe that was almost entirely exterminated during its wars with the Sioux, so that one no longer hears about it.[1] Scarcely twenty families are said to have survived, and these live at the mouth of the La Platte River under the protection of the Otoes. [13-4] The Missouri were, at one time, mighty and famous, and their language, which the Otoes [13-5] still use, is considered vigorous and melodious.

The elevation of the land is in pleasing contrast to that of the state of Illinois on the east side of the Mississippi.

On the south side of the Missouri the region containing lead and iron ore is very extensive, and there, as in most areas rich in ore, the soil is not particularly fertile. However, near the two main rivers (the Missouri and the Mississippi), as well as along the smaller rivers the Gasconade* and the Meramec, there are fertile areas of considerable extent. Along the beautiful banks of the Osage River there are, at this time, almost no settlements. [13-6] It flows into the Missouri River about a hundred and twenty miles from the junction of the latter with the Mississippi. At average water level the Osage is about eleven to twelve hundred feet wide at its mouth, and it is said to be navigable for over five hundred English miles. [13-7]

One acquires an idea of the Missouri River itself when one learns that, from its junction with the Mississippi to the cataracts, it is navigable without interruption for over two thousand five hundred miles, and from there again for over five hundred miles to its main tributary, the Jefferson. From the Gulf of Mexico, this navigable course amounts to over four thousand five hundred English miles. There is nothing like it in the entire world. It is also remarkable that in the lower part of the river (that is, from the mouth of the La Platte River) the water is never clear. To be sure, it is good drinking water, but it is muddy and precipitates silt. The wonderful fertility of its banks is attributed to this characteristic. The water of the Mississippi, above its junction with the Missouri, is entirely clear. The velocity of the current of the Missouri varies greatly according to the water level. The average is estimated at

---

*Many fir trees grow along the Gasconade, and sawmills there cut them into boards which are floated down the Missouri and Mississippi. A hundred square feet cost $1.25 at St. Charles.

five English miles per hour. The main stream, as well as the tributaries and creeks, abounds in fish. Catfish (*Silurus felis*, often weighing [13-8] over a hundred pounds), buffalofish, eel, and pike are considered the best. The waters are also said to have trout and a species of salmon.[2]

On the north side of the Missouri, the extent of fertile land is very great. The emigration of Americans from the older states has been tending to favor this direction. Here, at a considerable distance from the Mississippi, one finds sizable cities which have all been founded since 1812. Among them, Franklin and Columbia stand out.[3] They are situated on the Missouri, the former about 170 and the latter 150 English miles above its mouth. For several years, trading caravans have been traveling from Franklin to Santa Fe on the Rio del Norte in New Mexico, and soon a regular highway leading there will be built. The fertility of Howard County in which Franklin lies, and of Boone County in which Columbia is situated, has become almost proverbial. Several thousand families have already settled in these regions, and there one can no longer speak of a wilderness. To the east, however, closer to the Mississippi, much public land can still be bought and, with the exception of the valley plain of the Missouri and the neighboring hills, there are wide areas where no settlement can as yet be seen. How often on my trips have I thought of the reports of Mr. Friedrich Schmidt.[4] It cannot be gathered from his book through what parts of the interior of America Mr. Schmidt traveled. That he was never in the interior of the state of Missouri, however, and especially not in the parts lying between the Missouri and the Mississippi, is obvious enough. The most depressed state of mind cannot misrepresent reality as much as those reports. In the preface we read: "I should like to impress upon the minds and hearts of the inhabitants of Württemberg the fact that not one of the states of America which have been described as being so beautiful and so fortunate can compare with their own country, and that the farther they travel from their homeland the worse will be the conditions they will meet. This holds true from the borders of Württemberg to the shores of America, and from there to St. Louis and Council Bluffs, about seven hundred hours in the interior, where conditions finally become so bad that even the poorest European can no longer live there." Of the soil in the state of Missouri, Mr. Schmidt says (p. 206) that where it was not flooded, it was rough and infertile. The following note is added: "*bottoms* are areas that are flooded by rivers." From this we can see that the author did not concern himself in the slightest with agriculture. The word *bottoms* signifies nothing else but the valley plains of streams, rivers, and brooks, which are no more in danger of floods than the river valleys of Germany. Areas subject to floods are the last to be sold. Special purposes must attract one to buy them; otherwise they are quietly passed over. Whoever speaks of good soil in the interior of America excludes them from his thoughts. Where only rice is grown, this may be an exception. But in the state of Missouri, in Illinois, in Kentucky, in Ohio, and in Tennessee, at least, it is not the case. [13-9]

I ask you to take a look at the map. North of the Missouri you will see a range of hills that begins three miles below the city of St. Charles, in the angle where the Mississippi valley unites with the Missouri valley. This range of hills separates the waters of the Missouri from those of the Mississippi. Toward the Mississippi the land slopes northeast; toward the Missouri, southwest. Here originate innumerable brooks and small rivers that wind on one side to the Mississippi, and on the other side to the Missouri. The highest ridge of this chain forms undulating plains which are mostly natural meadows; but these are so interrupted and surrounded by woods that they appear to the traveling European as charming creations of cultivation. [13-10] On the sloping sides the ground becomes uneven because of the deep beds of the brooks and rivers, and here there is nothing but primeval forest which extends over the hills as well as over the ravines and valleys of the small rivers up to the two giant streams. Some of the hills enclosing the Missouri valley rise to knolls of considerable dimensions. Others fall almost perpendicularly for great distances so that masses of rock, seen from some distance, look like walls and towers fashioned by human hands. The entire surface of this region is covered for many hundred miles with the richest humus.

I must emphasize strongly that the meaning of the words *fertile soil* in these regions is very different from that in Germany. Good soil, or first-rate soil, does not require fertilization during the first century, and during the first decades it is too rich even for wheat. This is true of river valleys, especially those of the Missouri. Average or second-rate soil is of the kind that during the first twelve to twenty years fertilizer cannot increase the yield of the harvest. Because the hills adjoining the great rivers belong in this class the duration of natural fertilizer depends very much on the degree of the incline and the erosion caused by heavy rains. The poorest soil is found in the forests closer to the prairies. The prairies themselves, however, are again, for the most part, as fertile as the hills next to the river valleys. One sees stones nowhere except in the beds of the streams and along individual knolls. Nothing is more erroneous than to call the meadows dry steppes or even wastes of sand. They are all highland prairies. But the black humus is at most places approximately one and a half to two and a half feet deep, and below it is a good mixture of clay, limestone, and sand. They are covered throughout the summer with the widest varieties of flowers. Also the rocks sometimes show limestone (at times beautiful marble), sometimes clay, sometimes flint. In particular, there is no lack of springs that rise out of the sandstone. Here much importance is attached to this by some people who are of the opinion that calculus[5] can be traced back to the water that flows over the limestone. [13-11]

The trees of the forests are: oaks of more than sixteen species,* of which one species (the bur oak, *Quercus macrocarpos*) has acorns as big as small hen eggs; over eight species of walnut trees, of which the thin-shelled pecan nut tree (*Juglaus olivaeformis*) bears a nut very delightful to the taste. [13-12] The fruits of other kinds of walnut trees do not deserve this praise. The nuts of the black and white walnut trees are palatable enough when eaten fresh, but when dried, they are too oily. Futhermore, there are ash trees, sassafras trees (*Laurus sassafras*), iron-wood trees[6] (*Carpinus ostrya*), elms, and especially the red elm (*Ormus Americana*), the inner bark of which can be eaten without any preparation and turns entirely into slime when chewed. It is often placed in fresh wounds and is said to promote the healing of gunshot wounds. One seldom sees an undamaged trunk. Tame and wild animals know this nutritious substance. One finds mulberry trees (*Morus rubra*) mostly in the Missouri valley. Their fruit is valued highly. Plane trees (*Platanus occidentalis*), usually called sycamores here, flourish and attain a great circumference. I have seen several eight to ten feet in diameter, and they say that there are some in the Missouri valley more than twenty feet in diameter.**

I cannot describe the impression that the days of wandering in this river valley have made upon me. One can travel hundreds of miles between gigantic tree trunks without a single ray of sunlight falling upon one's head. The soil is so black here from the plant mold that has been accumulating since primeval days that one seems to be walking on a coal bed. I have seen grape vines whose trunks, over a foot thick, rise up about a hundred feet, free as cables, and then spread out in the crowns of elms with their heavily foliaged vines. Not infrequently the mighty support succumbs to its burden, which is swung back and forth by the wind, and in the fullness of its strength is uprooted from the ground. In the case of a dying tree this soon happens.

There are several kinds of grapevines here, and some hills are so densely covered by them that wagonloads of grapes can be gathered in a short time. The grapes of some varieties are sweet and palatable but furnish little juice. In the fertile river valleys they are mostly sour. I do not doubt that culture would produce the desired improvement. I have

---

*Germany has only three species.

**F. A. Micheaux (*Voyage a l'ouest des monts Alleghanys*, Paris, 1808) reports that on an island in the Ohio, fifteen miles above the mouth of the Muskingum, there had been a plane tree that was fifteen feet in diameter (over forty-seven feet in circumference). The banks of the Missouri were at that time still too unknown. The plane trees are also called *buttonwood* trees because of the shape of their fruit.[7] [13-13]

drunk juice from them that was quite enjoyable. I believe only red berries can be found here.

Among the fruit trees I must not omit the persimmon tree (*Diospiros persimon*). One does not see it very often. Seen from the outside, the fruit resembles a yellow plum. However, it contains not a single stone but several nuts like the medlar. Also the calyx is permanent (on top of the fruit). Before it is entirely ripe it has an astringent quality and is therefore recommended for dysentery. When it is completely ripe, its delicious taste surpasses that of most of our varieties of plums. Most striking to me among all the fruits, however, was that of the papaw tree (*Anona triloba*). The tree itself does not grow higher than about twenty feet and it is rarely six inches in diameter. The blossom is a beautiful dark-red bell (with five stamens and one pistil). [13-14] I might compare the shape of the fruit with a short sausage three inches long and one to two inches thick. The smooth green skin that surrounds the pulp changes upon ripening to a whitish yellow. Inside there are several stones, comparable to small chestnuts which, when eaten, cause vomiting. The pulp surrounding these stones, which makes up by far the largest part of the fruit, is hard to distinguish from a well-prepared (sweet) custard and for this reason it is a great favorite with children. Moreover, trees in the valleys as well as on the hills are the common indicator of rich soil. Palatable plums are also found in the woods.—I do not conceal the fact from you that the entire life of the inhabitants of these regions seemed to me like a dream at first. Even now, after I have had three months to examine conditions more closely, it seems to me almost a fantasy when I consider what nature offers man here. But I shall write of this in more detail later. I do not know the summer as yet, and I am prepared to meet with some disagreeable conditions because I do not expect so much good will to exist without some unpleasant features. For the time being I will add only the following.

I have settled down about fifty English miles above the mouth of the Missouri. There (near a stream[8] in Montgomery County above the small river *Osage Woman)*[9] I found very fertile, attractive areas that could be bought partly from the state [13-15] and partly from private owners. My companion [Ludwig Eversmann] also decided to live, for the time being, not so very far from St. Louis. We bought adjoining land, he about one hundred thirty acres, I about two hundred seventy. The land bought from the government costs one and one-fourth dollars (three and one-eighth Dutch guilders) per acre (*Morgen* of 160 square *Ruten*),[10] and that bought from private owners a little more.[11] It is extremely alluring to settle down in regions where one has such complete freedom of choice; where one, map in hand, can roam through beautiful nature for hundreds of miles in order to select land and its cover of woods and meadows according to one's own desires. Here attractive qualities are united with useful ones. Settling next to charming hills, near never-failing springs, on banks of small rivers near their junction with large rivers, all depends entirely on the option of the settler without taking the price into consideration. [13-16] And what is perhaps still more important, one can choose the climate. From the Canadian [Great] lakes to the Gulf of Mexico, the settler is faced with no difficulties. This is an area comparable to that extending from Northern Germany to Africa, within which one finds large and small settlements everywhere. When several years ago the lands west of the Mississippi were suddenly opened, hordes of speculators swarmed over them. The prices were driven too high and the result was that later they fell below their true value. [13-17] They are still very low now, and one can buy wonderful areas for two and a half to four dollars per acre that earlier were scarcely to be had for seven and eight dollars. To be sure, the price of grain during the European wars contributed to the rise in prices. [13-18][12]

It was too late to arrange for permanent settlements before the winter. For the time being we stayed with farmers in the neighborhood.[13] Now, however, the cold season is over and we shall try to transform part of the tree-covered hill slopes into a farm.[14] I say "the cold season is over." Those are the words of the Americans. I myself did not notice that it was winter. The woods never lost their green color entirely. Snow had not fallen and the temperature was so mild that one needed a fire only in the evening and in the morning. However, the inhabitants say that such weather is unusual and that the month of January is usually unpleasant. They also say that winter rarely comes earlier and that toward the middle of February navigation of the streams is already possible and no ice is seen in the rivers. Occasionally the Missouri as well as the Mississippi freeze over with such a firm layer of ice that large loaded wagons can be driven across them. This would not be true if it were not for the large masses of ice that float down the rivers from the far northern regions. [13-19] Also, they say that the ice layer remains for scarcely eight days. In general, they praise the American autumn, and I must testify that beginning with August we had excellent weather for traveling. [13-20]

At the present moment we cannot get workmen. Everyone is occupied with making sugar. Old and young are engaged in this activity, as if it were a continuous family celebration. I did not mention the species of maples among the trees of the forests. The sugar maple is so common along the Missouri that almost every settler owns his sugar grove (sugar camp), not infrequently quite near his farmstead, but sometimes one and even several miles away from it. In the latter case, the forest is usually government property. This manner of using public forests is as customary among the rich and the poor as if it were permitted by state law. The first occupant is considered to have the right of priority and only an actual purchaser of the land will disturb this arrangement. Toward the middle of February the favorable weather begins, that is, when warm days follow rather cold nights, which is often the case here in February. This change causes the sap of the trees to rise in such a way that it often does not drip but actually flows out of a damaged place in the wood. [13-21] As soon as the right time has come the entire family moves into the woods where there is a spacious hut with a fireplace built of rough stones and large enough for four or five iron kettles. Holes are bored into the trees several feet above the ground (large trunks may have several holes). Tubes of elder wood are then inserted in the holes and troughs are placed under them. One can preserve these utensils from year to year. Usually one person collects the content of the troughs in barrels and takes it to the fire (by means of a sled drawn by horses), and there, a second person, usually the housewife, is occupied with the boiling down of the sap. While the children play around in the grass, she transfers the sap from the first kettle to the last, where it remains until it attains the consistency of melted sugar, and it is then poured out for cooling. The firewood, as one can imagine, is easily procured. If it has been carefully prepared, the sugar is preferred in color and taste to the best light-yellow cane sugar ([13-22] powdered sugar) and requires no purification for household use. If the weather is favorable, two persons can easily prepare two to three hundred pounds in one week without being hindered in the usual work of preparing daily meals. Although sugar could be made in the fall also, this is rarely done. [13-23] At that time there is other work to be done, and the farmer does not overwork himself or the Negroes he may own. The price of maple sugar here is ten cents (fifteen farthings) per pound. Almost every household uses about a hundred pounds. No European poverty prevails here, where a day laborer with the heartiest appetite can earn as much in twelve hours as he consumes in an entire week in the way of meat, bread, vegetables, butter, milk, and brandy. I should add that the whites learned the uses of the maple tree from the Indians.*

---

*To prove how little is known in Germany about the interior of America, one should read what is said about the state of Missouri in the *Handbuch der Geographie und Statistik* [Handbook of Geography and Statistics] by C. G. D. Stein, Leipzig, 1826. In this book the following appears, p. 644: "The entire area is an immense grass-covered plain which extends 250 German miles from east to west and 300 miles from north to south. Human dwellings are rare and herds of buffaloes up to 10,000 seem to be the owners. Immeasurable coal beds are substitutes for the lack of wood. Along the Arkansas River there is a rock salt bed over 280 German miles long.—Also two great salt-water rivers flow into the Kanzes (Kansas). Near St. Genevieve there are rich lead mines, 150 German miles in length, and so forth." Such statements can only cause laughter in the United States. The Missouri territory, which is treated especially on p. 645, is obviously confused here with the state of Missouri. The area measurements in length and width conform rather closely to those of the state if one substitutes English miles for German miles. The same is true of the extent of the lead mines. The Kansas River is entirely

While I watched the boiling syrup, I noticed a piece of fat on the liquid, which is said to prevent the syrup from boiling over, and evidently it does so. If you will remember, the story was told years ago that when there was danger of shipwreck, barrels of oil had been broken open and that this oil had helped to calm the waves. At first everyone considered the report incredible, until [Benjamin] Franklin explained the reason for this phenomenon. The same reason holds here. Syrup is prevented from boiling over by the lower specific weight of the fat. This weight causes the fat, by its effort to maintain its place on the highest spot of the wave, to counteract the movement of boiling

---

excluded from the state by its western border (which passes directly through its mouth), and the Arkansas River with its slopes is a part of the Arkansas territory. But whoever speaks of a lack of wood in the state of Missouri reminds one only too vividly of the words: "They cannot see the forest for the trees." In the entire interior there is no place where the rich coal beds are being used, however easy it would be to do so. For it is still easier to make use of the woods. Immense prairies are not known here. Wherever their length amounts to one to two [13-24] German miles, the width is correspondingly less, so that woods are close by everywhere.—In the book about the United States by C. Sidons, Stuttgart and Tübingen, 1827,[15] there is a similar erroneous description of the state of Missouri. The author, as he himself states, was only on the border. If he had gone into the interior, he would not have mistaken as immense meadows the woods destroyed by the Europeans near St. Louis. What Sidons took for meadows was the undergrowth of felled forests. The meadows are of slight extent. At a distance of seven to eight English miles from St. Louis there are forest-covered hills everywhere. On the other hand, Illinois, which lies east of the Mississippi and which Sidons praises so highly, is the true prairie state.—That it is colder in St. Louis than in the national capital, Washington, is just as erroneous. I am referring you to the more detailed descriptions of the climate. Regarding the statements by Mr. Sidons concerning the basis of the political conditions, I should say that he places too much emphasis on the secondary basis. A close examination of what I have said about the main basis (the family life of the masses) will excuse me from further explanation.

According to Sidons, St. Louis is said to be a miniature New Orleans. There are said to be a great number of coffeehouses and dance halls there. It is strange that I, who often spent weeks at a time in St. Louis, did not notice anything like this. I know not a single coffeehouse in this town. The customs of the Americans support them as little in the interior as in the seaports; and the French population in St. Louis is very small. In fact, in 1810 there were only 1,600 inhabitants. The ceding of the land to the United States increased the number to 6,000. I remember that I inquired about a billiard room one rainy day in 1825. After a long search we found a poor building in the rear of which something was set up that resembled a billiard table. I was also struck by the distinction made [by Sidons] between the backwoods French and the Creoles (p. 126). By *backwoods people* they mean here the settlers living nearer the western borders. The word does not have a uniform definition. Many an American applies it to his countryman who lives farther west, whereas one living farther east applies it to him. There is less of a contemptuous connotation connected with it than in Germany with the word *Landvolk*. The Creoles (in other words, the persons born in America of European parents) are especially to be found among the "backwoods people." There are very few farmers in the state of Missouri who were born in France; however, French merchants and artists are not uncommon. [13-25]

which is foreign to it. A similar result can be expected from a large mass of oil on a stormy sea in bays and between islands, especially when the cause of the motion, the wind, has subsided.

Fourteenth Letter

Montgomery, September 1825

I have met with some inconveniences that I could easily have avoided if I had been better informed. When I landed on the American coast I was not familiar with the most recent laws concerning the sale of public lands. I had no further information than that the areas that had been announced for sale could be acquired merely by offering two dollars per acre and that the purchase price could, in part, be paid within four years. I had counted upon this when making my financial arrangements, and only when I was far into the interior did I learn that the price had been reduced to one and one-quarter dollars [14-1], but that it had to be paid at once. However, the land that I had chosen was so attractive to me that I could not await the arrival of more money. So my supply of cash melted away. I did not neglect writing to Europe immediately (November of last year) and could hope for additional money by the end of March. Unfortunately the letters were lost. Although actual embarrassment was prevented by loans from a friend in Baltimore,[1] the entire summer passed without my being able to make the place habitable. But the time was not completely wasted. After all, I had the opportunity to learn much that was useful for my purposes. [14-2] You will find some evidence of this in the following description, in which I shall tell you what happens when an American moves from already cultivated regions into the so-called wild country in order to establish a new homestead.

Every day during this season immigrants from Kentucky, Ohio, Virginia, Pennsylvania, and so forth arrive. If these people had to travel in the European manner, their desire to emigrate would soon vanish. However, things are entirely different here.

An *Ackerwirth* (generally called a *farmer*) [14-3] who has sold his property advantageously in Pennsylvania or Virginia turns as if by instinct to the western states, to the lands in the Mississippi valley. Usually he first undertakes a scouting expedition if he has not been sufficiently informed by dependable friends. For the time being he leaves his family behind and travels on horseback in order to survey the country. Usually he is in the company of other persons who have the same purpose in mind. This occurs either in the spring or in the fall. After his return, a plan for emigration is made in greater detail. Because of the continuously favorable weather, the plan is carried out in the fall.

A large freight wagon (or several, according to the needs of the family) is loaded with the household goods in such a manner that a covered space remains free for passengers. In addition to the household goods, tents and provisions are included: smoked pork, beans, peas, rice, flour, cheese, and fruit; also for the first week, bread, and maize for the energetic horses. Thus the journey is begun. Sometimes the owner rides with his wife and children in a special wagon, sometimes in a coach, or he rides on horseback. If he has male slaves, one of these will be the driver. Otherwise he or some other member of the family does it. On the entire trip of perhaps more than 1,200 English miles, there is no thought of stopping at an inn. During the feeding of the horses at noon the kitchen also goes into operation. A stopping place is chosen near a spring or a brook, either in the shade or in the open according to the weather. A fire is quickly lighted and housekeeping proceeds as if they were at home. In the evening, more thought is given to the selection of the next campsite. If something is needed, such as cooking utensils or provisions, they stop near a farm and tents are set up, especially if the weather is bad. Some members of the party tend to the domestic animals (if the journey is not too long even the cattle are taken along), and others are busy with the kitchen. Finally, the lodging for the night is prepared. Everywhere the wagon train stops for the night, the natives are polite and ready to supply what is desired. Household goods are loaned, provisions are sold at low prices, horses are granted places to graze if it is preferred to let them graze in the open. The latter rarely presents any difficulties. Usually it is necessary only to hang a bell around the neck of the leader of the herd and to make his walking more difficult by fastening hobbles to his legs. They are tired and hungry and will not easily leave a good grazing place. Also, a trained dog would easily find their trail. However, there are cases when they take advantage of a moment of freedom to run back home. No distance and no stream will then hold them back, and they know how to find the way back to their old homes even through great forests. In my neighborhood there are two oxen that recently returned from a distance of one hundred English miles, having swum across the Missouri. A horse came back alone from Franklin (a distance of about one hundred twenty English miles).*

The traveling families encounter no difficulties from the end of August to the middle of December. From the most easterly Allegheny ranges to the Missouri, inhabited places are not lacking where one can secure provisions. Danger from robbers is almost unknown, and there

---

*Horses are more hesitant to swim across the large rivers than cattle. Therefore, in the angle where the Missouri and the Mississippi unite, there are always stray horses that have escaped from the farms in order to return to their homes in Kentucky, Ohio, Virginia, and so forth.

is no record that such a family wagon train has ever been attacked. Everywhere the roads are easily passable for freight wagons. Moreover, an American on such a journey always provides himself with a good ax to quickly repair individual bad places or make a detour through the forest. A delay of several hours is of no importance for those who eat little more on a journey than at home. I really would have liked to travel in a similar way myself. I always had to depend on inns, as is the case with other individuals (in other words, merchants). Every evening some things in the wagon had to be unpacked and repacked again the next morning. A traveling household does not experience such inconveniences. It always has the same beds and the same responsibilities for the entire journey. The best inns cannot compensate for that.—In the spring, rainfall is more plentiful and roads are in poorer condition. In summer, however, it is too hot, particularly in the months of June, July, and the first half of August.

You will perhaps be wondering why I have not yet said anything about the summer along the Missouri, since in one of my previous letters I express some worry about this. I shall remark, in passing, that just as the first winter was called unusually mild, this summer [1825] was considered unusually hot and dry. Once the Fahrenheit thermometer actually recorded 104 degrees in the shade (about 32 degrees Reaumur). That the heat surpassed blood temperature was shown clearly enough by the fact that glassware and metal objects in the house felt very warm to the touch. However, the nights were mostly cool and I enjoyed uninterrupted health. In the future I shall have the opportunity to say more about this matter. For today, I request that you follow the traveling Americans.

As soon as a traveling family has arrived at the site of its new home, it stops at the exact spot where the buildings are to stand. Then an enclosure is erected as a temporary protection for household goods and tents, which are now set up for a longer period of time. Fencing is needed to keep out the cows of neighboring settlements. The young calves are also kept in this enclosure to restrict the movement of the freely grazing cows, which return regularly and, without the slightest attention or care, constantly provide the family with milk and cream. The site for the house is chosen near a good spring or brook. A small building is immediately erected over the spring to protect it from pollution and also to provide a cool place for storing milk, butter, and meat. [14-4]

The next concern is the building of a dwelling in the manner previously described.[2] The wood for it is not hewn and, in the beginning, only a barnlike structure is planned to provide temporary shelter. A second one is built for the Negroes; then a third to be used as a barn, and a smaller building to serve as a smokehouse. The tree trunks are felled in the neighborhood and dragged up by horses or oxen. The building itself is erected with the help of neighbors if the family cannot manage it alone. Not more than four or five persons are required to erect such a building. Boards are sawed for doors and floors, or trees are split into planks, for which purpose the ash and hackberry trees (*Celtis crassifolia,* or lotus tree) are especially suitable. The hearth, together with the chimney, is built very simply of wood, lined below with a stone wall and covered at the top with clay. If the chimney is six inches higher than the top of the roof smoke will not be a bother. The danger of fire depends on the construction of the stone wall and the clay covering.

Anyone who looks upon such a dwelling with too much contempt is not familiar with the local climate. I have been in some where cleanliness and good furniture made for a very attractive appearance. Many families desire nothing else, since in other matters they live a life of plenty. The only thing that I have to criticize about the houses is that they usually have no cellar (the hut around the spring takes its place). In the summer a moldy odor rises out of the humus under the rough floor. This rarely offends one's nose but obviously endangers one's health. A floor laid by a carpenter affords perfect protection. Whoever does not want to spend that much on it can take care of the matter himself by removing the humus from the building site, or by burning cut wood from the clearing on the home site. [14-5]

When the building is completed, which requires scarcely two to three weeks, the family already feels at home and the next step is to make the land arable. They usually begin by fencing in the chosen area in order to use it temporarily as an enclosed pasture for the horses and oxen which they want to keep close for convenience.

Nothing can be more erroneous than the European conceptions of the difficulties involved in turning mature forests into farmland. Even Volney[3] estimates at four years the time a farmer needs to thin out (*to clear* is the usual expression in America) a small field. In criticism of all the negative reports I merely remark that here, where a day's wage amounts to sixty-two and a half cents, the entire work required for a single acre (about 160 square *Ruten*) does not cost more than the small sum of six dollars, or fifteen Dutch guilders, provided that the area comprises about four to six acres. Otherwise the fencing, which is included, would cost proportionately too much. The field is then completely ready for the plow. Whoever has the work done by his own slaves or by those he hires by the year can do it much more cheaply. [14-6] Removing the tree stumps is completely out of the question. Such an undertaking would be considered ridiculous here. Only bushes and shrubs are removed together with their root systems. There is no heather here, and no bilberries[4] (these are found in other parts of the United States). On the other hand, on the treeless places now and then there are many hazel and blackberry bushes. Large trees are not even cut down. Only trees a foot or less in diameter are felled, and these are cut so close to the ground that the stumps do not disturb the plough singletree. All large trees are merely killed, in other words, notches are placed all around through the bark into the wood. This kills most of them in about two weeks so that they no longer withdraw nourishment from the soil, nor shade it. I say: most of them; this is true of all species of oak, ash, and walnut trees. In the case of linden trees the bark must be removed to some extent, and there are others that do not die until the third year. The plane trees and cottonwood trees (*Populus Canadensis*) that are frequently found in the valleys belong to this class. However, from the very beginning notching has weakened their vitality so much that they will not endanger the harvest. Since maize, cotton, tobacco, sweet potatoes, and so many other plants flourish only when planted a considerable distance apart, dried up trees do almost no harm. Large trees rarely stand so close together that they are a hindrance to a wheelless plow, and the ones of lesser diameter are, as I said, cut down. [14-7]

When preparations have been made for the crops, the dried-up trees can be removed gradually and used as firewood. However, it is customary to plan the location of the fields when erecting buildings, preferably so as to select lumber from this area. Trees suitable for fencing are likewise cut down. The stumps soon rot, and in twelve to fifteen years they have disappeared entirely. Of course, some trunks fall during heavy winds and others rot. But this does little harm to the crops and there is no danger that cattle or people could be injured by their falling. There are too many dead trees in the forests for that. With every strong wind, with prolonged heat without rain, during heavy rains, all of which cause loosening of the roots, one often hears within twenty-four hours more than fifty trees, close by or distant from the home, plunge to the ground with a terrible crash. Yet there is scarcely a case on record of domestic animals living in the open having been injured by them. Their alertness, especially that of the horses, is remarkable. In stormy weather they seem to avoid dead trees, and later when they are ridden or used for fieldwork the slightest cracking noise makes them restless. The people, too, are not careless during a heavy wind and postpone working among dead trees.

Very rarely is the cold said to interrupt outside work for more than two days. Even in January the weather is not always unfavorable for removing the roots of brush. Where horses, cattle, and hogs, not excluding the tenderest calves, can survive the winter without shelter, the climate cannot be too harsh.

It is remarkable how quickly all these domestic animals become accustomed to their homestead. Milk cows are kept near their fenced-in calves. Therefore, when a cow is sold its calf is part of the bargain. Calves are never slaughtered, partly because they grow up without any care or expense. During the first months cows return to their young at least twice a day at definite times. Often they wait for hours at the fence until the gate is opened. Then they are partially milked and enclosed with the calves who feed on the remainder [of the milk]. Usually a little maize is fed to them during the milking period. Afterward they are driven into the open again to forage for their own food, which is not difficult for them. When the ground is covered with snow they eat the tender twigs of the various shrubs. In such weather the fields are also open to them so that they can eat the stalks and leaves of the harvested maize. The remaining cattle obtain their share also, and in addition receive several ears of maize. But it is said that they can survive the winter without any food supplied by man. The same is true of horses. Hogs always find so much in the forests that they become very fat and are not often seen during summer. As soon as it becomes cold, however, they return to the homestead even if they have been gone for several months. They, too, are given maize to attract them to the homestead rather than to serve as nourishment. Only those that are selected for butchering are kept within fences and are generously fed in order to increase their weight more quickly.—Small amounts of salt are excellent lures for horses and cattle.—As soon as horses or oxen are used for work, however, they are also fed, even if only as a substitute for their lost grazing time. Ten to twelve ears of maize constitute a full ration for a horse, and thirty-six would be enough for the whole day without any supplement of hay or grass. A hundred ears amount to about a bushel, and fifty to sixty bushels are usually harvested from a single *Morgen*. A bushel of maize (in other words, a bushel of grain without the cobs) weighs about fifty-five to sixty pounds.

The manner in which the domestic animals habitually return is the most surprising sight, especially for the European. Cattle and horses follow the bell of the herd's leader. Only cows that have calves are an exception. These are attracted at any time by the loud barking of a dog in the neighborhood of the homestead. Often one sees them running from distant forests toward the homestead in great fear for their young, and they do not calm down until they know that the calves are unharmed. At night they lie down outside the fence while their calves rest close to them on the inside. On bright, clear days the horses appear, long after the sound of their hoofbeats has announced their coming, running at full gallop and leaping about wildly. They continue to frolic in happy abandon until they are given some food or salt. Sometimes one suddenly sees, after an absence of several months, several sows with litters of young, which have thereby increased the wealth of the farmer without his knowledge.*

---

*Every real farmer owns a tool with which he marks the ears of his stock (with the exception of the horses) and of which a copy is kept at the office of the county court. The hogs sometimes suffer from a disease called kidney worm disease in which a worm

When a settler has an insufficient supply of meat from his domestic animals, his hunting rifle will keep him supplied. Meat of domestic animals, to be sure, cannot be very expensive here; beef costs only one and a half cents and pork two cents (three farthings) per pound. But there is so much game, deer, turkeys, partridges, doves, pheasants, woodcocks, and so forth, that a good marksman supplies food for a large family without exertion.* In the entire United States hunting and fishing are entirely free, and anyone** can hunt in areas not fenced in, how and whenever he pleases, with dogs, with nets, with traps, with guns, small game as well as large. The deer, of which here (in the state of Missouri) there are two kinds (*Cervus Virginianus* and *Canadensis*), are usually very fat. The meat is palatable. But the hunter rarely brings home the entire carcass. He is satisfied with the skin and the thighs of the hind legs and hangs the rest on a tree so that anyone else who so desires can help himself to a roast. Turkeys are found in herds of twenty to fifty. Around Christmas they are usually very fat. Because I am not a good hunter, I have my neighbor deliver some every week, especially for soup. They must weigh at least fifteen pounds before the hunter will even take them home. I pay twelve and a half cents apiece for them.*** The bison (buffalo) has vanished from this region; he has moved farther north and west. One sometimes still encounters bears. Almost every evening I hear wolves howl, and yet sheep roam about without shepherds. Here, the farmer suffers as little from beasts of prey as from robbers and thieves. However, there are complaints that from the end of April until the middle of May young pigs are endangered by wolverines who give birth to their young at this time.

Although horse breeding is so easy here, horses are nevertheless rather expensive, far more expensive than in the state of Ohio. A strong draft horse is often sold for eighty to a hundred dollars. It is impossible to take advantage so quickly of all that nature offers. In New Orleans butter usually costs more than a half-dollar a pound, and yet this high price has resulted in only a few shipments from the state of Missouri. The waterway, to be sure, is good enough; however, in order to produce much milk and butter the cattle would have to be kept in barns at least

---

several inches long and about two *Linien*[5] in diameter eats away the tissue around the kidneys. [14-8] There are also instances when cows produced poisoned milk, the drinking of which had serious effects. [14-9]

*The hare is not found here. Some are said to be farther north. Rabbits are plentiful. They are rather annoying in the gardens and around young fruit trees.

**Slaves are not permitted to carry weapons; however, this rule is not strictly enforced.

***Board and lodging can be had here for one dollar a week. Feed for the horse is usually free. Such abundance explains the hospitality that most families practice. Wherever there is a house one can find shelter and food, and rarely will a farmer accept pay from a fellow citizen (an inhabitant of the same state), let alone demand it.

temporarily and this seems too inconvenient to a new settler. Grain, especially maize, and salted meat are sold in New Orleans at a great profit. The boats are built without difficulty on the banks of the Missouri.* Whoever knows that the lands along and in the Gulf of Mexico annually import from Europe many shipments of provisions [such as] butter, cheese, ham, and flour, cannot fear a poor market here. Also, most of the horses raised here are sold in the South.

At the beginning an acreage of four to five *Morgen* is sufficient for a small family. A half *Morgen* may be used for garden vegetables; a second half *Morgen* for wheat, although it is usually too late to sow it during the first fall. This leaves three or four *Morgen* for maize.

In the western regions of America maize is a main product of agriculture. One could call it the wet nurse of the growing population. It serves all domestic animals as food, as it is used for fattening. The flour from it is simply called *meal*. On the other hand, the ground product of wheat is called *flower* [*sic*]. When boiled with milk, it makes a very nutritious, healthful, and palatable food. If it is kneaded with the boiled pulp of the pumpkin (*Concurbita pepo*), however, a bread can be baked that I prefer to wheat bread, especially if the dough is fermented by subjecting it to heat for approximately twelve hours. A dough of cornmeal mixed with water or milk and then baked produces a bread that is too dry, but with fatty foods it is quite palatable. The bread is baked in covered iron pots which are placed on a bed of glowing wood coals on the hearth and also covered with them. In most households fresh bread is prepared every day, and in general, the cooking and baking are not very inconvenient because of the constant supply of glowing coals on the spacious hearth. Bread is also made of wheat flour. As well as I remember, the cornmeal is called groats in the Rhine region. There are many varieties of maize here. The most common varieties have white and yellow grains. There are also red, blue, and red-and-blue-speckled ones, and some that are

---

*Many families could derive a good income merely from gathering the ginseng roots, not to mention [14-10] many other medicinal plants. But the abundant supply of food, which they already have, is considered more convenient here. Even poppyseed oil and rapeseed oil are not produced here as yet, although the soil and the climate seem extremely favorable.—For immigrants from the Rhineland nothing is more important than viniculture. They do not need to worry about a ready market and high prices. For the Americans look upon viniculture as a national matter, saying the Old World has nothing to offer them except wine. But they have not the slightest knowledge or experience in its production. The descendants of the British could not learn it from their ancestors who themselves had not engaged in it, and that the descendants of the French, the Swiss, and the Germans have had as little experience can be explained by the fact that the first generation was so fully occupied with caring for immediate needs that they died without planting vineyards and their knowledge and experience were not transferred to their children. To be sure, attempts have been made here and there (at St. Louis and at St. Charles, for example); however, in such a manner that the vineyards soon resembled forests and no sunbeam could penetrate to the grapes. [14-11]

tansparent like beautiful pearls. These variations are preserved by propagation. The meal from all of them is the same. The stalks grow very tall, ten to fifteen and even twenty feet. [14-12]

The garden provides the best European garden produce. Peas and beans flourish beyond all expectation. Only the finer varieties of beans are found. In order to require neither poles nor a special bed they are usually planted in the maize fields where the tall cornstalks serve as support for the vines. Pumpkins, lettuce, and several other things are planted there also. In this fertile soil, without the least fertilization, all these plants grow at the same time just as luxuriously after twenty years as in the first ones. I assure you that there is no exaggeration in this statement and that I have convinced myself many times of its truth. One of my neighbors, by the name of William Hencock [Hancock],[6] owns a farm on the banks [14– 13] of the Missouri that was started twenty years ago. Every year without interruption these areas have produced the richest harvests which no fertilizer can increase. In fact, the only change is that wheat can now be grown on fields that have been under cultivation for so long, whereas formerly it always fell over. However, some garden produce requires natural fertilizer. The farmer provides this in a very simple manner. He quarters his sheep overnight in the area intended for beds. Every year there is an abundance of cucumbers and melons (watermelons [14– 14], and others), of course without any care. A good vegetable for the garden is the *Bataten* (called *sweet potato* here; the common potatoes are called *Irish potatoes*). They require a long summer and probably would not develop well in Germany. Prepared in steam they taste like the best chestnuts. I like them very much with coffee in the morning, although so early I can rarely eat the fried meat that is usually served in addition. Like the cucumber, the plant has vines that spread over the ground.

In the second year cotton is raised also; however, north of the Missouri only for family use. On the whole, the American farmer tries to spend no money for food or drink or clothes (with the exception of real finery). Therefore, flax and hemp are cultivated, and a small herd of sheep is kept. The products are all made at home. The spinning wheel is found everywhere, and if there is no loom, the housewife or one of the daughters goes from time to time to a neighbor who owns one. Just as most men are skilled at making shoes, few women find it difficult to make not only their own clothes but also those of the men. The demands of changing fashions are not ignored.

After housekeeping has been organized and the first purchases have been paid for, the whole family lives a carefree and happy life without any cash. And this is the real reason small sums are less important here than in Europe. [In Europe] when the husband brings home a little ready money, the wife immediately needs something, and usually there is no peace and quiet in the home until it has all been spent in the

nearest store, usually for tawdry finery.—The smallest coin is a silver
coin worth six and one-fourth cents (nine farthings). [14– 15] One does
not see copper coins in the western states.—Cash is needed only for
taxes. These, however, are so low that scarcely any thought is given to
them. Land acquired from the government is not taxable during the first
five years. To be sure, the taxes vary in accordance with the needs of the
state. Please take note of the fact that this year a fourth of 1 percent of
the value of real estate, adult livestock, and luxury articles (including
gold watches) must be paid as state tax, besides a small contribution
toward the expenses of the county (county taxes). Capital is not taxable.
The value of taxable objects is estimated so moderately that a tax of six
dollars is considered reasonable for a farm of considerable size. Whoever pays that much owns at least four to six adult horses, forty to fifty
head of cattle, a hundred hogs, and a herd of sheep. There is rarely a
direct federal tax, but individual states levy taxes every year.[7] With the
exception of the expenses mentioned, the farmer has no obligations at
all. He can send his products to the Atlantic Ocean or to the Gulf of
Mexico without the slightest tax or the least inspection. In Germany it
will cause surprise that here in the state of Missouri not only the
assessor but also the collector of taxes must come to every citizen. No
one is obligated to take the taxes to him, although most people do so in
response to his friendly request.

Here as in the entire West it is quite customary to arrange for the
payment of labor (for the common day laborer as well as the artisan) by
barter (called *trade*). This is done less because of an absolute lack of cash
than because of their effort to make trading easier through the
establishment of equivalents. Articles to be traded have no fixed price
but their true value in cash is estimated in each case by the traders
themselves or by a third party who has been requested to do so. This
procedure is based, naturally, on the conviction that these articles can
actually be exchanged for silver without any special loss. Under Spanish
rule things were different. At that time, certain wares, especially skins
and furs, had a fixed legal value. Formerly it was not unusual here
during a sale to judge by eye the number of small coins, piasters, and
half-piasters to be paid. In general, penny-pinching is foreign to the
American.

From this outline you may draw conclusions concerning the lot of the
local farmer in general, and at the same time answer the question of
what more can be desired for the welfare of the settler whose venture
we have been following here. I would know of nothing except the
comforts of a better dwelling house, and the expense connected with
this is again in sharpest contrast with the usual European ideas. Just
consider that this improved dwelling needs to be designed merely as an
abode for the inhabitants, since other buildings, which cost almost

nothing, provide for the rest. For fifty dollars one could build more than a half-dozen outbuildings, such as kitchens, smokehouses, sheds, barns, and stables, using hired day laborers, which is not a cheap way of building. A passable wooden dwelling costs about two hundred to three hundred dollars. For five to six hundred dollars, however, a presentable brick house can be built which would cost more than four times as much in the coastal cities. [14– 16]

If the farmer owns two slaves, he may devote his time merely to supervision without doing any of the work himself and, in this case, the housewife will have little reason to complain about keeping house. Food is abundant. Also beer can easily be brewed since enough hops grow in the forests. The apple and peach orchards found on every farm furnish cider and brandies. Although a very good whiskey can be made from corn, the apple and peach brandies are preferred. I have tasted old corn whiskey that cost thirty cents a gallon (about two Cologne quarts) and it was as good as the best French brandy. [14– 17]—Even without slaves, the farmer lives in a manner that surpasses by far that of a European farmer of the same financial status.

The soil is so fertile that the maize harvest requires nothing but a mere breaking of the soil (a single plowing). Then (with the same plow) furrows are drawn from two sides of the square field to the opposite ones at intervals of four feet. The field is now, as one says, ready for planting. Children then drop three or four grains of corn on the intersection of the furrows and an adult scrapes a little soil over them with a light hoe. This is done during the last half of the month of May. About four weeks later, as soon as the seedlings are from one to one and a half feet high, the soil between the rows is plowed (with a single horse) several times and the weeds destroyed. This comprises the entire work until the harvest. The general attention given to fences cannot be called work. Wherever dead trees still exist, one usually has to remove one or more of the fallen trunks or branches before breaking the soil. Here, too, the American knows how to make the work easier. Instead of attacking big trunks with an ax, he places glowing coals accompanied by single pieces of wood on the surface at definite intervals. Stirring the fire and adding a little more wood, repeated from four to six times, is sufficient to disintegrate within forty-eight hours the greatest trunks into pieces that can be rolled without difficulty by two persons. These will later be consumed altogether by fire.—Removal of corn stalks from a previous harvest is a part of the preparation for the next planting. They are either struck down (mostly by children) or rolled down, then raked together with a harrow and burned. If a farmer has no harrow, he simply makes use of a bundle of branches dragged by horses.

Much less work is required here in sowing wheat, oats, and rye than in Europe. With this method, to be sure, the grain suffers much from weeds. But the abundance of space, which does not need to be utilized so carefully, makes up for it, and European perfectionism would be a waste of manpower here.

For most of the harder work of housekeeping there are ways of making the labor easier. If, for instance, laundry is to be done, a fire is lighted next to a nearby brook and a kettle is hung over it. The bleaching ground cannot be far away either, and it is a matter of course that during the summer a shady place is chosen. If butchering is to be done, there are similar advantages. Usually, animals to be slaughtered, oxen as well as hogs, are shot. The animals are lured to a suitable place with a little feed and very rarely does a shot fail to serve its purpose. In this way a single person can do the entire job, although it is the custom that neighbors help each other in this work.

Finally, I must correct the erroneous opinion that the difficulty of social intercourse is the dark side of the vaunted lot of the American settler. One should dismiss from his mind the idea that the accomplishment of his purpose demands a great degree of isolation from neighbors and consider, at the same time, that a distance of from two to three English miles here is negligible, even for the female sex. No family is so poor that it does not own at least two horses. Everyone strives to make these animals, which are kept at so little expense, his first purchase. Next in line are good saddles, and it is not unusual to spend twenty-four to thirty dollars for a woman's saddle (which would suffice for three saddles on the Atlantic coast, for example, in Baltimore [14– 18]). Women and girls, old and young, ride (sidesaddle in the English manner) at a rapid or a slow pace without any difficulty, and they last in the saddle as long as the men. Not a week passes in which the housewife does not visit her neighbors on horseback either alone or with a companion. On Sundays, only the weather can be a hindrance. Often the whole family leaves the house without the slightest worry about thieves. Some houses are not even provided with [14– 19] locks, although the kitchen utensils alone are worth more than twenty dollars. Horse racing,* cock fights, and target shooting are here, as in North America in general, the most frequent occasions for the gathering of men.

---

*In some states racing is forbidden, for example, in New York and Massachusetts. In Connecticut cock fights are also forbidden. Unquestionably they are to be counted among the cruel games. The natural spurs of cocks are cut off and very pointed steel ones are attached, making the fight mortal in a few seconds.

Fifteenth Letter

Montgomery, 1 November 1825

In the last letter I tried to give you a true picture of the life of a local farmer. I well remember what ideas are widespread in Europe and especially in Germany about life in the interior of America. Sometimes they speak of terrible forest fires, which are said to endanger entire regions; sometimes of hostile Indians; then of beasts of prey, of poisonous snakes, of scorpions, tarantulas, mosquitoes, and other insects, and finally of a host of diseases caused by the climate and the soil. I anticipate, therefore, your objection to what I have presented so far and that I owe you far more information about the dark side. But do not worry about this. I shall not leave these regions for some time. I intend to live at least a full year on my own property in order to acquire a proper knowledge of all the adverse as well as the favorable factors, and I shall, now as before, express myself about every detail.

I experienced a great forest fire recently. I myself helped to keep the fire from the farms in my neighborhood, and I can now give you a full report concerning the danger and the means of meeting it.

It is a very common occurrence that during dry weather in some part of a savanna (prairie) or forest a fire breaks out as a result of carelessness or an accident. Lightning is also frequently the cause. But sometimes a fire is started for a purpose. In the regions where the Indians are in control, prairies and forests are set on fire to restrict game to a smaller area for hunting purposes. Dry weather, dead grass, and dry foliage are the main causes for the spreading of fire, and these conditions are usually all present in the fall. The spring is usually too damp.

About three weeks ago a fire broke out in a prairie six miles from my place. At the beginning the wind drove it in the opposite direction, and in a few hours one could see it spread a distance of fifteen miles.

One can easily understand why fire spreads very quickly on the prairie, but it disappears just as quickly since there is only dry grass and no wood to keep the fire burning. It is different in the forests, where fire spreads because of the foliage. It is also consumed quickly. However, it makes its way to the dead trees (already lying on the ground or still standing), which furnish fuel for the fire for several days.

During the first weeks we hoped to remain undisturbed because the fire had been driven away from the woods close to us. It could now reach us only by a long detour (through the forests on the opposite side of the prairie). In the meantime rain was expected. I was curious enough to ride up to the fire but found it hardly worth the effort. By daylight there is not much to look at, at least one cannot speak of a terrible spectacle unless there are evergreen woods nearby, which are lacking in our vicinity. To be sure, there are green deciduous trees

73

which catch fire immediately even when large logs [from them] are placed on the hearth. This is true especially of the hackberry tree (*Celtis crassifolia*). But standing trees burn only when they are dead. If a dry trunk leans against a green tree, the latter can suffer from the heat of the burning dry wood, but the fire is extinguished when the dead wood is consumed. I stated earlier that there is no heath here.

The fire kept at a safe distance from us for an entire month; only in the evening was there a bright illumination on the horizon.* But the rain did not come; instead the direction of the wind changed to our disadvantage and finally blew so strongly that there was no doubt that we would soon see the fire here on Lake Creek.

Lake Creek (in German *See-Bach*) [15– 1], next to which my farm is situated, derives its name from a lake that it forms before entering the Missouri. It flows from north to south. Its course to the lake is about five miles long, and after it has been joined by several tributary brooks its bed is rather wide and deep. It is never dry, to be sure, but it is full only during heavy rains. The upper part of the small river, as well as its tributaries, winds through deep, narrow valleys that are usually covered with sugar maples to the top of the adjoining hills. There are eight settlements within its drainage basin.[1]

The fire came from the northeast side and first reached the ravines of Lake Creek. Twilight was approaching when the owner of the farm where I had formerly stayed[2] invited me to take a walk in that direction. We wandered in a deep, narrow valley until we came close to its division into several ravines. It was dark when we arrived there and it seemed just the right moment to observe the terrible element at the moment of its greatest glory. It would be useless to try and give you a picture of what I saw. The imagination of the boldest painter would scarcely attain this reality in a portrayal of hell. The fire, driven by wind, had first spread along the bottoms of ravines and from there it rapidly climbed simultaneously in many individual trails to the tops of the hills. The black curves of ravines were strangely illuminated by burning trees 80 to 150 feet tall, and trails of flames on the hills resembled glowing streams plunging down the hills to be lost in the dark depths below. The entire spectacle retained its terrible character for a long time while most multifarious changes in detail occurred. The crashing and roaring of plunging oak and gigantic plane trees and the flying about of burning masses were the usual interruptions while the howling of the wind seemed to pursue the flight of desperate wild animals. I saw deer, squirrels, foxes, wolves, raccoons, opossums, horses, and cattle escaping the common enemy, all at complete peace with each other.

On the following day farmers began working to keep the fire away from buildings and fences, which would probably all have been de-

---

*A faint illumination (from distant forest fires) can be seen almost daily in the fall.

stroyed without these precautions. As soon as the fire is rather close and the hope of being spared by it disappears, a line is chosen by the people of the neighborhood to serve as the fire line. Generally they try to make use of a road. Along this line a space about three to four feet wide is carefully cleared of leaves and dry wood by means of brooms or rakes, including any dead trees that could fall across this borderline when set afire. After such preparation the foliage on the fire side of the line is set afire and extreme care is observed that flames do not reach the opposite side without being extinguished immediately. The work is easy and in a short time all combustible material near the fire line has been burned up. The fire can then spread only in the direction of the forest fire and the farms are safe from any danger without further effort. In carrying out these precautions they choose a moment when an adverse wind will not be too great a hindrance. If they wanted to let the forest fire come closer they would depend, in this case, entirely on chance. However, great difficulties would be encountered in fighting the fire because it spreads in an incalculable way.

Besides, fire does great damage to forests. The fertilizing foliage is lost and the young growth is partly destroyed, partly damaged. This reason alone makes it advantageous to limit the fire as much as possible. But the destruction of the pasturage is even more deplorable, and with reason if the fire has encircled the farm. The fire rarely extends to the valley of the Missouri; perhaps only during a severe drought. This fall there was danger of such an occurrence but the farmers there had already made preparations to meet it when suddenly a two-day rain fell and stopped all further spreading.

You may judge from this report how much danger there is from forest fires. If a farm suffers from such a fire the owner is seldom without blame. At least no one fears forest fires here.

The same is also true of all snakes, especially of rattlesnakes. There are three kinds of rattlesnakes here, particularly those with large yellow spots (*Crotalus horridus*).*[3] I have seen several and I have killed some. They are not so frequent in my neighborhood. At first, I went to see them out of curiosity whenever one had been killed. None are longer than four and a half to five feet and more than two and a half inches in diameter. [15– 2] Two months ago one this size was found in my fields and killed with an ax. However, I consider such an attack dangerous, because the weapon is too short. A long-handled hoe would be more suitable. The snake usually assumes a defensive position, coils up in a circle, rattles its tail, and extends its open jaws toward the attacker. In this position it can quickly move forward the distance of its entire length. One cannot call it jumping because the tail does not leave the

---

*This species is the largest; the smallest (*Crotalus miliarius*) and of a blackish gray color is called a *ground rattlesnake* here.[4]

ground. It can quickly coil itself again and strike again. The rattling sound is similar to that of a scissors grinder.* I cut the snake open and found rat and a species of thrush in its stomach. The two poison fangs in the upper jaw were more than an inch long. I extracted them and through one of them pushed a hog's bristle through its entire cavity so that it came out at the point of the fang—I did not notice any disagreeable odor.

I have also encountered vipers and copperheads. Neither is much more than a foot long but just as poisonous as the rattlesnake. Indeed, the copperheads are considered more poisonous. At any rate, I believe that they are more dangerous. If the rattlesnake is not attacked, either it crawls away from people or it reveals its presence by rattling. But the copperhead lies still and, as soon as a person approaches on foot too closely, tries to bite. The viper also retreats a little, emitting hisses through its jaws like an angry cat.

All these creatures cause less worry here than mad dogs in Europe. They usually appear only on hot days. A rider has nothing at all to fear from them. But one must bear in mind that Negroes and whites often roam barefoot through the woods for days in order to kill game. It is true that the nearness of a poisonous snake has some effect on everyone, especially on women, but only for a short while. Afterward it is completely forgotten. Areas where many snakes live together, in colonies, as it were, are rare and soon become well known. One of my neighbors showed me a place, an area of several hundred paces in length and width, which eight years ago had been completely covered with rattlesnakes. They seem to retreat from human settlements. Rattlesnakes love the south side of stony hills. Only on hot days do they leave their subterranean holes—a habit of land snakes in general. There are also poisonous water snakes here, in other words, those that stay in water most of the time but come to dry land occasionally. To these belong the so-called *water mocassins* [*sic*]. [15– 3] Near the first dwellings of farmers a species of small harmless toads is usually found whose presence is considered a sure sign that snakes are absent.

Stories are told of snakes crawling into houses and even into beds. Several weeks ago one of my neighbors found a snake sleeping quietly in a sugar barrel. It was an innocent, beautiful creature and is called a *garter snake* here. Once, the housewife went into the smokehouse to get some meat and heard rattling in a corner and when she stepped closer she saw a small rattlesnake. On another occasion a setting hen made a pitiful noise. Someone ran up and found her sitting on eggs encircled by

---

*One seldom sees snakes with rattles longer than two inches. The reason can be no other than that the thin, brittle members of which the whole consists break off from time to time. This is the unavoidable result of frequent violent motion. But I did see one rattle that was almost a whole foot long.

a black snake. There are many black snakes here, some of which are eight to nine feet long. Their bite is not poisonous, but they can be irritated to such an extent that they follow the enemy for long distances.

The caiman or alligator (erroneously called the American crocodile, as the true Nile crocodile is also found here)[5] is said not to exist beyond the 34th degree of latitude. There are none here. They are decreasing in number as their skins are sought after for saddlers' products.

More troublesome than the snakes are the ticks, a species of mite (*Acarus ixodes, Acarus Americanus*) called *carabatos* by the Spaniards. In Germany they are found on hunting dogs; but in the American forests both wild and tame animals are full of them, even mice. If one wanders afoot through forests in summer, one has to make a thorough examination of oneself before returning if one is interested in sleeping peacefully. If they remain long on the skin, they dig into it so deeply that they can be torn to pieces as they are removed. And although no species is as large as a bedbug, their abdomens become distended with sucked-in blood to the size of a hazelnut. The insect then appears to be all stomach, and head and limbs seem only an insignificant addition. Their bite is neither painful nor dangerous and the insect itself does not have a disagreeable odor. What Friedrich Schmidt says about it (vol. 1, p. 516), is not applicable, at least not to the United States.[6] There are several species. All are brown; some, however, also have neat white markings on their backs. One has a design that looks exactly like a crest. The very small, scarcely visible, ticks which cannot be seen until the end of July on the grasses and plants, never on shrubs and trees, appear to be the offspring of the larger kinds. They are often more annoying than the large ones.[7] But one should not believe that they are found everywhere. On arable land and in fields there are very few of them, and none at all where large areas are cultivated. There are none in the cities nor in the regions where the prairie predominates, nor in woods where the soil is covered with the strongly scented pennyroyal (a kind of mint). As soon as the nights become cold, they disappear, and if one has rubbed his clothes with tobacco leaves (green or dry) one will never be bothered.

Fleas are rare along the Missouri. On the other hand bedbugs [or lice] are all the more numerous, and in wooden dwellings protecting beds from these disagreeable guests is the first concern of cleanliness. I remember having read in Blumenbach's *Handbuch der Naturgeschichte*[8] that little is known about the original home of these insects in their natural state. I can say from my own experience that the *Cimex lectularius* (not the *corticalis*) is found in the forests along the Missouri, far from all human habitation, under the bark of dead oaks. There, bats also have their hiding places, and it is generally known here that bats are almost never free of lice. On the basis of this evidence, bodies of bats or dead trees are to be considered their original home.—Sand fleas (*Pulex penetrans*), which try to lay their eggs under toenails, thereby causing dangerous inflammation, are known here only through the reports of travelers. None of them are on the Ohio or the Missouri.

Yesterday I saw a spectacle here that, while not entirely foreign to Europe, can occur in only a few regions there. Not far from my house, in a small sugar maple grove, I heard a young ox bellow for quite some time. He remained at the same place, sniffed incessantly at the ground, and pawed the earth all around him. Finally several more oxen came running up from all directions at full speed, sniffed, roared, and pawed in a similar manner. They then fought each other so furiously that the owner of the farm considered it necessary to drive them apart and far from the spot mentioned above. He reminded me that several weeks ago some cattle had been slaughtered there and that the odor of blood was usually the cause of such scenes.

Sixteenth Letter

Montgomery, 10 December 1825

The day before yesterday one of my neighbors told me that he had caught a wolf. He wanted to turn the dogs loose on him and invited me to watch the fight. In company with others we immediately set out with four dogs. The pit or trap built of tree trunks was a mile away from human habitations. Through gaps between the logs we could see the beast of prey lying quietly on the floor of his cage. By means of wooden hooks the men pulled out his hind legs and cut the tendons, a procedure that could scarcely be accomplished because of the constant attempts of the dogs to attack him. Then the cover was lifted and immediately all the dogs fell upon the prisoner. Disregarding [16– 1] his serious injuries he easily forced his way from the trap and only then really began to defend himself. It was a full-grown male. The dogs were his equals in size and all were of a breed called butcher's cur. The wolf tried to escape, but since the dogs prevented him from doing this he squatted from time to time on his mutilated hindquarters and in a sitting position bit to the right and left so that even the bravest of his opponents emitted many a howl of pain. By his defensive tactics he tired the dogs so much that one after another ran to a neighboring ditch, cooled off by bathing in it, and then returned to resume the fight. Although my companions insisted that this cruel game was necessary to train their dogs, the courageous defense of the helpless beast finally aroused the sympathy of everyone and the torture was brought to an end by a well-aimed blow to his head.

Several days ago I visited my neighbor, Nathan Boone. He is the son of Colonel Daniel Boone who has become so famous in the cultural

history of America and whose name is used to designate various places.*
He died three years ago at the home of his son-in-law, five miles from
here.[1] To be sure, he was a tireless hunter, even in old age, but in
Europe tales have been spread about him that have no foundation in
fact. Among others, I remember reading eight years ago that he had
been found dead leaning against a tree with a cocked gun as if ready to
aim. His son, Nathan Boone, is a state surveyor and reputed to be a very
honest man. He lives eight miles from here on a beautiful farm on the
Femme Osage (Osage Woman) River. His house is built of hewn
limestone and offers the conveniences of an urban dwelling. Formerly I
had traveled about with him for several days in order to become
acquainted with the region and the salable land. He is considered to be a
good hunter. I am planning to go bear hunting with him next winter.
The people here like bear meat very much.

Occasionally one's sleep at night is disturbed in a peculiar manner.
The opossum [16–2], with whose strange natural history you are
familiar, an animal dangerous only to the smokehouse and the fowls, has
the habit of exploring at night a homestead's trees where a flock of hens
has chosen a resting place. Almost every farm teems with tame fowls,
especially hens which also find their food in the forests. Because they
hate to share a common, enclosed space, or perhaps because of the
hostility of cocks, they usually perch overnight in individual groups on
trees near buildings. The opossum creeps up to the trees with great
caution and often is already in the branches before the threatened hen
notices it. As soon as the slightest noise warns her, she utters a penetrat-
ing, piteous cry that immediately brings her rescuers, the dogs, to the
spot. At the first sound the opossum gives up its murderous plan and,
without the slightest attempt to flee, remains motionless in the
branches. The dogs now guard their prisoner with ceaseless barking
and, if they are not driven away, persist in staying near the tree until it is
cut down the next morning or their enemy is brought to the ground
with a shot. Often dogs from the neighborhood join them and increase
the noise until someone leaves his bed at night to deliver the mortal
blow and end the disturbance.

---

*On his hunting expeditions he discovered salt springs in several places which are still
being used; I am especially referring to the spring at Boone's Lick along the Missouri
River. Wherever there is evidence of salt on the ground, it is a good station for hunters,
as game gathers there to lick. Hence the name. I have noticed also that game is attracted
not only to soil that contains table salt but also to soil containing potassium nitrate, alum,
and sulphate of magnesia. On my property there are two licks where one can find deer
everyday. It is strange that these animals come to such places only early in the morning
and in the evening toward sunset.—At first Colonel Boone himself utilized the salt licks
which he discovered along the Missouri by shipping the salt obtained from them to New
Orleans.[2]

If one comes upon an opossum without being accompanied by dogs, the animal bares its teeth (which are large enough) and acts as if it wants to attack. But the slightest blow causes it to play dead. It permits itself to be touched, lifted, shaken, struck; in vain, it stays dead. It is interesting, however, to watch it when, after a time during which nothing has happened for a while, it simply opens its eyes and looks around without otherwise making the slightest movement. Only then does it get up in order to examine the situation further, and if it is favorable, it runs away in great haste.

Another curiosity of a different kind is the skunk *(Viverra putorius)*. It is generally called *polecat (iltis)* here. It has black and white stripes and is about twice as large as a squirrel, which it resembles in the way it carries its bushy tail. As soon as you meet it in the forest it assumes an offensive position and scratches the ground with its front paws as if in challenge. If you respond to this challenge and try to injure the animal it will take flight and while fleeing will direct a spray of liquid at you. If the liquid strikes you it will make the clothes unwearable for a long time. [16– 3] The disagreeable odor is so strong that a single small animal can pollute the air for a quarter of a German mile. Dogs that have pursued a skunk often have such an unbearable odor that they have to be kept away from the dwellings for several days. It has happened twice this year that the air in my house was polluted by such an odor for half the night. Perhaps the animal had been pursued in the neighboring forests without having been near the homestead. At first, this phenomenon was puzzling to me and I could scarcely believe that it could be attributed to such a small creature. The odor is pungent and easily causes headaches.

The weather is still very beautiful. Sometimes nights are rather cold but in the daytime it does not strike one as being almost the middle of December, all the less since here winter nights are considerably shorter (by more than two [16– 4] and a half hours) than in Germany. It seldom rains and, when it does, never more than three days in succession. In a region that is so distant from the ocean one does not need to fear such continuous rains as occur along the lower Rhine.

Seventeenth Letter

10 January 1826

Yesterday I went fishing with a large group. We had freezing temperatures for a few days and the lake near me (which is about three miles long but at no point more than three hundred paces wide) had a safe covering of ice.[1] It teems with many different varieties of fish. Especially tasty is the buffalofish. Holes were cut in the ice around which the fish crowded in large numbers. Poles were used to jerk them out. As soon as large fish weighing eight to fifteen pounds appeared on the surface they were stunned by heavy blows on the ice so that they could be pulled out without difficulty. The men also killed muskrats, whose skins bring twenty cents here.

When the lake is not frozen over one always finds it full of wild fowl of all kinds. [17– 1] Last year I went duck hunting there several times; such a hunt is always profitable.

A few days ago I saw parrots (*Psittacus Carolinensis*)² and discovered that they do winter here as I had earlier been assured. These birds [17– 2] are harmful to orchards. They descend in flocks upon apple trees in particular. [17– 3]

It is remarkable how quickly dead cattle are removed here by beasts of prey. A short time ago a cow weighing about five hundred pounds died. It was dragged several hundred feet away from the dwellings, skinned,* and left lying there. I expressed my concern about the odor that would soon spread. I was told that birds and beasts of prey would prevent that. Actually after eight days not a single bone was to be seen. Ravens, crows, the white-headed eagle, and a kind of vulture, called *turkey buzzard* here because of its resemblance to a turkey, had been active during the entire day. (At night the quadrupeds came, especially the wolves.) This species of vulture reveals to the farmer where one of his domestic animals has accidentally died or been injured in the forests by circling high in the air above it, which can attract the attention of anyone who misses some stock.

The cold weather has again driven back home some of my neighbors who had gone to the lead mines.³ According to a rather widespread custom they intended to spend their spare time digging for metals after finishing the harvest. Even after a few days some people succeed in discovering a mass of lead that they can sell immediately for a thousand dollars or more without any further work. Such luck is tempting, and farmers in the neighborhood of the mines love to try their luck. Usually they take along provisions, which are sold at high prices there. It is also a way of occupying Negroes if the homestead does not offer sufficient work.

Digging is rarely done with the care of a true miner. The metal lies close to the surface; therefore, even the crudest method pays rather well.

The nearest mines are on the south side of the Missouri about forty English miles from here. There are many, and they cover an area twenty-five miles wide and sixty miles long. But these ore deposits are said to extend much farther.

---

*Skinning is done by the owner himself or by his hired help without the slightest scruple. There are no knackers here. No one is of the opinion that such work is detrimental to one's health or honor.

One of the best places is Potosi. Formerly it was called *Mine a Burton* [Mine à Breton] after Frank Burton [Breton] who discovered the mine over forty years ago and began to work it after the Spanish government had granted him the area.[4] The ore was found in a prairie that is about a hundred feet higher than the brook into which the prairie's runoff water empties. It lies in masses of one to fifty pounds no deeper than two feet below the surface in a layer of gravel. Ruptured sandstone, which likewise contains ore, lies under the layer of gravel. A layer of red clay about six feet thick is under the sandstone, and below this stratum the best ore is found in masses of two to three hundred pounds. It produces 60 to 75 percent pure metal. Zinc, arsenic, sulfur, and antimony are found occasionally among the lead ore. The names of the mines are: New Diggins, Elliott's Diggings, Old Mines, Brown's Diggins, Mine La Platte, Joe's Mine, and so on.[5]

The pure metal is sold in St. Louis for four to six dollars for a hundred pounds. [17–4]

Eighteenth Letter

Montgomery, 16 May 1826

The money from Europe did not arrive until last fall. I decided to spend the winter at the place where I had stayed so long, but to live on my own farm at the beginning of the following spring. And that is what I did. Toward the end of March arrangements had been carried out to the point that the new homestead seemed habitable for American settlers, and since I had already become so familiar with their way of living I did not hesitate a moment to move in with my two horses, dogs, and cattle.* As I can remain here only until next year, I have restricted myself to the necessities. I had a secondary building made into temporary living quarters for me and had a roof constructed to protect the unfinished main house.[2] The yard covers about one and a half *Morgen,* the adjoining meadow about two and a half *Morgen,* and the arable fields four *Morgen.* Everything is well fenced and the fields have been prepared for cultivation in the usual manner. The cost did not amount to more than I had estimated earlier. An excellent spring in the pasture survived the drought of last year. I have had it surrounded with a protective hut.[3] The path from the house to the spring is shaded by tall oak, ash, walnut, and sassafras trees. The beautiful foliage of the white walnut trees bends

---

*[C.] Sidons sets the price of an ox or cow in the vicinity of St. Louis at twenty-five to thirty dollars (see p. 128).[1] How that estimate can be so high for 1825 is incomprehensible to me. Seven years ago it was accurate; but now the best young cow, together with her calf, nowhere costs more than ten dollars. [18–1]

the branches almost to the ground from a considerable height as is the case with weeping willows. In front of the hut, as I must call the place, a porch has been built. A few paces away, melons, cucumbers, and other kitchen plants thrive in a small garden.

A cook tends to my household wants and a young man hired for several months does the fieldwork. Formerly I had in my service a peasant who had emigrated from Germany in 1817. He had landed in Philadelphia and had given himself and his wife into indentured service for several years to pay for the passage money.[4] After many hardships fate had brought him here. The usual monthly wage for a male worker, be he black or white, is eight to ten dollars in addition to board and lodging; without it, from twelve to fourteen dollars. I pay the latter sum, as I do not care to be involved in providing board and lodging. A cook receives four dollars a month here. Several years ago the wages were twice as high, but with the rapidly increasing population the pay will decrease still more; however it will not be as low as it is in Europe in general. That is why it is easy here to establish a household. Immigrant Europeans who have no fortune and are skilled neither in arts nor crafts must earn their living doing ordinary house or fieldwork, and in the beginning theirs is a sad lot here. But more of this later.[5]

My fields are properly planted with corn, some cotton (merely as an experiment), potatoes, beans, peas, carrots, spinach, cucumbers, pumpkins, melons, and so forth. I can also obtain provisions of this kind from my neighbors at low prices.

I bought the necessary furniture and kitchen utensils in St. Louis, where such things are considerably cheaper than in the stores in my neighborhood,* so that when I leave I can sell everything to my neighbors without loss. I also provided myself with coffee and rice from there.

A good cow supplies me with fresh cream. Her calf, which is kept in an enclosure, keeps her from wandering far from the homestead even though she finds her food in the forest. I am accustomed to keeping one of my two horses in the fenced pasture in order to have it always at hand.

My daily routine is as follows: At sunrise I go outdoors, usually with a

---

*A German mile from here an attempt was made to found a town. It is called Marthasville. Its location was chosen unwisely and it will hardly grow. It has only a few houses. But there are two stores, a post office, and also a doctor. The city of St. Charles (San Carlo, founded by the Spaniards), about eight to nine German miles from here, has a better location, but it is too close to St. Louis, which hinders its development. Opposite it, on the south bank of the Missouri, there lives a merry Frenchman, who takes care of the transportation across the river, and he is also postmaster and inn-keeper. His name is Chauvin and he was born in Canada. He told me that Prince Paul of Württemberg[6] had stayed overnight with him some time ago. Several miles below St. Charles is the little town of Florissant, where Jesuits live (some Germans among them) who primarily devote themselves to the instruction of Indian children.

fowling piece. I roam around for about an hour, shoot partridges, doves, or squirrels, and also turkeys—which, however, can be shot better with a rifle—and return to eat my breakfast. After breakfast I read the books I had selected to include in my baggage in small locked chests. I then occupy myself, as calmly as I ever did in Germany, with the sciences. Shortly before the noon meal I stop [reading], walk in the garden, or go to the spring. After the meal I mount my horse either to visit my neighbors or to enjoy the beauty of nature in the forests, on the hills, or in the valley. To what extent one may call this a life in the desert you may be the judge, as I have recently permitted the neighboring farmers to build a schoolhouse on my land.[7] You must also take into consideration that newspapers from St. Charles and St. Louis always arrive here on the second day after printing.

Rainy weather rarely disturbs us here. [18– 2] I know of only one occurrence when there were more than three rainy days in succession. That was toward the end of March of last year. Rains are rather heavy and usually accompanied by storms. As soon as the rain stops the sun shines again and the roads are soon dry. At any rate, being near the large waterways they do not suffer from freight carts to the extent that a rider has cause for complaint. In the woods there are many paths made only by game and domestic animals.

I wish that you could see my present location even if only for a few moments. The hills and valleys are all covered with forests, but in such groupings that it appears as if an artist had laid out a park. Two hundred and six *Morgen* of private property surround my homestead, the rest is at a somewhat greater distance from it. Four never-ending springs spread a most refreshing coolness over it, and one of them is so elevated that I could run water into the house with considerable pressure. Even the water in Lake Creek on my property is as cold as well water during the greatest summer heat. This brook teems with fish and contains two kinds of turtles, one with a soft shell. Bullfrogs are also found there. Their croaking can be heard throughout the summer. They have a greenish color with black-brownish spots and are so large that they weigh about two to three pounds and hunt small chicks. At least I have never seen a larger one.* The French eat them with relish.

My house is situated on the level area of a hill that rises gently from the rather wide valley of Lake Creek. The plain changes to a slope which gradually reaches a height that offers a distant view of the Missouri valley and adjacent hills.

The splendor of the forests is, especially during this month, beyond all description. They are full of a vast multitude of flowering trees. Here

---

*No one here believes that there are some that weigh thirty pounds (Warden, vol. 2, p. 526).[8]

one beholds the purple of the Canadian Judas tree (*Cercis Canadensis,* English *redbud*), the leaves and branches of which are hidden under innumerable blossoms. There the cornel tree (*Cornus Florida,* English *dogwood*), covered completely with large white flowers, shines through dark foliage. The blossoms of papaws, persimmons, acacias, plum trees, mountain ash (service tree), cherry trees, fragrant grape vines—everything reminds me of the fact that I am in a country with wildernesses to which at least Tacitus's descriptions of Germania[9] do not apply. [18– 3]

In neighboring woods I see many species of walnut trees. The best species is the pecan tree (*Juglans olivaeformis*), which I have mentioned before.* Then follow: the black walnut (*Juglans nigra*), the wood of which is used by carpenters; the white walnut (*Juglans cathartica*), the bark of which is used as a purgative, *Juglans squamosa, Juglans porcina, Juglans amara.* The last four species are called hickory trees here. [18– 4] The young shoots of the *Juglans porcina* are so flexible that they are used instead of ropes, and some farmers constantly use them for their sleds** and plows. Among the oaks, the white oak is the best of all. Its excellent wood is also characterized by a degree of toughness such as I have never seen equaled in any other wood. The finest wickerwork can be made from its splints, and these baskets surpass by far those made of willow. In addition to white oak I have noticed here the *Quercus macrocarpos* [18– 5] with its conspicuously large fruits, the [18– 6] dyers oak (*Quercus tinctoria*), the red oak (*Quercus rubra*), and the Spanish oak (*Quercus Hispanica* [18– 7]). On the banks of the rivers, cottonwood trees (*Populus Canadensis*) and elms rise to a height of 80 to 150 feet. Among the varieties of maples I have seen the sugar maple (*Acer negundo*) and the *Acer rubrum* (English *water maple*) from which sugar can be made, but not in the quantity as from the *Acer saccharinum.* Sassafras trees, aromatic wood (*Liquidambra styraciflua*), various kinds of sumac [18– 8], weeping willows, ash, and linden trees—it is all this that usually attracts the eye.*** In some places the ground is adorned with the beautiful flowers of the Canadian bloodroot and varieties of lilies, in others, with asters, phlox, maidenhair, and mandrakes.

---

*It is found neither in the Atlantic states, with the exception of South Carolina and Georgia, nor along the Ohio, but it is found along the Illinois.

**One must not think of snow-covered ground in connection with the word *sled.* The sleds are used least of all on the snow, partly because the snowfall is light, partly because the farmer stays in the house during inclement weather. In many homesteads, a sled (which can be constructed with little effort) takes the place of carts and wagons, and is far more practical in the woods (for example, during the preparation of sugar).

***The wood of the sugar maple is also prized by joiners and carpenters. The hard wood of the acacias (*Robinia pseudoacacia*) is considered indestructible in water. Sometimes ships are built of it; but they are very expensive. The tree is called *locust* here. The *honey locust* is the three-thorned Christ's thorn, which I also see frequently here as well as the *Gymnocladus Canadensis* with its large pods, called the *coffee tree* here because its fruit

All my neighboring farms have orchards. These always produce so many apples that cider must be made of them. The abundant peaches are sliced and then dried. The peach tree thrives so well that one grown from a seed bears fruit in the third year. There is no need to consider grafting. Neither do apple trees require this. The seed produces a tree that is just like the original. Most apples are of a very good variety. [18–9]

While I am writing this, sitting in front of my house, I notice again the same kind of beetle that had earlier aroused my interest because of its industry. For the time being I shall call it the roll beetle* since I know of no other name for it.[10] I do not doubt that it has long been mentioned in printed matter. However, since you also have not concerned yourself much with natural history, perhaps the little creature is just as new to you as it was to me when I arrived in America. It belongs to the dung beetles, and it is very similar to the beetles that are found in Germany in pastures and in cow dung. Only I had never noticed a similar industry among the German beetles. The burying beetle, to be sure, resembles it in industry but not in method.—Several times before I had seen a black beetle, occupied with a round object the size of a walnut, without paying particular attention to it. Once, on a hot summer day, I was sitting in the shade of a plane tree when two such balls came rolling directly toward me. I looked more closely and found along with each ball two of the beetles I mentioned. Now I could see very well that the rolling object was formed of a soft mass and perfectly round. One beetle pushed with its hind legs, its forelegs supported on the ground, while the other beetle suspended its entire body from the opposite side. By this method the ball was made to roll. The pushing beetle never lost its position, whereas the one hanging on in front fell off at every revolution and rolled part way under the ball so that it had to attach itself to the ball again innumerable times. I wanted to see the end of their labor and waited until the ball was scraped into the soil next to the trunk of a dead tree. Then I investigated the mass and found that it was kneaded horse manure.

Meanwhile I had not lost sight of the other working pair. Without touching the beetles I changed the form of their ball by a light pressure. They soon noticed this and stopped to make repairs. However, only one beetle occupied himself with it and the other remained completely idle. When the curve was restored (by pressing and trimming) the work of rolling was resumed.

I thought I noticed a slight difference in the beetles and attributed it

---

is sometimes used as coffee. Hackberry, ash, oak, and hickory wood are considered best for firewood. They say that no dry wood burns better than these trees even when they are entirely green. It is therefore unnecessary to fell them in advance.

*I learned later that this (*Scarabacus volvens*) is also its technical name.

to the sex. The following observation confirmed this opinion. Not far from the balls mentioned above I saw a third ball which a single beetle was trying to move. Soon I saw a second one approach, which, without doubt, was on the lookout for such an object. The first beetle seemed to keep on working, and the one that joined it began to push in the manner described above. I succeeded in moving the two balls closer together without interrupting the workers. Then I removed the ball from one of the pairs, and since both beetles thereupon proceeded to search for their lost ball, I tried to direct the pushing beetle toward the other pair, specifically at first to the beetle working on the front side. This beetle welcomed the stranger, and the latter was about to begin its usual activity without further ado when it came in touch with the beetle on the rear side. Instantly a furious fight broke out which the beetle on the foreside seemed to watch quietly. The repeated clashes were so violent and made such a noise that I scarcely trusted my ears. Finally one of the fighters withdrew, but whether it was the one I had induced to come there I could not determine with certainty. Afterward I brought the second beetle, which had been searching for the ball, to the beetles rolling the ball. It was welcomed by the pushing one but violently attacked by the beetle on the front side; after some attempt at defense it was put to flight.—It was interesting to see how strenuously these little creatures exerted themselves to overcome the hindrances in their path. Often the ball would roll far back down a slope. They immediately followed and did not give up the endeavor. When special obstacles appeared, the beetle in front regularly assumed the work of investigation; it circled the ball completely, obviously for the purpose of ascertaining the nature of the obstacle.—I was told that these balls serve [as nests] for the development of the brood.

Nineteenth Letter

Written in May 1826

Surely you must think it strange that in all my former letters I have devoted scarcely a syllable to the Indians. But who in Germany would believe that one could live for years on the distant Missouri without being visited by Indians a single time? Because of various reports about them, they had been the chief cause of my concern for peace in the countryside. But I must tell you that no Indian has been seen in my neighborhood for perhaps ten years. To be sure, almost every week groups of them come down the Missouri River in order to exchange wares in St. Louis or to collect annuities for relinquished areas and then return by land; but they do not leave the direct [19– 1] route and they are seen only there. I met a number of Sacs in the neighborhood of St.

Charles where they had set up their tents. One often sees Indians in St. Louis: sometimes Osage, sometimes Kansas, sometimes members of the Fox tribe, sometimes Sioux, and others. They molest no one in any way, as little as do Negroes and whites. To be sure, there are still many tribes on the east side of the Mississippi of which some, for example, the Choctaws, have adopted the European way of life and customs, even owning Negro slaves and keeping inns; but [19– 2] few live in the state of Missouri (I say state because it is to be distinguished from the immense Missouri territory). About fifteen English miles from here on the south side of the Missouri a Shawnee town of about fifty houses existed. [19– 3] Some time ago they abandoned their settlement [19– 4] and moved about a hundred miles farther west. I do not know of any tribe west of the Mississippi that would be closer to me at present than these Shawnees.[1]

When the English incited the Indians during the war year of [19– 5] 1814, settlers along the Missouri suffered severely. According to an old custom the Indians scalped every human being they could get ahold of. No child in its cradle was spared. Usually individual Indians crept stealthily up to farms at a time when the men were absent. The scenes, which are remembered so vividly here, must have been frightful. The father-in-law of my nearest neighbor, by the name of Ramsay [Robert Ramsey], related again a short time ago how he had found his house after an absence of several hours. Whites and Negroes lay on the ground, murdered and scalped. Only a five-year-old boy (a grandson of Ramsay's [sic]) was still breathing. At the sight of his grandfather, he tried to sit up and then said: "Granddaddy, the Indians did scalp me." He died soon afterward.[2]—Rarely does a scalped person survive long. Usually death by bleeding (or apoplexy or inflammation of the brain) follows. However, if the wound heals the scar is protected by an airtight plate. I saw a man who wore such a plate. He also had been stabbed in the abdomen.—Now such occurrences are no longer to be feared. The white population has increased too much. In case of a war a number of small forts, erected earlier on the upper outermost borders of the state, would afford effective protection. If the Indians are not stirred up and given considerable assistance by another power [19– 6] (as formerly by the French and later by the English), their great fear of the United States easily keeps them within bounds. [19– 7][3]

The inhuman behavior of the Indians, moreover, is by no means based on hatred toward the white man. In their feuds they do not treat their red brothers any better. There is nothing more one-sided than the fanatical haranguing against the expansion of Europeans [in America] together with sentimental paeans of praise to the Indians. The person who looks for virtue among undeveloped people connects entirely erroneous ideas with this word and introduces vague images of a biased imagination into a field that should be reserved for rational thinking. Among children many evil acts are not committed because temptation is lacking. One can call such a negative state innocence, and to that extent the Indians can undoubtedly be compared with children. But one should bear in mind that the innocence of an adult child (if I may express myself thus) should never be confused with that of a real child. It will be unnecessary to remind you of the impulses common to all adults. When the direction of reason is lacking, adult children, as with real children, are controlled by the impulses of the moment, except that their impulses when combined with physical strength result in urges and actions very different from those of a child. The weaker the influence of [19– 8] basic principles (which are to be expected only as a result of culture) the more uncertain is the moral condition of a society within itself; the more dependent on inner contingencies without any consideration of dangerous outside influences, the lower is its true [19– 9] value. If after such observations, one studies a group of human beings who are incited by a national custom to murder women and children [19– 10] in order to acquire a claim to public praise for the scalps collected, one may dare to make the assumption that this custom did not sprout in the garden of innocence. [19– 11] Similar atrocities [19– 12] can be compared to cancerous evils which develop on an already rotten base. Such phenomena do not occur suddenly. [19– 13] Who does not know how common the practice has always been among Indians to kill their own children? Just as well known here are their atrocious sexual aberrations. Bestiality and lewdness with boys are found among most tribes. What Bernhard Romans (in his concise natural and moral history of east and west Florida, New York, 1776)[4] relates about the Chicasas [Chickasaws] holds true also for many other tribes.

Their preference for the roaming [19– 14] life of a hunter not infrequently results in famine which transforms them completely into monsters. There are instances when fathers and mothers have eaten their own children. Old persons are put to death merely as an act of mercy. After such a famine human nature must remain in a state of tension remembering such incidents, so that a feeling of innocence is forever impossible.

Fantastic representations are read with pleasure. Reports of strange customs, stories of individual characteristics, and naive remarks concerning European prejudices have their value as entertainment. For that purpose the darker side will be omitted. Nothing is more harmful than fanciful illusions when they become opinions that direct one's life.

The remarks by Indians about European follies are often correct. But one must not rate them too highly. The Indians are by no means stupid. Wisdom, however, is as foreign to them as innocence. Their religious legends and tales contain not only beautiful poetic characteristics of a mind sensitive to the glory of God but also repelling [19– 15] traces of brutality and moral distortion.

Instead of limiting oneself to vague ideas in using the word *nationality,* one should consider that essentially human nature in all creatures to which the name *man* is applied must be assumed similar. Therefore, as far as essential characteristics are understood in the above-mentioned word, only the study of human nature can supply the answer, and mere phenomena of an unessential character are exempt from a more profound research.[5]

The ambition of uncultured people is always based on low ideals. Their efforts are directed toward physical superiority and everything that (in their eyes) gives the appearance of greater physical strength. Just as the mental world is important to children only because of its spatial power, and as in their play they love to give themselves the appearance of greater strength, adults of inferior culture also have similar ambitions. Even with regard to mental superiority their [Indians'] ambition is directed solely to the external, to that which produces an outward show. From this source originate [19– 16] those characteristics of the Indian that philanthropic visionaries attribute to a high nobility of soul. Especially attributed to this is the feigned indifference in the presence of objects to be admired and in cases of suffering, which those visionaries confuse with Pyrrhonist stoicism, therefore, finally, the striving for formality in relationships and the ambition to shine through externalities, especially through speeches in which they refrain as little as children from boasting. All barbarous people are and were, in this respect, rather similar to the Indians.[6] Indeed they must be called fortunate where ambition does not lead to worse aberrations— unlike the Indians who methodically murder women and children. [19– 17]

Also, are there not incidents in Europe when the most barbarous criminals endured all degrees of torture and met death with unshakable defiance? Do we not find similar characteristics among beasts of prey? A passion that borders on madness makes man resemble these animals more closely. How may one speak of spiritual fortitude in connection with such paroxysms? To restrain the tendency toward pride, toward vengeance, and toward passionate defiance has always been the primary task of a good education. Among the Indians the opposite is true. They seek to attain their greatness by inflexible nurturing of these tendencies. European youth has the same predisposition toward such Indian greatness, and it certainly would not be difficult to develop it fully. The best travel reports agree on this matter. I recall only John [19– 18] Carver, Volney, Romans, Oldmixon, and La Peyrouse.[7] They declare [19– 19] the Indians to be extremely frivolous, inconsistent, and also arrogant; they say their pride is easily incited to cruelty, making them bloodthirsty and implacable. It is especially worth reading what La Peyrouse in his account of the unfortunate incident near the Friendly Islands writes about the Indians and the enthusiastic bias of one of his companions toward them.

I am not speaking here of the treatment that the Indians suffered [19– 20] from the first conquerors. Such an indictment can be applied in general to all people of this earth who have everywhere and at all times been guilty of atrocities. I am speaking of the manner in which the Indians are being treated by the United States. Slavery is out of the question. On the other hand, if the measuring rod of moral values is applicable also to the Indians then all evils that have resulted from associating with citizens of the United States must seem negligible in comparison with the good. Especially in comparison with the effect of the abhorrence that every European, not excepting the crudest hunters and frontier traders, feels concerning the above-mentioned faults. A collection of individual incidents has little weight [19– 21] for one who knows the exaggerations and distortions and the credulity of fanatic anecdote collectors. It is not difficult in this manner to have every people on this earth [19– 22] appear as offsprings of hell. Careful observation of human nature itself and of the source of information is [19– 23] the primary prerequisite for criticism.

That more could be done to further civilize the Indians does not justify a disregard for what is actually being done. Europeans should not take the trouble to offer advice to the United States concerning the promotion of the welfare of mankind. I should think that a mere [19– 24] glance at the need for it at home would deter the friend of his own country from this.

It has long been the endeavor of the United States to influence the Indians to adopt permanent homes and a steady cultivation of the soil. This is the indispensable condition of culture. [19– 25] Some tribes have already adopted this way of life and now realize what they owe to their white brothers. If the Indians are constantly decreasing in number, the United States has no cause to blame itself. The real reason can be found in their way of life and in their constant feuds. These feuds start mostly over hunting. This is not hard to understand if one considers how easily the pursuit of game in Europe, where in general it is only a sport, leads to border crossings and ensuing violent quarrels. For Indians, hunting is their sustenance since they abhor the breeding of cattle and farming. At most they have their women and children cultivate small gardens. To speak of the rights of a few persons to the exclusive possession of large areas is just as ridiculous as to complain about the increasing numbers of whites. The good sons of the forest [Indians] would thereby be restricted in their hunting grounds and perhaps even be forced to make use of several of the millions of *Morgen* of fertile soil to raise grain or for pastures in order to escape the pangs of hunger. The reasons that move the United States to buy the land from the Indians have nothing to do with the conviction that the aborigines have a sacred right to it. In immeasurable expanses such acquisitions have not even caused an irksome restriction, not to mention dispossession. The United States acquires only such areas as are used by the Indians solely as hunting grounds. The few tribes that engage in agriculture are spared even the suggestion of selling. In order to protect the Indians from fraudulent greed, private citizens have been [19– 26] denied any direct acquisition of their land. Even the individual states no longer possess this right. The federal government has reserved for itself the exclusive right, and its execution is directed on the basis of principles for which no civilized people on this earth need be ashamed. What the situation is at present concerning the affairs between the state of Georgia and the Creeks I do not know. But one must feel no concern that the national government will ignore those principles in this matter.[8] It is incredible how vehemently some German [19– 27] publications criticize the treaties of the national government with the Indians. As if the moderate procedure of the United States had any similarity with that of our honored ancestors who founded their rise to power upon the downfall of all old nations of southern and middle Europe!

You must not expect me to describe in detail the mode of life of the Indians [19– 28] as innumerable reports already exist about it. However, I must mention that I have seen true Kalmuck faces among them, faces in which the cheekbones not only projected but also seemed to be pressed upward so that the outer corners of the eyes also seemed to be pushed upward and the slits of the eyelids, instead of forming a horizontal line, converged downward. In general, I was reminded of the Asiatic warriors who appeared in Germany in 1813 and 1814.[9] Even the color of the skin seemed to me more yellow than red with some. Another point, which perhaps is less well known, is that some tribes eat no salt at all despite the fact that they exist almost entirely on meat. They maintain that eating salt impairs free breathing.

Twentieth Letter
Written in June 1826

Among the necessary tasks of the local farmer, which the European immigrant at first is inclined to regard as mere sport, is that of shooting squirrels. Yes, shooting or catching squirrels is considered work here, without which no corn harvest can be expected. As soon as the seedlings appear above ground whole hordes of these little animals attack them. If they are not prevented from digging up the sprouting kernels they will surely eat them all. They do not appear earlier. The first little sprouting leaf is their signal. For about the next two weeks the farmer must walk the fields in the morning at sunrise and in the evening at sunset (the little guests cannot be seen at any other hour) and shoot as many as he can until the crop is sufficiently developed. He must repeat this work several weeks before the grain ripens. At this time raccoons (*Ursus lotor*) [20-1] may also appear. These must be hunted with dogs, which drive the game into trees.

Some farmers use shotguns, but the majority use rifles with such skill that a ball scarcely ever misses its mark. Within a span of eight days my workman took about twenty-four shots and did not miss a single one, although the squirrels were usually forty or more paces distant and his rifle was supported only by his hands. These rifles are very long and of small caliber. They are made in the United States, mostly in Lancaster, Pennsylvania.

There are various kinds of squirrels here, but the gray species is the most numerous and the one that is a menace to cornfields. The better the walnuts develop the less the cornfields suffer. The little thieves soon learn what they have permission to do. One must creep up to cornfields in order to get within shooting distance. As soon as they see a human being approach they retreat quickly into the forest. On the other hand, they eat walnuts without the slightest fear of man. Often six or more of them sit for hours close to the houses of farmers and gnaw on the nuts.—The skins of squirrel are an article of trade, to be sure, but so little value is placed upon them here that no one picks them up. Superabundance gives rise to waste everywhere. For the same reason, only goose feathers are used. Although it would be easy in a short time to collect feathers from other fowls, especially wild ones (for example, wild ducks and turkeys), in sufficient quantity to make a feather bed, this is never done anywhere. A pound of goose feathers costs thirty to forty cents.

It is probably time to anticipate your curiosity and to tell you more in detail about the people I am living among here. I came to America with the opinion that it was really nature that had most to offer to the immigrating European. I was not mistaken in this, and therefore, I gave less attention to people in my first reports. I shall now try to make up for that.

You already know enough about the Indians. I cannot really say that I live among them. It is the white people, the Europeans and their descendants, I shall write you about now. All the more so because to a certain extent they furnish the background for a picture of the Negroes and mulattoes who live among them.

The first general point in my ideas should undoubtedly be the remark that the English language is the prevailing one here as well as in the United States as a whole. This is generally connected with the idea that the English way of life has emerged as the main element among the masses of the North American population. Small colonies of Frenchmen exist here and there in the Mississippi valley, along the Wabash, the Arkansas, and the Red rivers, where along with French customs the French language also predominates. At the mouth of the Mississippi in the state of Louisiana, the French population is very large. The French along the upper Mississippi are largely from Canada. Some German families also immigrated to the Mississippi and the Missouri from there. They were living here when the Spanish were still rulers of the land. But the children as well as the grandchildren speak English and do not know their mother tongue. As a rule, even the old people cannot read or write German.

Among all those who have ever immigrated from Germany to North America very few were capable of instructing their children themselves, and rarely did enough well-to-do families settle together to establish a regular school. Faced with the alternative of letting the young people grow up without proper instruction or of sending them to English teachers, sensible fathers chose the latter. The children's own judgment told them that there was no evidence that the German language had been of any special value to their parents. The speech of German peasants and mechanics, which had never been refined by education and instruction, especially that of the immigrants from the Palatinate, Swabia, and Switzerland who had brought with them their dialects in all their harshness, was not suited to recommend German culture.[1] As with regard to language, these immigrants were also the only representatives of the German people in everything else, in their customs and their habits. Beginning with the first attempts at colonization, the English and the French never lacked men who belonged to the most highly cultured families of their mother countries. It is easy to understand how, far from the influence of European views which earlier were never so favorable to us as to cope with disagreeable circumstances without our assistance, the opinion could develop that Germany was culturally far behind England and France. This is the opinion of the masses in all of North America. Only a few highly educated natives judge differently. Therefore, it must not seem strange if some descendants of Germans treat the later immigrants from the land of their own ancestors with some disdain. Whoever wanted to improve this attitude would have to begin by making them understand what a miserable education their own fathers had. Fluency in the English language is a sure protection against the annoying arrogance of such Americans. One then immediately notices that their conceit loses all its support, and only the immigrant's ignorance of the language of the country will confirm in them their delusion of imagined superiority. Moreover, it is not advisable to speak German with this class of Republicans in case they do understand it. Aside from the embarrassing sensation of seeing the mother tongue subjected to ridicule because of poor articulation, it also seemed to me that the same people [Germans] assumed better manners when they spoke English than when the conversation was carried on in German. This may seem paradoxical, but one should consider that only the English language could separate them from their inherited crude customs, and that their German language was an integral part of these customs. The use of *du* and *ihr* instead of *sie*, which is almost universal in the interior of America, probably biased my judgment somewhat, but there is certainly some truth in it. Almost all who were born in the United States understand English, and those who also understand German speak it very poorly. They have learned it without instruction, mainly from the immigrants mentioned above and intersperse it with innumerable corrupted English words. There are only a few descendants of Germans for whom English has remained an entirely foreign language. In Pennsylvania there are such individual families. Usually religious differences keep those who settled near each other isolated [from others].[2] They are considered still more awkward than the semi-anglicized ones; however both groups are praised everywhere as models of sobriety and domestic industry. In general the cultured inhabitants of present-day Germany will prefer to associate with the British and, as a rule, with Americans who understand only the English language and not the adulterated kind of German mentioned above. Among the latter one also finds a more favorable view of German culture, which they partly derive from Great Britain and partly from a comparison of the various German immigrants themselves. [20-2]

The Dutch, Swedes, and other North Europeans were always too limited in numbers to exert any significant influence on the masses of the population. Their descendants have merged almost completely with the British.

Only the French could limit and modify the English way of life in the western states. The French immigrants were certainly not lacking in culture, and each one had an innate attachment to the language and customs of the mother country. But they were given up too soon by their mother country. After the cession of the Mississippi territory to England and Spain, immigration from France was very insignificant. French settlers sought to forget their grief over the political dominance of the rapidly increasing English population by finding solace within family life. The less they were inclined to sacrifice anything concerned with their nationality, the more they were bound to lose in regard to their influence on the whole. The new immigrations from the eastern states only caused them to retire into stricter isolation.

The immigrants from Great Britain were thus greatly superior to all others, partly in numbers, partly in political power. At the same time they were so advanced culturally that in this respect no influence by the minority seemed possible, least of all by the Germans. Immigrants from

Great Britain did not come, as did those from Germany, from the poor, uneducated masses but from the very beginning from all classes. They were so numerous and followed so closely upon each other that for this reason alone, aside from the great political and commercial intercourse, the essentials of English culture could be transplanted to America and there progress at the same pace as in the mother country. There was no fear of a retarded intellectual development among the English population unless they considered the new home itself (the land and climate of the United States) unfavorable for the sons of Great Britain. On the other hand, the situation of the other immigrants was entirely different. It is easy to see that the more they kept to themselves the more they had to lag behind. It was possible for the English population alone to keep pace with Europe. And it is particularly true that the more foreign the English language has remained to the present-day German descendants the further they lag behind.* (This serves also as an explanation for the arrogance of the semi-anglicized Germans, which I have mentioned before.) It is not a cheerful phenomenon that here devotion to the old homeland has produced such detrimental results, and very often one wishes that under the prevailing conditions Germans would yield to its loss.

The present can only be understood in the light of the past, and without doubt the correct method to understand life in North America is to investigate the derivation of the North Americans. The most general information is found in the language. History alone can supply the details. But Bülow made an incorrect application of this method,[3] and all who followed him were guilty of the same error. It is entirely contrary to the facts of history that the British immigrants usually came from different classes. In his passionate enthusiasm Bülow forgets that the first undertakings of the British were animated by the same spirit that at that time inspired all of western Europe to discover new lands. After reports of the great finds had become widespread and had excited young and old, everyone who felt himself restricted and limited in any respect in Britain cast longing eyes upon regions that, especially at the beginning, were depicted with exaggerated praise. But in order to know who at that time felt especially restricted and thwarted in Great Britain and Ireland, one need only make a brief observation of the earlier conditions in these countries.

One will then discover what interests clashed there in those times and realize that even centuries ago there were dissatisfied persons in all classes of society ready to exchange their own country for America. It was not merely a struggle between the rich and the poor, the freemen and the slaves, the cultured and the uneducated, the enlightened and the fanatics which agitated the human race. It was a period when,

---

*They call themselves Dutchmen instead of Germans.

besides physical interests in material goods, which are always present as long as men have mortal bodies, in most of the European countries human nature began to focus upon itself instead of depending solely on individual impressions, as was the case formerly. The mind of man began to be conscious of itself, to sense itself as a constant under all conditions, and based upon this created a demand for independence from the entire outer world and especially from other men and their opinions and actions. However, in all stages of development the relation [of man] to the Supreme Being represents, among all other relationships, the primary one. Therefore, here too it had to be the mind's first object of more careful consideration when examining its environment with a freer vision. For each person, the history of his own development will furnish the commentary for this thesis. What is more explicable than as soon as insurgence of intellectual life occurred anywhere in Europe, a struggle with hierarchical limitations followed as the initial consequence? This struggle also had to consume one's vital energy for a considerable time, although not exclusively, but yet chiefly, partly because the mind was fully occupied with the ideas in question, and partly because external restrictions could not be removed so quickly. Only later could the investigating thinkers gradually succeed in mastering the significance of the other relationships so that an influence on volition and action became possible, an influence that not only agitated against religious and political pressure but also instigated an unremitting struggle for general independence. The history of England presents no exception. Because the entire population of Great Britain took part in this development all classes were affected by the interests connected with it.

To the interests in material possessions were added religious interests in overwhelming strength. Later religious interests were crowded more and more into the background by political ones.* How can one be surprised that during a time when all of Great Britain was embroiled in religious feuding the masses of people emigrating to America were not unbiased? As little as the struggles in the mother country stopped with the emigrations, just as little could the colonists be expected to remain free from them. Bülow assumes that when the various religious sects were developing in England only fanaticism and prejudice prevailed on one side, and on the other side quiet circumspection and reason. He does not expressly say that, but it is the basis of his deductions. Nothing

---

*Whoever thinks in this connection of the older struggles for political rights and the Magna Carta should consider the different kinds of aspirations that started the struggles. In the earlier struggles there was no thought given to the effect of universal rights of man. These are founded on the most general basis possible, on universal independence, whereas formerly more limited endeavors strove for individual freedoms for more limited reasons. Only interests that are based on such ideas really deserve to be called political.

can be more erroneous. The sky was dark in England as well as in the rest of Europe. Whoever defended old traditions obstinately was as unclear in his thinking as those who attacked them fanatically. Where insight is lacking, it cannot rule. The times were ruled by base impulses even more than now, and they alone attained their purpose, to which every fighter contributed without knowing it. Therefore, it is a serious mistake to speak of immigrating Puritans, Presbyterians, and so forth, in order to draw conclusions about the characteristics of present-day Americans. Nothing in particular can be deduced from that, even if one could assume that only these sects emigrated. They as well as those who remained in Europe possessed the seeds for further development. But such an assumption contradicts historical facts. All the main interests that had influenced the English, the Scotch, and the Irish to action since the first discovery of the Atlantic continent also had an effect on the emigrations; those who have prevailed to the present (I repeat) without active commercial and political intercourse have been able to maintain the intellectual development of the North Americans at the same level as that of Great Britain.

Finally, if one mentions the criminals sent to the United States one should consider whether their number was ever as significant, in comparison to that of good colonists, as the rabble, sentenced or not sentenced, that remained behind was and still is in comparison to the respectable inhabitants of these countries.

These remarks hold true for all states of the Union. The history of the population of older states is approximately the same. One cannot speak of characteristics peculiar to individual states, at least not essential ones, no matter what may be said on this subject. In newer states it does not come into question because of uniform emigrations from all Atlantic states. In Ohio, in Kentucky, in Tennessee, in Indiana, in Illinois, in Missouri, and in the rest of the Western states, the immigrants from Pennsylvania and New York live beside those from Virginia, Maryland, and Carolina.—I have already made an exception of the state of Louisiana where, up to the present, the French population has predominated. Almost all of the few Spanish families that had settled on the Mississippi departed as soon as their king was no longer the supreme ruler.—Even the difference between states where slavery is permitted and those where laws forbid it is not yet so striking. The reason is: even in the latter states there are many Negroes and mulattoes who, while they are free, almost all serve as day laborers, servants, and maids, and because of the general prejudice against their dark skins, have scarcely better relationships with their employers than real slaves. Derisive nicknames that the individual provinces give to each other are hardly worth mentioning. They have no more significance than similar chaffing in other countries. One often hears the expression here, "He is a Yankee." This name is given to the inhabitants of New England.* The name is derived from the Yanko Indians in Rhode Island, and New Englanders are said to have assumed it themselves at first as a kind of joke. Now it has the connotation of the craftiness in business of which the inhabitants of other states accuse New Englanders.** Warden (in his account of the United States of America)[5] derives the name *Yankee* from the Cherokee work *Cankke,* meaning cowardly or servile. Southern tribes applied it to the New Englanders because they had refused them their assistance in a war against the Cherokees.[6] He bases this statement on Anburey's journeys.[7]

Only after such a historical introduction may we proceed to the study of the present. Without it, life in America, as it is now, can be neither properly comprehended nor evaluated. Just as only the person who connects with it a knowledge of the characteristics of the new land itself is completely prepared, it is equally true that the proper use of historical data must in itself prevent many misconceptions now prevalent in Germany.

How absurd, for instance, seems the assumption that in religious matters the United States lags behind Europe when as long as a half-century ago its people had by way of freedom of thought concerning human nature progressed to the point of decisive political struggles? The general law that no one needs to account for his religious opinions is as old as the Union itself. In the charters of the constitutions of individual states we read that only those who are confessors of Christianity can hold office; in others, everyone who believes in a Supreme Being. Who can still speak of traces of puritanical persecution in the light of such results brought about by the votes of the entire citizenry? What would the present-day inhabitants of Germany and Switzerland say if one were to judge them by the frenzy of olden times, which incited even the reformer Calvin to the murder of Servetus, or by the burning of witches, which occurred as late as the middle of the past century?

---

*New England is the name given to the territory east of the Hudson River. It includes the states (1) New Hampshire, (2) Massachusetts (named for an Indian tribe), (3) Rhode Island, (4) Connecticut (from the Indian name of the river, which signifies long river), and (5) the state of Vermont, added after the Revolution (1790, deriving its name from the mountains covered with evergreen forests).[4]

**Many stories are told of the thievish cunning of the Yankees. A Yankee brought clocks to the western states, which are much in demand there, and for which a high price is paid. He made good sales everywhere by promising to exchange the clocks on his return if demanded. So he sold all the clocks but one, and on his trip back, he gave this one to the first person who complained, keeping the first one for the second person who made a complaint. The third received the clock of the second, the fourth that of the third, and so the speculator could return home without any worries, since he seemed to everyone to be a man of his word.

On the contrary, there would be more basis for the assertion that this highly regarded toleration approaches a certain indifference toward religion and cult. But this criticism is just as warranted with regard to European Christianity. In Europe one believes that when the future is threatened by the action of inner forces it can be met by outer forms. In America, on the other hand, one puts trust in these inner forces themselves and seeks comfort in the thought that a people living in a situation such as that in the United States will not soon turn away completely from the eternal voice of truth and that the essentials of Christianity must be preserved beneath all outward forms. They regard any coercion in a cult as an interference in the relationship of the individual to the Supreme Being and fear more harm from it than any fanatic aberration could cause to the existing freedom of religion. It is foolish to think that such aberrations would gain the approval of the majority of the people. Public opinion tolerates a sect's troublemaking here as little as in Germany. However, they are convinced that forms of coercion against them are worse than the evil itself. One can only say to the person who judges prematurely the condition of the whole on the basis of individual details that he should consider what would probably happen if the masses of the European countries were suddenly left to their own devices as the North Americans actually are.

That Americans are not entirely indifferent to cults is proved, among other things, by the conformity in the laws of all states regarding the observance of Sunday, which shows just as clearly how well in North America freedom of religion is distinguished from license. As far as I know, only Louisiana, where French customs prevail, is an exception. In the other states the lawmakers were unanimously of the opinion that noisy pleasures were least fitting for Sunday. To hunt on Sundays is also punishable by law. [20-3] Whoever believes, however, that they have gone too far in some respects, for instance that not all music but only dance music should have been forbidden, does not consider the nature of democratic procedures, which does not permit such distinctions.

Aside from a rather large number of Jews, all inhabitants of the United States confess to be Christians, but in very different ways. For example, in my neighborhood there are Lutherans, Catholics, Presbyterians, Episcopalians, Methodists, Baptists, and Swedenborgians. Where there is no building for church services, private homes are opened during the hours of worship; and where there is no local pastor, itinerant ministers appear from time to time. This depends, of course, very much on the population. Moreover, these religious differences never cause any friction in social intercourse.

From what I have written up to this point one could still be inclined to think of the North Americans simply as Englishmen in America. But this would be far from the truth and coincide merely with the superficial outlines of the picture. To be sure, I would not know how to formulate the basis of my description better than by the advice to think of the North Americans for the time being as Englishmen in America. But one should make note of the expression *for the time being* and beware of keeping too closely to this idea so that one does not dream of an England in America. Everyone knows that in America there is no noble class, no personal rank at all, and this alone distinguishes it significantly enough from Britain, as well as from the rest of Europe. But the fact is not so well known in Germany that in North America no distinction at all is made between city dwellers and country people, and yet no characteristic of local life strikes a European more than this. To consider the American farmer in the same light as the German peasant would be a great mistake. In dress and in manners country people and city dwellers are completely alike, and peasant women, in the German sense, are seen nowhere. All trades have the same status, and the new order of society has overcome the seemingly unconquerable Old World prejudices of the Europeans. Only in harbor cities does one notice that European ideas have some influence. But everywhere farming is a respected occupation and the highest official of the state would not hesitate to do manual labor on his own farm. It will occur to no one who can do something better to spend all his time in physical activity, but no prejudice will hinder the person who, through inclination or motivation, decides to cultivate his fields himself, whether he has the title of doctor, judge, or colonel. It would be useless to describe further to anyone who does not recognize this great advantage of the Americans. Aside from the effects of some physical activity on the health of the body and the mind, only he who is more closely associated than a mere observer with the manifold aspects of life in the country can supervise them. Then one should reflect how much it contributes to his independence if the educated man feels capable of wresting from nature enough to satisfy his needs without the help of others and does not have to consider the physical labor involved as the utmost of necessity.

I by no means deny that the rural simplicity of the inhabitants of some remote regions in Europe is very attractive, and I would consider it a misfortune if the customs of the cities gained a foothold there. Their situation is not that of the Indians and they can only lose by an accidental or basely motivated association with the world. To be sure, one seeks in vain for similar fields of rural innocence in North America. However, it has not been supplanted by what usually follows in Germany. When culture penetrates to the country people in Germany it will first be evidenced in a greater inclination toward sensual pleasures and in a desire to attract attention. From this develops, furthermore, doubts about the mandates of religion and the value of old customs simply in defense of the new desires hostile to them. There is no thought of an increased activity of the mind. More ostentation, irregular work, deterioration of body and mind, poverty, deceit, theft, and worse crimes are the successive products of such enlightenment. Young people who find themselves on this path could be helped in no better way than if they could be offered more that would attract them to business and enterprise. For this there is no opportunity in overpopulated Germany. In North America, however, every possible one exists. In the interior of North America the tendency toward enervating pleasures is balanced by the greater incentive to industry. It is clear to each young couple that the founding of their own homestead depends only on themselves, on moderate exertion in order to gain a carefree existence. Thereby they are introduced to their first independent activity, and the rewarding results are sufficient to maintain them in it. Health remains unspoiled, the mind becomes more active, and poverty, which usually makes the moral depravity of German country people incurable, is completely unknown. This is the reason one sees no beggars in all of North America. There, where it is so easy to make one's living, begging must be judged more harshly by public opinion, and general contempt will incite the laziest to work. The same is true of theft. Most of the thefts in Germany are committed for minor things, especially thefts of provisions. In North America one hears of such a case very seldom. In two years I can remember only one case among more than three thousand individuals in my neighborhood, and that was the pilfering of objects of feminine adornment for which the motive was vanity. That is why there are so many dwellings here without locks for their doors. On our trip here from the Atlantic coast our worries about the effects in the wagon while we ate our noon meal attracted attention everywhere. The thief finds no receiver for stolen goods and everyone helps track him. Even the Negroes and mulattoes here are nothing less than thievish, although they are not trusted as absolutely as the whites.—In St. Louis we met a German stablehand at our inn who recommended that we watch our possessions because in this country one encounters all kinds of people. We had been in the United States too long for such talk not to seem strange to us. At our departure we actually missed some things, such as a whip, traveling flasks, and so forth. The innkeeper immediately instigated a thorough search, and the result was that our countryman had wanted to furnish proof of how necessary his warning had been.—Of four thefts, scarcely one is committed by native Americans.

Some travel reports are full of harangues against the vices that are said to prevail among the inhabitants of North America. I repeat that one cannot look for the characteristics of an idyllic people here. Also it would be a mistake to equate the new Free State with such Free States, the basis of which can be formed only by educational legislation over a number of years. The citizens of the United States are Europeans in America and will develop into nothing more than can develop out of the present-day Europeans in general. Without strict isolation of youth from the adults, without a planned universal education, the present inhabitants of Europe will not, in any place on earth, turn into Romans or Spartans, let alone anything better. This attempt will not be made in America. The freedom prevalent here would be a hindrance. As in Europe, there are here also few in relation to the entire population who would make the necessary sacrifices. In Europe such an attempt could still be decided upon by the aristocracy or by monarchs; in America the matter would not even come up for decision. The political condition of the North Americans gets its real support from the fortunate external conditions, which assure independence to the first generations without requiring the characteristics of Romans or Spartans. In this regard the worry before the election of General Jackson to the presidency was entirely without foundation.[8] Even a Caesar or a Bonaparte, without external support, is not dangerous to any Free State. It was easy for Caesar in the Rome of his time, as well as for Bonaparte in France, to obtain such support. But where would there be any possibility of it in North America? Until now there are few here who could be classed as rabble. The number of indigent people is infinitesimal when compared to that of the masses. For a healthy body there is ample subsistence everywhere; for those who seek more, there is full scope for enterprise. Mere rank is too much in conflict with prevailing ideas for much to be accomplished by it without a previous transformation of general thinking. For years so much has been said publicly and written about this that for the present a simple feeling of shame would keep one from exchanging exertion and risk for a patent for arrogance (as the bestowal of rank is called in America). What can be offered then to win so many adherents that plans against independence would not appear completely ridiculous? To be sure, pointless riots could be incited; there are always enough dissatisfied people for that. When in time the favorable external conditions have changed, then the political conditions will also change. But that time lies in the far distant future. A monarchy, however, cannot develop until individual citizens so distinguish themselves that they represent, as it were, guiding lights for a large part of the masses. Since birth does not provide any advantage, there remains only the distinction acquired by outstanding deeds. Therefore long wars must come first. Only in the event of such wars could the historical basis develop that gives individuals a permanent ascendancy over the people. Similar political guiding lights are rare phenomena, especially among the newer nations. Between them and good generals and excellent statesmen there is still a great gap. Even if the North American people were ready for a monarchy, the monarch himself would be lacking. Someone from a foreign country would not be accepted, and he could not easily rise from native soil. Before that happens, aristocracies will appear. In the states where slavery exists, the number of slaves can become a dangerous factor. The mass of the free and unfree Africans is too much of a foreign element that a complete isolation from the whites would not be desirable. For the present, the influence of slavery on the customs of the masters is the most important point.

Without overestimating the moral standards of Americans, I nevertheless see no reason to prefer any nation in Europe to them. I have noticed no faults that would not also be found in Europe. Especially one should not speak of avarice [20-4], as if Frenchmen and Germans would not have cause to leave this point completely unmentioned. In North America, they still remember very well that during the Revolutionary War Germans who had been sold man after man by their princes for several pounds of sterling fought against them.[9] If one accuses the Americans of frequent bankruptcies, one does not consider how many European adventurers are among the American merchants. If one sees the same business firms go bankrupt three or four times in the same place and always begin anew, then the undiminished confidence of their fellow citizens is stronger evidence of their misfortunes than of any suspicion of swindling. That the Americans are daring in their business transactions is known well enough.

In spite of the fact that Europe sends, besides good men, so many ne'er-do-wells to America, it is not able to found a settlement of beggars and rabble there. The greatest advantage of the United States is that it is free of all the ills of overpopulation without having to complain of a lack of people. This brings me back to the point that it is really space that the Europeans are looking for in North America. If they can also enjoy all the advantages that nature offers to the citizens of the states, and if the behavior of these citizens prevents the foreigner from worrying about molestation of his property, as well as of his person, it is only fair that he should at least refrain from casting aspersions. But let me add something more: no foreigner needs to fear the rudeness in North America that is so common in Europe and especially in Germany. Nowhere is there a trace of the impudent mischievousness so many are guilty of in Germany, who still cannot be considered rabble.* Because even the craftsman is accepted in good society, he also has made an effort to show himself worthy of it, and everywhere one meets with a sedate propriety so that it cannot even occur to the traveling German that in some inns

---

*Sidons says a great deal about the rude behavior of the Kentuckians. Either I was very fortunate on my trip, or Mr. Sidons was very unfortunate. In Missouri I was also surrounded by immigrants from Kentucky. To be sure, they have the reputation of a disturbing liveliness and a tendency to boast, but one should beware of placing more weight on this than on the reciprocal accusations among the German states. Under such circumstances individual instances are not infrequently the cause of reputation that goes far beyond the truth. Kentucky has no extraordinary legislation. Its population includes immigrants from most of the older states, and the emigrants to the western states are still being supplanted by immigrants from the East. This alone shakes one's belief in national vices.[10]

he finds himself among joiners, carpenters, saddlers, and tailors. Their behavior toward the feminine sex is admirable. In no inns are dirty jokes told in the presence of women. This strict rule has been well preserved from the English customs and has not remained without effect on the descendants of the Germans.

After these statements, Europeans will not be very much surprised to hear that the white hired man claims a seat at the table of his employer and demands to be addressed as "mister" (master, gentleman).* Such white people do only a certain kind of work and would not consent to be waiters for any price. The natives dislike very much to hire themselves out as servants. If they do it, of course they have to be satisfied with another kind of treatment. It is just as unusual that white women hire themselves out as maids or cooks. Negroes are usually hired as maids and farmhands. In the large cities, as well as in the states where slavery is forbidden, this custom is not quite so prevalent. Yet even where slavery is against the law, the domestic servants are, for the most part, Negroes and mulattoes, who, however, are free. The recently immigrated Europeans, to be sure, are less particular in their hiring, but later they adopt the American customs. In no shop in North America have I seen white women except as customers. There are no shopgirls here. [20-5]

Continuation of the Twentieth Letter

Concerning slavery in the United States, together with an investigation of the moral principles involved in slavery in general.

Do not be concerned that I consider the picture complete that I have given you of the American people. I shall always try to describe so many features that I shall at least be safe from the reproach of incompleteness. Only you must not expect this in the next letters. You have asked me for more than a general description of people, and I am adding a few pages to this letter that seem to me to be most fitting at this point. They deal with the Negroes and slavery.[11] This subject has such deep roots that no superficial investigation is possible, and yet perhaps there is nothing that has been subjected to such boldly shallow treatments. My pages resemble a short treatise, which I gladly submit to your judgment, since you, in no case, will be of the opinion that one can present the matter in a more popular vein.

It is well known to you that in the United States people are not

---

*In all of North America one merely touches his hat in greeting, even when he meets a lady. But inside the house, the hat is removed; in inns, however, it is optional, and in the country not much attention is paid to it even in private homes.

insensitive to the lot of the Negro. The Americans are trying to counteract the evil at its source by establishing the settlement Liberia on the same African coast where the English have established the Negro colony Freetown.[12] The United States is just as much opposed to the slave trade as are the British. However, just as Britain still tolerates slavery itself in her colonies, so the United States has been able, up to now, to limit it to certain states; and especially the state of Missouri is among those in which slavery is permitted.

For immigrants from Europe this phase of the social condition is of the greatest importance. No European, unless he belongs to the lowest classes, will be able to refrain from considering the moral implications of slavery when he arrives with plans for settlement beyond the Allegheny Mountains. The decision as to whether or not one wants to keep slaves has such an influence on the choice of the state, on the place within that chosen state, and on all one's arrangements, that every settler should make up his mind on the subject before he crosses the ocean. I was by no means satisfied with what I learned about the treatments of the morality of slavery in the literature that had appeared on the subject up to that time. I therefore found it necessary, several years ago, to study the matter independently, and what I am writing you now is the result of the investigations I made at that time.

It is obvious enough that everything that deals with the exportation of the Negroes from their native land does not concern us here. In 1808 Congress passed a resolution forbidding this as well as the importation of slaves from foreign territories,[13] and therefore one may refrain completely from discussing the atrocities connected with such practices. The question is not whether more Negroes should be taken from their fatherland, but what view one should take concerning the situation of those who look upon America as their native land, who feel no longing for Africa, and who would not make use of their freedom to return to the land of their ancestors without some special reason.

Also the horrible descriptions of the lot of the slaves in tropical regions, where they are kept like herds of cattle to make possible the exportation of colonial products, must not disturb us. The southern regions of the United States are not suitable for German settlers. If they do not want to sacrifice health of body and mind to the climate, they must abstain from raising sugar, indigo, coffee, and so on.* Wherever, however, the raising of grain is the main occupation of the settler, slavery exists in a milder form. In the state of Missouri, the lot of a slave with regard to care of the body, protection against diseases, and the amount of work expected of him is much to be preferred to that of the domestic servants and day laborers in Germany.

---

*The climate of Florida is said to be well adapted to the raising of coffee. But up to the present, no large plantations exist.

It is true that all this does not touch upon the essentials of the situation and nothing can be derived from it concerning the moral nature of the institution. My purpose at present is merely to remove the effect of the abhorrence that Europeans feel at the mere words *Negro slaves*. Only if this can be done will a calm investigation be possible. For this very reason it may also serve a purpose here to remember European serfdom and to consider that among most of the nations in history, the crude as well as the cultivated, slavery has been a part of the legal order. One meets it among the Egyptians, the Hebrews, the Persians, the Greeks, the Romans, the Arabians, and the Germanic tribes: the Alamannians, the Franks, the Goths, the Lombards, and many others.

There seems to be something in our minds that opposes the significance of all historical factors; something that, like a direct verdict of reason, condemns slavery and declares it to be an unacceptable evil. Therefore some consider the matter closed and any further investigation superfluous. It is hard to deal with minds of this caliber. Only those who are more capable of investigation will decline to succumb idly to an emotion, with the basis of which they have never concerned themselves. These will attempt to examine more closely what is at the bottom of this damning verdict. They will strive to determine what ideas are really connected with the word *slavery* and to what extent this image of slavery appears as something repugnant.

Unquestionably we connect with the word *slavery* the idea of dependence on the will of other people. But as soon as we question merely the degree of dependence, we shall again have the opportunity to notice on what vague, untested ground the most decisive statement is often based. Most people are dependent to a certain degree on other people, but we think of nothing less than slavery in connection with them. Let us take, for instance, the relation of the poor to the rich. If, on the other hand, we wanted to interpret slavery as complete dependence, it would be difficult to find such a condition anywhere on earth. Aside from other restrictions, the executive power itself is against it in many nations. To be sure, at the beginning the Romans had the right of punishment by death in regard to their slaves; but later this was restricted and finally entirely revoked. Among the Lacedaemonians, where the lot of the slaves was in general very hard, an individual citizen was nevertheless not permitted to increase arbitrarily the burden of their work. In Athens, mistreatment of slaves was often punished very severely; and among the Greeks there was a law that a slave, if he had been cruelly treated, could demand to be sold to another master. In North America also, the murder of a slave is not exempt from punishment and in most states is regarded in the same light as the murder of a white man. There are also alimentation laws here, and especially the regulation that everyone who frees a slave must give assurance that he will be cared for during his old age.[14]

Other difficulties appear in that even the same degree of dependence that we demand for the word *slavery* at the same time applies to relationships that no one would connect with this word. I call your attention to paternal power, to the dependence on the state, and especially on an absolute supreme ruler. Among the Romans fathers had the power of life or death (at the time of the Republic) over their children, and the power of the Caesars over the citizens was entirely unlimited. But it would never have occurred to anyone to connect the institution of slavery with these two relationships.

The following statements will lead to the standpoint that will solve all difficulties.

(1) The actions and regulations of our fellowmen effect our sense of morality only because of their aims, and the aims again only because of the endeavors from which they seem to originate. Inexpedient measures arouse a moral disgust only when an evil endeavor can be recognized in them. Actions and measures that can only be attributed to evil endeavors we therefore, without further ado, declare to be evil.

(2) To be sure, it is a basic characteristic of the human mind to attribute a certain value to everything that exists next to us in space. But the element in space that is connected with animal life has a very special effect on us. It demands the recognition of a certain independence; it makes claim to coexistence and demands consideration of the conditions of its coexistence. This holds true to the highest degree when creatures attract our attention that seem fit to compete with us in value, when human beings are in question.

(3) If the side of our nature that recognizes that claim as well-founded is fettered and obscured by impulses so that we can recognize in our actions the overpowering influence of these impulses, then we must feel remorse when passion subsides and we regain presence of mind. The actions themselves will then appear as monstrous images, as indestructible offsprings that one's own mind condemns, whose continuous effect is all the more distressing the more important past considerations seem. We then accuse ourselves of evil actions and declare the endeavor that has given birth to them a wicked endeavor.

(4) Therefore all institutions that are based on and preserved by a continuous emotional disregard (by the calm mind) of the recognized value of other human beings must seem evil to us. It is revealing that the above-mentioned verdict, which declares slavery as a moral evil, is apropos of this and makes it evident also how little it deserves the epithet of a direct verdict (of reason). Like so many other verdicts, it is based on a combination of ideas that unclear minds label as simple emotions, and in order to realize its meaning, one must study these ideas themselves more closely. For in order to decide whether an institution is really preserved by a continuous passionate disregard of the value of other human beings, clear opinions about the purpose of

the institution and about human nature are necessary. This is most important in the investigation of the moral implications of slavery. The usual erroneous statements concerning slavery can be traced back partly to incorrect opinions about the purpose and partly to confused ideas about the value of human nature. This should become clearer after the consideration of the following theses.

(5) Paternal power is considered equal to the power of the state by everyone, as far as its aim is concerned. The welfare of those over whom it is exerted is accepted as the aim of both, and where reality does not correspond to this assumption, we complain about misuse, without criticizing the institution itself, however far the power of the fathers may go beyond the borders of mere guardianship.

(6) On the other hand, the idea that the welfare of the slave is not considered at all is almost as generally connected with the word *slavery* as the idea that power over them has been granted to the master for his sake alone and that he is to look at them merely as beasts of burden. Such an idea must naturally lead to a condemnation to which only a madman could refuse his approval. The cruelest of all slaveholders will never be convinced that his slaves are really only domestic animals, even if his wild impulses cause him hourly to treat them unmercifully. It is very strange, however, that it is just at this point that the misuse of power is looked upon as being as much a part of the nature of the institution as its purpose, as if it were unthinkable that, besides paternal power, another similar power of a citizen over his fellowmen could arise for irreproachable reasons, or could continue to prevail even for a while. It is just this view that leads to the so-called direct verdict of reason. Whoever does not consider it direct, will easily recognize the insufficiencies of its basis after the following remarks.

(a) That innumerable Africans have been reduced to slavery because of greed proves nothing more than that this institution, as some others, is capable of an evil origin.

(b) If the state subordinates the life and work of individual persons to another, this means nothing more than the bestowal of a power, the use of which is made dependent on the nature of the master. In case of doubt, one must believe that the one who bestows this power will expect a wise use of it, and that he desires that the master will pursue his own interest not without consideration of the welfare of those so controlled.

(c) Who can maintain that, besides the immature and the imbeciles, there are never any other individuals whom one could put on the same plane with the citizens just as little as one could drive them out of the domain of the state? The more important and the freer the status of a citizen is, the more should be required before one is accepted as such. To tolerate within the state a large number of adults who are not adapted to citizenship without subjecting them to special supervision and restriction is without danger only where the citizens themselves live under the greatest restrictions. Therefore it must be clear that a class of unfree individuals could arise among the free citizens without the latter being accused of oppression. If these individuals live under the immediate supervision and guidance of the state, then they deserve, in contrast with the free citizens, the name *state slaves*. But if the executive power is vested in the citizens themselves, if the entire state depends entirely and alone on their behavior, why should not such citizens consider themselves capable of exercising a family rule over human beings who must unquestionably be kept under close supervision and guidance?

Wars result in slavery even among nations that look upon it as an evil. It is an evil that cannot be avoided without permitting far greater ones. Those who hold the opposite view belong to the dreamers of everlasting peace. It is striking to what follies wishful thinking leads. Long books have been dedicated to projects for permanent peace, although a complete transformation of human nature in its basic elements is the primary condition for this.

(7) Without stopping to discuss the objection that for the mere education of children, no paternal power but only guardianship is required, I shall proceed to the truths that furnish the guiding points for human relationships in general and political dilemmas in particular.

In the comparison of the various interests, it will soon become evident that the earthly welfare of every human being has only a limited value and that this value is not to be confused with the absolute value of the person; that, as a man may according to his own nature regard the risking and the sacrifice of his own life and his earthly welfare as proper to attain certain conditions and purposes, he may also not place the value of the life and welfare of individual fellowmen above all purposes.

With this is connected the further thesis that as little as we are capable of deciding the absolute value of human beings, we, on the other hand, can estimate their value on this earth (the value of their earthly existence) only to the degree that our minds can grasp it; and that, because to the individual observer there appears a great gradation in this, there must also be a great gradation for him in the value of the mortal lives of various human beings.

The assertion that all human beings deserve to be given the same value is based on a confusion of the conceptions of the absolute value with those of the value of earthly existence. The value of an existence can be conceived only as that of a relationship in which existence is perceived by the ego. Decisions concerning value must therefore be exactly as the original relations present them. Concerning absolute value, we are entirely incapable of making a decision because the thought of it leads to the origin of all things, to God. Insofar as we must assume that everything originates from God, everything is of equal value, and every gradation must therefore be discarded. From earthly beings only individual rays of the deity affect us, and because various rays and also similar rays of various intensity from various objects fall upon us, therefore we have the right to speak of various values. Whoever realizes this, will be led astray just as little to absolutely damning statements as to an absolute equalization in a field where differences do occur that one must consider as phenomena, if one does not wish to declare all earthly existence as nothing. The human mind must consider its relation to all other existences, especially to those with its fellowmen as something given, as a restrictive matter. To want to oppose the limitations of nature with arbitrary statements is madness, which in some individual cases is not treated as such.

During a war, everyone acts in accordance with these views. But those who do not understand their basis then speak of necessity, without considering that only in a situation where a free decision is absolutely out of the question, where man is driven like a machine, such an excuse is permissible. If urgent circumstances can permit us to violate so-called fundamental principles, then, for that reason, they are not fundamental principles and can, at most, only be considered rules that permit modification and exceptions.

If it must be admitted, however, that certain situations can cause us to make an irreproachable decision to sacrifice the earthly existence and the earthly welfare of individual human beings, then the thesis is also acceptable that whether human beings are to be subordinated to the unrestricted power of other men depends entirely on the circumstances, on changeable situations. It is also acceptable that moral criticism can never be made of the result but only of the investigation, insofar as the lot of fellowmen might not have found the consideration that one could have expected from an unbiased judge. It is a vain undertaking to draw up rules for the judgment of future cases in advance. The manifold situations permit so many modifications that the difficulties of the investigation would lie in the correct interpretation of these situations. Whether there is a conflict, and to what extent, can only be decided for each individual case and by a separate fundamental investigation.

These theses are then also in conflict with the all too hasty condemnation of the states of antiquity. It has always seemed suspicious to me when I saw persons of our day so audaciously condemn ancient nations, whose moral and intellectual values were at least completely equal to those of more recent Europeans, because of institutions that have been preserved through all the stages of domestic and political development. At the present time, when so much is unknown about what contributed to the origin and the preservation of those institutions, it remains a meaningless presumption to oppose decisively the unanimous judgment of the leading men of those nations. The source of the presumption can be found in nothing else than in vague confused ideas and a code of ethics based on them.

For political institutions, history usually furnishes future generations with material that cannot be modeled so arbitrarily. The passing generation bequeaths to the following one an inheritance of situations that only madness can declare as absolutely without importance. Just as the head of the family must subordinate his well-intentioned plans to many so-called unforeseen occurrences, a whole nation will have the same experience. Where slavery already exists, whether its origin was commendable or not, it is not easy to abolish it if one does not believe one can control by mere words something that has hidden roots in human nature. Only he who makes no distinction between *without a master* and *free* will judge differently. If, in the abolition of slavery, nothing else were to be considered but the welfare of the slaves themselves, it could not escape the most limited view in what a sad situation some of them would find themselves as a result of attaining a freedom for which they were not prepared. In their helplessness many would resemble domestic animals that having grown up under the constant care of men are suddenly left to their own resources. In the United States the master is obligated to assure the maintenance of the slaves, whether they are capable of working or not; and granting them their freedom does not release him from this duty toward the indigent. If one considers mental welfare, then the mere relinquishment of power over primitive human beings does not deserve any special praise. When history tells us that individual Romans used their power over their slaves to train them to become capable persons, the subsequent granting of freedom must seem negligible in comparison with the excellent results of slavery itself. As one desires good teachers for children, the greatest advocate of freedom can only wish a wise and virtuous master for all uncivilized men. Whoever permits a crude subordinate to live according to his nature and thereby relinquishes his wholesome influence on him disregards his true interests just as much as a slavemaster who considers only the physical welfare of the slaves as it works toward his advantage. The purpose of the one may be far nobler than that of the other; but the effects it produces are not very different, disregarding the aid of accidental occurrences. [20–6] Where the masters are worse than the slaves, there slavery is the greatest of earthly evils. Just as reason deplores it when bad rules over better, stupidity over sensibility, it must, on the other hand, approve fully when the uncultured obey the cultured, and man driven by passions finds a check in his fellowman whose actions are directed by insight. However, as no regulations can be formulated against passion and ignorance that always attain the purpose for which they were made, and just as everything finally depends on that which animates intrinsically lifeless regulations, and this animating spirit is itself subject to human frailties, the same also holds true for the institution of slavery and of paternal power. Nevertheless, in the best states, where the endeavors of intelligent men control the executive power, calm judgment will not always prevail. Thus, the domestic rule of the father of the family must also suffer from weaknesses that are an inevitable part of human nature. The further the fathers are removed from possessing the characteristics that qualify them for participation in state rule, the less promising their aptitude is for family rule. It follows, therefore, that family slavery (if I may use this expression for the subordination under the domestic rule of a single citizen) stands in a reverse relationship to political slavery. In other words, the more political freedom must be restricted, the more the power over children and slaves must be limited; for the same basic reasons that exclude a person from participation in political rule speak equally strongly against his ruling as such. This condition occurs in reality only where citizens lose their political power because they are no longer capable of exercising it, where, for example, with an increasing degeneration of the masses a democracy gradually becomes an oligarchy of the truly better men. If the citizens, without mental degeneration, lose their participation in executive power, perhaps to a conqueror, then this is an unnatural event in the development of the nation itself. If the conqueror deprives such a nation not only of political rights but also of domestic power, then he acts in a twofold war against the true welfare of the nation, and it is a foolish opinion that in a state where the political rights of the citizens are not many, family rule must also be limited in order to avoid an apparent contradiction.

Because of this result, I cannot therefore criticize unconditionally the holding of slaves by Europeans in lands where slavery exists. It will depend mostly on the master whether the purchase by him was good fortune for the slaves or not. And especially here in America Europeans can console themselves with the thought that the black population in the United States could not be set free en masse. Their color distinguishes them so much from the descendants of Europeans that there can be no thought of a general interbreeding. The male whites, to be sure, have always caused fewer difficulties; but the feminine sex, in spite of all enlightenment, has never approached the necessary degree of abstraction. The union of a white woman with a Negro is still a seven-day wonder.*[15] Also the Negroes themselves would never be able to disregard the difference in color to the extent that they would not tend toward a political segregation from the whites. What happened in Domingo was,[16] to be sure, partly the result of the former pressure of slavery, in part the reaction against the doubts expressed by Europeans

---

*Sometimes the marriage of whites and Negroes or mulattoes is forbidden. In Virginia, for example, whites who marry Negroes or mulattoes are sent to prison for six months and the minister must pay a fine.

concerning the human rights of Africans. But the opinon of the Negroes that, aside from educational advantages, nature had destined them to a closer bond with their black brothers than with white persons was certainly not without its effect in this case.—Similar observations have already given rise to various projects to remove Negroes entirely from the vicinity of whites. To these are added naturally the views concerning the receptivity of Negroes to culture and especially to the degree of culture without which a political freedom, such as that of the North Americans, is impossible. There was really a time when the lack of receptivity to the cultivation of the mind was deduced from the black color and the conclusion was reached: The Africans are born to slavery because they are black. Since this deduction has lost its validity, the attempt has been made to use their facial features as a point of departure. In this area there is such a great latitude that if heaven had not created in the same Africa black people who can compete with every European in regularity and beauty of facial features, all anatomical research would scarcely completely destroy the belief in a descent from the apes (which some Negro tribes themselves hold). In the United States one rarely sees a Negro with handsome facial features. Among mulattoes there is more regularity, but their yellow color is often more repugnant than the color of Negroes. However, as little as the facial features of the North American Negroes recommend them, in ordinary matters of business they show the same skill as the whites, and in Europe there are innumerable people who do not show the slightest advantage over them. But none rises above the average, although some have enjoyed a good education. Also, there is scarcely one well-to-do Negro among the many free ones. They live only for the moment. The desire for enjoyment predominates in them to the extent that even the best education finds an unconquerable hindrance in it.*

I am not among those who consider the effect of education greater than that of all climatic influences. As history shows us, the inhabitants of intensely hot Nubia, as well as the Samoyedes of the icy North, will never flourish as will the inhabitants of the moderate zones. The inability to correlate these differences with the wisdom and kindness of God has caused several critics to deny these phenomena themselves. They are the same who maintain that even among the Europeans training can cope with anything. But the earlier generations continue to live in the present more actively than one knows. They exert a power over the basic elements of our nature in their dependence on the physical, so that the education of a single generation can often have little influence on it. This seems to me to be true especially of the

---

*It is a well-known fact that the confectioners in the larger cities have their greatest number of customers among the Negroes and mulattoes.

Negroes.—All reveal their descent by a conspicuous sensitivity to cold; on the other hand, they never complain about the heat.

The mental level of free Negroes in North America is nowhere superior to that of the servant class in Europe, and slaves are much better off physically than the European domestic servants. There would still be the question whether the limited mental span of an underprivileged European day laborer has so many advantages over that of a Negro slave that it balances the better physical care the latter receives. How much the Negro or mulatto in North America would gain by being set free can be judged by the rank in society granted to a free Negro.*[17] Such emphasis is placed upon color that no Negro, whether he be free or a slave, rich or poor, may dare to sit down at the same table with a white man. In the inns where the drivers stop, one sees Negroes and mulattoes eat at separate tables [20– 8]; a slave suffers little from this insult, because he, as a servant, makes no claim to equality. Since the belief of the slaves in the inborn superiority of the masters furnishes a strong lever for obedience, it is not to be expected that in the slave states there will be violent opposition to such assumptions. But it seems all the more amazing that the zealous promoters of freedom for Negroes in the other states no longer fight against them.

Therefore I do not consider slavery in the central states an evil so much because of the lot of the slaves as because of the danger to the moral nature of the masters. I repeat that this statement by no means holds true for the southern regions where colonial products are raised. There slavery in general takes on a form that the old nations of Europe [20– 9] have scarcely known. This type was reserved for the greed of the more recent Europeans. In the state of Missouri, in Kentucky, in Tennessee, a disobedient slave is threatened with sale to the sugar plantations.

In the western part of North America the population, in comparison to the amount of fertile, cheap land, is too sparse to permit anyone who either cannot or does not wish to be actively engaged in physical labor to carry on farming on a large scale without slaves. [20– 10] Even if one wants to supply only one's own needs, domestic affairs would suffer because of the lack of whites who would have any desire to be hired for this purpose. [20– 11] But one who could decide to hire a slave would probably not hesitate to buy him.

The usual price of a male slave from nineteen to thirty years of age is

---

*In no state do the free Negroes or mulattoes enjoy political rights; in other words, nowhere are they equal to the citizens in regard to rights and duties to the state. They take part neither in the legislation nor in the election of officials. Neither are they themselves eligible to be elected. But even aside from this, there is no thought of equality. In the state of Ohio, for example, where slavery has never been permitted, the (free) Negroes and mulattoes have no right to testify against a white person. [20– 7]

four to five hundred dollars. The price of a female slave is a third less. Sometimes there is a guarantee against running away; often not. It is always advisable to take this into consideration. [20– 12]

One who keeps slaves here has their living quarters near his own house. They do all the work that is done by domestic servants in Germany. It is in the master's self-interest to treat them with consideration and to make their lot bearable. He encourages young slaves to marry so that they learn to like a regulated life. The children are also slaves and follow the mother if perhaps the father should have another master, which can easily be the case.

It happens in the United States that male and female slaves try to avenge insults and mistreatment not only by running away but also by murdering one or more members of the family. Sometimes they resort to open violence, sometimes to poisoning.[18] Only recently there was a case of the latter about twenty miles from here. A seventeen-year-old Negro girl wanted to poison the entire family. But the dose of arsenic was so large that it caused immediate vomiting and therefore the attempt failed.—The public papers recently told of the following incident. A farmer, the father of several children, had a small Negro girl about seven years of age in his home. One day this girl came back from a nearby wood and announced to her master and mistress that their four-year-old child had fallen into the brook. They ran quickly to the place and found the delicate creature already drowned, although the water at that place was not at all deep. They censured the Negro girl severely, saying that she should have helped the child herself instead of running for aid. A year later it happened that a younger [20– 13] child of the family failed to appear for a meal. The mother asked the Negro girl, who was accustomed to playing with the child, where it was, but received such a strange answer that, driven by great anxiety, she got up immediately to look for her. But she searched and called in vain, and then, as if filled with gloomy forebodings, turned fiercely to the Negress and demanded that she should tell her where she had left the child. Thereupon she obtained without difficulty the information that the child was lying in the brook. This indeed proved to be true, and this child also was lying dead at a place in the brook where she could have been saved by merely raising her head. They became more and more suspicious of the Negro girl and soon urgent reasons for a severe cross examination became apparent. As a result she confessed that both children had been choked to death in the water, and that the culprit had committed a similar murder while at her former owner's (who likewise had found a child suffocated in the water).[19]

Such details, however, must not prejudice anyone against Negroes in general. There is no lack of gruesome deviation from nature among the whites either. I remember, among other things, that several years ago, on the Lower Rhine, a seven-year-old boy twice reduced an entire village to ashes in revenge for a minor punishment (which some German law professors would attribute good-naturedly to a curious urge to see fire).

Twenty-first Letter
16 June 1826

Yesterday, as I was roaming through the forests in my usual manner, I came upon two bee hunters. To be sure, the procedure followed by these people in an occupation so foreign to the European had long before been described to me, but this time I was interested in becoming acquainted with it in actual practice. First of all, you must know that in the forests of the state of Missouri there are very many wild bees, which establish their colonies in hollow trees. If one knows how to find these hollow trees, one can in a short time collect a considerable amount of honey and wax. It is the general opinion that originally there were no bees in America,[1] and that the wild bees are descendants of the swarms brought from Europe to the east coast. Be that as it may, in bee hunting the Indians are as skilled, if not more so, than the whites. The bee hunters I met yesterday were whites and inhabitants of the state of Missouri. They proceeded as follows: They chose their first stand on the ridge of a hill between two valleys. They lighted a small fire in a spot free of trees and placed honeycombs on it so that the wax produced a column of smoke without being consumed by the fire. A strong odor of honey spread in all directions and in a short time attracted all kinds of flying insects and also some bees. Now it was the business of the hunters to keep their eyes fixed on the lure, in order to be able to watch the bees as they flew away. Soon three of them rose and flew away in the same direction. This was noted as accurately as possible, in the previously verified assumption that a bee bound homeward with its load of honey would fly directly to the swarm. Thereupon one of the hunters took a glowing coal and walked about two hundred paces farther on the same ridge, leaving his companion behind at the first stand. He repeated the previous procedure and again caused a strong odor of honey to spread. Here also the bees did not let him wait for them long. Several came, and then flew away in two directions almost opposite from each other. The hunter made note of both and without delay called to his companion to pursue the direction taken by the first bees. He himself started out in one of the other directions indicated, which seemed to be leading toward the first one. I accompanied him. We had walked scarcely three hundred paces through the forest when we met the first hunter. Now both searched for a while until they found the colony for which they were looking. In a dry oak, about fifty feet above the ground, one could see a small opening, where bees were swarming in and out. The skill of these natural mathematicians surprised me and I was more delighted by the discovery of the tree than they themselves. But I confess that soon this feeling gave way to the consideration of the sad lot of the good little creatures, who cannot hide the products of their persevering industry from human robbers even in the great wildernesses of America. These particular ones, to be sure, were given a period of grace because, judging by the season, the hunters thought that not much honey had as yet been collected. But being robbed in the fall only places the colony in greater jeopardy.—Last year I watched a Negro lad taking out a bee's nest. He found about four quarts of honey and was exceedingly glad to get some extra money. He was a slave, to whom such a find, to which his master had no claim, seemed like a gift from heaven. While he was tying his booty together, I asked him what would happen to the robbed little creatures now. These words visibly affected him and caused him to consider the matter; and after he had answered regretfully that the cold weather would probably cause them to starve to death soon, he shoved a large slice of honeycomb back into the hollow of the felled tree, which was constantly being encircled by flying bees.—The bee hunters of today marked their find with cuts in the tree, which is generally considered an inviolable symbol of possession, and set out in the third direction.

Twenty-second Letter

18 June 1826

You can scarcely imagine how much pleasure I derive from the wild birds of this country.[1] That there are no good songbirds in North America is a ridiculous exaggeration, which the contrast of the voice to the beautiful colors of their feathers seems to have given rise to. Actually one misses only the nightingale. The rest of America's songbirds can compete very well with those of Europe. Of how little value this contrast is,* is proved by the purple thrush [sic] (*Turdus phoeniceus*). The whole body of the male has the most beautiful purple color and his song resembles the sweet notes of the flute, like that of the ouzel (black thrush), which is not found here. (To be sure, there are birds here that are black and closely resemble the ouzel; but I have never heard them sing and have seen them only as migratory birds.) The mockingbird (*Turdus polyglottus*) [22– 2], which may also be called the American nightingale, is found just as frequently. Instead of the cuckoo

---

*Who would not call to mind here the reports on the South Sea islands, where there are likewise said to be wonderful songbirds with the most splendid feathers? [22– 1]

of the old world, one hears everywhere here the soft, plaintive notes of the turtledove, to which the cooing of the European species cannot be compared. Because these inoffensive creatures (which are not called pigeons here, but doves) are harmed by no one, they prefer to live near human dwellings. Sparrows do not disturb the country dwellers, one would look for them in vain in all of America. On the other hand, there are also no chad finch *(Fringilla caelebs)*, and the American lark resembles the European only in its feathers.

In my cornfield a large number of colibris [hummingbirds] swarm around on the flowers. I can approach them rather closely and notice especially the jewel colibri *(Trochius mosquitus)* among them. This little creature is adorned with colors of remarkable splendor. Its flight resembles that of a large hornet, for which I took the first little creature of this species in its humming flight. The English, with good reason, call it the "humming bird." On one side of the field is a small ravine in which grow many different flowers, especially beautiful asters. There I can watch the play of hummingbirds on every clear summer day. They are constantly teasing each other, as I have never seen any other birds do. It would be easy for me to kill a half-dozen with water or sand,[2] but my love for natural-history collections is not strong enough for that. I have not yet been able to discover a hummingbird nest. But there are enough nests of other birds near my house. Several weeks ago I was busy removing some shrubs near the fence around my yard. I was working on a small sassafras tree in the crown of which a grapevine was entwined when the anxious restlessness of a purple thrush attracted my attention. I looked around and saw a nest in the endangered tree. Of course, it remained unharmed. It is quite near the gate, and whenever I pass by I see the female or the male sitting on the eggs. Instead of flying away, they threaten me every time with their open beaks, as young doves are accustomed to do when one approaches their nest. Indeed, one day a very pretty blue bird came into my room and sat down fearlessly on the table, but a tomcat chased him away. Every morning a long line of partridges wanders past my house to look for the grains of corn left from the feed of the domestic animals. I provide the same protection for this family that the turtledoves find everywhere.—Sometimes one comes upon little partridges that have scarcely slipped out of the shell. Then the mother defends them as a tame hen would and immediately takes recourse to a ruse that has fooled me several times. She acts as if she were obviously lame and tries thereby to attract the pursuit to herself, so that the young can escape in the opposite direction. At first I did not trust my eyes, but repeated observations convinced me, and when I finally mentioned it to my neighbors, they said that such behavior had been a matter of general knowledge for a long time.—In the spring (and only then) one often sees single partridges on trees, where they utter a flutelike sound, which one never hears at any other time.

The whippoorwill (named thus because of his song) is also a remarkable creature. It belongs to the night ravens *(Caprimulgus Americanus)* [22– 3] and is the certain harbinger of summer. As long as there is still frost, one does not notice it, nor before sunset nor in cloudy weather. As soon as twilight begins to fall, it appears, and repeats, close to the houses of the farmers, its strange notes until toward midnight. One never hears more than one bird at any one homestead. On the other hand, there are few homesteads without one. Wherever a new settlement is made in the forests, a whippoorwill will soon appear. Folk belief interprets its behavior as omens of future events. [22– 4]

Owls frequently produce a nocturnal noise so that the whole forest reechoes from it; and wild doves at times appear in flocks that resemble dark storm clouds. The branches of the trees break where they settle down. This sounds fantastic, but it is nevertheless true. There are also countless flocks of wild ducks. In the neighborhood of St. Charles a heavy hailstorm occurred in the course of this year, which killed so many ducks that a farmer was able to collect about three hundred of them on a flooded meadow.

Everywhere one hears the hammering of various woodpeckers. It has happened to me several times that I took a hammering woodpecker for a man knocking at the door. Among these there is one the size of a dove, the entire body a dark brown color, the head and the one-and-a-half-inch crest crimson. This bird utters a sound that is very similar to loud, shrill laughter. It is called *woodcock* by the farmers, although it undoubtedly belongs to the woodpeckers.

In general there is so much life in the local forests that the word *wilderness* scarcely fits. The gobbling of the wild turkeys I have mentioned before as well as the drumming of the pheasants, and night and day one hears the familiar sound of the herd bells. This indication of the proximity of domestic animals grazing near the farms is doubly pleasant at night. The stars shed their light over everything with an indescribable shimmer, and in addition the air is full of myriads of fireflies, which for a stranger from Germany naturally lend the glow of enchantment to the forests.

You cannot imagine either how tame fowls thrive here. Ducks, geese, chickens—all find sufficient food in the forests. The fear of beasts of prey keeps them from straying too far. Every evening they return to the human dwellings, where they know they will be protected by the dogs. And these faithful animals never betray their trust. At the slightest noise at night, they are ready for action. The cry of a hen or a goose will bring them to the spot immediately. A farmer rarely knows how many chickens he has. If he needs eggs, he sends his children to the nearby woods to look for them. They often gather one to two hundred eggs at a time, but even the most careful searching does not prevent one from being surprised by new groups of baby chicks from time to time.

One cannot live here without dogs. Tame fowl would be killed within a few nights; and the dogs are just as necessary for the protection of the calves and lambs at night. The wolves, to be sure, are certain of so much game that they never expose themselves to obvious danger. But if a homestead is not guarded, they will pay it a visit very soon. They immediately know where there are dogs, and as little as they fear them in the open woods, far from mankind, near the houses even the voice of a weak pug or a Pomerainian will keep them outside of the fences.— Some dogs are too timid to go outside of the fences during the nightly howling of the wolves, others immediately run in the direction of the howling and bark for hours until the beasts of prey have disappeared. This kind of challenge sometimes ends in fights, in which, however, the guards are soon put to flight.

Twenty-third Letter
6 August 1826

Now I can tell you about the mosquito plague too. About six weeks ago there appeared everywhere, in valleys and on elevations, such swarms of mosquitoes that in shady places it was difficult to keep them away from one's mouth and nose. On the basis of my experience I would scarcely have believed this possible. The insect is the same as our gnat or midge *(Culex pipiens)*.* Just as these are found in Europe, from Italy and Spain to Lapland, they also appear everywhere else on the entire earth. But I would have expected them in such numbers only near swamps, never on hills and mountains. That the phenomenon was very unusual I could believe all the more readily, as I had noticed nothing of the kind in previous years. It was attributed to the floods along the Missouri.

In the summer of 1824 the river had left its banks and had flooded the largest part of the valley plain.[2] Such a flood is said to occur only once in about thirty years. [23– 1] Almost no homestead has taken precautions against it, and aside from the resulting diseases many farmers suffer great hardships and danger because of it. I cannot advise strongly enough against settling in the Missouri valley itself. If one lives close to

---

*These are not to be compared with the bloodsuckers of the tropics, especially those of the Orinoco. According to Humboldt,[1] the mosquitoes found there are not gnats, but insects resembling flies. These are not known here; neither are the species of gnats (culices) of Spanish America, the *Zankuden* or *mariguenen.* Humboldt says it is characteristic that the European *Culex pipiens* is also found in mountainous areas, but not the *Culex* species of tropical America. Besides the common gnats, small, barely visible gnats, called nettles, appear in the morning and evening. Their sting causes a slight, very temporary burning sensation.

the riverbed, one has nothing to fear from the bad air.[3] But there are few places where the bank is firm and safe enough for the construction of good buildings. Just where the soil is richest, it furnishes little resistance to the floods, the ice, and especially the masses of wood;* and permanent protection, which goes beyond the interests of individuals, cannot be expected soon from the state. I know of several instances when beautiful farms, houses, barns, orchards, and hundreds of *Morgen* of cultivated land have been washed away in a short time. But to want to live far from the currents of air along the river, surrounded by thickets, on forested hills or mountain slopes, is the worst plan of all. Until a clearing of several thousand *Morgen* has been made, such a settlement is constantly subject to fever. The basis for all the complaints about an unhealthy climate is almost entirely due to the situation of the dwellings in wooded river valleys (bottoms) and along swamps. If one constructs one's buildings on hills, far from swamps, one will be affected by the climate here as little as in Germany. And this procedure does not exclude one from utilizing the fertile soil of the valley plains. In no city in Germany can one lead a more healthful life than in St. Louis on the Mississippi because it is surrounded by several miles of open country. Also in St. Charles on the Missouri one seldom hears of diseases.

But I shall now return to the mosquitoes. It is believed that because of the backwater in the depressions of the valley plain, the breeding places increased very greatly. During the first year the effect could not have been felt; it would in any case be of only short duration since the entire valley was again as dry as before the flood. Dwellings that were surrounded by broad, shadeless areas did not suffer very much, because the mosquitoes avoid the rays of the sun and cannot endure much heat. They are most active in the morning and in the evening. However, one can keep them away from the inside of the houses without much effort. Since they fly low and swarm around the ground floor, the smoke from a small fire built in front of the entrance will drive them away, without being at all annoying in itself. The livestock suffered much from them. Now they have disappeared completely. But one always finds them along shaded waters from June until the frosty nights begin, only not in such numbers. In the cities along the rivers it is customary to protect the beds by net curtains. One finds these also in most of the good inns under the name of mosquito bars (bars against mosquitoes). However, if one takes a trip of considerable length during the summer or fall, it is wise to include mosquito netting in one's luggage. Farther down the Mississippi, there is more standing water in the valley plain, and consequently one must expect more mosquitoes. The highland prairies are

---

*On several places enough wood is piled up to supply cities of considerable size for several years.

not bothered by them at all. The mosquitoes do not love such sunny places.

Along with so many advantages offered by the Mississippi states, a German finds some disagreeable things that, like all unfamiliar evils, strongly excite his imagination and really harm him more than they do the natives because he does not know how to protect himself against them. If one relies on first impressions, he will not fare well. There is no lack of immigrants who at the beginning were just as intoxicated by the attractions of the new situation as they later were abhorred by them. That is due to human nature and not to the country. If one wants to report only what is attractive, these regions will seem a paradise to all Germans. [23–2] But it is just as easy, with some exaggeration, to paint a horrible picture of the disagreeable aspects. If one has a tendency in this direction, one will find sufficient material in my letters. I could offer even more and tell about the poisonous plants, the mere touching of which causes leprosy in the case of some people. Beside the most beautiful flowering trees stand the poisonous varieties of sumac; especially frequent is the rooted sumac *(Rhus radicans)*.[4] As with many other things, the danger here is also exaggerated to a ridiculous degree. The inhabitants are familiar with the injurious effects of these plants, but no one lives in fear or worries on their account.

Twenty-fourth Letter
12 August 1826

Several days ago I had the opportunity to become more closely acquainted with the nutrient matter of the previously mentioned American elm tree. On a walk through the forest, I got into an impenetrable thicket, and after searching a long time for an exit I finally became confused as to the directions. The position of the sun told me that it was only one and one-half hours to sunset, and after a vain effort of over four hours, I was preparing myself to spend the night in the open. I was tired and very hungry. I sat down and looked around for an open place where I could build a fire for the night in order to ward off beasts of prey without setting the whole woods on fire. At the same time I was thinking of finding some kind of fruit to satisfy my hunger, when my eyes fell upon a group of elms. Without delay I took out my pocketknife and began to peel off a handful of the inner bark. This was accomplished quickly and the food, just as nature offered it to me, tasted very good.[1] A second and third helping followed and together with some water from a nearby brook so thoroughly restored my strength that I had nothing to complain about except the short time left before nightfall. With the increasing darkness I could have resorted to attracting the attention of a neighboring farmer to my plight by repeated shots. This signal is understood very well here. But I thought (and rightly so as I found later) that human habitations were rather distant. I therefore made another attempt to find my way out and had spent perhaps a quarter of an hour at it when the scarcely audible sound of barking dogs gave me a direction, which I then pursued steadfastly. At sunset I came upon a familiar path. I was about two English miles from my house, and now had no more difficulty in making my way toward it. For such cases a pocket compass is very useful. I had procured such an instrument at the beginning of my trip, but this time I had not taken it along.—When one speaks in Europe of impenetrable forests, in which tree trunks stand close together, a correction is necessary. Large tree trunks rarely stand so close together that they prevent passage among them. Neither the crowns nor the roots would permit this. The more fertile the soil, the larger the trees usually are, and since the large masses choke most of the smaller growth by robbing it of light and nourishment, passage is usually freest in the most luxurious forests. The bottoms, especially the Missouri valley and the nearby hills, offer the best evidence of this. It is not at all difficult to wander through the forests there on foot, since even a rider can make his way through them fairly well. Climbing plants are not very numerous. But where the large trunks have died for some reason, for example, because of frost during blossoming time, a thicket usually shoots up very soon that, intertwined with grapevines and other creeping plants, makes progress impossible without an ax. Likewise, after many years individual trunks would get a head start and gradually destroy the rest.—It was such a thicket into which I had strayed and was laboring to find a way out. In such places are found the true lairs of beasts of prey, and for this reason my prospects for the night did not seem exactly pleasant.

If one has seen only German woods, one will certainly be struck by the variety of tree species in this region. Spruces stand everywhere in rather compact groups.[2] I have not noticed a deviation from this in the Mississippi states either. In fertile areas none is found, except on some rocky slopes. But most of the other kinds of trees grow here in the most colorful variety. Only on less fertile knolls do oaks and hickories predominate, with other trees rarer. In the fertile bottoms the oaks (with the exception of the *Quercus macrocarpus*) do not thrive.[3] On a single *Morgen* of my farm I found four kinds of walnut trees, three kinds of oaks, two kinds of elms, the Virginia cherry tree, plum trees, a mulberry tree, ash, the broad-leaved linden, sassafras trees, storax bushes, papaw trees (*Anonen*), the Canadian Judas tree, the flowering cornel tree, the ironwood tree, the hackberry tree, plane trees, grapevines, hazelnut bushes, blackberries, and elders.[4]

Twenty-fifth Letter

19 August 1826

On the afternoon of the day before yesterday I was at home occupied with writing when I heard my cook call anxiously that a large snake was coming toward the house. I stepped out and saw a rattlesnake about five feet long at a distance of twenty paces. It had coiled itself up at the foot of a nut tree and positioned itself to attack my dogs. Its tail was in constant motion and made a noise that I have previously compared to that of a scissors grinder, while the neck extended its open jaws toward the dogs. Both gazed motionless at the threatening reptile as if extremely amazed. Neither dared to attack it, even though one of them was never too timid to do battle with the wolves. Two cats also stood around overcome by the same surprise. I was worried about the fate of these domestic animals. But the snake suddenly changed its position and continued on its course. It came straight toward the house door, but soon turned aside to a grassy spot. The dogs and cats carefully kept out of its way, but nevertheless pursued it, as it seemed, out of sheer curiosity. Meanwhile I had brought out my shotgun. I shot a full load into its body and then made an end to its tenacious life with a stick. It belonged to the species with large yellow spots (*Crotalus horridus*) and was about two inches in diameter.[1] I could not persuade any of the domestic animals to approach the lifeless body more closely than when it was alive.

This is the only rattlesnake I have seen in the current year. I repeat once more; no one worries here about these creatures, although the deadly effect of the poison is never doubted.*

My garden has given me much pleasure. Beans, peas, cucumbers, and melons have grown very well. The watermelons become unusually large, and the juice is so sweet that perhaps they might be cultivated advantageously for their sugar content. It is a strange feeling in the midst of these forests, five thousand miles away from home, and on land only recently fenced, to wander among garden plants to which one is accustomed in his native home.

Every day turkeys with flocks of their young appear on my homestead. They often sit so trustingly on the fences that it is difficult for me to shoot at them. Nothing is easier than taming them. One frequently comes upon nests with twenty or more eggs, which one only needs to place under a domestic hen. The brood will become tamer the more often the hen brings them to human dwellings. Their feathers are gray

---

*The poison is deadly even for the snake itself. Two rattlesnakes were incited to bite each other, and another one to bite its own tail. Each time death ensued within an hour.

like those of the common owl. Otherwise they resemble the tame turkeys quite closely. In the spring their gobbling sounds come from all directions, and I at first took it as an indication of the vicinity of farms.

One can almost always see deer at a distance of several hundred paces from my cultivated field. Sometimes one finds young ones that can be tamed. They become so tame that they, like the cattle and horses, return from time to time from the woods to the homestead and not infrequently bring along wild ones, which they thus innocently deliver up to their destruction. It is strange that the deer like to mingle with the grazing cattle so much. Many thus fall as booty into the hands of the farmers, who always carry guns with them while looking for their cattle, which sometimes do not return early enough to suit the housewife. It is said that the wild oxen are driven away by the bells of the tame cattle.

Several weeks ago a cougar (American panther, but called *tiger* here) was shot about four miles from here. It was a male, about five feet long from the mouth to the beginning of the tail, and weighed about ninety pounds. With the exception of small black spots on the ears and the mouth, the color of the body is yellowish but under the belly more whitish. There are few of these beasts of prey near the farms. It is unusual for them to attack a human being. It is said that they never dare to attack an adult. Beyond the state of Missouri in the Missouri territory they are more abundant. There is found also the gray bear, which is said to be a great danger to the fur hunters. I have already told you that I hear the wolves howl almost every evening. A short time ago a newborn colt was torn to pieces by a pack of these beasts. In the twilight I suddenly heard a barking as if a dozen dogs were being set upon some animal, and the next day the remains of the victim were found along with much evidence of a furious defense by the mother. No one here remembers a similar case, and one may almost say that the beasts of prey do no harm at all to the inhabitants of the state of Missouri. An abundant supply of young game is available to satisfy their hunger, although they cannot catch the adult animals, and it has long been well known how bold and dangerous they become in times of need (hunger). This is especially true of the wolves, as the annual reports from Poland and Russia inform us. This explains the striking phenomenon that in Germany a single wolf is more dangerous to a number of villages than packs of wolves are to a single farm here.—The bison (called buffalo here) has retreated farther to the West. Several months ago herds numbering many thousands were still seen along the Kansas River. Also one will not find the wapiti (*Cervus wapiti*), the elk, and the "moose-deer" within the settlements. [25– 1]—In St. Louis there lives a Mr. Ashley[2] (general) who annually goes on long hunting expeditions. He usually hires thirty to forty hunters with whom he journeys to the Rocky Mountains and beyond in the spring and returns toward the end of the fall with furs and skins. He is said to have discovered a place, west of the sources of the La Platte River, where for several miles the Rocky Mountains are so low and flat that one could easily reach the Pacific Ocean with beasts of burden and wagons. If it is true, it will surely be announced to the public soon, together with a fuller description of the place.

Twenty-sixth Letter
12 September 1826

Nature has deposited here many things that are waiting for an increased population. Several miles from my house I found in the bed of a small brook clumps of the richest iron ore that weighed more than sixty pounds.[1] It looks like pure metal; but as soon as it is heated, it explodes with a dangerous force. It does not pay as yet to search more closely in this place, however, as farther toward the west, in Washington County, whole mountains of the same material have been discovered. Several foundries have been built there, so that one can buy iron kettles and other castings here rather cheaply.[2] There is also a great abundance of salt. We are supplied here by the salt works in Boone County.[3] Among the cliffs of the Missouri valley I found Epsom salts. I was very easily able to gather several pounds of very pure pieces. There is no lack of saltpeter either. There is an abundance of bituminous coal of the finest kind near me, not far from the Missouri River about twelve miles away and again forty miles above its mouth. There are also large beds opposite its mouth on the east side of the Mississippi. These recently became the source of supply for St. Louis. Formerly only wood was used as fuel, and this will be true of the interior of Missouri for a long time. There is no copper nearby, although a small river, which empties into the Mississippi about forty miles from here, has been named after the metal. On the other hand, the copper mines on the upper Mississippi in the neighborhood of St. Anthony's Falls are all the richer.

Recently, rich lead mines have been discovered along the upper Mississippi at the mouth of the Fever River about three hundred fifty English miles above the mouth of the Missouri. Many people are going there.[4]

Twenty-seventh Letter
28 September 1826

I have not told you anything as yet about the antiquities of these regions, about the remains of the constructions erected by the tribes who lived here in past ages. One cannot think of them as works of art (such as those of Hindustan, Egypt, Persia, Greece, and Rome). The American monuments are of historic interest only. In this respect, of course, they are important enough, but my main purpose demanded so much of my attention that on the whole I had to be satisfied with printed reports. On the trip here I could repress my curiosity all the more easily as I knew that a considerable number of these antiquities were in the neighborhood of St. Louis. These I have seen, but not those near Wheeling, nor those in the states of Ohio, Kentucky, Indiana, and so forth.

The most nearly complete information can be found in the *Archaeologia Americana,* published in Worcester in the state of Massachusetts in the year 1820 by a society of archaeologists; in the above-mentioned work by Heckewelder on the habits and customs of the Indian tribes; in Humboldt's picturesque views of the Cordilleras; and in the second volume of the aforementioned work by Friedrich Schmidt.[1]

Most striking within the territory of the United States are the fortifications and mounds that spread from the southern shores of the Canadian lakes in a southwesterly direction through the western part of the state of New York and the Mississippi states to Mexico. Closer to the Mississippi these monuments are larger. In the state of Ohio the most important ones are along the Muskingum, the Scioto, and the two Miamis; in Kentucky, along the Kentucky River; in Indiana between the White River and the Wabash.[2]

These are the works of vanished generations and as foreign to the Indians of today as to the Europeans.—According to the traditions collected by Heckewelder, they date back to the Talligewi or Allighewi, to the same tribe that gave its name to the Allegheny Mountains. This tribe is said to have been very powerful, to have lived in cities, and to have surpassed all other American tribes in culture. The fortifications are said to have been built as protection against the Lenni-Lenape (Delawares) coming from the West, and at that time allies of the Mengwe (Iroquois). The powerful Allighewi are said to have been defeated, and on their retreat to the South to have buried those who had fallen in various battles in high burial mounds.—On some structures there are trees as old as the oldest in the forests. This alone takes us back more than a thousand years in time and must also rather radically change the opinion about the youth of the new continent.

The fortifications (square and circular entrenchments), as well as the mounds, are built of earth. Walls are rare, although they do exist. The mounds are found chiefly in fertile regions and along rivers with abundant fish, but also on high, stony hills.

The mounds are generally taken for graves, and investigation of their interior confirms this. They can be compared with those of the old world, especially those of the Germanic tribes (for example, those along the Rhine) and also those in Russia (for example, along the Volga), even in regard to the utensils, pottery, swords, axes, and ornaments that are found along with the skeletons. Their height varies from two to one hundred fifty feet. However the mounds inside the fortifications seem to have been built partly because of the view. Not all are conical; some are hemispherical and others angular like pyramids.

Opposite the city of St. Louis, along the Kahokia River [27– 1], there are more than a hundred fifty of these graves, divided into two groups. Therefore the fertile valley plain there (called *American bottom*), about nine miles wide and eighty miles long [27– 2], is considered to be the center of a large vanished population. Everywhere in this region, they say, one finds human bones when turning over the surface soil. Close to St. Louis, on the east bank of the Mississippi less than a mile from the river, is the upper group, which from a distance resembles immense haystacks. They are usually round and some have room for several hundred persons on their high tops. The largest stands close to the bank of the Kahokia, and its construction must have provided work for thousands of people for years. The base is a parallelogram eight hundred yards (2,400 English feet) in circumference. It is ninety feet high. Several years ago, some Trappists[3] settled close to the pyramid and turned part of it into a garden.

There are also burial mounds on the western bank of the Mississippi close to the city of St. Louis, and a structure that is known by the name *Fallen Garden* seems to have served for tribal meetings.[4]

Three (English) miles below St. Charles on the north side of the Missouri, where the Missouri valley unites with the Mississippi valley and the hills bordering the two valleys form an angle, there are also two elevations that are considered to be man-made. The French call them *les mamelles* because of their shape. In spite of the skeletons and utensils that reportedly were found there, I must consider them as products of nature, as layers of earth deposited by the two great rivers in times of floods. I confess that the wonderful view that one enjoys from there diverted me from a closer examination. If one faces the Mississippi, one sees to the right the mouth of the Missouri, to the left that of the Illinois, and straight across (on the east bank of the Mississippi), a row of cliffs near which Portage des Sioux is situated. [27– 3] To be sure, the ground of this large valley plain has long been private property, but hardly any settlements can be seen. The owners are speculators who are waiting for higher prices. I wrote you earlier that the Missouri valley and the bordering hills are everywhere densely forested. Here at the junction with the Mississippi valley, meadows prevail, however only in the plain.

The other monuments west of the Mississippi I have not seen. According to the written reports of Lewis and Clarke [*sic*], Picke [*sic*], and Nutall [27– 4], there are extensive fortifications as well as burial mounds as far west as the Rocky Mountains.[5] Only recently has the closer attention of scholars been directed toward these objects. Probably the next decades will furnish more information about their origin as well as the origin of the American tribes than is at present available. The rather general tendency is to believe in an emigration from eastern Asia not only of Mongolian tribes but also of Malayans. Even Scandinavian tribes are said to have immigrated long before the discovery of America by Columbus. To the latter are ascribed the antiquities of the Atlantic coast in the state of New York and in New Jersey, and so forth (fortifications, walls, and rock drawings). Indeed, some even attribute the monuments in the Mississippi territory to them.

Twenty-eighth Letter
October 1826

The strangest ideas about health conditions in the United States have also been disseminated. There is no distinction made between the North and the South, the life in the cities and in the country, the settlements near the swamps and low-lying forested regions, and those on airy hills and highland meadows. There is no thought of distinguishing between foreigners and natives. Of course there are some upon whom these misrepresentations make no impression. However, the people as a whole are deluded by this blatant propaganda which is intended to cover up the insufficiencies of the reports. In a country that extends over twenty-five degrees of latitude in the moderate zone, that is surrounded on the one hand by the icy waters of the North and on the other by the hot currents of the tropics, that encloses mountain ranges many hundred miles in length and contains rivers and lakes among the largest in the world, and where extensive prairies and unlimited forests extend over the greatest varieties of soil, one could certainly expect the most varied influences on the human body.

The most common diseases in the United States are bilious fever, malaria, feverish colds, and tuberculosis; among the children croup and "whooping cough."[1]

In western America there are many adults who have had neither ordinary smallpox nor cowpox. Inoculation against cowpox is not a common practice here as yet. To be sure there is no prejudice against it, but compulsory measures could hardly be taken here unless the danger became very great.[2]

Yellow fever prevails only along the Gulf of Mexico. In New Orleans there are cases almost every summer. But there is no fear of it during the winter months, from November to the first of April. [28–1] It also occurs occasionally in the large cities on the Atlantic Coast, although it is said that on several occasions other diseases were diagnosed incorrectly there as yellow fever. Along the Ohio there are said to have been some cases. [28– 2] There have been no cases along the Missouri.*[3]

Feverish colds and tuberculosis are not as common in the western states as in the eastern ones, where, again, they are found more in the northern regions than in the southern ones. On the other hand, there is more bilious fever and malaria in the western states, excepting the notorious coastal regions of Georgia and the two Carolinas.

Everywhere a main cause of malaria is decomposed vegetable matter. When the heat of the sun falls upon the damp vegetable humus, matter is extracted from the aqueous portions which volatilizes either automatically or in interaction with water vapor. Where this occurs, only a hindrance to the free circulation of air is needed to produce malaria or bilious fevers.[4]

At the beginning and at the end of summer (here in May and September) fevers occur most frequently. This is due partly to the condition of the human body and partly to poisonous influxes. The more abruptly the summer heat sets in, the more the first hot days weaken the body and increase its sensitivity to adverse influences. On the other hand, the vegetable mold has accumulated during the colder season without undergoing the harmful decomposition already mentioned. The first damp heat must therefore have an especially potent effect.

At the end of the summer, only heat and polluted air are needed to complete what has been in the course of preparation during the preceding months as far as health conditions go. The sensitivity of the body is increased by the duration of the weakening influences just as it was

---

*Yellow fever is to be considered a high grade bilious fever (caused by swamp air). In its original form, yellow fever is no more contagious than simple bilious fever. But air polluted by human excretion easily causes a simple bilious fever to assume the characteristics of typhoid (similar to jail fever). The same is true of yellow fever. The air in the seagoing ships soon effects such a change; and when similar fevers are carried from the Mexican Gulf to Europe, they have certainly come to resemble typhoid. In trading vessels, at least, there are no arrangements on stormy days to counteract pollution of the air in areas where the sick are kept, and outside of the tropic circles the sea seldom remains calm long enough for a trip from America to Europe. If, however, in exceptional cases it should remain calm enough, it would still be a second exception if the solicitude of the captains and their own willingness to follow precautionary rules would satisfy all the requirements for the care of the sick. There is no main cause for the development of jail fever poison in the tropical countries. Cold weather does not crowd people together so closely, nor for so long at a time as in German huts. Therefore bilious fever and yellow fever do not change their character so easily along the Gulf of Mexico that they become contagious, although there is not a complete absence of such instances.

earlier by abrupt change. At the same time, the development of impure air has probably reached the maximum the length of the hot season can produce.

It is strange how definitely these poisonous soil products show their effect here. If one works in a recently cleared forest in the damp humus which has been warmed by the sun for only one or two days, one will almost always suffer consequently from bloody abscesses, or from malaria, or even bilious fever. A similar result is caused by the drinking of brook water when the summer heat has raised its temperature.[5] Cold springs are quite safe as is the harmful brook water just as soon as it has become cold again.* During the hot season I sometimes worked in the garden and felt the effects every time. I was not able to prevent them entirely by a previous or accompanying use of medicines, neutral salts, sulfuric acid, salicylic acid, and naphthas.[6] The water, however, could be made entirely harmless by adding drops of sulfuric acid until it had a slightly acid taste.[7] These phenomena are too common to consider individual differences. To be sure, Europeans suffer more from them than the natives, but even the latter are not exempt; Negroes are more immune than the others. The harmful air of the overturned earth offends the sense of smell very little or not at all.

The use of sulfuric acid is very important for the inhabitant of recently cleared forest ground. During the first two years he should never drink water during the heat of summer without adding a few drops of sulfuric acid (which he can find in all American cities). Mixed with rum, with French brandy, and even with common brandy and water, perhaps with the addition of sugar, it is a pleasant drink and for the health far preferable to citric acid. A few ounces will be sufficient for many months. Since ancient times** vinegar has been considered a preventive against all bilious disorders, and rightly so, especially when it is made of honey.[8] But sulfuric acid is better by far. [28– 3]

Last spring the well-known illness called influenza appeared in the Mississippi states. It came from Georgia to the lower Mississippi and gradually spread to the most remote settlements on the Missouri. About the twentieth of March it had reached St. Louis, eight days later St. Charles, and about the middle of April Columbia, and Franklin on

---

*Everyone knows here that a person who has recently recovered from malaria suffers a relapse when he occupies himself with laundry work. This happens more frequently in hot weather than when it is cold. The soap, which is only too often made of rancid fat, certainly is not beneficial to the body when it is is inhaled for some time in a warm atmosphere. But the lukewarm water of the brooks, which is used so much in washing clothes, I consider still more harmful when, as here, the brooks are full of decomposed vegetable matter. That malaria and dysentery seem to have a common cause is often noticed here because of the frequency with which they follow each other.

**In the Roman armies its use became so common that every soldier had to carry some with him. In the last wars the French adopted this custom with success.

the Missouri. At first it was thought to be only a simple catarrhal ailment. However the regular spread of the malady and its contagious nature were already attracting attention when the warmer weather revealed its character beyond a doubt. When the weather turned warmer, very painful swellings resembling those of erysipelas on various parts of the body, especially the thighs, were a common symptom.[9] Before that, only the respiratory organs seemed to be affected. Almost invariably the patient suffered from headaches. Very few persons escaped it entirely. In its mildest form there was merely a feeling of unusual weariness. But even with the slightest catarrhal difficulties, the black color of the excrement was a conspicuous enough symptom of the malady. Old persons suffered most. The wandering pains in the chest soon became localized and some also lost the use of their voices and did not regain them until they were completely recovered.

Purging induced by Epsom salts and cream of tartar, and plasters to alleviate the local disorders of the chest, repeated incisions in the surface of the painful swellings for the purpose of causing slight bleeding, and the use of sulfur-naphtha and sulfuric acid very quickly put an end to the danger and completely restored the patient to health in six to eight days. Only old people recovered a little more slowly. Bleeding the patient is said usually to have been detrimental and to have caused death. In my neighborhood about thirty persons contracted the disease and at my instigation used the above-mentioned measures, and all recovered without difficulty.

Some immigrants from central Europe suffer here during the first two years from a rash that is very similar to the itch. However, it does not attack the joints or the skin between the fingers, but the lower extremities. There are never any inner disturbances connected with it, neither is there any disagreeable odor noticeable, and sulfur has absolutely no effect on it. In healthy persons, the rash is limited to the feet. It induces scratching until the affected area bleeds. Usually the itching begins at sunset. After a discharge of lymph and blood the itching ceases until the next day. This affliction does not occur before the hot season and disappears with the coming of cold weather.[10]

It seems to me that there are no causes other than a general heightened activity of the circulatory system due to the heat and the usual sensitivity of the lower extremities to such disturbances as local irritation caused by insect bites, especially by the slight injuries caused by ticks (*Acarus Americanus*), which no rural inhabitant of the state of Missouri escapes entirely. [28–4] Where there are no ticks, in other words, in cities, in the prairies, and also where the homesteads are close together, the rash is less prevalent. The lower extremities are most exposed to the ticks.

A European who settles neither in the neighborhood of swamps nor in the forests of the river valleys, who builds his house on an elevated area, does not work in the recently cleared forest soil during the hot season, and does not exert himself too much on hot days, has, as soon as he has made satisfactory domestic arrangements, just as little to fear from fevers as at any place in his homeland. [28– 5]

Besides neglecting to follow these rules, the immigrants from poorer classes often do not have a sense of moderation, especially in the eating of meat dishes, which are so inexpensive here.

The greatest danger lies generally in a depressed state of mind, which especially at the beginning is so easily a result of glorified memories of the old home in contrast to the minor unavoidable unpleasant experiences that one has before one is established enough to enjoy the safety of good domestic arrangements.

The too frequent eating of meat produces unpleasant results especially among members of the feminine sex,[11] because their household tasks demand far less of the exercise necessary for digestion than the men have in their work in forest and fields and during their hunting. It is easy enough to understand that men who have been working in the open since five or six o'clock in the morning, or have roamed around hunting, enjoy a breakfast of meat dishes, pork roast, and fowl toward nine o'clock. But that a city woman (with whom the American women can be compared in delicacy of physique and manner of living) can eat the same food without leaving her rooms is rather remarkable. A number of prevalent ailments are due merely to the excessive eating of fatty meat dishes. As soon as the patients restrict themselves to coffee, bread, and butter during the morning, they feel better.

Most of the ailments from which the natives suffer are their own fault. They have little relation to the climate. But the manner of living, which is the common one here, would very soon kill half the population in Germany. Children and adults, whether they are healthy or ill, eat and drink, in summer as well as in winter, whatever tastes good to them. To fast in times of illness is considered great folly. It never occurs to anyone to protect himself against colds either. In every season one sees the children run half-naked into the open from their beds or from the heat of the hearth. Some houses are open to the wind on all sides, and the householders do not take the trouble to guard against the penetration of the cold northwest winds by using a little clay. Every day they would rather drag a cartload of wood to the hearth, around which the whole family gathers.*

It is probably to be expected that the medical situation is not so excellent in the state of Missouri, which is such a "new country" (an expression with which one tries to excuse, and sometimes with reason,

---

*One hears some complaints in the Atlantic states about losing one's teeth early, but there is probably no more danger of that here than in Germany. In no way can it be attributed to the soil or the climate; with far more reason, however, to the diet.

all the inadequacies of domestic and public institutions); especially when one knows how the American laws are in regard to the medical profession.[12] The trade in medicines is completely unrestricted in all of the United States, and in most regions the practice of medicine is not contingent upon passing examinations or possessing a license. To be sure, provisions for universities have been made, and in the western states Lexington in Kentucky is well attended. There, as at the universities on the Atlantic coast, many doctors are graduated every year. But the title of doctor is not required for practicing medicine. The people are the judges of the ability of the doctor as of that of an artist, whose business depends entirely on the approval of the masses, and everyone who makes medicine his profession assumes the title. No investigation is ever made of his right to it.

I believe that the unrestricted sale of medicines causes more harm than the lack of restriction regarding membership in the medical profession.

Since there is no lack of real physicians at the public educational institutions, a man will soon establish himself in places where the population is not too sparse, and no quack can compete with him. As I have already said in detail, the inhabitants of all the states are capable enough of recognizing within a short time the great difference when a man has been trained. Where there is no competent doctor, people try to help themselves as well as is possible. If one trusts a quack, a midwife, or some other person in the neighborhood more than himself, he consults this person in times of trouble. Often the advice received is worse than his own opinion. That cannot be avoided anywhere. It is not so important either as some believe. Everywhere, even where the best doctors are available, folly has enough play, and without conquering this folly itself little can be done against the many troubles resulting from it.

In regard to the medicines, however, the situation is worse.[13] Innumerable differences in quality, whether as the result of ill intentions or not, are recognizable only by scientists. The masses of the people, in spite of their confidence in an honest, well-qualified salesman, will not refrain from time to time from succumbing to the temptation of a bargain supported by dishonest advertising. Nothing can be done without state control, and efficient control leads to monopolies. Perhaps it will later come to that in the United States also. For the present, physicians can do nothing but sell the medicines themselves, and most of them do so. Only in the larger cities are there exceptions. There some passable pharmacies can be found that depend entirely on their reputations. Surgeons are also found only in such cities. In other places, the physician (called doctor) is at the same time surgeon and apothecary, and in a short time (especially in the smaller towns in rural areas) acquires a considerable fortune.

A natural result of this situation is an excessive trading in quack medicines. In almost every newspaper secret remedies are advertised. Far more noticeable, however, is the ridiculous boasting of bona fide physicians. A Doctor Anderton (in New York) for instance, recommends his "superior method of curing a certain disease," and, while he promises the greatest secrecy, he characterizes his house with the concluding words: "where that integrity and candor may be found, which thousands can testify, has always been the ruling principle of his practice."—A Dr. Horne talks about his "profound attention" and says of himself (in the third person): "His experience is very great, his success is astonishing." (Excerpt from the *New Hampshire Journal.*)— Such notices usually have a motto, such as Neither quackery nor imposition, or To prevent the abuse of mercury, or *Salus populi suprema lex,* and so forth; at the side is the picture of Hippocrates of Galen, or Aesculapius and others.—Among the secret remedies are, as one can imagine, many panaceas. "Swaim's Panacea" with Hercules vanquishing one of the Hydras, appears in almost all the papers together with laudatory certifications by various professors on the medical faculties in Philadelphia and New York.

Some quack doctors even call themselves Indian doctors and assert that they have acquired their knowledge from the Indians.

Twenty-ninth Letter
Written in October 1826

In Germany no one has any idea how quickly roads are constructed in the forests of America. Because of the great waterways most regions do not feel the need of hard stone surfacing. Here in that part of the state of Missouri between the Missouri and the Mississippi, it is sufficient to adjust the direction of the road to the localities, and to clear away the timber on the sides. In the first respect, the value of the ground presents no difficulties and the timber can be removed much more easily than one would think. Also bridges over the small rivers are soon built; and all this is done by the farmers themselves. Every male between the ages of eighteen and forty-two is obligated to work on these connecting roads or to have the work done.[1] A male slave must also meet this obligation, so he cannot represent his master.[2] He must hire someone from a neighboring road district if he wants to absent himself without an excuse. The counties are divided into districts for the purpose of maintaining the roads or for the construction of new ones, mostly under the direction of the townships. In each district one of the inhabitants is appointed as overseer for a certain period of time, and he must assemble his fellow inhabitants [29– 1] from time to time to do the necessary work. The work is done by the group as a whole. No one is obligated to work individually. Hardly a third of the work is done that could be for the number of hours spent on it. But people are not in such a hurry here. The meeting is regarded as recreation. For this reason hardly anyone sends a substitute. Even physicians and lawyers are requested to come and if they are not detained by their business, they appear in person, although merely to converse with someone or other. No one unaccustomed to physical exertion is expected to help. But I would not advise anyone who does not care to be present in person to send a substitute at the beginning. This could be interpreted as pride and that is not easily forgiven here. Besides, he will meet everyone there with whom he usually associates, and he will not be less respected because he performs physical labor, as I have already told you.

In the state of Missouri residency of two months obligates one for the upkeep of the roads. Even a foreigner is not permitted to disregard it when he has acquired property. I was notified on several occasions and always appeared in person. But I was told that it was not their intention to ask me to work. Later all those who were obligated agreed (without my requesting it) to spare me the summons because it was difficult at times to find a substitute. The main reason could not be misunderstood. They wanted to maintain the principle of equality before the law, and that certainly was not to be criticized.*

I scarcely need to mention that almost everyone appears on horseback.

I have mentioned above the term *citizenship.* (In Germany the too-limited expression *Bürgerrecht,* civic rights, is the usual term.) In some states of the Union one cannot acquire any landed property without being a citizen or without having made a legal declaration of one's desire to become one. In the state of Missouri the situation is different. Here even a foreigner can buy land from the state as well as from private persons, and absence does not endanger his rights, as long as the legal real estate taxes are paid. To be sure, he has no political rights, he takes no part in the enacting of legislation, nor in the election of officials, neither can he himself be elected to an office. But in the beginning he finds enough to occupy himself in his domestic affairs and in the effort to become thoroughly acquainted with his new situation. Therefore he can consider it a special privilege to be entirely free of all personal service to the state such as jury service or membership in the militia. Citizenship is important to the merchants in the coastal cities insofar as only citizens can own seagoing vessels.[3] If the newcomer wants to retain his above-mentioned status, he is entirely free to do so. However, in

---

*Later a tax will probably be levied, as has been done elsewhere, so that one can pay a small sum annually in order to be free from any obligation.

order to become a citizen he must, according to the most recent laws, present written evidence that he has lived in the United States for three years without interruption and declare his intention under oath before court and afterward continue to live in the territory of the Union for two more years. When the latter condition has been met and certified, he receives his citizenship papers.

By this means, however, civil rights have been acquired only in relation to the Union. In order to become a citizen of an individual state also, a definite period of residence is required by this state. Both terms can be met at the same time if one has a permanent home. The person who moves from one state to another acquires citizenship in his new home only after an established time of residence there, in most states after one year. However, the eligibility for election to some offices is dependent on a longer residence as well as upon age, and so forth.

The civil and criminal law is very similar to the English, particularly in the case of civil lawsuits, where sworn jurors are called in. The sources of the law are (1) the common law of England; (2) the decisions of the English Parliament (naturally the ones made before the separation); (3) the decisions of the Congress; (4) the special laws of the individual states. Every state is free to change the civil and criminal laws that it has passed, even without the consent of the other states, as long as there is no conflict with the expressed laws of the Union. The state of Louisiana (at the mouth of the Mississippi) has adopted the Napoleonic Code with few modifications. [29– 2]

Besides the concurrence of jurisdiction in lawsuits, notarial and administrative functions have been given to the justices of the peace. Aside from the fact that far more of them are appointed for a definite population than in France, their office is in itself very different from the French justices of the peace.

The rest of the courts are divided into governing bodies that are peculiar to the individual states (state courts) and those that serve the Union (federal courts). The latter courts settle, among other things, the disputes between the individual states. There is therefore in every single state a supreme court and another one for the federal courts. The latter has its seat in the capital of the Union at Washington. It consists of a chief justice and six additional judges. Only in certain cases can an appeal be made to it from the state courts. To call it simply the highest court, the court of last resort in the United States, would therefore not be accurate.

The court trials are open to the public, but the judges and other participants appear in their usual dress.[4]—No rhetorical torrents of words can influence the judgment of the cautious American, and in general an effort is made to express points with a calm clarity such as is proper in the close scrutiny of legal affairs. If such simplicity does not appeal to someone, he lacks a clear comprehension of the purpose of criminal and civil laws, and if he calls himself a lawyer, he lacks still more. I must, however, mention that in a trial in Cincinnati I saw in an otherwise respectable place the judges eat fruit during the trial, stretch their legs out over the table, and otherwise act in a manner that can hardly be attributed to a difference in customs. Some Americans expressed their astonishment about it to me in such vigorous terms that if only for this reason I was inclined to consider their behavior exceptional.

The executive power of the Union is vested in a president, who is elected by all the states for a definite time (four years) [29– 3], whereas the executive power of the single states is vested in a governor chosen by the people of that state, in some states for one year, in others for several years. And as the legislative power of the Union is administered by two chambers, there are also institutions similar to these chambers in the individual states. Only one of the twenty-four states, Vermont, has one chamber. The chambers, to be sure, are distinguished by the words *Senate* and *House of Representatives,* but one must not forget that the members of both are determined by free election by the people. The main difference between the chambers of the Union (which together form the Congress) consists in the fact that in the Senate all states have the same number of representatives, namely two.[5] The number of the so-called representatives (a word that could also be applied to the senators), however, depends on the population, and now* there is one representative for every fifty thousand persons. [29– 4]

These matters are so well known in Germany that I do not wish to say anything more about them. Moreover there are, also in America, men of so-called culture who attribute a profound wisdom to such arbitrary institutions, which could assume quite a different form without violating the basic idea.[29– 5]

It seems wonderful to a European when in this wide circle of human activity he can discover nothing of all the evidence of government rule and policelike surveillance which causes so much commotion in the old world and especially in Germany. On my whole journey here and on my later short trips I did not see a single official except in the court sessions and in the bureaus. Not the slightest outward distinction, not the least trace in the behavior here will call attention to the judge, the governor, the representative, or the minister. Even the police agents are recognizable only as they discharge their duties.[7] It is unnecessary to remind you of the total absence of rank here, and that any claim to it would be ridiculed. One sees the highest officials, ministers, and generals travel

---

*In the constitutional laws one reads: As soon as the number of representatives amounts to two hundred, fifty thousand souls are required for every additional representative; and this condition occurred several years ago.—In the constitutional laws enacted by a new state, sixty thousand is the number required.[6]

in ordinary stagecoaches. It often happens that they choose this mode of travel in order to avoid being suspected of pride, although they would prefer special wagons for the sake of comfort. However some, here as well as in Europe, do not conform to this practice. President Monroe, who held office previous to the last president, used to tie his horse in front of the Capital just as everyone else did who had state business there.[8] In contrast to this, however, is a certain mania for military titles. The titles of Captain, Colonel, and so forth, which are officially conferred only in the army, are quite commonly used in addressing persons who have no connection with the military service. Let no one therefore believe that the liking for rank has completely disappeared here. But it would be just as inaccurate to speak of a sansculottic quality. Some European immigrants bring such crude ideas with them, but they are soon corrected. The difference in intellectual power is respected in no European country more than here, and everyone accepts the distinctions attendant to the differences in material possessions without submitting to any arrogance.

I have talked earlier about the bases of American freedom. It is based far more on domestic order and rational moderation than one dreams of in Europe. This and the respect of Americans for the law are just as much in conflict with a fanatical striving for uncontrolled freedom as with restrictions of an arbitrariness motivated by hatred, arrogance, or lazy ineptitude. It is ridiculous self-praise when Germans maintain that there is more intellectual activity among them than in North America. Americans can well overlook this overcompensation in the field of the imagination. But I consider myself obligated to give you a true picture of conditions. Only in Germany can one express such thoughts without being ridiculed. They are connected with such equally ridiculous assumptions as: Americans have no history; material life makes too many demands on their energies, and so forth. If it were necessary to refute such statements, it would suffice to point out the old Asiatic and Egyptian colonies along the Mediterranean, and especially the glorious development of the Greeks in Italy, who, because of the conditions of navigation prevalent at that time isolated themselves from their mother countries much more than the Europeans did in America. One should call to mind that the Romans, as well as the Greeks, in spite of their glorious history, later degenerated intellectually to such an extent that all lamentation about their disgraceful defeat by the crudest northern hordes must be silenced. And besides, is the former history of Europe less the heritage of the Europeans in America than of those who remained behind in the old home? [29– 6] But whoever says that American material life demands too much of one's efforts should become better acquainted with the land of which he speaks and should not confuse the conditions under which the first colonists lived with the situation of a present-day settler in the midst of an area that is crossed by highways running in all directions. At the same time he should investigate how much is being done in Germany for the sciences merely for the sake of the sciences; whether it is not the lot of most scholars to live in a kind of mental drudgery so that their bodies will not suffer for lack of food. Would these scholars be worse off if instead of engaging in this drudgery they enjoyed untroubled supervision over fields yielding food? Finally, I ask what difference is there between men who discuss the most important events of the present and the laws pertaining to them, and those who, completely remote from the present and unconcerned about its legal conditions and demands, anxiously strive to determine to the letter the legislation some ruler used millennia ago to make his people happy or to oppress them? I do not think that a comparison of the number of these two classes of thinkers and scholars in Germany and North America would be entirely fruitless in judging the intellectual life.

But I am saying all this not to praise the intellectual capacity of the Americans but solely to oppose the presumption of others and to counter a foolish self-conceit, which, because it is the greatest hindrance to the progressive education of the individual, can never truly benefit an entire nation. I repeat again that the political situation of the North Americans is based more on fortunate external conditions than on the advantages of a high intellectual culture. It is the masses of the people that here appear in more favorable light than elsewhere. In their fortunate position they find the most varied incentives to engage in innocent occupations and far more stimulation to rational thinking than any other nation of recent times. In order to convince one's self of the truth of this assertion, one only needs to consider the ordinary knowledge and skills of the farmers who at present comprise more than two-thirds of the total population of the United States. For the sake of clearness, I shall enumerate them here.

Every American farmer: (1) knows how to judge the soil and can distinguish the organic fertilizer from the various types of soil proper very well. He can quickly determine this from the plants and trees growing in it. (2) He knows the various kinds of wood suitable for buildings, furniture, field implements, fences, and firewood. (3) He can build houses and barns, break stones, calcine lime, so that he has no need of a carpenter, and of a cabinetmaker and a mason only for the finer work in his dwelling (not in the hut used temporarily as a home). (4) He has a good knowledge of everything pertaining to the transformation of a forest into arable land as well as to the tilling of the fields for grain, for garden plants, for tobacco, for cotton, hemp, flax, and several other products. (5) He can manage everything pertaining to the breeding of cattle himself. He knows how to foal horses, mark hogs, cattle, and sheep, shear the sheep, and perform all the tasks of a butcher. (6) He can make shoes and prepare potash soap and maple sugar. (7) He is a good hunter and can process the skins of game, especially the deerskins, as well as can the best tanner.*

The housewife knows how to sew and knit, spin, weave, dye, and make clothes.

From time to time because of state affairs such a farmer is brought into contact with the most informed persons of the great Union, who solicit his vote for public purposes. Let us take, for instance, the election of a governor. Often the candidates for similar offices have their views on various points relating to state government printed in periodicals quite early. This alone is an incentive to many kinds of discussions among the qualified voters. Besides, these candidates may also appear personally in the homes of individual citizens, as well as at places where they will meet a crowd, for instance, at races or at reviews of the militia. Or political friends of the candidate travel around in order to comment on his ideas and plans. The other candidates make similar efforts. And thus there is so much and such emphatic talking on the one hand about demands of the general welfare, on the other hand about the ability and the purposes of the various candidates that even the most stupid cannot be entirely uninformed. Is it any wonder that under such influences, in the midst of a new development of a great continent, which is daily flourishing more beautifully because of the free, joyous interplay of human forces, men develop within a single generation who are entirely different from ordinary German peasants or artisans?

I have often listened when simple farmers deliberated at length about [John] Adams and [Andrew] Jackson in regard to the presidential election.[9] Jackson, they said, could not bear any contradiction; that as soon as he himself was convinced, he hated all procrastination involved in further discussion; that he was better fitted for a general than for the president of a council. Such remarks were common.

However, one must not think, therefore, that this is the land of idle political talk. The American farmer loves nothing less than to spend his time on state affairs. Only because he sees the necessity of using his vote for legislation and for the execution of the laws does he speak about them, and he looks upon his participation as serious work, which he likes to see completed as much and as quickly as he does every other task. Also in the cities there is so much incentive to productive activity for the respectable citizen that less idle talk about politics is heard there than in Europe. The person who, although he is not an official, takes a prominent part in state affairs must be prepared for severe criticism concerning his private business. In all public meetings, from the beginning to the end, an order and a calmness usually prevail here of which

---

*They have learned from the Indians to use the brains of the deer for this purpose. This method makes the skins especially soft and smooth without weakening them.

there is no conception in Europe.* It would be very incorrect to conclude from the vehement words of journalists that the opposite is true. The laws of the press permit an ardent politician to relieve his feelings by expressing them publicly. The people read and smile. They know all too well that with regard to their main interest no real opposition is possible in the Union at present. The opinions and declarations of individuals cannot affect this conviction and therefore cannot disturb the calmness of a large assembly. [29– 7]

Continuation of the Previous Letter

Concerning the political parties. Higher education in North America.

It is pardonable if in Germany, when political life is so very different from that in North America, erroneous ideas prevail concerning party spirit here. A comparison with the French factions during the time of the Revolution could only confirm this misunderstanding. The ability to see clearly the complete inapplicability of such a comparison presupposes a knowledge of the political conditions of both countries, which is general in Europe just as little as it is in America. The next pages are intended to develop more accurate views.—As you know, the political parties in the United States are designated as the Federalists (or aristocrats), Democrats, and Royalists.[10] But it does not seem easy to me to explain the meanings of these words, or rather of the first two. The real reason is that few of those who use them have a clear concept of them. This ambiguity of words and vagueness of thought can only be improved by illuminating somewhat the whole field to which they pertain. This is in itself necessary if the political factions are to be traced to their sources.—At present there are no longer any Royalists, with the exception, perhaps, of a few recently immigrated Britons. The most zealous adherents to the crown of England have long since realized that any further attempt to restore royal power is entirely hopeless.—The name *Federalists* (or aristocrats) was originally given to the friends and defenders of the older federal constitution, which gave way to the present one in 1787.[11] According to the older constitution, the individual states were less dependent on the power of the Union, but on the other hand, more on their governing bodies and were in this case more similar to the Swiss cantons. After the separation from the mother country a trace of an official aristocracy, hostile to equality, began to develop among the official holders through the mere administration of the republican

---

*It happened that next to my apartment in Baltimore a political organization of about forty persons met several times for hours of discussion. Is it credible that such quiet prevailed there that although only a partition with a connecting door separated me from the meeting place, I could nevertheless sleep entirely undisturbed?

offices, on the same basis of a common interest in the new order, although there was no thought of striving for a formal patriciate. In order to understand this process as only natural, it is only necessary to remember that regardless of their own characteristics the North Americans still are Europeans in America. This happens in every free state, and the earlier, the more extensive and complicated its legislation is, the less its study is considered a part of the educational process. But everywhere, when intellectual forces become active among the people opposition very soon results, namely a certain antipathy toward those who know how to maintain for themselves and their families the tenure of offices and the administrative power. In no organization in the world, unless all the members are genuinely wise men, can a similar division be avoided; and in the states of North America the opposite could be hoped for if among the officials only models of moderation and unselfishness could be expected, and among the citizens always a calm judgment completely free from envy and other passions.

It can easily be understood that the one party was interested in maintaining its advantages with regard to the holding of offices and therefore in general not very much in favor of a change in the constitution, let alone a change that would directly limit the influence that they had won at the expense of time and effort and would introduce new and higher governing bodies. To the other party, the people, on the other hand, a change that threatened to destroy the tender roots of an aristocracy of officials had to seem quite welcome. And since they, and not without reason, looked upon their striving as an attempt to assure the rights of the people and political equality, the name *Democrats* was rather well chosen. Likewise there was no milder designation for the officials and their followers than that of *Federalists* (the defenders of the existing federal constitution), which indicated nothing as yet concerning their secret motives.

In order to assess the political life of Americans correctly, it is absolutely necessary to consider the original source of the cleavage mentioned above. With that in mind it can be clearly seen that the cleavage first neither originated with the struggle for or against the older constitution [29-8], nor could it disappear with the end of this struggle. Even if all the complaints about the weaknesses of the new constitution were obviously without basis, there would still be factions; because, as I have said, a perfect protection against these is to be found not in the constitution, but only in the perfection of the citizens. Second, in addition to the obvious duration of the division one should also bear in mind the fact that it extends over the whole population. And third, one should pay attention to the direction which is given to the two parties by the cause of the division, and which was only more apparent in the above-mentioned struggle regarding the older constitution. With the Federalists, the emphasis is on the preservation of the status quo, on that which has been confirmed by time; with the Democrats, on changes and innovations.

These three characteristics of long-term duration, of extension over the entire population, and of the general directions easily explain the fact that most of the other causes for political differences must, in their practical expression, be attributed to the indicated basic cause. They show why transient political feuds, as soon as they attain a certain importance, assume more or less the colors of the original parties. For every political effort follows one of the general directions in that it emphasizes either the preservation and the enjoyment of the old order, or change and the introduction of a new one. All special political purposes coincide in a sense with the general direction of one of the two original parties; and since these comprise the entire nation, it is not surprising if the proponents for such purposes choose to join a party in order to win support for themselves and to strive to transfer party influence to their own particular causes.

However, one should not be led astray to attribute too much importance to the basic split and should not overlook the following limitations. I have said that the direction of the Democrats is toward changes and innovations. But these words must not be interpreted to be more than a general indication that excludes neither closer definitions nor deviations. There is neither a rigid adherence to the old nor a blind striving for the new. The Federalists cling to the old because of their influence in the government. Changes that do not endanger this influence or even increase it they will certainly not oppose. The Democrats try to undermine the roots of the aristocracy of officials and strive for innovations only insofar as these seem to lead to this end. This alone leads to the assumption that the constant fighting for and against so many political aims can by no means be explained solely on the basis of the interests of the basic division, although the strength of these interests has not even been discussed as yet.

If one wants to judge the effects of the party spirit in North America, one must not object to a closer examination of the interests that, in general, animate Americans. All of these interests, more or less, obviously or not, have a part in it. In order to avoid confusion, however, such an investigation demands that one divide them into two main classes so that there are on the one hand the interests that support and further the division, and on the other hand those that decrease it, that have a negative (conciliatory) effect. This can easily be done if one merely knows the aims of the various interests. But the end result, the explanation of the effect of the reciprocal forces on each other, presupposes a complete investigation of the individual interests, in other words, an investigation that covers not only the aims, but also the duration, the greater or lesser extension over the population, and its inner strength.

If one proceeds according to this method, one will soon realize that in the North American Union the number of all the interests that tend to dissension, when compared with the strong interest in internal peace and order, does not cause the slightest worry. One will find that with the exception of the relationship of the people to the officials, there is no other [29-9] source of dissension that is so widespread among the people, that is so constant, and produces such generally opposite forces or aims. On the other hand, one must realize at the same time that the degree of tension based on this single relationship as yet requires no vigorous counteraction for the prevention of dangerous struggles, and that the purpose of the arrangement, which is obvious to every citizen, is entirely sufficient to at least maintain calmness. [29-10]

One could believe that it is principally the love of power and ambition that increases the tension to the point that can be noticed at times during political conferences. But these moods are not frequent enough that they, except for the stir which they cause, could have much influence on a nation with no rabble class. Also their purposes are rarely so closely connected with the general interests of one or the other party that there would not be danger of various differences and obstacles, or even crossovers to the opposite party. It would be very inaccurate to attribute the actions of the officials to a real love of power or to ambition altogether. Other factors play a far greater part. One needs only to consider a preference for a certain way of life, for a certain activity, for a place of residence that has become dear to one because of habit or associations with people. Such factors alone can make the holding of an office very attractive without being accompanied by motives of ambition and the love of power. Also few offices in this large Union are associated with areas adapted to such considerations. Usually there is only the opportunity for the satisfaction of petty vanity, and here, with the local [29-11] views on rank, this is much less important than in the old world. To be sure, there will never be a lack of individual ambitious and power-loving members among the Federalists, and perhaps there are still more of these among the Democrats—impetuous natures, who fight not so much for the rights of the people as for the power and glamour of the highest offices. But it is a question whether the vigorous efforts of such persons, among a people who are not so entirely blind to their own interests, will not decrease the party spirit rather than strengthen it. Exaggeration in the case of minor grievances arouses ridicule; with more serious ones, distrust.

The result is that the spirit of faction, insofar as one interprets this to mean a general, constant frame of mind, is too weak in its sources to provide decisive factors for individual political aims. Its effect is limited almost entirely to the fact that, with its opposite poles, the parties, within which a single purpose itself creates and animates, serve as a means of attracting followers and never permit the general party names to die out completely.* The violence that sometimes characterizes the conflicts is, on the other hand, to be attributed to the peculiar interests of individual aims. The party spirit contributes little to it. It never leads to important sacrifices without these special interests. But these interests are, aside from a general political split, no different from the ones that are generally expressed among the Europeans. They can spring from noble or ignoble sources. When a proposal is made, one person battles for himself alone, another for his family, his friends, his district, for the state, or for the entire Union. One is motivated merely by the material advantages of money and the value of money; the other is interested in the higher values, the ennoblement of mankind, and above all, of his fellow citizens. On one hand, the immediate advantage is emphasized; on the other the promises of the future. Thus the particular situations and inclinations of individuals, together with their views and opinions on the aims and advantages of state regulations, always provide the most various causes for disagreements without the necessity of having a constant aim in mind and being moved by a continuously active party spirit. On the other hand, the only cause of this kind that exists in North America requires rather those particular interests and stimuli if serious steps are to be taken. Therefore it is entirely contrary to the truth to attribute the new constitution to the victory of a faction proper. The opinions of the advantages of a greater concentration of power had infinitely more effect than the vague inclination toward innovations. It was these that decided many (by no means members of the Democratic party) to accept the new constitution.

If the picture I have given you concerning the incentives to dissension is really a true one, then a fleeting glance at the other class and its motives toward unity must also reveal the miserably insufficient basis of all complaints about the dangers of the North American faction spirit. A brief study of the family life of the Americans must convince one thoroughly that the interests that support and strengthen the division into Federalists and Democrats are controlled so much by other interests that a fear of tumultuous revolution must be considered purely a product of the imagination at present. A serious danger to the general freedom would unite the parties more quickly than the factions of the Romans were united by the threat of foreign enemies. In order to realize the full importance of this assertion, one must not forget that the most cogent reasons for dissension among the Romans are lacking here,

---

*Because the name *Federalists,* derived from a single purpose, does not accurately describe the general aims of the party, it can more easily be subject to change than that of the Democrats, which will be retained as long as the cause itself exists. The word *Aristocrats,* to be sure, expresses the contrast more exactly, but it does not seem to be popular.

namely the advantages of birth and great inequality in the possession of wealth. The laws and private opinions are against the former. Nature itself prevents the latter by its gift of a national territory such as was never before offered to a young state for its free development. If the area were not larger than England or Spain, the nation would long ago have been divided into the rich and the poor. That all the causes that usually produce inequalities in wealth can for the present create no rabble class here is an advantage that no state comprised of millions of citizens has ever enjoyed. Where everyone can enjoy prosperity with slight exertion on his part, the abundance of individuals is not dangerous. Wealth produces dissension only where it is confronted with poverty, and that is unknown in the United States. At least the number of poor people will not be able to create an opposition as long as it remains so easy to make a living by farming. Therefore, if the word *Aristocrats* is used instead of *Federalists*, one should not think of Roman aristocrats nor of those of the newer states of Europe. In North America the richer citizens are not exposed to any inordinate desires, which only need arouses. The value of wealth consists primarily in the influence on independence and livelihood, and wealth is very limited in this respect here. Therefore a passionate struggle for treasures is rather rare among the American farmers (the majority of the population). I then repeat once more that of the constant causes of a general split, only the least important exists in North America—since the far more powerful ones based on the contrast between nobility and common people, as well as on wealth and poverty, are entirely lacking. Also, the black population is important enough neither in population nor in intellectual power.—With that I shall proceed to the incontestable statement that the enjoyment that their domestic situation offers to all families, and especially to those who utilize the land, is the prevailing factor in all the states of the Union. This factor ameliorates the inclinations of the rulers who are hostile to equality as well as the criticism of the people regarding the official class. It furnishes promoters for the valid improvements of state regulations from among the most zealous Federalists and makes many Democrats so distrustful of innovations that one can look upon them as the most determined opponents of real demagogues and persuasive public speakers. [29-12]

Dissatisfaction with the constitution is, in most cases, the usual dissatisfaction of people, who even when they are in a fortunate situation do not suppress complaints and desires for changes when minor irritations, moods, and envy incite them. [29- 13] The Democrats do not take revolutionary projects at all seriously. But the thought that the desire for power should direct such projects toward a loss of freedom is, for the present, to be considered only a bad dream. The interests of the parties are so far from being uniform that the young people, even among the Federalists, in accordance with the natural spirit of youth, frequently entertain visionary hopes of innovations. [29– 14] (In their desire for action) they also turn instinctively to the military profession, which, the more warlike it is, the more it must hate the quietness of peace.

The army is too small for its aims to have a great effect. Moreover, in its desire for innovations, it can scarcely be surpassed by the Democrats, although its other aims are far from being democratic. One might say that, aside from the influence of individual commanders in chief, it is about midway between the two parties. But one must not forget that the interest in domestic life is lacking here and with it the mighty counterbalance of all restless desires.

In Europe there is much complaining about the great influence of lawyers in North America, and this certainly does not indicate that the matter has been given serious consideration. One should realize that in a country that is governed primarily by law, those persons who know these laws must necessarily have more influence in public affairs than others who are less familiar with them. To complain about this means to grumble about the power of better insight. To be sure, there is a real reason for this dissatisfaction, but one is seldom conscious of that. I am referring to the fact that the study of the laws, which pertain to all situations, instead of being considered a part of a good education, is here, as everywhere else, looked upon as a professional matter. It is this that gives the lawyers a greater influence than they should have. If one realized more clearly that there is no freedom without laws, and that in the field of law there is freedom only for the one who knows the law, because only such a person can move freely in this realm, at least the education of the richer classes would be planned differently. It is not to be denied that the mass of the North American people, through their participation in public affairs, can judge better the intellectual and moral quality of a man who is versed in the law than any nation in Europe. But the closer study of law is a professional matter in America as well as in England, and it is not the fault of the lawyers that higher considerations do not have more influence over the thinking and the desires of the present-day world. It is unreasonable to believe that simplification of the laws would make a study of the law unnecessary. Much can be done by clarity of expression, conciseness of enactments, and a good summary, and it must strike everyone that so little has been done in this respect in North America also. The North American system of law, as well as the English and most of the others, seems like historical chaos. But the laws can be simple and easily comprehensible only when the relations of people, which they must cover completely and in detail, are themselves simple and easy to comprehend. The more a newer nation is governed by laws, the more influential the lawyers are. Where the standing of individuals is more important than the law, naturally its interpreters cannot be very influential. In a free state, such as North America, however, the legal profession has still another significance, which despite its great importance has not as yet been mentioned in any article as far as I know. It is undeniable that in case there were no lawyers and the legal battles were prepared for judgment only by paid judges, an oppressive aristocracy of officials could develop far more easily than now, even if the people were to choose every official directly instead of through representatives. For it is understandable that the individual citizens will, as a rule, elect only such persons to important offices and as representatives who have become knowledgeable through study and practice. The fact that the people always become acquainted with capable men among the lawyers weakens the influence of the officials in favor of their families more than anything else. In North America the lawyers are not only the chief political guardians against the presumption of the officials, but it is also they who can be used immediately as substitutes for these officials. As a whole, they belong without doubt to the popular party, because they share with the governed the natural antipathy to aristocracy, which is never quite foreign to official life. But their own prospects of attaining a high office in the future compel the majority to show a certain moderation, and although the interest that induces the farmers to maintain public order can have less influence on the lawyers, there is on the other hand something else in the process of development (because of the closer acquaintance with the laws) that rarely permits the more intelligent ones to attack that order thoughtlessly. Thus the legal profession forms an intermediary link between the rulers and the ruled that cannot be omitted without causing the most disadvantageous changes in the political situation. The frequent transitions to the official class weaken the spirit of the profession as little as the number of its members, since it offers in itself much that is attractive, and admittance is completely free to everyone without election or favor.

The strength of the political parties, as can easily be seen, must differ a great deal in various states. One has reason to expect more Democrats in the newer states than in the older ones. But I cannot emphasize the fact enough that the general interests that justify the assumption of a constant opposition are so weak, especially in their effect on the large agricultural population, that they are hardly noticeable during important deliberations, however much individual groups who seek some private advantage may attempt to excite them. If anything causes a diversion from the right path and from harmony in the case of federal decisions, it is usually the special interests of individual states. In the state resolutions it is the special interests of the districts and the families. Often a whole state is guided by its preference for a single official. For example, the state of Kentucky wanted Henry Clay to be president because he had won the gratitude of Kentuckians by special services. Such feelings not infrequently unite the parties of a state to the extent that it sometimes is considered entirely Federalist, sometimes entirely Democratic by the other states, depending on the manner in which they interpret its aims. Thus it can happen that a state's party designation changes at short intervals to the opposite one, whereas there has not been the slightest change in the situation. That, of course, is playing with words, but not unnatural among a multitude of people who do not like to concern themselves with sharp distinctions in complicated matters. The ordinary citizen who considers himself a Democrat will be inclined to declare everyone who does not completely agree with him in political affairs to be a Federalist, because he lacks a name for a closer distinction which might give him some guidance.

General Jackson did a great service to the whole Union by his brilliant victory over the English (at New Orleans in 1814). [29–15] [29–16] Those states that were in the greatest danger are very grateful to him for this and wish to see him rewarded by election to the presidency. But one must not believe that aristocratic ideas are lacking there. Other states are more receptive to accusations against the violent temperament of the general. They accuse him of several arbitrary actions. It has even been said that in the above-mentioned war he condemned to death by hanging two Englishmen who were suspected of spying and inciting rebellion in spite of the fact that a properly appointed court-martial had acquitted them.[12] It would be very wrong to assume that there are not many Democrats in the provinces where the general attitude is against Jackson. The general split is too ineffective in this matter also, and the names *Democrats* and *Federalists* (or Aristocrats) are scarcely heard there. A great many Democrats are for Jackson, many are against him, and the same is true of the Federalists. But it cannot be denied that, on the whole, those who for some reason desire important changes, in other words, in general the dissatisfied and restless ones (including the young people), are more for Jackson than for anyone else. So, on Jackson's side there is more of a Democratic element and more of the element that usually joins the Democratic view than of the Federalistic (Aristocratic) element. The majority of the officials and the fighters for the status quo are against him. Only one must not be confused by the fact that really many persons vote for Jackson who have always previously been counted among Federalists. If one examines them more closely, one will find that among them most harbor the special reasons that usually move the aristocrats to remain for a while with the great mass. Among these reasons, the prospects for office are not the weakest. It is clear that no circumspect man, be he Democrat or Federalist, who considers the accusations against General Jackson valid will vote to make him the president of a republic. But among the people there is not so much agreement concerning the basis or lack of basis for these accusations that the above-mentioned victory would not prove to be a decisive factor. Then, too, during recent years, the general has won many followers by his exceptionally genial manner, which made all the greater impression, as his opponents tried to picture him in the public periodicals as a haughty scorner of all bourgeois virtues. He may win the presidency, or he may not, but it is folly to fear that the power connected with that office is sufficient for the execution of plans for sovereign power that would imperil the general freedom. One must give the general credit for too much intelligence to believe that he has not long ago thoroughly realized this, no matter what his secret inclinations may be.

As the people have always wished to limit the powers of the officials of the individual states, who were closely connected with them by a more remote general federal power, so, true to their original aims, they now demand a greater influence in the appointment of federal officials. They want to elect the president directly, and no longer through representatives (who themselves are looked upon as officials).[13] Perhaps their wishes will come true. But even in that case there is no danger of their being misled because of schemes for sovereign power, for the rabble class is lacking. The majority has too great an interest in public order and realizes it too clearly. Who can outbid this interest by bribery? The slightest suspicion of plans against the general freedom would arouse the entire nation against the person elected. To be sure, he can scatter seeds of evil, but their harvest would come far beyond the scope of his lifetime, in the distant future. This striving of the Democrats is, one must confess it, an expression of their general aims; but just because no special interests strengthen it particularly, it is coupled with circumspection and can never cause dangerous incidents. The officials of the Americans are not Roman aristocrats, who were more irksome to the people than the Caesars. [29-17]

I therefore maintain my opinion that most of the people in North America are better than those in European nations, and that in regard to a higher education, which is everywhere limited to a short time, North America is surely second to no nation on this earth. This characteristic of the masses explains why the need for differentiation in social life is felt less here than in Europe. On the steamships along the Atlantic coast, for example, there is only one class, and no European will have the slightest reason to complain about this. If a person lacks none of the qualifications for good society except proper clothing, he can soon be helped in America; and every craftsman in America has enough tact not to forget to dress properly when he enters public circles.

Regarding higher education, the Republicans are to be considered in all respects an English colony. English literature is also theirs, and in all cities, in those along the Atlantic coast as well as those far in the interior, one finds the works of the best English poets and prose writers. I found them in Cincinnati, in Louisville, and in St. Louis on the Mississippi. I also found an English translation of *Werthers Leiden*[14] in an inn in St. Louis. There are theaters, not only in the coastal cities but also along the Ohio and the Mississippi. The latter, to be sure, are usually poor (as is the case in smaller cities in Germany). However, the theater in Cincinnati is said to distinguish itself. In architecture, painting, and sculpture one cannot expect to find here what in Europe is the fruit of many centuries. At first, architecture must serve a predominantly useful purpose, and in this respect its structures have already aroused the amazement of the rest of the world. It is a matter of course that where there is a love for poetry, there is also an interest in music. It is childish to draw general conclusions from the practices of some austere sects. To be sure, not such great emphasis is placed on instruction in music as a part of the general education as in Germany. But it is hard to see what is lost by this if one knows that the greater number of music teachers in the newer nations considers technique the main object. Although everyone admits that versification is not poetry, nevertheless anyone who has mastered the technique of music will straightaway be declared a musician. It is never taken into consideration whether he is familiar with the field in which the norms for higher musical creativity are alone to be sought. It is really strange that someone who has never approached these norms by a training in poetry is considered a musician; and just as incomprehensible that the skill of young people in playing musical instruments or in song can be valued highly if poetry remains such a foreign subject to them as it must be with the usual education. The old nations knew very well that the ideals of music and the ideals of poetry belong to one and the same field. Meaningless playing with notes was respected as little as empty playing with verses, however much difficulty might be involved. They thought that the outlines of musical images were more indefinite, to be sure, than those of language, but not without their laws. The abiding condition of the higher enjoyment of sounds is that they give rise to ideas, however vague (which we probably would call emotions). Music provides higher enjoyment only insofar as the arrangement of the notes awakens or strengthens poetic emotions. The old Greeks therefore found it to their purpose to recommend to the musicians poetic creations for their guidance and support in order not to be annoyed by arabesques, by aggregates of fragments. The musician should help to represent more clearly the ideals of the poet than is possible even by the most felicitous choice of words. Through the words of the poet the musician was to arrive at the ideal and, as soon as he realized it, to try to clothe it with a garment of notes that corresponded best to the ethereal picture. The greatest masters were not permitted to be ashamed of such tasks, and only crudeness and bad training can reject them as degrading or easy. Through this treatment of poetry an enjoyment was created for the people that music can offer in no other way. Even more recent times have furnished individual successful attempts of a similar nature. The people have crowned them with the greatest applause. But most musicians themselves respect them very little. They want music to follow its own course independently. These words, however, can have no other sensible meaning than this: The musician must choose his ideals himself without being dependent on poetry, and this then obviously requires that he must be completely equal to the poet in spirit. If the latter were taken seriously, then the fact would be incontestable that the development so necessary for the poet would be just as necessary for the musician, and that there is only one and the same way for both to approach these ideals, which they want to present to the world in a more tangible form. For both, instruction in poetry is absolutely essential and in this training that technique would still play a very subordinate part. After actual training of this kind even the greatest genius among the musicians would soon have to realize that music only very rarely succeeds in producing creations that, without the help of speech, would bring to the awakened longing of the human spirit for the ideal world a relaxing enjoyment. This experience would certainly cause him to relinquish the idea of a ridiculous independence when nature and reason so urgently demand a union. Without concerning themselves with similar considerations, the newer musicians create a type of music that exists for themselves alone. In most of the creations, therefore, one can discern so little of the ideal that only technicians whose entire vital energy is focused on the difficulty of execution can find delight in them. Very ludicrous, at the same time, is their assertion that the Greeks, whose ideal life is so splendidly depicted by all the works that could be passed on to posterity through poetry, sculpture, and architecture, must have had poor taste in music—because it seemed to contrast so much with their own.

All Americans with a higher education look upon Europe with an interest with which more recent Europeans perhaps regard the Orient. Therefore, it will not be due to America if in the future the cultural bonds between the inhabitants of the two continents are broken. The names of many cities are good evidence of this interest, and the thought of it must also be tinged with amusement when one comes upon a Rome, a Paris, a London, a Vienna, or a Madrid that, except in the imagination of the founders, has scarcely a few huts in common with the European cities. One finds the most famous names in history in the United States, even a Memphis on the lower Mississippi, a Utica in the state of New York. In this manner Americans try to bring the youthful charm of their country into a closer relationship with everything in the old world that has remained dear to them and prove by this that the history of the countries of their ancestors is no less their heritage than that of those who think they are gloriously continuing it.

With regard to the institutions of higher learning complaints are expressed in North America which also have always been applicable to Germany, namely that energies are diffused too much, that instead of twenty average universities, two or three excellent ones should be founded.

Thirtieth Letter
Written in the month of February 1827

While I have been in this country I have occupied myself a little more with weather observations than I was formerly accustomed to do.[1] From the very beginning a striking regularity, which one expects nowhere far from the torrid zones, attracted my attention. Here in the state of Missouri the wind, in constant repetition, runs through all the points of the compass within twelve to twenty days, always in the sequence of from east through the south to the west, and through the north, again to the east. I have never noticed a pervading counter-movement. Although the wind sometimes returned from the south to the east, or from the east to the north, and so forth, it was only for a short time of about twelve to twenty-four hours. Without having re-passed through all the points of the compass, it returned to the course mentioned above. The only deviations were that it remained longer than usual at the individual points and thereby retarded the completion of the cycle. However this rarely happened and mostly during the summertime in the western areas.—In Germany also it is known that the east wind is never constant if the transition through the north has not taken place. Perhaps a similar sequence prevails there, only not so clearly evident as here on the Missouri because of oscillations. Natural scientists have up to now paid less attention to this circumstance than it deserves.*[2]—Such a simple change of winds must naturally make a prognosis of the weather very much easier, and therefore it can be predicted with a fair amount of probability if one has noted once and for all the effects of the various winds.

For the summer months, or rather for the time from April until the end of October, one can assume that a northwest wind will bring clear weather with refreshing coolness. The north and northeast winds bring some clouds and occasionally, although seldom, light rains. The east wind brings warm clear weather, which becomes warmer when the wind shifts to the southeast, and because of a strong south and a violent southwest wind it then attains a rather high degree of humidity, which

---

*The constant electric currents discovered by Oerstädt and Ampère, which have revealed so much concerning magnetism, may in the future also be able to shed some light on this matter.

usually results in the formation of storm clouds and then heavy rains. Then the wind shifts through the west again to the northwest, and all the southern rain clouds yield to the clear, cool weather already mentioned above.—During this time the temperature ranges from 13 to 26 degrees Reaumur[3] (61 to 90 degrees Fahrenheit). This holds true, however, only for the daytime. The nights are considerably cooler. During my first summer here, the Fahrenheit thermometer actually registered 104 degrees (in the shade), the same as it was supposed to have been in Paris in 1720. But everyone assured me that no one had ever before experienced such heat. Volney[4] reports that at Kaskaskia on the Mississippi (about seventy English miles below St. Louis) the Fahrenheit thermometer had once registered 110 degrees. With a clear sky, a temperature of 104 degrees is not so uncomfortable as one might think. With a cloudy sky a far lower temperature is often much more oppressive. This difference in sensation depends on more or less free transpiration. For if the air contains little vapor, then transpiration remains unhindered, but if the opposite is true, if it already contains as much water as it can absorb at a certain temperature, perspiration of our bodies is hindered and we feel the oppressiveness of the humid weather.

In the remaining months, from November to March, the northwest wind is cold. But until the end of December it causes frost only at night when the sky is entirely clear; after sunrise the thermometer rises to 14 or 16 degrees Reaumur. However, as early as October there are also some cold nights that destroy the blossoms of the cotton plants; and in December it is sometimes cold throughout the day, but not for more than forty-eight hours. The north and northwest winds bring milder nights, but also a cloudy sky; less often cold rain or snow, which before New Year's Day remains on the ground for hardly a day. With the east wind the nights become still milder and the sky clearer. The southeast and south winds bring a clear sky and weather that is quite warm; the southwest wind follows with recurring rainstorms. After these rains, the wind shifts further toward the west and northwest to begin anew the cycle I have been describing. In the months of January and February violent west and northwest winds sometimes cause the thermometer to fall to 5 to 8 degrees Reaumur, which, however, rarely lasts more than forty-eight hours and at no time, it is said, has it lasted more than three days. I have not been able to find any records of frozen limbs or chilblains. In January and February a snowfall usually occurs when the winds come from the north and northeast; it may occur with an east wind, but rarely with a west wind. The northwest is accompanied, as I have said, by clear, frosty weather; and the south and southwest winds, even in the midst of winter, by warm weather and thunderstorms. On 25 January of this year heavy rains fell during the entire day, accompanied by violent thunder and lightning, and when toward the evening the wind shifted more toward the west it became so cold that the next morning the ice was strong enough to bear the weight of horses. A similar rapid change of temperature, which is often talked about, never takes place during the months from April to October.* The snowfall rarely amounts to six inches and usually the sun melts it completely in a short time. In trees that are bent under the weight of melting snow one hears the birds singing as if it were May. This year also (as is said always to be the case) shipping on the Missouri and the Mississippi was entirely unobstructed before the middle of February,[5] and no ice was to be seen anymore. Naturally this is not the case in the higher latitudes. Both rivers were frozen over in January so that heavy freight wagons drove across them. The ice comes down from the colder states in the higher latitudes; otherwise such a cover could never form here. Those who estimated the climate of St. Louis from the freezing over of the Mississippi did not take this into consideration. [30– 1] If the temperature is merely low enough so that the ice produced in the far north does not melt, then soon such masses will accumulate that a moderate freeze of forty-eight hours can combine them into a firm cover. When the Missouri was frozen over, I tested the earth's crust at various places on the nearby hills where neither snow nor grass nor foilage protected it and found that the frost had penetrated less than four inches. In the highland meadows the cold west and northwest winds are far more cutting than near the river valley. Along the upper Ohio and especially at Cincinnati it is colder than along the lower Missouri, because of the neighboring Alleghenies and their not unimportant branches. Warden[6] says of Kentucky that although the Ohio froze over every two or three years, the (Fahrenhiet) thermometer did not often register a temperature below 25 degrees (7 degrees under the natural freezing point).

The west winds, namely those from the southwest, the west, and the northwest, are the strongest. Therefore one sees the trees growing in an open space, for example, the apple trees, leaning toward the east. Strong winds from the east are very rare. But terrible storms sometimes come from the west, which tear down the most vigorous trees.[7] I was told of such an air disturbance that had passed through the states of Missouri and Illinois. It had partly uprooted, partly broken all the trees, not excepting the largest oaks, along its entire course, which was about several hundred paces wide. I can only report what I have heard about this. Shortly after my arrival in this area (on 8 November 1824, I think) a storm raged, the effects of which extended far beyond the area of my

---

*The rapid change of temperature is not so much to blame for the illnesses as people say. Evidence of this is found in the fact that during the cold winters there is the least illness, in spite of the fact that people change from hot rooms to icy atmospheres. During the fall and spring weather, which scarcely call for heating, most cases occur.

trip of sixty miles through the Missouri valley and beyond the adjoining hills. It was not so violent as the ones mentioned above and spread out over a wider area, but the trees lying on the ground made it possible everywhere to recognize the direction it had taken. [30– 2]

Others may investigate to what extent these data agree with Volney's theory* concerning the American winds. I remember that the same traveler expresses great surprise at the number of uprooted trees in the forests of western America and sees in it a singular phenomenon that could be explained only by a second singularity. He claims actually to have discovered this in a characteristic deviating completely from the nature of European trees, namely in an almost general lack of taproots. He is all the more convinced of this as he has discovered further reasons that also make such a deviation explicable. For he reminds one of the fertility of the earth's crust in the western states. This, he says, directs the roots upward, and must thereby prevent the development of taproots. To that I answer, first, that the number of uprooted trees is not so especially striking if one considers that here a fallen tree remains just as untouched as a standing one. Most of those that plunge down with their roots partly exposed are still attached to the ground on one side and continue living until other trees meet a similar lot. Thus a stranger can easily be misled to contribute the effects of a half-century to recent years. But I must also contradict the assertion that the taproot is so frequently lacking. To be sure, there are instances of this now and then; but at the same places one sees the opposite so frequently that it is out of the question to speak of a general difference.

It is probably unnecessary to mention in this connection that not all species of trees have taproots. Finally, as far as the explanation for the deviation is concerned, this is applicable here least of all. In western North America the fertile soil (vegetable humus) is very deep. In the Missouri valley it is common to find rotten wood at a depth of twenty to thirty feet, and for this reason, well water is not satisfactory in many areas. And in the Missouri valley certainly as many trees are uprooted as anywhere else. Gusts of wind and the porous consistency of the soil are the primary causes of the uprooting of trees here as well as elsewhere.

---

*With astonishment I read in Warden's works, vol. 1, p. 154, the following: "the winds, which chiefly prevail, are the northwest, the southwest and the northeast. The first, which blows from the mountains and high table-land, predominates in winter and is by far the driest and the coldest. But along the atlantic [*sic*] coast, where it meets warm clouds and warm currents of air, it produces snow, hail and sometimes rain; along the banks of the Ohio and Mississippi rivers it produces rain in winter and storms in summer." The contradiction in these sentences is inexplicable to me. After such exceptions, what part of the United States is left over for the general character of the northwest wind? The northwest wind never brings rain along the Mississippi, least of all in the winter. Also the storms come from the west and the southwest far more frequently than from the northwest. It is when the northwest wind brings coldness that it blows most violently.

In Volney's work we read also that earthquakes are completely unknown in the western states, that in the Indian languages the words *earthquake* and *volcano* are completely lacking, and that south of the Great Lakes there is no trace of them.[8] I do not know how the Indians designate such phenomena, but I have been generally assured that from the earliest times earthquakes have been felt here, and that a few years ago several chimneys were destroyed by them here in my neighborhood. New Madrid (at latitude 30° 34′) and the surrounding region [30-3] suffered from earthquake shocks every week from December 1811 to February of the following year during the time they caused such disaster in South America; for example, they reduced the city of Caracas to a heap of ruins.[9] Everywhere in my neighborhood there are traces of volcanoes.[10] Most striking is the iron that is now half slag. At the same time, however, there are petrified shells on the high hills. At the time of Mr. Volney's journey, the country west of the Mississippi was still so inaccessible that similar errors should not surprise one. Among them also is the opinion that from the Mississippi to New Mexico the land consisted of nothing but immeasurable plains full of swamps. Now the regions along the Red River, the Arkansas River, and the Missouri River are better known. In general, the land west of the Mississippi is higher than that east of it, and there are extensive mountain chains between all those rivers. Also it is entirely erroneous to think of steppes here, such as those described as existing in middle Asia. Beginning with the Mississippi valley and extending five hundred miles toward the west [30– 4], forests predominate, with the exception of the regions near the Gulf of Mexico, especially in the provinces of Attakapas and Opelousas. [30– 5][11]

In recent times it has become more and more customary to compare the climates of countries according to their average temperatures. The mean daily temperatures of a place are calculated from the daily observations of the thermometer registrations at different hours of individual days; the monthly ones from the average daily temperatures, and the annual ones from the average monthly temperatures. The results of such observations have established the probability that in all countries the mean temperature of the month of April approaches more closely the mean annual temperature than that of any other month. Furthermore, the almost constant temperature of the earth at a certain depth (of about eighty feet) is everywhere approximately the same. For instance, the mean annual temperature of Paris is nearly 52 degrees Fahrenheit, and the temperature of the earth at a depth of ninety feet is 53 degrees and is said to vary about a half-degree only during very cold years.

Partly on the basis of the daily observations made, partly by the application of the above-mentioned principles of probability, it has long been believed that the North American temperature is at least ten degrees of latitude lower than that of Europe; that, for example, the mean temperature of the regions at the fortieth degree of latitude does not exceed that of the fiftieth in Europe. But some later observations most obviously contradict this. Washington on the Potomac, for example, has a mean annual temperature of 55°, 5′ Fahrenheit at 38°, 52′ latitude according to Humboldt,[12] whereas the mean annual temperature of Paris at latitude 48°, 50′ is given by the same natural scientist as nearly 51°, 15′ Fahrenheit (10°, 7′ Centigrade). If one might compare the location of Cambridge in Massachusetts with that of Vienna, the exaggeration would be still more obvious. Vienna is located at a latitude of 48°, 12′ and has a mean annual temperature of 50°, 56′. The location of Cambridge is latitude 42°, 25′, and the temperature 50°, 36′. Vienna's location could more aptly be compared with that of Cincinnati on the Ohio, which, situated at 39°, 6′ latitude, is said to have a mean annual temperature of 54°, 25′ Fahrenheit.

To what extent an idea of the climate can be gained from the mean annual temperature will become apparent from the following comparison of European cities. At a latitude of 48°, 50′ Paris has a temperature of 51°, 15′; while Amsterdam at 52°, 22′ is said to have a mean temperature of 53°. The mean temperature of Padua, at 45°, 24′ latitude, is estimated by Kervan[13] at 52°, 2′. According to more recent investigations it is said to be 56°, 66′. Genoa, at a latitude of 44°, 25′, has, according to the most recent investigations, a mean temperature of only 50°, 21′, whereas that of Mannheim, at a latitude of 49°, 21′, is calculated to be 51°, 26′. I shall pass over several other examples.[14]

It is hard to be convinced that not many serious errors were made in observation as well as in calculation, and this, of course, does not affect the method itself. A usable result can only be expected from a combination of the number of degrees and the duration of the individual thermometer registrations. Therefore, three of four observations made after sunrise are insufficient. In countries of differing geographical latitudes, the difference in the length of the days causes great differences in duration. Between Germany and Chesapeake Bay, the state of Ohio, or that of Missouri, the difference in the length of the days amounts to two to three hours. In winter the days in Germany are so much shorter and because that makes the nights longer those states in America receive heat from the sun from two to three hours longer [30– 6] in a twenty-four-hour period. Therefore, for the same time less heat is withdrawn from them. Mean temperatures, the calculation of which does not take this into consideration, do not deserve the name, and some European as well as American ones seem to belong to this class.

But the most careful observations and the most exact calculations cannot give to a list of mean temperatures the significance that it lacks because of its nature. Whoever, without further ado, wants to compare lands of different zones according to this list, uses it just as wrongly as the person who does not take into consideration the altitude of the areas to be compared.

Two differences that play a primary part in the phenomena that we are accustomed to designate by the word *climate* are completely ignored in determining the mean temperatures.

The one difference is based on the greater and the lesser direct effect of the rays of the sun. Thermometer observations made in the shade, which serve as the basis for the calculation of mean temperatures, give information only with regard to the indirect effects.

The other difference is obscured by the generalization of calculation of the mean temperatures themselves: the change of the actual temperatures. But this very change of temperature has the greatest effect on organic nature. Whoever speaks of climate thinks first, or should think first, of the plant and animal kingdoms. Climatic investigations are of interest to us precisely because of the dependence of plants and animals on cold and heat. Therefore, the extremes of heat and cold should certainly not be overlooked if one is trying to get only a fairly accurate idea of the climate of a place. With the most striking differences in regard to extremes, the mean temperatures can nevertheless be exactly the same. Due to the forests, the nights in America are in general colder than those in Europe. If the mean temperatures of European and American cities are exactly the same, one may nevertheless always assume that the daytime temperature in America is higher than that in Europe and that the temperature at night, on the other hand, is lower. I am not the first one who has made this objection to the overhasty conclusion about the similarity of the mean temperatures. But in general only a change in degrees is mentioned. There seems to be scarcely a thought given to the distribution of the temperatures among one another, and yet this is of the greatest importance for plants and animals. One should consider what a difference it makes whether there is a succession of six cold days followed by twelve mild ones, or whether the cold days occur distributed among the mild ones, surrounded by them, as it were. I have told you that in the state of Missouri the cold seldom lasts more than forty-eight hours and is said never to have lasted over seventy-two. It is followed then by a temperature that causes the ice and snow to disappear noticeably. This explains why here the most delicate calves and lambs, regardless of their European ancestry, need no protection against the weather.[15] The cold of winter along the lower Missouri may at times be as intense as the cold along the upper Rhine, in the Palatinate and in Alsace, but only in degree, never in duration.

The direct effects of the sun's rays are no less significant for the climate. This becomes clear when one imagines a plant or a person alternately at the fiftieth degree of latitude in a land without forests and at the fortieth degree in the midst of endless woods. The coolness of

these forests perhaps permits no considerable difference in the temperatures in the shade. But in objects exposed to the sun the ten degrees of
latitude will be evident clearly enough. The forests cannot prevent that,
since the earth that is covered with ice and snow cannot even do that, as
one often experiences on clear winter days. But the nearby coolness
does not lower the temperature of an organic body exposed to the sun,
as it does that of a stone. With the cooling of the stone, every noticeable
effect of the sun's rays disappears. But the stimulation of the vitality of
plants and animals has results that by no means disappear with the
receding to the former temperature. That European domestic animals
can survive the winter as well in the open here as in the best stables in
Germany can be attributed to the direct effect of the sun's rays as well as
to the short duration of the cold. In the middle of January along the
lower Missouri the sun has the effect that birds and other creatures,
surrounded by melting snow, show the same liveliness as in the spring.
And since most trees, even in the densest forests, are exposed to this
great direct effect of the sun, at least from above, the complete difference of the vegetation here from that of Europe should cause just as
little surprise. [30– 7]

These remarks show that areas that differ by several degrees of
latitude can be compared with each other only inadequately. If, however, such a comparison is to be made, I should without hesitation
compare only such European areas as lie south of the forty-eighth
degree of latitude with regions along the lower Missouri. I do not
believe that Italy had a much milder climate before its cultural era than
that which the Mississippi areas at the same latitude have at present.
Horace, Virgil, and Pliny still speak of the Tiber freezing over and of
catching fish under the ice, although cultivation of the southern as well
as the northern parts of the peninsula had advanced quite far by that
time. The endless forests north of the Alps once had the same effect in
Europe as they have now in America. It is the forests that make the
Mississippi areas so hospitable to the new arrivals from central Europe.
If they should, in a later century, disappear completely, the hills and
valleys that are now so charming would have the same scorched,
repellent appearance that the destruction of past ages has given to the
greatest part of Persia.

Finally, to the person who attributes the proper importance to the
happy development of human beings, the information about the clear
skies will seem as important as that about the temperature. The sky of
the Mississippi areas has such an advantage over that of middle Europe,
and especially over the cloudy sky of Germany, that it abundantly
compensates for every disadvantage that is to be feared for the health of
the Germans who settle in the so-called wildernesses. It is generally
assumed that there is more precipitation in America than in Europe.
But it is still more certain that there are far fewer rainy days in America

than in Europe. Whether the exact amount of water is greater or less is of little importance for the climate. In America the individual rain showers are heavier than in Europe. But that cannot make the climate damper. On the contrary, a heavy rain does not penetrate the earth so deeply; the water collects quickly and the effect of the evaporation on the atmosphere will not be as great as with a continuous drizzle, which seldom occurs in America. Most of the rains along the lower Missouri are thundershowers.—There are also numerous traces of the effect of lightning here. In the forests there are places where in an area of several *Morgen* almost every tree is damaged.

To speak of a climate of the United States in general is absurd. One cannot put Vermont and South Carolina or Georgia* in the same class, any more than Sweden and Italy. Since Volney's journey, it has become customary to divide the whole territory into four climatic regions. (1) The coldest region comprises the northeastern states from the ocean to the range of hills where the Delaware and the Susquehanna have their sources, approximately to the forty-first degree of latitude. (2) The central region includes the southern part of the states of New York and Pennsylvania and the state of Maryland to the Potomac River. (3) The hot region comprises the southern states: the level land of Virginia, the two Carolinas, and Georgia, in addition to Florida, where it never freezes. (4) The fourth region includes the western areas, the Mississippi territory; that is, a surface area, the northern part of which is just as different from the southern as Norway is from Sicily; but at present no agreement has been reached about a more accurate division. Jefferson was the first who (in his remarks about Virginia) tried to show that the Mississippi areas enjoy a milder climate than that along the Atlantic coasts.[16] Volney and others accepted this opinion and it has now become rather general. For the Mississippi valley itself the difference is estimated at about three degrees of latitude. More recent writers, however, have taken the opposite view, especially Darby in his above-mentioned work.[17] In answering this question, obviously the time of the estimation must be the deciding factor. It is well known that the climate of the Atlantic states has changed very much because of their cultivation, and even since Mr. Volney's journey (in the years 1792 and 1793) it has become considerably milder. The land east of the Alleghenies was at the time of the first settlements covered everywhere with forests, while in the Mississippi areas the extensive plains always gave less resistance to the sun's rays. At the time it was unquestionably colder along the Atlantic coast than along the Mississippi. About the

---

*The average annual temperature of Rutland in Vermont is calculated to be 44 degrees Fahrenheit; that of Cambridge, in Massachusetts, 50°, 36'; that of Philadelphia, 53½°; that of Richmond in Virginia, 57°; that of Charleston in South Carolina, 63°; on the other hand that of Stockholm, 42½°; that of Rome, 60°; that of Naples, 63°.

present condition I can only say that according to the information I received in Baltimore, I consider the winter along the upper part of Chesapeake Bay to be far more inclement than the winter along the lower Missouri. To be sure, these regions differ by more than one whole degree of latitude. Toward the end of April, the market at Baltimore already offers a plentiful supply of new peas; but these come from the southern shores of the bay, for example, from Norfolk in Virginia, which is two degrees farther south than Baltimore. The Allegheny Mountains are also more distant from the coast of Virginia, which is not to be considered a less important factor. Nevertheless I should believe the rains are more frequent in the Atlantic states. The winds from Newfoundland bring them much cold rain, which seldom reaches the Mississippi. The distance from the ocean has a powerful influence on the clearness of the sky; there is sufficient evidence of this in the eastern and western areas of Europe. However, the vicinity of the ocean does not necessarily presuppose a damp climate. But the waters of Newfoundland nevertheless seem to have a peculiar influence on the coasts of Europe as well as on those of America. Around Newfoundland the sky is almost always cloudy; this is related to the temperature of the Gulf Stream and the polar currents, which meet near this island. For our (the Atlantic) half of the Northern Hemisphere, this seems to be the main source of the rain clouds that move in part toward America, but in denser masses toward Europe.[18]

Continuation of the Preceding Letter

Volney's temperature scales will be of little help to anyone who desires to study the climatic phenomena of the United States more closely. The matter is not so simple that everything can be traced back to two lines connected at a right angle. No one will deny that it is colder in the Allegheny Mountains than at the same latitude along the Atlantic coast and on the plains of the Mississippi. However, with the exception of the latitude scales from north to south, I do not see how scales from east to west can make a survey of temperature variations any easier. How can such a scale be applied to the hook-shaped formation of the Alleghenies, even if one were to disregard all other deviations, especially the many branches that spread out through the entire west and do not differ very much in height from the main chain? One could not easily add anything to a scale from north to south (which has a purely mathematical basis) that would be suitable for a considerable extent of the earth's surface. But Volney's suggestion is entirely impracticable.

It is a fairly well-established custom to permit someone who has visited a distant country to give his opinion on anything that concerns this country and to treat with special leniency even hasty judgments on subjects the thorough understanding of which requires more than journeys. I should not like to claim such consideration for my statements about the climate and present the following remarks merely as the results of a study made for my own information. That it was made under the guidance of well-known writings I probably do not need to mention. I place the greatest value on methodology, and it is perhaps suited to obtaining a simple overview of the most important factors of this subject matter.

Of course I must begin with the meaning of the words *heat* and *cold*. The ideas connected with these words obviously relate to an inborn conception of temperature that is merely awakened, not created by the sensuous impressions. Our concept of temperature is such that we cannot exclude any substance from it. It is a part of the conception of its existence in space. Insofar as we think of an object as existing, we also conceive of it in connection with a characteristic that we call temperature. Accordingly, whoever believes that the temperature of an object is completely dependent on the sun, would have to believe that the existence of the object is completely dependent on the sun; which means that the sun was the original source of the existence of the object. Such a conclusion, however, would be opposed by the thesis that everything that is itself limited and dependent, that does not contain the source of its own origin, certainly could not contain the primary source of another existence.

However much a certain kind of existence of our earth may depend upon the sun, the existence itself cannot be dependent upon it; and, however much the variations of temperature are dependent on the sun, the temperature itself is something that is characteristic of every object and depends only on the existence of that object.

Just as we must attribute a temperature to the sun itself, we must also attribute a temperature to the earth itself. But just as little as we can know what part the sun plays in the special kind of existence of our earth, just as little can we learn the degree of temperature of the earth itself, independent of the sun. We can only make variations of temperature the subject of our investigation, as they are revealed to us in the dependence of our earth on the sun. And with regard to these variations themselves, we are again limited almost entirely to the surface of this earth. Of what happens in its depths, of what influences the temperature there, we can learn extremely little, although one must assume that through the long years the effect of the sun must penetrate also to the core of the earth. The investigation of the climatic phenomena must, in general, be limited to the earth's crust and the air masses surrounding it.

In this field all temperature changes seem to us finally dependent, on the one hand on the various effects of the sun's rays, on the other hand on the varying sensitivity of the solid and liquid matter that form the earth's crust together with the atmosphere surrounding it.

If one wants to become acquainted with temperature changes, one has to observe them in that double dependence; one has to concern oneself with their twofold roots, of which they are the products, and one's procedure in doing so must necessarily be similar to that which a mathematician follows in studying analytical problems of two variable magnitudes. His task also is to investigate results that can originate only through the influence of two variable factors. In order to establish the influence of each single factor in the whole scale of its variability, both factors must be assumed, alternately, as constant, and it is advisable to study first the influence of the factor whose variability can be surveyed most easily. This is the case with the dependence on the various influences of the sun's rays. For all the differences in the effects of the sun's rays, which I shall call variations of the first class, have their bases (a) in the shape of the earth, (b) in its rotation on its axis, (c) in the direction of this axis toward the axis of its revolution around the sun, and finally (d) in its course on this path. This results in variations:

(1) in the number of effective rays, because of the varying distance from the sun,

(2) in the direction of their radiation toward the earth, which is also to be traced to differences in their number,

(3) in the duration of their effect; and

(4) here one can add another great difference in the number of rays because of the different passage through the atmosphere, due to the angle at which they strike the earth.

Only the number of rays and the duration of their effect are subjects of consideration in the first class, and since here most things can be determined by continuous closed calculations, all the temperature changes could be ascertained with almost mathematical accuracy, unless the dependence on the variations of the other class involves insurmountable difficulties.

Accordingly, in order to become acquainted with the dependence of the temperatures on the variations of the first class, the natural scientists abstracted, for the time being, from the variations of the second class; in other words, they assumed the susceptibility of the earth's crust to the sun's rays to be equal and made an effort to learn what the climates would be if they were based entirely on the variations of the first class. Usually these imaginary climates were called sun climates,[19] in contrast with the actual climates.

At the very beginning of the experiment, which, as is self-explanatory, could only be directed toward an approach to the truth, they were confronted with the question of which of the various degrees of susceptibility of the earth's surface would be most adequate for the purpose. The answer had to be the one that appears to be the clearest, the expression of which seems to be changed least by the expression of the other susceptibilities; and thus it was soon realized that the ocean would give the best information. The susceptibility of the waters is revealed to the observer more clearly the further they are removed from the influence of land. For testing the various effects of the sun's rays on a homogeneous susceptibility the regions of the sea that are far from solid earth are the better adapted since they are found at all known latitudes. Such places on the earth's surface bear the name *stable regions*. With the aid of travel reports and ships' logs, a temperature record of these stable regions has been completed for most of the latitudes, which corresponds with reasonable exactness for the purpose of a record of the sun climates.

It is evident that if the surface of the earth were really completely covered with water, these sun climates would be the actual climates everywhere. To be sure, this is not the case. On the solid earth the sun climates are more or less different from the actual climates, and only on small islands in the middle of large seas may the difference become insignificant. Nevertheless, the usefulness of that record is striking enough, as it thus has been found what part the differences of the first class play in the climates. Now it is permissible to study the differences of the second class, which could not be considered at the beginning. The climates of the stable regions furnish the basis for the study of the climates that differ from them. In the former, only the susceptibility of the waters to the sun's rays was taken into consideration. If now this susceptibility is compared with the susceptibilities of the various parts of the solid earth, then the modification of the sun climates to the true climates has been completely prepared for, and therewith everything has been done that can be demanded of a general investigation.

It is easy to see that in the further research indicated above, the reciprocal effects of the various susceptibilities will be the most difficult to determine. In this matter we shall always have to be content with incomplete results which, however, still sufficiently reward the effort of investigation. But as far as the execution of the work itself is concerned, the investigator, as soon as he approaches the solid earth on the aforementioned basis used in the study of the sea regions, may no longer disregard the question whether the heat-giving characteristic of the sun's rays can be compared with that of a glowing body; whether the sun, like a glowing body, emits heat, or merely causes heat. The affirmation of the former is subject to very important objections. It is far more probable that the sun's rays, without being hot themselves, incite the heat in the bodies, develop it in them, and that the characteristics of the bodies themselves determine the development.

If this is the case, then heat can exist only where there are terrestrial bodies, and elsewhere only insofar as these terrestrial bodies transmit it. From this there follows the productive thesis that it can be warm only near the earth, and that the cold must increase the more the farther one removes oneself from the earth. To be sure, the air is a terrestrial substance; but its susceptibility to the sun's rays, in regard to the development of heat, is so slight that it owes its heat almost entirely to the transmission from the earth. Therefore one may interpret this thesis to mean that it becomes colder the farther one leaves the earth's crust behind. To be sure, the warm air is lighter than the cold, and therefore the layer of air warmed by the earth's crust must rise, and the upper colder one must sink because of its greater weight. But the rising of the warm air is eccentric, the sinking of the cold air concentric, whereby the warm air, gradually spreading out in wide areas of cold air, disappears. The experience of aeronauts coincides perfectly with this.

It is this thesis, that heat emanates from the earth and is withdrawn from its immediate surroundings by the more distant colder areas, that furnishes, even at the first glance at the characteristics of the solid earth, the explanation for the temperature on high mountains. High mountain peaks are surrounded completely by cold air and the sunbeams cannot develop as much heat from the surfaces of these heights as is withdrawn from them from all sides. Let us consider a dense crowd of people under an open sky. In moderately cold air they will warm each other. But if we assume that one individual towers far above the heads of the others, then we can compare his temperature condition with that of a mountain peak. Also the same rays of the sun would have a more concentrated effect on the base of the mountain than is possible on the far larger surface. But that is of less importance.

If the investigator proceeds to the study of other characteristics of the solid earth, he will find the reason the bare, firm earth's crust is more receptive in general to the sunbeams than water surfaces. He will also discover why the sun, under conditions that are otherwise the same, develops more heat from the bare, firm land than from the expanses of water. It is easy to see that this—aside from the characteristic of water not to transfer its temperature quickly to the areas not reached by the sun's rays and aside from the size of the masses not subject to the rays of the sun—is due mostly to evaporation, whereby much heat becomes latent and does not affect the temperature.

In case of types of soil that are very susceptible to moisture, clay, for example, a similar reason counteracts the rise in temperature. Therefore the sunbeams have far more effect on the sandy soil than on areas of clay.

Bodies that reflect rays most are not easily warmed. Therefore a snow cover is a great hindrance to the development of the sun's heat. There is no doubt that snow also evaporates.

The sunbeams have an entirely different effect on animate bodies (including in a wider sense plants) than on inanimate ones. There is no question of a direct development of heat, as when stones are irradiated by the sun's rays. At first the effect of the sun is received by the vital forces, and development of heat is only an indirect result. Plants (as well as animals) seem to reject superfluous heat by evaporation as water does, that is, as latent heat. But they differ from water in that their bodies themselves permit no particular rise in temperature, at least none that could be compared with that which the water can assume in the evaporation process. From this it follows that after the sun's rays have lost their effect, the heated water continues for a long time to affect the nearest layer of air, while forests have no special power to do this.

If now, after similar general observations, one wants to study the climate of a particular area of land, he must, above all, disregard the influence of neighboring portions of the earth's surface in order to study first of all the nature of the surface of land itself and the effects of the sun's rays on such a surface. Only when this is done may one look beyond the borders of the area in order to learn what changes the temperature could undergo from the influence of air currents from other land areas.

After what I have previously said, the entire investigation is reduced to the indicated differences in the development of heat and its disappearance through vertical and horizontal air currents.

If, for instance, the climate of the state of Missouri is to be investigated, the irregularities of the surface of the land will themselves present no particular difficulties. The highest peaks of the Ozark Mountains, between the Osage and the White rivers, are said to be less than two thousand feet high. That is the mountainous part of the state (the region of the lead [30–8] mines). To be sure, with the exception of the river valleys, the surface of the entire state is hilly; but this altitude is not great enough to affect the temperature noticeably. It is really the forests and the plains that (aside from the rivers) are to be considered. The plains, however, cover the smaller area, whereas the forests extend in all directions.

The sun's rays penetrate to the soil of the forests only when there is no foliage; that is, when their strength is weakest. In the plains, up to the second half of the summer, the grass proves a similar hindrance to the warming process. However, the difference is still significant. About the month of August many grasses and other meadow plants are already dried up and very susceptible to the sun's rays. But when they are later consumed by fire, which often happens as early as September, the sun has all the greater effect on the black surfaces.[20]

As soon as the sun has set, the warming of the air by the dense forests cannot be continued because they themselves are not warm. However, the air of the high areas does not cease to withdraw the heat, and so a temperature condition of the lower air layers soon develops that cannot absorb the mass of vapor that has developed during the day. The heated earth, for example, the sand areas, emits much heat even after sundown, whereby the temperature of the air is preserved for a while. Therefore it is easily understood that where forests are interrupted by open areas of land, the dew must fall mostly upon the forest region. In the middle of the summer the dew does not fall so frequently even over inland lakes as over the forests. In the forests along the Missouri it occasionally falls as a thundershower, which is a simple result of the power of the sun's rays at that latitude, the great evaporation from forest regions, and the rapid cooling of the atmosphere over them. In the daytime one feels the full effect of the sun in some open places. But as soon as the rays disappear, the warming of the soil of a small area is negligible in contrast to the rapidly cooled [30–9] air over the immense forests. Because of the dew at night, it is necessary to light a small fire in the morning in every house, even in midsummer. If this is not done for some time, the iron utensils become rusty, the leather covered with mold, and silk materials spotted. But the effect of this dampness on the health is far less harmful than is generally maintained. In any case, the pollution of the air in closed small rooms is more to be feared. Except in the cold winter night, I always sleep with open windows.*

Although the plains of the state of Missouri do not themselves have special effect on the climate, those of the bordering regions affect it all the more. Two-thirds of the state of Illinois consists of plains. From the Arkansas territory, wide plains extend to and through New Mexico, and from the upper Missouri to the Rocky Mountains. Along the lower Missouri, forests predominate; along the upper Missouri, plains cover the greater area. The same is true of the areas along the upper Mississippi. But one should not think that forests are entirely lacking.

I attribute it to the plains that the western states enjoy a milder climate than that which, at least formerly, prevailed over the eastern areas.

Furthermore, the climate of the state of Missouri is determined on the one hand by the heat of the Gulf of Mexico and its northern coastal areas; on the other hand, from the northwest by the ice of the Rocky Mountains. The high temperature of the Gulf of Mexico is well enough known, and the air currents between it and the Mississippi territory find few obstacles. The Mississippi valley itself is, on the average, rather wide; but, what is more to be considered, the ridges that extend from west to east to the Mississippi are not very high. The average height of all the ranges between the North River (Rio del Norte), the Red River, the Arkansas, and the Missouri, can be estimated at five hundred to eight hundred feet. In this wide area individual knolls have very little effect.

---

*If viniculture in North America is really more difficult than in Europe (as some believe), probably only the coolness of the nights is to blame. For the first experiment I would choose regions on the high plains, and not the hills along the streams, where everything is covered with dark forests. Micheaux also advises this, when he speaks of the barrens of Kentucky.

One could call to mind that toward the north there are also no obstacles for the air currents and that the polar zone is completely open. It is true that the regions around the sources of the Mississippi, the St. Lawrence, and the streams that flow into Hudson Bay and into the Polar Sea, are no more elevated than the moderate fall of these waters requires. The entire space between the Great Lakes and the Rocky Mountains is said to contain no real mountains but many prairies and smaller lakes. But this is just the reason the winds coming from that direction are milder than the ones from the eternal ice of the northwest.

With this I shall break off, so that what I had designated as remarks will not turn into a book. Besides, I do not like to concern myself with hypotheses about the influence of electricity.

Concluding remarks about the climate along the lower Missouri. Swarms of flies in the plains. Concerning settlement there. Settlement on the unsold state property. Manner of surveying the public lands.

I have now spent two summers, three falls, three winters, and two springs along the lower Missouri and must confess that I do not wish for a better climate. Above all I like the clear sky. Even in January and February there are more clear, mild days than wet and cold ones. The resurrection of nature, which can lend a wonderful charm to early springtime in Germany, is, to be sure, less noticeable here. The vegetation is not so dormant, and the grasses and some shrubs begin to sprout very early.* On the other hand, one does not have to complain about the prolonged cold and rainy weather that characterizes the German spring still more than the beautiful days when nature awakens. The German fall cannot compare with the American one. Along the Missouri the hot weather lasts no longer than two months, namely from the middle of June to the middle of August. But even then it is a pleasure to travel through the dark forests for the entire day. Last summer the temperature did not rise higher than 90 degrees Fahrenheit (almost 26 degrees Reaumur). This is not infrequently the case in the Rhine region also and is more unpleasant there than here along the Missouri because of the lack of shade during the longer days. Only one must avoid the plains in July and August if one cannot in some way protect the horses from the flies. There are countless numbers of them there and one species that is

---

*The trees are not in full foliage in Missouri before the middle of April. This is due to the cold nights. These do not permit the vegetable garden to be sown earlier than in Germany. After the blossoming time of the spring flowers the local climate can therefore not be compared with that of Germany either.

an inch long and a half-inch in diameter. If a person must take a trip of several hours through uninhabited prairie land, he is in danger of losing his horses, as they become extremely exhausted by the bloodsuckers. If the trip cannot be avoided, which is possible almost everywhere, it is the custom to add the juice of wormwood, or of another bitter plant, to vinegar and to wash the horses with the mixture. Nets are not effective and covers are too warm. As soon as the prairies become inhabited, the flies decrease in number. This fact is attributed to the grazing domestic animals, which destroy the brood attached to the grasses.

It is very easy to settle in these prairies. After a place is found near the encircling forests and a good spring, the dwelling is immediately erected, and the area chosen for the field and garden is fenced in the usual manner. This area can then be plowed (with a wheel plow) and seeded immediately. There is no need for fertilizer here either since no one would choose such a poor place that fertilizer would be needed during the first decade. The same field will be seeded and planted without interruption and yields a second harvest of vegetables after the wheat and rye harvest, which falls in the first weeks of June. The turnips, which are then sown, thrive particularly well. I have never tasted better ones. Nevertheless, the soil in the Missouri valley and the adjoining hills is more fertile. [30– 10] And however beautiful the range of colors of innumerable flowers in the natural meadows may be, I prefer the forested regions. The cost of clearing is too insignificant. The difference amounts to not more than three dollars per *Morgen,* and if the forests have little underbrush, scarcely half of that amount. I have been told also that the grass cover of the prairie must be removed by hoeing, if the wheat, the rye, the tobacco, or cotton is to thrive in the first years. The corn stalks, which attain a height of twelve to eighteen feet and sufficiently overshadow the wild grasses, demand less attention. For the person who comes from the dark forests, which are closer to the river, the prairie region has a dreary, dried-up appearance in late summer and fall and becomes still more unattractive during the winter months. However, one must not compare the desolate mountain ridges of Germany with the prairies because of this appearance. There are also more good springs close to the hills near the river. Of course one could substitute wells for them everywhere. But the new settler seeks to avoid the costs and difficulties of digging a well. Where the land is so cheap, no sensible person will chain himself immediately to a definite place by making large investments. Not until its advantages have been proved by time and the population grows will finer buildings, wells, and water piping be constructed. Many of the poorer farmers do not even buy the land at first. This use of public lands is, to be sure, forbidden by federal laws, and the felling of trees is punishable by high fines. But no one pays any attention to this, and no case is known when a settler was actually driven away by [30– 11] the governor of the state, whose duty it is to attend to such evictions. The law seems to serve more as a means of protection against wanton destruction, or similar misuse. There are families here who live throughout their entire lives on farms for which they have paid nothing at all, nor will they pay anything. Naturally no real estate taxes can be levied on them. No censure is connected with such behavior, as one might believe erroneously from some German publications. Quite respectable persons continue to live in this manner without their reputations suffering in the least. The only disadvantage is that a buyer can evict them without reimbursement for their investments. That happens occasionally, but in general this procedure is subject to public criticism. Moreover, they are careful to choose a fertile area of small size for such a settlement that, compared to the less useful remainder of the lot, is too small to attract anyone to buy the whole.* The smallest lots of public land amount to eighty acres.

This reminds me that I have not as yet said anything about the surveying of state lands. The procedure is as follows. [30– 13] The course of a parallel of latitude is determined for a number of degrees of longitude, and the direction, the individual degrees, and also every distance of six English miles is marked by mounds of earth, stones, and by their relation to unchangeable, easily located landmarks of an inanimate nature, such as rocks, springs, rivers, and so forth. From a point in this line, which is called the basis, the course of a meridian is pursued in both opposite directions for a number of degrees of latitude, and its direction, the individual degrees, and the intervals of six miles are indicated in the same manner on the earth's surface.** Thus a general point of reference has been established and the surveyors are instructed to divide, by means of the magnetic needle (box compass), individual areas enclosed by parallels of latitude and meridians, into townships, sections, quarter-sections, and eighth-sections. Because the measuring is done individually, according to the directions of the two main lines, all other lines must also be directed toward the four cardinal points of the world, and all parts of the network, comprising only a few degrees, must be at right angle. The townships are squares containing thirty-six square miles, for the sides directed toward the four cardinal points are six English miles long. Such a mile is equal to 1,760 yards or 5,280 feet, London, or 5,135 Rhenish feet (a foot, which stands in the ratio to the London foot as 13,918 to 13,511, and the Parisian foot as 13,918 to 14,400). Each side of this square is again divided into six equal parts, and by the drawing of crosslines the whole is divided into thirty-six smaller squares, the sides of which are one mile long. These smaller

---

*That the natural meadows are nevertheless very important for the poorer settlers can easily be seen from this. [30– 12]

**One can imagine that this work requires no less skill and exertion than the measurement of geographical degree that was made during the previous century.

squares are called sections, and each contains 640 acres. Therefore the large square (or township) equals 23,040 acres.* The sections are divided into quarter-sections, and the quarter-sections finally into two equal halves by a line running from north to south.—Eighty acres is therefore the smallest lot that can be bought from the state. [30– 14] The sections of a township are distinguished by numbers. One begins with No. 1 at the side opposite the basis and counts toward the left up to No. 6. Then No. 7 is directly under No. 6, and from here one continues to count toward the right to No. 12. No. 13 is again below No. 12 and so one proceeds from the left to the right until No. 36 forms the bottom of the perpendicular column of 1, 12, 13, 24, and 25.** The parts of the sections are designated according to the four cardinal points.—The townships following each other from a common basis in a direct line from north to south or from south to north are known by the collective term *range.*—It must not be forgotten that fractions of townships and sections occur frequently where navigable streams, lakes, and acknowledged previous property rights interfere with the surveying grid.

The exact designation of a piece of real estate in the western states therefore requires:

(1) the stating of the number of the section, and if it is a quarter-section or an eighth-section, the designation of this portion in its relation to the four directions;

(2) the number of the township;

(3) the number of the range; and

(4) whether the ranges are located west or east of the meridian;

(5) whether the north or the south side of the basis (or the parallel of latitude accepted as the basis) comes into question. Finally,

(6) one must give the number of the meridian, which does not mean the astronomical number of the degree, but merely the number given to the individual meridian lengths for the purpose of locating them when surveying the surface of the earth. So, for example, my real estate is in the area of the fifth meridian, very close to the line. The fourth meridian passes exactly through the mouth of the Illinois, and the third through the mouth of the Ohio. [30– 15]

The political division into counties and states is completely different from the geographic and topographic division. Because the latter had been made earlier (in the western areas), it has been used for the political one. However this also could not be done consistently, if only

---

*An acre is also calculated at 1,053 toises,[21] or at 37,908 Parisian square feet. In the country itself, one calculates 160 square rods to an acre, a square rod at 272¼ London square feet, a linear rod at 16½ feet. This makes 43,560 London square feet to an acre, which does not quite agree with the above estimate in Parisian square feet. For according to this the ratio of the London foot to the Parisian would have to be 1,071 to 1,000 (instead of 1,065 to 1,000).

**The sixteenth section is reserved everywhere for schools.

because in a political division various kinds of natural obstacles of unity could not be ignored.

As a result of this surveying, there are splendid charts of the United States. Charts of the individual states, which approach the topographic charts as closely as possible, can be found in all good inns. It is easy to see what an advantage this is for the traveler, as well as for the planning of new roads, highways, and canals.

As long as the sales by private citizens do not deviate from the given divisions, border disputes can soon be settled. To be sure, this condition cannot be met entirely; but at any rate, border lawsuits lasting several years must be a rare occurrence. Where most of the areas become private property only by documented sales by the general federal government, the situation concerning the proving of property rights will be more favorable for quite some time than in other countries. A feeling of insecurity, such as exists in the states east of the Allegheny Mountains, is not to be feared here.

Thirty-first Letter

In the month of March 1827

I am now making preparations for my return. I have rented my farm for a period of three years. The rent will be paid in kind and is based on the amount of arable land. From every acre, ten bushels of corn are to be paid. At present a bushel costs only twenty to twenty-five cents. I am chiefly interested in the maintenance of the present improvements and of the good timber, which can be transported from here also. Why I bought any land at all, you will know from my former letters. It was the best and cheapest way of acquiring the information that was the purpose of my journey. I do not need to tell you that the use I intend to make of it will not keep me in America. [31– 1]

I confess that I am leaving these regions with a feeling of sadness. The only thing that I missed here was the proximity of German families who were my friends. The Germans and the North Americans do not differ at all in what is usually called nature and temperament. Also the domestic customs of the natives cannot repel the German immigrant. They are largely adapted to the situation, and one can easily become accustomed to them. Even the language barrier soon disappears. But the bond of common memories will always be missing. However well a German may adjust to the manner of life and the situation of the American, the charm that social intercourse derives from the past is felt all the less the longer the immigrant has lived in his native country. The newcomer from Great Britain has less cause for complaint about this. He is by nature more closely related to the American and also everywhere finds himself surrounded by fellow immigrants from every class of society in his fatherland. Which classes Germany has sent to America up to now, and what the situation is regarding their descendants, you know from my former statements. Only a few of the first generation of German immigrants cross the Allegheny Mountains and still fewer come as far as the Mississippi. This good fortune is preserved for the grandchildren, after the parents have perished in misery. Most of them remain in the Atlantic states. Who would direct them here? How could they meet the expenses of the long journey? Only a few can afford the trip across the ocean. Also, many inhabitants of the eastern states look with envy upon the flourishing development of the Mississippi areas and try, above all, to detain the Europeans whose arrival has, up to this time, increased the value of their landed property so greatly.

How often I have thought of the poor people of Germany. What abundance and success would the industry of a few hands bring to whole families, whose condition in their own country an American-born farmer cannot imagine to be possible. There is still room for millions of fine farms along the Missouri River, not to mention the other rivers.

The great fertility of the soil, its immense area, the mild climate, the splendid river connections, the completely unhindered communication in an area of several thousand miles, the perfect safety of person and property, together with very low taxes—all these must be considered as the real foundations for the fortunate situation of Americans.

In what other country is all this combined?

If one wanted to paint the picture more colorfully, it would suffice to call to mind the rich forests, the abundance of bituminous coal, salt, iron, lead, copper, saltpeter, and other minerals; the active interest of almost all inhabitants in cheerful industry, the utilization of the advantages of their location, and the thriving steamboat services that have already resulted from it; finally, the contrast to all European prejudice with regard to the rank in society of the tradesman and the respect in which physical activity is held.

Only the person who has engaged in agriculture in Europe, and especially in Germany, will be able to comprehend the full significance of these seven main characteristics. [31–2] He will know what it is worth if the domestic animals require no care, if neither the breeding of horses nor the feeding of cattle and hogs is dependent on an extensive cultivation of the soil, if it is essentially sufficient to procure breeding animals and to leave the rest to nature. He knows how to judge the value of a soil that with no fertilizer and little work will produce the most abundant harvest year after year. The soil in Germany is almost useless if it is not cultivated. Here, on the other hand, the farms are separated by areas that compared to land of the finest quality will, to be sure, find no purchaser for a long time, but that are nevertheless covered with dense forests of oak and nut trees and luxurious grazing land that any farmer, without exception, can use for his stock.

It is very easy to understand the doubting remarks of Europeans as to how it had been possible that such a territory (where one, in addition to all the other advantages, can also select the climate and can change one's residence from one climate to another without special cost) had remained unoccupied until now. The answer is the following. It was discovered by the French only shortly before the end of the seventeenth century. They came from Canada, later from the Gulf of Mexico. The inhabitants of the United States at first found so much to occupy them on the Atlantic coast that for this reason alone they did not consider settling beyond the Alleghenies. Later, however, the French, who claimed the entire Mississippi River territory as their possession and even tried to exclude the English fur traders from it, prevented it. They incited the Indians; and settlements by the English could not be established until, in the Peace of Paris, 1763, the French gave up their claim to the land east of the Mississippi in favor of England. However, no move was made toward an actual settlement for some time. The first attempt was made in Kentucky, in 1775, by Colonel [Daniel] Boone from North Carolina, after he had first become thoroughly acquainted with the region on his hunting expeditions. At that time, Kentucky was considered a part of Virginia. From then on it became a chief speculation of the North Americans in the Atlantic states to sell their farms at high prices to immigrants from Europe and, at little expense, to establish new and better ones west of the Alleghenies. The area between these mountains and the Mississippi is so immense, however, that for the present it should easily suffice for any number of newcomers. In the same peace treaty, the area beyond the Mississippi had also been ceded to Spain, which considered it a buffer for its silver-rich Mexico, and did not exert itself to fill it with colonists. Finally, in 1803, these lands also came into the possession of the United States. However, the territory was not actually opened to settlers until a few years later (after the surveying had been completed and the grants of land made by the former rulers had been examined). Meanwhile the possibilities of steamboat services had been discovered, and therewith began a new era for all of North America.

Many times I have said to myself and to my traveling companion (whom I shall leave behind in the most fortunate situation)*: People in Europe will not and cannot believe how easy and how pleasant it can be to live in this country. It sounds too strange, too fabulous. Believing in similar places on this earth has too long been consigned to the fairy-tale world. The inhabitants of the Mississippi area, on the other hand,

---

*His name is Ludwig Eversmann, a son of Chief Surveyor of Mines Eversmann of Berlin.[1]

consider the reports of need in Europe exaggerated. The citizens of the state of Missouri, together with their slaves, doubt so much that there are so many white people in Europe who with the greatest exertion can enjoy scarcely as much meat in an entire year as is here thrown to the dogs in a few weeks. They cannot believe that some families would even starve or freeze to death in winter without the charity of others; they are accustomed to attribute such statements to the intention and desire to praise and flatter America. However, sometimes one hears a person say: "Yes, yes, my grandfather told us that life was very hard there."

And yet I must advise against moving here by oneself and without careful consideration. Success depends completely on the way emigration is carried out; and without special preparation or adequate guidance, everyone will be exposed to chance more than he might expect. If a person has successfully survived the first two years, he is safe. But that is a difficult condition to meet. The initial effects of the new climate, the lack of domestic stability and service, attacks of homesickness—all these general causes hardly require the inevitable minor nuisances to produce disturbances in the healthiest body, which, even if they do not endanger life, usually decrease one's means considerably and cause one to lose the courage to use properly what remains.

Most of the unsuccessful attempts at colonization in distant lands have failed for such reasons. They have no relation to the land itself. The native-born descendants of the immigrants are not affected by them. I am sure that if several German families (perhaps ten to twenty on friendly terms with each other) had spent a year here together in the peaceful situation that the Americans so quickly create for themselves in the uninhabited forests, they would no longer yearn for Europe. They would indeed want to see it again, but not to remain there. Therefore I say once more that the success of the emigration depends entirely on the way it is carried out. When everything has been attained that an American himself can attain, then a single immigrant family will feel the separation from friends left behind all the more keenly the less it lacks for a satisfactory living. In Germany, most of the people are so deeply absorbed by domestic cares that friendly intercourse with other families seems to be of very minor importance. Here, where these cares usually disappear because of the abundance with which one is surrounded, the mind is freer and a person naturally turns to those things with which the noble classes have always occupied themselves.

The talk one usually hears in Europe about the wilderness and lack of cultural products is without basis. Here one can at far less expense have everything that is expected in Europe from living in the country. The inexpensive upkeep of horses, the lack of any kind of obstacles, the safety from thieves and robbers [31–3] make social intercourse so much easier that only a lazy fool could ask for more. There is also no lack of schools, and a German who does not value the loss of his native tongue very highly has no reason to fear that the education of his children will suffer from his immigration.

Moderate means, efficient guidance, with medical protection for the first two years, and the vicinity of friendly families from the native country are the true conditions of success. [31–4]

After what I have said previously you surely will not interpret this to mean that the climate is more unhealthy here than in Germany. Because in similar undertakings even slight illnesses can cause the greatest disturbances, medical aid is more necessary here than in one's homeland, even if there were nothing to fear from the hardships of the first settlement. Because of its clear skies the state of Missouri is far more conducive to health than Germany. The person who considers Germany and central Europe a very healthful area has no means of comparison with other regions on the face of the earth. The inhabitants of the Pelew Islands will, in remembering their Li-Bu, not praise Europe; just as little as the Sandwich Islanders will after the loss of their rulers.[2]

If a small city were founded with the intention of serving the American Germans as a center of culture, one would soon see a rejuvenated Germania arise and the European Germans would then have a second country here, such as the British have. If only a live interest for such a project would develop in Germany! No plan of the present day can be more promising to the individual and to the whole than such a plan for the founding of a city as the center of German culture in western North America, and especially in the areas west of the Mississippi. It would immediately make the new continent a home for the Germans and would add to all the direct gifts of nature that which must always proceed from human beings themselves. No one should fear that any political obstacle or envy of the Americans would oppose it. German immigrants are generally welcome here, and as soon as they have set foot on the new continent, they are considered equals of the citizens (aside from political rights, which are dependent on a residence of five years and in the beginning are more of a hindrance than a help). I have already told you that in the state of Missouri even a foreigner can acquire landed property. A plan could easily be made that would combine the interest of the sciences and the consideration of gain very well. The purchase of land in connection with the founding of cities is a sure means of increasing one's means. The lands west of the Mississippi are almost a terra incognita for the natural scientist. At a slight expense natural science societies could support representatives here who could from time to time be replaced by new ones. And these delegates would not find it in conflict with their main interest to serve the young colony as teachers of the advanced sciences.—How many men there are in Germany who have funds amounting to four to six thousand *Thaler* without any other prospect than to use them for living expenses! But this sum is more than abundant to provide a happy life for an entire family on the banks of the Missouri, even if eight hundred to a thousand *Thaler* should be spent for traveling expenses,* provided that they did not lack guidance. Such a financial status is very common in Germany among persons who are forced by what is called propriety and decorum to make expenditures that, without providing pleasure for the present, veil the future with anxiety. With the above-mentioned sum the immigrant can buy two adult slaves (one male and one female), which cost about twelve hundred Prussian *Thaler,* and establish himself in such a manner that he can live more happily and, especially in regard to the future lot of numerous descendants, with many less worries than if he possessed six times that amount in Germany. But if he is capable of cultivating his own soil, a thousand Prussian *Thaler* would more than suffice, except for traveling expenses. I am estimating 150 to 200 *Thaler* for eighty *Morgen* of land; 45 to 60 *Thaler* for clearing and fencing from five to seven *Morgen;* 120 *Thaler* for two horses; 26 *Thaler* for two cows; 12 *Thaler* for two sows; 100 for the buildings; a like amount for goods and chattels. That makes at the highest estimate 618 *Thaler.* So almost 400 *Thaler* are left for other, less essential things and for the ability to live without adhering quite so closely to a strict budget. If 200 *Thaler* more are spent on the dwelling, the immigrant is surely established far more comfortably than is usual for peasants who cultivate their own fields in Germany. A quarter of a mile from me there lives a farmer by the name of Jacob Haun. Seven years ago he began to establish a homestead. Because he possessed scarcely a hundred *Thaler,* he at first lived on state property and there tried to earn enough for the purchase of 160 *Morgen.* Then he continued to farm on his own property after the usual fashion and prospered, so that in seven years, without any assistance, he acquired a fortune of three thousand *Thaler.* Meanwhile his wife bore him five children, and now his household annually consumes over twelve hundred pounds of pork, an oxen weighing five to six hundred pounds, and several dozen roosters and hens. Also, at least ten to twelve deer are killed and a large number of turkeys. (No powder is used for partridges; it is left to the children to catch them in traps.) Who would believe that so much meat could be consumed in one household of two adults and five children, of whom the oldest is scarcely six years

*A single individual (traveling in respectable fashion) could get here from Holland for four hundred *Thaler* (*Cleve* currency), or about 450 Dutch guilders if he could utilize the information from someone who has already made the trip. For children and servants it would cost about half as much. Only one should beware of bringing men servants. They would leave him soon after the crossing unless they were bound by an agreement made in Germany. During the first years they do not earn half the high wages paid the natives, and even if one would consent to grant them, the calculation of the traveling expenses, the initial confusion of the mind by the political equality, and the self-conceit aroused by the insinuations of envy and gloating (which demons do not spare America either) would in a short time spoil even the best individuals. [31–5]

old? Some, of course, is contributed to hospitality. But most of it is due to the extravagant use of an article of food that is almost cheaper here than the most common vegetables in Germany.

There is much complaint in Europe about the decrease in the number of marriages, and superficial moralizers therefore declaim about immorality without considering that need is the true cause of this phenomenon, whereas immorality is merely the result, even the inevitable result. Only a thoughtless person can indulge in propagation without considering the future of his children. Among the low class of people, marriages have not decreased, although their morals are worse than ever. This is a deplorable, unnatural situation in our poor fatherland, which will never change automatically. The only charitable aid is the general promotion of emigration. There is no more sacred duty for the states of Germany now than to provide efficient guidance for these emigrations. To want to prevent them when they occur, as it were, instinctively, means working against nature and reason, and all unfortunate results are to be attributed not to the urges of the crude masses, but to those whose vocation it is to assist them with advice and guidance in the difficulties of life. If the associations among the well-to-do emigrants were facilitated and promoted, if the states would take an interest in helpful guidance to the new home, if philanthropic organizations were formed to help even the poor to emigrate to lands where the abundant offerings of nature accustom even the beggar to regular activity, then the unfavorable reports about emigration would cease very soon. Unfortunately, exactly the opposite has been done in Germany [31-6] up to this point. But time, which has erased so much systematic nonsense, will in a few years also abate the frenzy of the population epidemic in states that have long been overpopulated. It is a terrible folly to declare something as an advantage for a group of several families that an individual family must consider an absolute evil. If the hierarchy, in conflict with temporal power, considered the poverty of innumerable people dependent on the charity of the monasteries as a part of its basis, if Asiatic despots crushed the prosperity of the country in order to increase to the highest degree the willingness of the people to serve, then at least the expediency of the means must be recognized. But if our statesmen, who are surely honestly attempting to make us really happy, give thanks to heaven that the number of automatons controlled by their need for bread increases annually by the millions, then it only remains for us to be astonished at the wonderful capability of the human brain to create from the most airy nothings—forming, as it were, a ganglion by means of a web, or rather a maze, of errors—a firm political center that has such a terrible effect on the fate of great nations.

The above conditions of emigration concern only those who want to make use of the soil (by farming) in making their living; just as I have, up to now, been talking almost exclusively about the prospects for farming, which, however attractive they are, still cannot deteriorate during the present century even by the immigration of millions. Moreover, it is easy to see that in a country that enjoys similar physical advantages, it is almost sufficient for the thriving of most trades if the legislative power merely remains passive and avoids foolish intervention. There are few trades that do not thrive here. The situation is most favorable for tanners, skilled craftsmen, joiners, masons, carpenters, saddlers, and smiths. The tanners may find that the skins and the materials used for tanning are extremely cheap here, but that leather is expensive; and the saddler can make note of the fact that no one goes on foot here. There is a great lack of glass factories. In St. Louis an ordinary bottle costs twelve and a half cents (eighteen *Kreuzer* [groats or farthings]). The same is true of pottery ware. There is no lack of good clay, and since private rights are no hindrance, a type can soon be found in this large territory that is adapted to finer vessels, together with a site near navigable rivers and dense forests. Beer brewers would soon become rich along the Mississippi; however, they themselves would have to attend to the culture of barley and hops, as up to the present there has not been much interest in raising them here. St. Louis gets its beer from Pittsburgh and even from the Atlantic coast. An expert in the production of chemical medicines will find an excellent sphere of activity in the western states. I probably do not need to mention that architects are very welcome because of the continuous building of cities.

Emigrants who intend to make their living by similar trades must keep to the cities themselves, or at least settle near them, and in such a location they can depend on medical aid as well as in Europe. Also the condition of social intercourse with friends from the native country will seem less important to them. But one condition holds for every single emigrant, namely that he must bring some funds with him. Even though his trade requires no capital, it will always be a matter of chance whether a foreigner immediately finds work. It will depend still more on whether he can at the very beginning earn enough while coping with the new world to assure some savings for himself in case of illness. If he would ask for charity, as he might in Germany, he would encounter such contempt that rapid advancement would be impossible. I must warn the German emigrants especially not to expect to earn a living merely as day laborers. Most of the work done by day laborers in the interior of America is new to the German. He first has to learn how to do it and slowly accustom himself to it. Otherwise his health will be ruined in a few weeks, and yet the greatest exertion on his part will not bring him what another earns quite easily and without danger to his health. Such work consists of: grubbing out bushes, killing trees, felling trees, and splitting them into rails for fencing. The last named kind of work is not known in Germany, and without practice most of one's strength is wasted. [31-7] Finally, I scarcely like to mention the lot of those unfortunate ones who become slaves in return for the payment of traveling expenses. Only a galley slave will find his lot improved in this situation. They are called redemptioners here, and perhaps also white slaves. Their fate is far worse than that of the Negro slaves, and it is incomprehensible to me that some German publications can pass over this so lightly. The health of the Negro is, after all, to the owner's advantage. Negroes are acclimatized; most of them call America their home and have never known freedom. The poor Europeans who think they have purchased the land of their desires by the hardships endured during the journey across the sea are enslaved for five, seven, and more years for a sum that any vigorous day laborer earns within six months. The wife is separated from the husband, the children from their parents, perhaps never to see each other again. [31-8] Just because so little is expected of such workers during the first years, their term of service is extended so much. But let no one believe that these first years will be years of play. They are indeed the most oppressive ones. That individuals survive and later become rich does not alter the general prospect. Ten perish miserably, while scarcely one prospers.

Therefore, let me repeat: Without any funds, emigration is a risk to which only the greatest need should drive one.

Finally, a few words about direction. The artisan, the technician, or the craftsman will also be freer in this respect than the farmer, insofar as the nature of these skills and trades (especially with a certain degree of training) prevents great differences. However, everyone must orient himself in the new surroundings before he proceeds to extensive undertakings. The native has the advantage over the immigrant that only a longer stay in the country can supply. When a European has once come to feel at home here, then everything that promised him an advantage over others in his own country will prove of value here. But the person who wants to proceed immediately in the European way and wants to spend considerable amounts in doing so has to beware that he does not lose his means before he is capable of using them.

The last remark is important for no one more than for the farmers, because they have the most to learn in America and need guidance most. It should occur to no one to plan to introduce a European type of agriculture in the western states at present. Such overly hasty action would soon have serious results. If a person has engaged in agriculture in Europe, he will know much that is also applicable here. But the important thing is that he comes with an open mind as far as the standards and practices of European agriculture are concerned, instead of being ruled by them. The immigrant must approach his new life with a mind that can comprehend easily what the climate, the soil, and its location offer in the midst of the changing relationship of social and political conditions. Such a person will, instead of beginning with adverse criticism of local procedure, consider carefully whether he will not have to adapt himself to a similar one. He must not expect the Americans to take the trouble to disprove his criticism. The more decisively the stranger airs his opinions, the less they will try to teach him. They become politely evasive or even agree with him, well aware of the fact that the practical results will teach him more effectively than words.

The great difference between German agriculture and the local type can be summarized as follows. (1) In Germany the land is expensive due to its capital value and the state taxes; labor, however, because of the dense population, is very cheap. In the areas west of the Allegheny Mountains the reverse is true. The land is very cheap and the labor expensive. From this it follows that a very careful utilization and cultivation of the soil, which in Germany is absolutely necessary, would be wasted here. (2) The farm buildings cost very little here. (3) The breeding of livestock (including horse breeding) can be left almost entirely to nature. (4) In Germany fences are built to enclose the cattle, horses, hogs, and so forth; in America to keep them out of the fields—a simple result of the different relationship between pasture land and cultivated fields. There is as yet no region in North America where it would be easier to fence the pastures than the fields, for all forests are used as grazing land. Although it is folly when farmers value their wood too little without thinking of future transportation, or when cities that have no access to water carelessly allow the neighboring forests to be ruined, yet it will not soon be necessary to limit the livestock in its pasturage, at least in the state of Missouri. (5) In erecting the fences, here again the material is not expensive, but the labor all the more. In Germany, the opposite is true. (6) Fertilization of the fields where the soil is of the first or second quality is entirely unnecessary in the state of Missouri, with the exception of where vegetables are grown that demand animal fertilizer. (7) Now one should consider the difference in the products: (a) cornfields are the basis of all agriculture; (b) every family grows at least as much cotton as it requires for its own use,* (c) the use of the sugar maple forests is an important branch of farming; (d) in some places the cultivation of rice and everywhere that of tobacco** is very profitable. (8) If one further considers that although for all

---

*The cotton plant continues to produce new blossoms almost until Christmas, while the earlier ones mature and are picked from time to time. In the areas north of the thirty-seventh degree of latitude, it happens more frequently that the later blossoms are destroyed by night frosts. Therefore the harvest cannot be so plentiful as farther toward the south, and other products, which do not thrive so well in the south, are more profitable. Two hundred fifty pounds of clean cotton is the usual harvest per acre. [31-9]

**Tobacco is raised mostly for export to Europe. The Americans do not use it very much. Smoking is not so frequent as chewing. On the seacoasts, as well as in Europe, chewing is considered a crude habit; but not in the interior. There one also sees some fairly well educated women who smoke. Among the younger generation, however, the habit seems to be losing ground. [31-10]

products there is a ready market, the farmer, in order to utilize his location, must sometimes undertake river trips of many hundreds of miles; that he must know how to construct boats, how to select his helpers, and to supervise the entire business transaction; and if one adds finally (9) the unfamiliar situation that slavery presents to the European, then it can easily be seen what the immigrant must bring with him in addition to some funds.

According to the above description, the local country life is so different from that in Germany that the former occupation of the immigrant is of special advantage only insofar as it has trained him in the accurate analysis of actual conditions. Therefore many a German peasant is less adapted to engage in agriculture here than the more skillful artisan.

Nevertheless, all I have said does not contradict the statement that the western states comprise the real area where even a European who is entirely inexperienced in agriculture and domestic economy can still learn the essential requirements without damage. It requires no other precaution than to limit the first facilities to one's own needs, and this is absolutely necessary for a stranger with modest funds. Here there are no oppressive taxes on a high capital evaluation nor real estate taxes, which in Germany make all temporizing impossible.

Everyone whose business affairs permit his living in the country finds so much to attract him here that only a lack of funds or insensitivity will keep him from doing it. At the same time, the immigrant should not forget that in the western states some families (and not only foreigners) have been completely ruined by purchasing too much land. The land is so beautiful, so fertile, and so cheap that a European especially has to struggle with dangerous temptations. It is a common preconception in Germany that the regions along the Mississippi are immeasurable, treeless plains. I have shown in my letters how much reality differs from this idea. The surface of the state of Missouri, for example, with its mountains, hills, and valleys, rivers, and creeks has a topography that, with its forests and meadows, offers all the charm that may be expected from an unspoiled landscape. Therefore it is certainly not unnecessary to warn the immigrant urgently not to buy too much land at the beginning and always to keep the disposable capital in mind. The stranger from Europe will find it difficult to believe that such splendid areas can be had for a song for a long time to come. But no one should be led astray to engage in speculations, when to wait for the outcome goes beyond his powers. Utilization of the soil will always remain the main object, and it is the greatest mistake to deprive oneself of the means required for this purpose.

Continuation of the Thirty-first Letter

Prosperity of the United States. Finances.
War Potential. Postal Institutions.

The intellectual powers that have developed in Europe throughout generations find a sphere of activity in North America which one seeks in vain in the old [31-11] world. In North America construction jobs, which the European countries do not accomplish in centuries, are completed in a few years through the voluntary cooperation of individual citizens. If anyone suspects the slightest exaggeration in this statement, let him consider the three-hundred-and-fifty-mile-long canal in the state of New York, which connects the Hudson River with Lake Erie;* let him think of the two-hundred-thirty-mile-long [31-13] canal that will connect the Ohio from the city of Portsmouth with the same lake and within two years has already been half-completed. [31-14] ³ Last year work was begun on the canal around the falls of the Ohio near Louisville in Kentucky, and it will be completed during the next eight months. [31-15] Work is also being done on a canal from Lake Erie to Lake Ontario around the great waterfall at Niagara, not to mention many others. Several days ago I heard that in Baltimore there is a plan to construct a railroad from Chesapeake Bay across the Allegheny Mountains to the Ohio.** But I do not need to concern myself with plans.—For in no country in the old world is steamship transportation so important as in America. The utilization of distant regions is made so much easier by it that one can scarcely draw conclusions for the future from past accomplishments.

Those mathematicians who want to persuade themselves and others that the prosperity of every state can be reduced to a simple mathematical formula are justly ridiculed. To whom would it occur to speak of retrogression if a private individual incurs expenses for extensive investments in real estate that exceed his income for several years? Who will dare to calculate the wealth of the person without taking into consideration the value of the real estate? And yet some writers do this when they dispute the national wealth of the North Americans. A mere

---

*By means of ninety locks this canal runs over an elevation of eight [31-12] hundred feet. Passage is very rapid and also very cheap and convenient.

**This is now no longer merely a plan; execution of it was already begun in the summer of 1828 by a sale of shares of stock amounting to several million dollars. This was collected within a few weeks during my stay in Baltimore. When it is actually completed this construction will arouse amazement in the entire world. The arrangement will be such that twelve to twenty freight cars connected with each other can be quickly pulled by a single steam engine. Aside from steam power, it is calculated that a man of ordinary physical strength can pull a load of four thousand pounds on rails. Moreover, railroads have the advantage over canals that they will never be hindered by ice. [31-16]

balance of trade is supposed to give a complete picture here in a country where in a single day more is spent on landed property than in Germany in a whole year. If during a definite period less is sold to foreign countries than is bought from them, it is said to be a sure sign of impoverishment. That attention has meanwhile been directed to inland projects, that canals several hundred miles in length have been constructed, that forests have been changed into beautiful cities, that a hundred more steamships are furnishing transportation, that thousands of new farms have been established—all this is immaterial; it has nothing to do with the prosperity of the nation. I have always been a friend of mathematics, but mostly because its study trains the mind and is directly opposed to such an application of its elements to the calculation of national wealth.

The income of the federal government varies, for the chief reason that no more is ever demanded of the inhabitants than will presumably be needed.

In 1823, income was almost 25 million dollars ($24,778,093 and 55 cents),[4] including a surplus of about 4 million from the previous year; expenditures were a little over 15 million ($15,314,171). Income for 1824 amounted to almost 34 million dollars ($33,845,135 and 60 cents), including a surplus of almost 9½ million from the previous year; expenditures to almost 32 million ($31,898,538 and 47 cents). I have taken these figures from the annual reports of the secretary of the treasury, dated 31 December 1824 and 22 December 1825. In the latter report an estimated calculation for the year 1825 is set up according to which the income would probably amount to almost 28¾ million and the expenditures to almost 23½ million.

The nature of the expenditures and income is indicated by the individual items given below for the year 1823:

Income	Dollars	Cents
(a) Tariff, about 19 million	19,088,433	44
(b) Sale of public lands, almost 1 million	916,523	10
(c) Dividends on stocks in the Federal Bank	350,000	00
(d) Taxes, outstanding debts, and miscellaneous	131,951	69
(e) Loans paid back by Ministry of War also	53,758	03
(f) Surplus from previous years	4,237,427	55
Total	$24,778,093	81

Expenditures	Dollars	Cents
(a) Total civil administration, diplomatic service, and miscellaneous, about 2 million	2,022,093	99
(b) Military affairs including fortifications,		

	pensions, outstanding debts, and Indian affairs, about 5¼ million	5,285,294	77
(c)	Navy, about 2½ million	2,503,765	83
(d)	Interest on national debt, about 5½ million	5,530,016	41
	Total	$15,314,171	00

[31– 17][5]

I have stated above that income varies chiefly because no more is demanded of the nation, or more specifically, the people do not demand more of themselves than will presumably be needed. It is not necessary to call to mind that the variations in the items of income mentioned above depend on such a reason only insofar as it affects the creation of sources of income. The formulation of the tariff law was influenced chiefly by the interests of the national treasury not only in general, but also in the determination of the percentage itself. However important this law is for inland industry, it would probably not have been passed without the aforementioned interests, nor would it have been preserved in its present form. [31– 18] Approximately the same situation exists regarding the income from the sale of public lands. Recently a decrease in price was proposed, but without results. If the needs of the national treasury were not urgent, the proposal would have been approved, as the other reasons for maintaining the present price are of less significance.

On the other hand, until the present the direct taxes have always been dependent on the annual decisions of the Congress. They have not been needed since 1815.

A person who judges the financial condition of the nation on the basis of its foreign trade (balance of trade) will find in the report of the secretary of the treasury, in his remarks about the income from tariffs, that in the first nine months[6] of 1824, exports amounted to about 76 million dollars; imports, however, to 80½ million.—The tonnage of the American ships used for this purpose was 1,769,311; that of the foreign ships used for trading with America, 204,919.

In the report of the secretary of the treasury on 31 December 1824, we read: The entire income from 1 January 1817 to 1 January 1825 would, including the expected income of the last quarter, amount to 210¼ million (210,275,899 dollars and 11 cents). Included, however, in this amount was 16⅓ million (16,336,747 dollars and 34 cents) received as loans. The expenditures during this same period would amount to about 205¾ million (205,769,230 and 20 cents). Almost half of this sum had been used for the payment of interest on the national debt and for reducing the capital of the debt itself, namely:

	Dollars	Cents
	101,365,900	67

Furthermore, for demands of American

citizens in accordance with the Florida agreement	4,891,368	56
For pensions to soldiers of the Revolutionary Army	9,400,000	00
For new fortifications	4,200,000	00
For increasing the navy	6,000,000	00
For compensation demands from the last war	4,500,000	00
For all the other usual expenditures of a nation, namely: Civil administration, military affairs, navy, pensions, defense, building of lighthouses, payment of Indian claims, surveying of public lands, and so forth	75,400,000	00

If one distributed the last sum over the individual years, the result would be an annual requirement of 9 million and 425,000 dollars for national expenditures.

According to present prospects (the report continues), the future annual income could be estimated at 21½ million dollars, and the annual expenditures for all branches of national administration and gradual retirement of the national debt could be calculated at 18½ million, not including the sums necessary for new fortifications and expansion of the navy. The surplus of 3 million would rise to 13 after 1835 because by then the sum of 10 million estimated in the list of presumable expenditures for the retirement of the national debt would, with the actual payment of this debt, be added to the surplus. [31– 19]

During peacetime the national debt decreased steadily. In 1804 it amounted to almost 86½ million, in 1813 to almost 56 million; and in the following war it was increased by 68 million, so that in 1817 it exceeded a total of 123½ million. At the beginning of 1825, however, it had again been reduced to 86 million.[7]

I repeat here once more that the budget of the federal government is not to be confused with the budgets of the individual states. Every single state has its own budget, and its income is derived almost everywhere from direct taxes, licenses for individual trades, auction dues, and so forth. But there are no inland tariffs, and no single state has the right to institute anything like that.

According to the report of the secretary of war, dated 1 December 1825, the standing army, including the general staff, the corps of engineers, the medical corps, and the accountants, numbers altogether only 5,719 persons. A cavalry unit did not exist.* Also provisions for field artillery were still to be made. The military school at Eton and the

---

*Almost everyone knows how to ride and care for horses, and most of the horses live out in the open in all kinds of weather. How easily a good cavalry can be formed here!

School of Engineering at Monroe have an excellent reputation. [31– 20]

It is not necessary to remind you that the defense of the country rests upon the shoulders of the citizens who are capable of bearing arms. Regular periods of training are mandatory in all the states, and every citizen from the eighteenth to the forty-fifth year must take part. However, not more than four or five days in an entire year are devoted to this and only so that psychologically they will remain in a state of preparation for war, which, of course, is the main purpose everywhere. I have already reported what marksmen are to be found here. Such universal skill in shooting rifles as is common in the western states can scarcely be met with anywhere else on this earth.

According to the annual report of the secretary of the navy of 2 December 1825, the navy at that time consisted of: 7 battleships with 74 cannon, 6 first-class frigates with 44 cannon, 4 second-class frigates with 36 cannon, 2 corvettes with 24 cannon, 5 sloops with 18 cannon, and 9 small men-of-war, such as schooners and brigs, equipped altogether with 69 cannons. At the wharves there were, in addition, 5 battleships, 4 frigates, and 3 war sloops.[8]

Especially worth noting is the report of the postmaster general, dated 24 November 1825. It shows that since July 1823, in other words, in one and one-half years, 1,040 new post offices had been established. The number of postal officials is not given more definitely than that there were between fifteen and twenty thousand. The income of this branch of the administration amounted from 1 July 1824 to 1 July 1825 to approximately 1¼ million, the expenditures during the same period to approximately 1 1/5 million dollars. [31– 21].[9]

Thirty-second Letter
10 March 1827

Day after tomorrow I shall start on my return trip. I am sending my effects to St. Louis by land. Steamboat navigation on the Missouri River is not very flourishing as yet. To be sure, one sees steamboats from time to time, but the population is still too small for a regular schedule. The state of Missouri, the twenty-fourth and the youngest of the Union, was not organized as such until 1819 [32– 1][1] and up to the present has sent only one representative to the Congress. From this one can draw conclusions as to the number of citizens. They amount to approximately 80,000 [32– 2] (settlers who are not citizens not included). [32– 3] The mail coaches run twice a week up to Franklin. In St. Louis I shall board a steamboat and travel down the Mississippi to the mouth of the Ohio, then up the Ohio to Pittsburgh. That is a trip by water of about fourteen to fifteen hundred English miles. [32–4] From Pittsburgh I shall travel by mail coach to the town of Erie on the lake that bears the same name (about 120 English miles); from there again by steamer across the lake to Buffalo. I shall make a detour of 20 miles to the Niagara Falls and then travel in nice yachts on the large New York canal to Albany on the Hudson River. From Albany, steamboats sail daily to New York in less than twenty-four hours.—To be sure, I could travel more conveniently and more quickly by way of New Orleans. But ships that sail from there to Dutch ports are rather scarce, and from a French port the journey by land to my home is too expensive because of my baggage. Also the crossing from New Orleans is disproportionately more expensive than that by way of the eastern coast. [32–5]

For the last four weeks the weather has been so beautiful that I was able to go on the most pleasant excursions every day. I visited once more all the valleys and hills to which my customary walks and rides had been directed. Also it really grieves me to take leave of the domestic animals. Entirely contrary to what is believed in Germany, the horses and cattle become far tamer and more attached to man in the freedom in which they live here. In the cities, man seems, especially to the horses, more like a tormentor; here as a benefactor, who, in return for moderate exertion, gives them a generous amount of food and then leaves them again to enjoy their sweet freedom. Therefore, on clear days, at a time when they are least interested in food, they return too happily to the homesteads, leaping and racing playfully. If one comes upon them in the forest, some of them immediately walk toward their master and stop good-naturedly in front of him. Others dance around him at some distance, as if they wanted to make fun of his intention to fetch them to work. If he really wants to use them, there is nothing he can do with the latter but drive them home, which presents no difficulties. To this treatment and freedom is also to be attributed the love for home that brings some horses back from a distance of a hundred or even two hundred German miles through streams and wildernesses. On his return from a trip they are accustomed to announce the rider by their joyful neighing at a distance of several miles from home. I own a spirited six-year-old animal that I usually keep in the fenced pasture in order to have it always at hand. It responds to my call like a servant; if it does not see me, it immediately answers by neighing and comes to me wherever I may be. I regret that now I must sell it. It will astonish you still more to hear that one of my neighbors has a hog that follows him and his children like a dog for miles through distant forests. Its mother died, and out of pity they kept the young pig (which was the only one left of the litter) in a corner of the house, and therefore it became very tame.

I would never have hoped to find the abundance of everything concerned with the conveniences of life together with the security of person and property as is the case here. In no region in Germany can one risk leaving women or children without the protection of men, especially in remote buildings in which there are articles of value. Here the master of the house can leave without any worries. In midst of dense forests his family and his possessions will be safer in an unlocked dwelling than in the strongest houses in European cities. I probably do not need to repeat that this is not due altogether to the lack of people, but only to the scarcity of thievish and predatory ones. Because of the spread of population far toward the west and because of a chain of small fortresses, the worries about Indians have completely vanished and will never recur here along the lower Missouri.

Thirty-third Letter
Pittsburgh, 30 March 1827

I have arrived again at the border of the Atlantic states. In Germany it will not be believed that one can travel far more comfortably and more cheaply from the distant Mississippi to this point than in any country in Europe; and yet there is no exaggeration in this statement.

With the exception of January and up to the tenth of February, steamboats from New Orleans or from the Ohio arrive almost daily in St. Louis. One can travel to New Orleans in five days. The cabin fare is twenty-four dollars. This includes all meals and bedding. The trip back requires about nine to ten days and costs forty dollars. [33– 1]—Such a round trip formerly took longer than half a year (on ordinary ships). In view of this one can estimate of what value navigation by steam is to the interior of America. Formerly there was no thought of utilizing distant areas profitably. One had to wait until the increasing population would gradually come closer. Now that the spatial separation has almost disappeared, human energy can be directed chiefly to the tilling of the best soil, and that of poorer quality will for the present be left to wild game.—The cabins of some steamboats are spacious and have high ceilings like the largest guest rooms and are furnished excellently with expensive carpets, chandeliers, sofas, and so forth. Thus one can justly call the steamboat *Atlanta* from Louisville a floating palace. The floors of the cabins in the steamboats on the Mississippi and its tributaries are considerably above the water level and one does not have to climb downstairs as in the steamships on the Atlantic coast. For the ladies there is a special smaller cabin, but they always take their meals in the large one in the company of the men. A second type of accommodation, which is over the cabin and is called the deck-room, costs about a third of the cabin price with no meals; including meals it costs half the cabin price. On these steamboats there are therefore two classes; on those of the Atlantic coast, however, only one. The second-class area is well roofed and on some boats it is completely protected from the weather. If one has to save, one can well live here. The inconvenience of second-class on ocean vessels (steerage) need not be feared here.[1] There is also never a lack of individuals whose company is quite bearable, and at the same time one always has the choice of changing to the cabin class later. The food is usually very good, the breakfast as well as the midday and evening meals. Alcoholic beverages, except those that are properly a part of the meal, are paid for separately. Moreover, everyone can bring similar provisions on board according to his desire. Some passengers tip the steward, others do not. It is never expected. In general, the custom of tipping is not practiced in North American inns. No barkeeper—who can be compared with a waiter in Europe—would accept a tip unless he were a Negro or a mulatto, which is seldom the case. Only now and then one is secretly asked by a Negro or a Negress for a few cents in return for the blacking of one's shoes. A stableboy does not dare to demand anything.

The entire trip from St. Louis to Pittsburgh took thirteen days and cost (by cabin) no more than forty dollars. I had about four hundred pounds of baggage, for which there was no extra charge. The steamboat from St. Louis did not go any farther than to Louisville in Kentucky; actually only to Shippingport, up to the falls of the Ohio, about two English miles below Louisville, which took five days. To this point the fare was eighteen dollars; from Louisville to Pittsburgh twenty-two more dollars. One must look upon such an American steamboat as a traveling inn, in which the captain is the host and which one does not leave until the destination of the journey is reached. One could not wish for a more convenient and pleasant way of traveling long distances. Every day we met six to eight steamboats that were sailing down the Ohio. The water was at average level, and the speed of the current of the river was on the average four English miles (per hour), and yet every hour we progressed approximately seven to eight miles. Going downstream we would therefore have covered fifteen to sixteen miles. The ship sailed day and night, except for short stops to take on or disembark passengers as well as to load firewood, which one sees piled up on the banks everywhere. On every steamboat there are accurate river charts, which the pilot can depend upon completely.

The passengers of the ship consisted of merchants from the western states, who are accustomed to buying their wares along the Atlantic coast, and farmers, doctors, and lawyers. I also met a mechanic from London, who had delivered steam machinery for the mines in Mexico. He had been in Real del Catorze for five years and painted a sad picture of those regions.[2] Robbery and murder, he said, were the order of the day there. In that city, which had a population of approximately forty thousand, murders were committed every week. Seven times, shots had been fired into his house. Victuals were exceedingly expensive because the people were too lazy to farm. He had paid seven dollars a bushel for corn (along the Ohio and the Mississippi it costs a quarter or three-eighths of a dollar). He considered himself fortunate to be among human beings once more in the territory of the United States. Concerning the mining operations of the English, he reported that five of the six companies had stopped payments after a loss of 30 million dollars.

Near the city of St. Louis, the river valley is very broad on both sides, so that the mountains and hills appear at a great distance.[3] The east bank is low, but not exposed to floods; the west bank is high. Several miles below St. Louis one sees beautiful hills close to the river, but the east side still remains low.

This east bank is the American bottom (American valley), famed for its fertility.[4] It extends from the mouth of the Kaskaskia River to the neighborhood of the Missouri and is, according to the course of the Mississippi, about eighty to one hundred miles long, with a width of three to nine [33– 2] miles. The hills bordering it are between one hundred and three hundred feet high, terminating, in the direction of the river, in steep, rocky walls of limestone; toward the east they gradually become lower over an area of two to three miles. It is in this valley area that the numerous burial mounds (cones of earth) are found, of which I wrote you earlier, and it is considered to have been the center of a large population that perished in ages past. The soil is inexhaustible here, as is proved by the isolated settlements which have existed here for a full century. The owners are mostly speculators. Therefore one still sees few settlements. One can buy land more cheaply and more quickly along the Missouri; the soil is no less fertile there, and the woods are far better.

Farther down the river, the hills on the west bank increase in altitude. Then they retreat again and the east bank becomes higher. Finally high knolls appear on both sides and decrease the width of the riverbed for a long distance. The rocks and groups of trees afford many splendid views. Below the city of Cape Girardeau, the hills and mountains disappear entirely, and at the mouth of the Ohio, which lies exactly at 37° latitude, the region is flat in all directions and, in part, subject to floods. Some travelers speak of the beautiful sight that the union of two great rivers offers. I must confess that I was not so much impressed by it. It is the surroundings that lend charm to the picture. With flat banks, the broad waters are more offensive than attractive. Even the most vigorous growth of the trees cannot change the scene enough. The trip on the Ohio is least interesting at its mouth. From the hills near Cape Girardeau, the region may have a better appearance. But one does not see any desolate places along the entire twelve hundred miles of its course. This description does not fit the plains either. For that the most manifold species of trees are grouped too beautifully: colossal plane trees, cottonwood trees, silver poplars, weeping willows, tulip trees, elms, maples, oaks, beech trees, walnut trees, chestnuts, and so forth. The banks remain rather low far beyond the mouths of the Tennessee and Cumberland rivers. On the other hand, farther upstream, the hills are only a short distance from the river for many hundreds of miles, up to Pittsburgh. This constant closeness of beautiful hills lends a certain charm to a trip on the Ohio such as perhaps can be found on no other river on the earth. If a person wants to take a trip to the Mississippi, beginning at Pittsburgh, in an ordinary skiff or boat, he will need thirty to forty days to do it. He will travel thirty to forty English miles a day (about six and a half to eight and a half German miles), and gliding over the surface of the water, where the strength of a child is sufficient to guide the ferry, he is always surrounded by a natural scenery such as the imagination of a poet is wont to select for an idyllic world. Therefore the French call the Ohio, not inaptly, the beautiful river *(la belle riviere),* with which the English pronunciation *Ohio* seems to present some contrast to the German ear.

One should not believe that landed property along this beautiful river is, in general, expensive. That is the case only in the neighborhood of the cities. There is enough land along the entire course that can be had for four to five dollars per *Morgen*, and this is fertile land that requires no fertilizer during the first years. But one must not look for areas on the upper Ohio such as those along the Missouri. On the lower Ohio, the layer of humus is deeper and more extensive. But the valley plain is mostly narrow, and where it is broad, it is rarely entirely safe from a water level that rises about fifty to sixty feet. The hills, however, are very precipitous and therefore subject to erosion during heavy downpours. In general, the banks are better adapted for pleasant country estates with viniculture than for large farms. For the latter, the land at some distance from the river is better. In any case, settlers would do well to turn to the areas below Cincinnati. [33-3] Because of the flourishing river navigation, settlement on the Ohio has at present a considerable advantage over that along the Missouri. But that will soon change. In Ohio the scenery is pleasant and lovely everywhere. But along the Missouri it is so striking that there is no region in Europe with which to compare it. I have, to be sure, often spoken of the size of the Missouri, nevertheless I do not consider it superfluous to add the following summary. The Missouri itself, before its union with the Mississippi, is navigable for 3,096 (English) miles. Among its many tributaries, the Osage is navigable for 600 miles; the great river (Grand River), 600 miles; the Kansas, 1,200 miles; the LaPlatte with its tributaries, 2,000 miles; the Great Sioux, 200 miles; the Jacque, 300 miles; the White River, 600 miles; the Chien, 100 miles; the Little Missouri, 200 miles; the Yellowstone, 1,200 miles; the Maries River, 200 miles.[5] Rivers having a shorter navigable course are not mentioned here.

At the mouth of the Wabash, several miles above Shawneetown, I learned that the colony of the Württemberger pastor [George] Rapp had moved back to the vicinity of Pittsburgh. A Mr. Owen of New Lanark in Scotland bought their establishments at New Harmony on the eastern bank of the Wabash.[6] Mr. Owen had acquired a considerable fortune in his country from factories in which he employed the children of poor parents and at the same time gave them some school instruction. While he was increasing his worldly goods, the good results of his praiseworthy efforts in the education of these helpless children seem to have developed in him the idea of working on a large scale for the betterment of mankind. In New Harmony he undertook the establishment of an institution whose purpose is no less than to transform the whole human race completely by means of a culture that is different from the usual one. Some of the passengers claimed to know him intimately and told many droll stories about his maxims, his method of teaching, and the mode of life that he had introduced in his school. But everyone seems to agree that Owen is sincere in his efforts, that his purpose is good, even though his methods might be wrong. Men of some reputation are connected with him, as for instance, the well-known mineralogist Maclure.[7]

As I left the state of Illinois, the eastern border of which is formed by the Wabash, I remembered the famous region along the Sangamon River. The chief city of the township of the same name is Springfield. For several days on my journey to the Missouri I was in the company of a wealthy resident of this place, who praised his home very highly and tried to direct me there, at least to see the region. But in spite of the otherwise very attractive picture he drew, he could not deny that the wooded areas were far superior in Missouri. At that time I was so tired of the plains we had crossed that this admission was sufficient to prejudice me against all other prairie districts of the same state. Later also, I found no reason to return to the eastern bank of the Mississippi. For the newcomer from Europe it is a disadvantage that one cannot keep slaves there. However it remains very probable that the state of Illinois will at some time attain an excellent ranking because of its large fertile plains and its excellent waterways, which connect it with the far North by way of the Canadian lakes, with the Atlantic coast by the St. Lawrence, and with the Gulf of Mexico via the Mississippi. But for the present, the extensive prairies have something that repels most people, which can only be remedied by settlements and parks. Also the land is considered less healthful than that on the higher western bank of the Mississippi.

From time to time our boat disembarked passengers and took on new ones. I saw several families who were leaving the regions along the lower Ohio in order to return to their former homes on the same river, but more toward the east. Since moving is connected with so few difficulties here, reasons of minor importance may naturally influence people to do so. If it happens that illnesses occur in the family in their very first year in the new settlement, the women are almost always overcome by nostalgia for the old home place, and for this reason alone they often decide to return. In the state of Indiana a group of such settlers, returning with all their household goods, joined us. They had two dogs with them, but these were refused passage since even the second-class passengers are not expected to tolerate the company of dogs. In general, few Americans permit dogs to come into their houses. However, I was just as indignant because of the callousness with which the dogs were abandoned by their masters as I was touched by the pitiful complaints of the forsaken creatures. One was a cute little Pomeranian, the other a setter. While the household goods were being loaded on the ship, they carefully guarded the articles still lying on the bank. When the last one was picked up, they wanted to follow the families, who had come on board earlier. Whining pitifully, they ran after the ship for a while. But soon the rocky bank hindered their progress, and they gave way completely to their misery, their howling reaching us for a considerable distance.

Almost everywhere I noticed groups of buildings that had been constructed only recently. In this region it is not unusual to travel through forests and after three or four years find them transformed into flourishing towns. If one considers that the founding of a city immediately increases the value of the surrounding land four to tenfold, one will not be surprised that there is a great tendency in this direction and that the bringing together of families succeeds so easily.

At Cincinnati we stopped for half a day. I made use of the time by looking the city over once more. It is astonishing how rapidly this city is progressing. I had not been there for two and a half years and found that a considerable number of beautiful buildings had been erected during that time. Also the bank of the river had been strengthened against floods by expensive masonry in such a manner that a gradual decline was formed that offered ships the same convenience in loading and unloading at every water level. I do not think that any city has more attractive market buildings than Cincinnati. They are several hundred paces long and yet they were entirely filled with provisions.[33-4][8]

Several miles below the mouth of a large Kenhava [Kenawah], which rises in the highest mountains of Virginia, there appeared on the right bank of the Ohio the town of Gallipolis (or Galliopolis) in the district of Gallia. It consists of about eighty houses and is the seat of a court of justice. It is said to engage in some viniculture, but I could not see any evidence of this as we were passing by. This town was founded by the French in 1791 and 1792. A company formed by owners of extensive areas along the Ohio had spread enticing pamphlets throughout Europe, which influenced some people in France, and especially in

Paris, to buy landed property that they themselves had never seen, nor had they had it inspected by agents. They were mostly people of the middle class, who, as all of France in those days, intoxicated by chimerical hopes and fanciful projects, sailed for America on chance, without any leadership or preparation, in order to settle in a region that at that time was swarming with Indians. It would have been a miracle if such an undertaking had succeeded. The number of emigrants amounted to about five hundred. They met with much bad luck, and most of them perished. Naturally occurrences like this one discredit emigration plans in general among the unthinking masses, who believe there should be only successes.[9]

About eighty English miles below Wheeling our steamboat and the steamboat called the *Pilot* collided. The latter was coming downstream. It was during the twilight. The cabin passengers had just finished their evening meal and the passengers at the second sitting had taken their seats. I was conversing with a fellow traveler at the railing of the gallery when the steward, hastening to the cabin from the forepart of the ship, called out in sheer fright, "We are all lost; the *Pilot* will sink us." At the same moment we saw a large steamboat sailing straight toward us. It was scarcely two hundred feet away. We clung to a post of the gallery and awaited our fate. The impact came. Only those who were prepared and braced themselves in some way, or held tight to something, remained upright. Most of the passengers fell headlong. Tables, chairs, stoves—everything flew around chaotically. Hopelessly the people awaited the immediate sinking of the ship. The lights were extinguished and the weak gleam of the twilight could not pierce the dense steam that spread throughout the entire ship. Fire broke out on deck, caused by the embers in the dislodged stoves. No one could say how far we were from the bank. The confusion was extraordinary. Everyone crowded aimlessly from one place to the other. Some men vied with the women in their complaints. The children screamed and whimpered. A few of us were able to detach the boat attached to the ship and to put the women and children (ten or twelve persons) into it. Now it was discovered that we were close to the bank. I returned to the cabin, hastily pocketed some papers and objects of particular value, and stepped again to the gallery, from which I thought to reach the bank by swimming if the ship should really sink. But the captain appeared and assured us that there was nothing more to be feared. Only unimportant parts in the prow of the boat had been damaged. The boiler had not been damaged either; the lid had merely flown off. He said that the fire on deck had been extinguished and that we would continue our trip in a short time. This actually proved to be true. We owed our deliverance to the fact that we had run into the side of our opponent. If the reverse had been true, the far larger *Pilot*, which the current made all the more powerful to the same degree that it weakened us, would have scuttled us completely.

Actually it had suffered more than our boat. A large opening in the side forced it to sail quickly to the bank. On the whole, there would have been little to complain about if a worker had not suffered a serious contusion of the chest and a baby a dangerous burn. In the other boat the feeling of alarm had not been less intense, and also several persons had been injured.

There was much arguing on both sides about who or what had been to blame for the accident. But there was a general tendency to believe that the helmsman of the *Pilot* was an evil person and that private revenge was at the bottom of it. The matter has been turned over to the law. [33-5]

The waterway from Wheeling to Pittsburgh is calculated to be ninety English miles. The Ohio has a rather swift current for this distance; below Wheeling this is not at all the case. During the last night we twice ran onto a sandbank, and it took several hours before we were afloat again.

Thirty-fourth Letter

Pittsburgh, 1 April 1827

The city of Pittsburgh (at the site of the former French Fort Du Quêne) has a splendid location at the fork of the Monongahela* and Allegheny rivers, which form the Ohio. The former comes from the south, the latter from the north, with charming valleys bordered by picturesque hills. Both are navigable for more than sixty English miles before their union. Their width at Pittsburgh is considerable; that of the Allegheny about twelve hundred feet, and that of the Monongahela two hundred feet more. Over each river there are beautiful covered bridges resting on stone pillars. Only there is a complaint that the bridge over the Monongahela is not at the right place; that it should have been built farther down, closer to the junction. I actually saw that men and beasts of burden were ferried across in boats in order to avoid the detour of half an English mile to cross the bridge. This can be explained only by the great industry in this region. This is the most important place for steamboat service in the entire interior. Here most steamboats are built, and this is also the center for the transportation of wares. The wares to be sent from the Atlantic coastal cities to the western regions are brought here (by land) to be sent on by steamboats or other means of transportation; and in reverse, many wares from the west reach the Atlantic coast by this route. The highway built from Baltimore to

---

*According to Warden, this word is derived from the Indian,[1] "Meck mon a wan getulak," which means a river with eroding banks.

Wheeling at the expense of the federal government has caused some loss to the city of Pittsburgh.[2] But there is probably far more to be feared from the projected railroads as well as from the canal to Lake Erie, which will join the Ohio at Portsmouth on the Scioto and is already half-finished. [34–1] I found fourteen steamboats here that were being loaded.

The city and its surroundings are full of iron factories, among them the strange rolling mills for the transformation of thick masses of iron into thin sheets which, in part, are cut into nails. Nearby there are inexhaustible coal mines, which are utilized with the greatest ease. To the stranger the all-pervasive coal fumes are annoying, and for this reason alone few persons would stay here long merely for pleasure. The population is said not to exceed ten thousand. Not far from the city, however, there are various smaller cities and hamlets, and agriculture flourishes there as much as industry.

The construction of steamboats has been brought to such a state of perfection that a vessel that cost twenty thousand dollars about ten years ago is now produced for six thousand. I saw people working on a small steamboat that had in its two cabins four bedsteads for ladies, twelve for men, and a storage room capable of holding 150 tons. The owner was asking something over five thousand dollars for it.

On the Mississippi and its tributaries there are only steamboats with so-called high pressure. The English consider them too dangerous, and a motion has even been made in Parliament to forbid their use. However the difference between the power of low pressure compared to that of high pressure is almost negligible. Also machines with high pressure need scarcely half as much fuel and take up far less space. This difference is so great that in an English steamship of three hundred tons there is less available space than in an American one of two hundred. The equipment with high pressure also does not seem to be as dangerous as it is believed to be in Europe. At least the Americans laugh at this great concern about it. The difference is due to the essential fact that machines with low pressure are propelled by the compression of water vapor. As soon as the cylinder is full of steam, a sudden cooling and condensation is caused by the cold water in an auxiliary mechanism. Thereby a vacuum is created in the cylinder and the piston is driven in by the external atmosphere. This power is always the same in every single machine because the pressure of the atmosphere undergoes only insignificant changes. The amount of power depends solely on the surface of the piston. It may amount to about eight to nine pounds per square inch. Later, to be sure, the use of outside air was completely discontinued in favor of a stream of steam, but not much more than is necessary to replace natural air pressure, so that the basic idea remains the same. Machines with high pressure, on the other hand, are propelled directly by the steam itself. It is said that here the power can be raised to more than a hundred fifty pounds per square inch of piston. The former method is more ingenious and was also invented later. But because of the advantages mentioned, they have returned to the simple one.[3] America already owns several steam men-of-war,[4] among them some that can expose themselves without danger to the strongest batteries because the side walls are so thick than no cannonball can penetrate them. The equipment with high pressure may or may not be dangerous, but England will find herself forced to adopt it, at least for the navy; otherwise all her *colossi* with a hundred and more cannons can do very little damage to the Americans. [34– 2]—The words *high pressure* and *low pressure* should moreover be translated as *strong* and *weak* pressure.—In the United States there are at present more than four hundred and fifty fully active steamboats [34– 3]; in Great Britain, not over a hundred and fifty.[5]

My trip to Lake Erie, from which I am now about a hundred to one hundred ten English miles away, will not materialize. The great New Yorker canal (from Erie to the Hudson River) is not expected to be free of ice before the end of this month of April.

Thirty-fifth Letter
Philadelphia, 26 April 1827

In about two weeks I shall leave America. In Baltimore I found a large, beautiful ship of more than four hundred tons, which is bound for Rotterdam and is now in the process of loading. It is called *Armata,* is known as an excellent sailing vessel, and the captain, Joseph Harwey [35– 1],[1] has a fine reputation. From New York ships sail almost daily for England; but Baltimore has more traffic with Holland than any other American city. Moreover, I had sent my baggage to Baltimore.

Excellent provisions have been made for connections between Baltimore, Philadelphia, and New York. During the summer, steamboats sail twice a day between these cities; in the winter only once provided, naturally, that ice does not prevent it. If one leaves Philadelphia at six o'clock in the morning, one will be in Baltimore or in New York at about five or six o'clock in the evening. The distance by water to Baltimore is about 120 English miles, and that to New York about 130. [35– 2] Both waterways are interrupted by narrow strips of land, however. [35– 3] From Philadelphia to Baltimore one travels by steamboat down the Delaware River to Newcastle in the state of Delaware.*

---

*The state and the river are named for Lord Delaware, who sailed toward these regions with 200 men in 1618 and died at sea. The Delaware River was first named the New Sweden River. The Delaware Indians call themselves Lenni Lenape (Aborigines).[2]

There, enough coaches are ready to transport the passengers without delay a distance of 15 English miles to Frenchtown (on the Elk River), where a second steamboat picks them up in order to convey them into and through Chesapeake Bay to Baltimore. This is accomplished within twelve hours. Provision is made for beds on the ship, which sails throughout the night. The total cost (including meals) amounts to five dollars. From Philadelphia to New York, which costs five dollars without meals,* the ship sails up the Delaware River to Trenton in the state of New Jersey. From there coaches transfer the passenger across an isthmus, which is about thirteen English miles wide, to the small river Rariton to meet another steamboat, which sails through Rariton Bay to New York. A second steamboat usually lands a short distance above Trenton, at Bordentown, where the former king of Spain, Joseph Napoleon, has settled. I came past his country estate. The soil is rather poor and the surrounding vegetation looks scanty. The buildings make no impression of luxury. Now they are of stone; the former wooden ones were destroyed by fire two years ago, it is said, together with many costly paintings.[3]

Philadelphia seen from the Delaware [35– 6] fulfills completely the conception of size and wealth that its reputation has given it in distant places. The population may be approximately a hundred thousand souls. [35– 7][4] It is built systematically throughout and has many attractive houses. It is divided by the long marketplace into two parts, a southern and a northern one, and most streets in both parts run parallel to this marketplace. They are numbered from east to west with ascending numerals. Locating dwelling places is thereby facilitated immensely. The designation of a house would therefore be as follows: No. 20 on 2d Street, south of the marketplace; or No. 20 on 3d (4th, 5th) Street, north of the market. The streets that cross those leading to the marketplace at right angles make some modifications, but these too are easily understood. The most remarkable building is the Bank of the United States. [35– 8] The front with its Doric columns was modeled after the Parthenon. Neither in the interior nor on the outside is there anything that could be destroyed by fire. Everything is constructed of stone or iron. Even the frames of the doors are of iron.

Very noteworthy also are the waterworks on the Schuylkill. In this small river there is a not unimportant waterfall,** about three English

---

*I learned shortly before the printing of these letters that the trip from Philadelphia to New York, a distance of 130 English miles [35-4], now costs only two dollars. This is due to the rivalry of several boats. During my stay in America, the competition once went so far that one steamboat transported travelers without charge and even presented each one with a bottle of wine. [35– 5]

**This fall is formed by a range of granite, of which Volney[5] speaks in his first volume, chapter 4, number 4. It says there that this granite ridge (in which the mica is very predominant) runs from the Hudson River in a southerly direction direct to North

miles from the city, which is used to drive large wheels that move a threefold pumping works and with the water of that river fill a basin that lies over eighty feet higher and is large enough to provide the whole city with water. Formerly the pumps were driven by steam engines. These works are very important for Philadelphia since there the wells cannot be used. This is due to a layer of black, stinking mire filled with bushes and tree trunks which one encounters at a depth of fourteen to eighteen feet.

What shall I tell you about New York? The whole world knows of its flourishing trade. Ships from all parts of the world arrive here daily. Here there is never any lack of opportunity to travel to northern, western, and southern European countries, to Asia Minor, to Africa, to the East Indies, to the West Indies, and to South America. For trade with foreign countries New York has a better location than Philadelphia. Its surroundings are also more appealing to the eyes. The high western banks of the Hudson [35– 9] (the North River), the hills of the nearby islands (Staten Island and Long Island) are covered with beautiful clumps of trees, friendly little towns, and country houses. Broadway (probably to distinguish it from Broad Street) runs from north to south through the entire city and is bordered by many splendid buildings. Its southern end is at the same time the end of the island (fifteen miles long and one mile wide) on which the city is built.* It has public parks extending to the harbor, which are good for strolling and afford charming views of the surrounding islands and the incoming and departing ships. There is nothing striking about the other streets. The inner section of Philadelphia is more beautiful. If a person likes excursions into the country, he will probably prefer Philadelphia; if he prefers water trips, New York will be his choice.—New York lives almost entirely for trade. In Philadelphia the sciences and the arts have more admirers.—The city hall of New York is by no means a model of good taste.[6] It is one of the unfortunate combinations of the new bourgeois architecture with the idealistic style of the Greeks.—The population of New York may surpass that of Philadelphia by twenty to twenty-five thousand souls. [35– 10][7]—It is well known that it was named for the Duke of York (brother and successor of Charles II of England). Formerly it bore the name New Amsterdam, and the city of Albany on the Hudson was called Orange. The Dutch were the first to settle in this region. In 1664 they were deprived of their rule by the English. However, I can hardly believe that in 1792 there was still significant evidence of Dutch customs in New York, as Bülow maintains. Now

---

Carolina, is almost five hundred miles long, and only two to six miles wide. The falls of the Potomac at Georgetown also owe their origin to it.

*The island is formed by the Hudson River, which divides above its mouth into the North River and the East River. It is called York or Manhattan.

there is no sign of them. The later growth of the population wiped out all traces.

In New York the inns are somewhat more expensive than in Baltimore and Philadelphia but not as expensive as in Amsterdam. In the first-rate inns in Philadelphia, for example, in the United States Hotel, which is opposite the beautiful Bank building, complete board costs one and a half dollars per day; in the City Hotel in New York, one and three-forths dollars. In the large cities every good hotel keeps a large number of newspapers for the guests. Besides the lounges, there are also special reading rooms for their convenience.

Thirty-sixth Letter

Helvoetsluis, 22 June 1827

I hasten to report to you my safe return. My trip to the United States took ten weeks, and now I have spent only twenty-nine days on the ocean in spite of an eight-day calm near the American coast. For seven days we were detained in Chesapeake Bay, which is often crossed within twenty-four hours.

About two hundred nautical miles from Land's End (the western tip of England) we were surrounded by more than forty large vessels, which were coming from South and North America, from the East and West Indies, and from the Mediterranean Sea. Here we had the pleasure of realizing that our ship was the best sailing vessel among them all. It floated with ease ahead of every other one. If a ship was about twenty miles ahead of us at sunrise, we had caught up with it by noon. The whole company watched its winged flight with wonder. It was built in New York. At night great caution was necessary to avoid ramming another vessel.

Even before the Scilly Islands we met pilots for Amsterdam and London, but throughout the entire Channel none for Rotterdam.[1] Fishing boats, which sold fresh vegetables in addition to fish and crabs, were everywhere.

About two hundred (English) miles west of the Channel, sea charts indicate the depth of the sea to be eighteen hundred feet, and here they first mention the bottom. From this the depth of the distant ocean, where there is never any mention of a bottom, can be inferred. As one approaches the Channel, the depth decreases to four hundred feet. In the Channel itself, there are few places where it is greater than two to three hundred feet.

The captain proved himself to be an experienced mariner. Using the customary calculation he had missed the length of the journey by only ten (English) nautical miles. To be sure, we had been spared any storms. But near the shores of Newfoundland we had sailed farther north than we had wished. Shortly before our departure from the port of Baltimore, it had been announced in the newspapers that an American sailor had seen many icebergs between the forty-ninth and fifty-second degrees of longitude (from Greenwich) and the forty-first and forty-third degrees of latitude. Among these degrees of longitude, we touched the fortieth degree of latitude and for twenty-four hours felt a cold that lowered the thermometer recording under the (natural) freezing point. Such a sudden change in temperature during the summer months is generally attributed to floating masses of ice. The current from the poles to the equator predominates during the summer, and this not infrequently brings the polar ice far toward the tropics. The main paths for this are near Newfoundland. Many a ship has sunk because of it. Usually the icebergs, which often rise several hundred feet out of the water, are veiled in fog, which greatly increases the danger. We had evidence of the ice only by the temperature.

We sailed close by the coasts of England. We saw Cape Lezard,[2] the regions of Falmouth and of Plymouth, and the foothills of Saint Alban, the Isle of Wight, the foothills of Beachy, and those of Dungerness, where the current was a great hindrance. Opposite Dungerness lies Boulogne, of which, however, we saw nothing. The French shore is generally too low to be seen at a great distance. We could distinguish only a few dunes. We passed the city of Dover at nightfall.

The captain, to be sure, had been in London, but never in a Dutch harbor. But with the aid of his excellent chart he came close to the west side of the island of Goree,[3] where we found a pilot. There we had to wait for the high tide, which made the passage over the shallows to Helvoetsluis possible the next morning. The course taken by large ships passes along the north side of the island. Here there are two places where the water is ten to twelve feet deep at low tide and eighteen to twenty feet deep at high tide. Our ship required fifteen feet. With the next high tide we were able to cross only the first shallows. In the meantime the water had fallen so much that we were forced to stop. According to maritime law the pilot replaces the captain during his time of service and the commands are then given by him alone. Our interim commander gave the order to cast the anchor before the speed of the ship had been decreased by the lowering of the sails It was not more than six English nautical miles [36– 1] (per hour) and yet it severed the half-foot (in diameter) cable like a piece of thread. This exposed us to the scarcely avoidable danger of being grounded. The pilot, who realized this most clearly, expressed his dismay without restraint. The sandbank was only about five hundred paces away and although the sails were speedily furled, we had every reason to fear the second anchor (with a weaker cable) could do just as little to counteract the power of the ship. To be sure, there were several other, smaller anchors, but they were too insignificant and therefore not in readiness. For our consolation we saw a large East Indian vessel, which after a quick, safe journey from the East Indies had met with the same fate that now threatened us. The masts projected out of the water like three crosses. Also the wreckage of two other ships could be seen. They had foundered two years before. At the most critical moment, the second anchor was cast, and we experienced the relief of seeing our dangerous course checked. However, if we had really been stranded, all lives would probably have been saved, as the sea was not very rough and the coast rather close. During a stormy sea, the shallows are dangerous even at greater depths, for the ships borne by the falling waves can approach the bottom in such a way that the keel is either broken or rammed into the mire and sand too firmly to be able to rise again quickly enough with the rising waves. In this way many a vessel is drawn into the depths.

Here in Helvoetsluis we shall take on another pilot who will pilot us to Gravendeel (two English miles from Dordrecht), which is considered the port of Rotterdam for large ships. We are now floating in quiet water and the hardships of the journey are at an end.

Concerning the
Nature of the North American United States
or
Concerning the
Bases of the Political Situation
of the North Americans

Introduction

Few people will be able to read these letters without being motivated to make a closer examination of the domestic and political condition of the Americans. At the conclusion, most of them will ask to what main causes the striking success of individuals and of the whole can actually be attributed, and which among the various factors should be considered the essential ones.

Certainly for years much has been printed about America that was worth reading, but one will nevertheless seek in vain for a comprehensive answer to this question.* Because of the research I had done on the differences in the states, which I mentioned in the Preface, I considered myself prepared to attempt it myself, and if my previous remarks have justified the expectation of an acceptable result, I hope that the following will also not be disregarded.

The purpose demands, however, that the presentation be concise. It would be easier for me merely to mention what was most important. Thus, to be sure, I could inform the reader of my opinion, but could by no means explain my reasons in such a way that he could make them his own. I could, for instance, say that the stability of the entire Union, as well as that of the individual states, depends entirely on the conduct of the citizens. There exists no power except theirs; on the contrary, legislative power, and through it all power, emanates equally from all individual citizens. As soon as the conduct of the citizens changes, legislation and therewith the entire political situation will have to change. Then I could say further that because about two-thirds of the population is farmers everything depends mostly on the conduct of the farmers. The conduct of the farmers again depends on their external situation, and finally the external situation depends on the relation of

---

*This is especially true of the publication by the American A. H. Everett entitled: "America, or a General Survey of the Political Situation of the Various States of the Western Continent." I shall refer to this again below. Here I merely remark that it is known to me only in the translation by Hoffmann and Campe, published in Hamburg in 1828.[1]

the population to the amount of land. To be sure, this train of thought will be evident in my presentation. But such a bare indication will satisfy only the person who is already familiar with the results. Brief explanations are of little help, and detailed ones would perhaps become longer than a methodical development, but certainly not more convincing.

In similar investigations one must not limit oneself to general hints, to a loose gathering of fragments of information. As convenient as such a treatment may be for comprehension, the area of research is not clarified thereby to the extent that it removes further doubt of the solution of the problem and permits the matter to be considered closed.

Accordingly, I am requesting the reader to forget those intimations and to follow the course of methodical development, beginning with the second section, and to pay close attention to the intrinsic connection because only thereby can the importance of the end result be determined. [C-1]

First Chapter

Posing of two main questions

If anyone seeks an explanation of a composite whole, he must examine the details of its parts. This principle certainly holds for the nature of the United States of North America. There is no power aside from that of the citizens of America. The condition of the whole is a product of family life. Therefore, if a person wishes to judge the United States of North America, he cannot avoid careful consideration of the characteristics of family life.

The various stages in the development of man, however, can be thoroughly comprehended only in their natural sequence, and in order to become acquainted with the stages of the development of men and their strivings, a mere observation of the present is entirely insufficient. Just as the present has developed out of the past, it can only be understood by studying the past.

Without violating these principles there is perhaps no shorter way for the necessary examination of the family life of Americans than by posing and answering the following two questions. [C-2]

First Question. How can pupils from contemporary Europe develop differently merely by being transplanted to the lands of North America?

Second Question. Besides that which is implied by the first question, what else has influenced the inhabitants of North America so that an essential difference between the development of North Americans and that of Europeans can be detected?

Obviously the purpose behind these questions is to divide the large field containing the solution of the problem into areas, which can in no way be avoided without complete confusion. [C-3]

Moreover, I believe that the words I have used outline the content definitely enough so that no explanation will be needed. [C-4] It will suffice to remind the reader of the Twentieth Letter. I merely repeat the warning to beware of the error of interpreting the expression "Pupils from contemporary Europe" as if the emigrations had been limited exclusively to individual classes. In order to remain close to the truth, one should rather assume that they had been carried out, as it were, by lot, without distinction, from all classes of society. This will avoid in particular the restriction to uneducated and poor people, which as I have said in more detail in the letter referred to applies only to the emigrations from Germany. In Germany up to the present only poverty has been able to effect what entirely different motives were able to bring about in Great Britain many years ago. [C-5]

Therefore I proceed immediately to answer the questions themselves, with which I shall begin in the next section. [C-6]

Second Chapter

*In answer to the second question
with a temporary deferment of the first*

The course of this discussion will show that it is advisable to occupy ourselves at first with the second question, and for the time being, defer the first. The area of the second question is much easier to survey, and it will therefore be to the purpose to assure ourselves by its examination that the solution of our problem is probably to be sought in the far more extensive area of the first question.

It is very well known to me what importance has been attributed in the written and oral [C-7] treatments of the political situation of the Americans to their legislation and to their statesmen. But the results of my investigation concerning the nature of the states are in conflict with this view, and anyone who has carefully examined these investigations will certainly agree with me if I answer the second question rather briefly with the following statement.

Neither the history of the colonization nor that of the separation from the mother country nor the history of all later political formation points to any influence (except that belonging to the area of the first question) that could develop in the characteristics of individual citizens that could not also be met with in Europe.

One should think that the political events of the last decades alone, aside from all more profound reasoning, had destroyed forever the dreams of the powerful effects of constitutional forms on the sense of freedom—if the publication of the American, Everett, had not recently proved the opposite. What the basis of this feeling of freedom is, I have shown in detail in my work on the differences between the states. There I have shown that it could become the basis of public order only by means of a high development of reasoning power. Before attaining such a stage of development, it would remain in its first stages, restricted to the expressions of other aims, for example, desires for individual pleasures. Also, it would reveal no independence, and perhaps, as in the case of children, lead to expressions of opinions merely because of willfulness. Later, however, with increasing development, it could produce first a lust for power. This wild passion would turn into a calm, circumspect striving for independence only through clearer insight (the fruit of constant thinking).

Mere freedom from political pressure does not in itself benefit human nature. This can be noted in so many primitive peoples—in American Indians and those of the South Sea islands. The difference between primitive people who live in political [C-8] slavery and those who are not subjected to it consists rather in the fact that in the former the sense of freedom is not only undeveloped, but has even been decreased. They have even become confused in regard to their inborn right to independence, which is expressed so unmistakably in every person whose spirit has not been crushed if one opposes it in order to arouse his will to enmity. [C-9] The comparison to nations enslaved has often misled people to see in others more than actually existed. One found pleasure in attributing the difference in the expression of a sense of freedom to the increase of mental powers in one nation instead of to the suppression of the spirit in the other. [C-10] Calm consideration of individual human characteristics will guard us against such errors. And this then leads to the realization that in the characteristics resulting solely from a higher education, Americans cannot be distinguished from Europeans; they are neither superior nor inferior to them. Especially the striving for independence in that rigid, uncompromising purity, which can provide the surest foundation for the States, has not been met with in America, to the present time, any more frequently than in Europe. [C-11]

It is the realization of this that has caused me to state that the political situation of Americans is based mainly on their fortunate external situation. The connection is easily seen. It requires only [C-12] a keener glance at the significance of the statement, which at the same time will also counteract the erroneous ideas to which the word *external* might give rise.

As far as the conduct of a person is dependent on the effects of [C-13] his environment, we say that the person himself is dependent on external things, and that the situation, which is a result of his conduct, is based on external things. Insofar as we consider his conduct and his situation dependent on fundamental principles, on norms of the mind that are fixed and not subject to the change in his environment [C-14], insofar do we speak of an inner cause.

Fixed norms of the human mind presuppose a superior education. Therefore the conduct of all people who lack this education is dependent almost completely on external influences [C-15], and everything that seems to be a result of their conduct is based almost entirely on the external situation.

If one may now assume that the political situation in North America [C-16] is actually a result of the conduct of such people, then its foundation must undoubtedly be attributed to external circumstances. It is clear, therefore, that it is finally a question of the justification of this assumption, which again depends entirely on the validity of the following two statements.

First, legislative and executive power derives equally [C-17] from all the citizens; it depends therefore completely on their conduct and, to be more specific, on the conduct of the majority. Second, the masses of Americans have, in regard to a higher education, no advantage over Europeans. If it therefore cannot be denied that the conduct of the majority of Europeans is determined less by prevailing mental norms than by their external conditions (by their surroundings), the same must necessarily be true of Americans. [C-18]

In the statement concerning the basis in external things, I by no means intended to point to the protection that is given to Americans against attacks by foreign nations by the isolation of their country and by its forests and mountains. [C-19] If it is a question of discussing the factor of safety, this must be well considered. But my words referred only to the inner situation, to the relation of the citizen to the executive power. Since this relation is founded on the conduct of the citizens, it is clear that we can speak of external things here only insofar as they influence human conduct.

The present section is to serve as a preparation for the following one. Its purpose is to show where the lever of national power is *not* to be sought; and in its negative direction it is rather well adapted to banish the usual vague ideas of political miracles. I wish to direct the full attention of the reader to the important truth that all phenomena in the conduct of human beings, which without finer distinction are called phenomena of order and moderation, are always derived from the reciprocal effects of two factors. One factor is human nature, the other is environment. One can chiefly attribute the phenomena to the first factor only insofar as something independent has developed in it. If this has not happened, then the chief importance is placed on the other factor. Within the range of these alternatives everything is included that is to be considered in the examination of the political situation of Americans. With this idea in mind, as a preparatory step, one should now consider my statement concerning the culture of Americans. Then it will become clear that the political difference between their country and European countries is not to be found in the flowering of a higher intellectual [C-20] development. Characteristics of a high cultivation of the mind, which differ greatly enough in their aims and actions from the mere semblance of it, are as rare in America as they are in Europe. [C-21] One cannot attribute the advantages of the United States to a larger number of intellectuals, not even to the greater influence of intelligent minds. Only a fool can doubt that the cultivation of the mind produces an elevating influence there. [C-22] But whatever gives it this influence differs from the cultivation itself, and it is just this on which the situation of the American nation is truly based. One cannot attribute the blessings of the new land to the wisdom of a Lycurgus or a Pythagoras. In nothing that statesmen have done for North America is there the slightest evidence of anything that could give to the innermost development of man a definite direction different from that of the European nations. [C-23] Their efforts for the public welfare were undeniably of great importance and perhaps as highly effective as the total conditions, as the nature of the given subject permitted. [C-24]

But it is a great mistake to declare them to be the actual causes of the present political situation. To repeat once more, since in the United States power derives from the masses, since the votes of individual citizens create and maintain the state institutions, that which keeps the majority on the beaten track of order must also be considered the main basis of general order. And precisely because the conduct of this majority is more dependent on external influences than on prevailing norms of the mind the state has its foundation chiefly in external things. On the other hand, the few persons who, animated by loftier aims, work for the preservation and ennoblement of society appear only as secondary supporters. However important their influence may be on the separate actions of the nation, they have to avoid any conflict with the efforts of the masses. Everything that is to succeed must be represented as corresponding to the aims of the masses, for the unveiled demands of loftier aims will be accepted only by those of a higher culture.

So much concerning the second question. As I have said, the answer had only a negative function by stating where the solution of our problem was *not* to be sought. But the discussions chosen for this purpose have really supplied a positive statement, namely that the foundation of the political situation of Americans must consist in keeping the majority within the bounds of order and moderation, and that this can be nothing but the external situation. We should not let this distract us from the line of my argument. One could think that the continuation of the investigation would demand that we now proceed immediately to the examination of the external situation of the Americans. [C-25] If one recalls, however, that the external situation is of importance only insofar as the conduct of the citizens depends on it, it might soon become apparent that in such an examination it depends chiefly on keeping human nature constantly in mind (as that which is affected by the situation). Then a slight postponement and roundabout method of procedure would seem less tedious. With that I am requesting the reader to assume that the area of one of the two questions has been investigated without results and that we shall now have to turn to the other area all the more decisively.

Third Chapter

Narrowing the field of the first main question

As you will remember, the first main question was what could become of the pupils from contemporary Europe merely by transplanting them to North America.

To be sure, the field still seems to me rather extensive if one thinks of the manifold directions and occupations of the various immigrants; and the attempt to find a satisfactory answer may at first be rather difficult. The difficulties will disappear as soon as one recalls the purpose for which the question was posed and considers that this must guide us so that we do not roam around in vain in this wide field. [C-26]

The purpose of the question, however, is no other than to become acquainted with the nature of the political situation of Americans. We found this situation so different [C-27] from the situation of European nations that the general conclusion could [C-28] not be avoided that there was a specific cause for this. It has already been shown in the previous section that this cause could consist only in whatever influences the majority of the citizens to maintain a conduct that supports the public order. [C-29]

Accordingly, the question itself can be restated as follows: "What influences the majority of the citizens, or the family life of the majority, so specifically that it makes their conduct so different from that of the majority of Europeans?" [C–30]

This restatement should now be supplemented by the statement that the families [C–31] of farmers outnumber all the other families almost threefold. With this in mind an investigator will involuntarily turn his attention to the former; a more exact consideration of nonfarmers can only justify this more and more. [C–32]

Nonfarmers are largely merchants, craftsmen, and artists. Most of them live along the seacoasts and in important cities. No one will discover any significant difference between them and Europeans of the same class. An American merchant carries on his business like a European, and this business life prescribes a direction for him and his entire family. A similar condition holds for craftsmen and artists, insofar as they do not concern themselves with agriculture.

Those citizens who make their living by agriculture, who utilize the soil of the new country, are the real supporters of the present political situation. [C–33] As soon as the conduct of the American farmer deteriorates, this living support of the Union as well as of the individual states will give way. Therefore investigating the foundation of the present* political situation is synonymous with investigating the reason for this conduct.

The question of what could become of the pupils from contemporary Europe merely by transplanting them to America is finally limited to the question of what effect the American country life has on these pupils.

In the first section it was mentioned that the words *pupils from Europe* (in order to keep close to the actual emigrations) should be interpreted

---

*Whoever investigates the former political life will, with the guidance of the following sections, realize quite easily what a favorable influence the growing preponderance of agriculture has exerted.

to be applicable only to such persons as one ordinarily meets in Europe, in the country, and also in the cities. [C– 34] The content of the second section, however, justifies us in disregarding the products of a high culture. It teaches that the main foundation of the United States of America is not to be sought in the aims of clear insight, because there also a high degree of mental development can be found in only a few, and in this aspect conditions are no better in America than they are in Europe. And given the more limited framework of the above-mentioned question it obviously permits one to abstract even from a sporadically high culture. Accordingly, people whose conduct (under the influences of American country life) is to be investigated are sufficiently characterized, and the question is put in the form required for reaching an understanding with the reader.

Nothing more can be said now concerning the outer limits of the investigation. The following concerns the heart of the matter as it has been defined for the present.

Fourth Chapter

Concerning the inner nature of the
area of the first main question

According to the previous chapter our next task is to become acquainted with the influence [C– 35] of American country life on Europeans, that is, such Europeans as one usually meets in the cities and in the country, exclusive of individuals of high development.

With regard to the full [C– 36] meaning of the words *high development* I must refer you to my work on the essential differences between the states. In general one can find the more fundamental bases of my statements about the nature of the American states in that more general work. Here I must limit myself to quotations concerning the results obtained. [C– 37]

If one seeks information about the actions of men, one must study their driving forces. [C– 38] If one wishes to judge the conduct of human beings in certain surroundings, one must, before inquiring into their environment, study the people themselves and investigate their receptivity in general in order to determine by what motives their aims can be directed; one must investigate their aspirations.

This is completely applicable to our problem. In order to solve it methodically and to arrive finally at a clearer understanding, let us isolate [C– 39], for the present, a simple German farmer from the mass of emigrants, a farmer who has enjoyed perhaps no or only little formal schooling. Let us not disdain to devote some time to the study of such a person and examine especially those aspects of his nature that influence his aims and his actions. [C– 40]

First, let us consider his instinct for self-preservation; second, his individual physical instincts; third, his attachment to other human beings; fourth, his sensitivity to praise and criticism; fifth, his sense of freedom; sixth, his conception of higher beings, especially the hopes and fears connected with them.

The striving to reach a higher state of perfection will, except for slight response to praise and criticism, become effective only when connected with the conception of God's will, as if there existed a direct command from God. This must be true especially in the case of remorse. This remorse will consist less in an inner dissatisfaction with one's self than in the fear of a punishing God. However, we must not forget how strictly church religion [C–41] and politics are separated in the United States and that the influence of priests of all confessions carries very little weight in external considerations. A theocratic guidance of families therefore is completely out of the question.

In regard to the effects of the sense of freedom I refer you to the second chapter.

After a slight effort the reader will soon realize that one has not much reason to hope to discover a calm, ruling inner principle that would be the basis of the aspirations of such an individual just described.

Only a successful occupation gained from the environment can (disregarding threatening external evils) make it possible for the weak influence of the as yet very dim guiding star, gleaming in the background of the conception of higher beings, of the striving for perfection, and of the general interest in the lot of mankind, to maintain its leading role.

In persons of a similar type [C–42] almost everything depends on external conditions, on external influences. The weaker the inner guiding principle is, the more power impulses have. They can endure the difficult tests of trouble as little as those of good fortune. Both will destroy them.

A situation that will satisfy the physical demands without increasing them, that offers a rewarding or at least an unrepulsive sphere of activity to the desire for an occupation, that is innate in every healthy body, without giving free reign to the intoxication of wild desires and hopes—a situation that offers an abundance of innocent pleasures in rural surroundings, and at the same time keeps them away from the sphere of vanity, ambition, and desire for power—it is this which is suitable for human beings whose inner guiding star sends out only faint beams.*

---

*It would be digressing too much from my purpose if I wanted to show in detail why a domestic and political life similar to that found in the United States could not flourish in the Spanish and Portuguese parts of America. Aside from the nature of the colonists themselves and their religious and political relations with their mother country, the products of the land itself, especially the precious metals, had to produce different results.

The more reality deviates from it, the worse is their behavior. To be sure, wealth is a great danger to them, but poverty presents a far more difficult test. I shall speak more about this later. For the present it is more to the purpose to remember my experiences in North America and to recall what that country offers our simple farmer who meets those conditions of good conduct. [C– 43]

When I touch upon this subject, it is always with the fear that I will be thought guilty of exaggeration because I have things to report that in Germany have always been a part of the fairy-tale world. [C– 44] I am speaking of the interior of America, especially of the Mississippi territory, not of the coastal cities. If a person has been only on the Atlantic coast, and not beyond the Allegheny Mountains, he knows very little of the abundance that nature offers in the United States. To be sure, European povery is not found on this side of the Alleghenies either, but good soil costs perhaps more there than in Germany and without a considerable fortune nothing of first quality can be acquired, although if the land has once been paid for, it will surely afford a living to its owner. Because of the moderate taxes and the few hindrances to trade and industry, tracts of land in the Atlantic states are under cultivation that in Germany always remain untouched. I saw many such tracts in Pennsylvania from Pittsburgh to the coast. Rocks adjoined rocks, so that a plow could not be used, and yet the spaces between them had been sown and the whole fenced. Other fields were full of small pieces of a reddish clay-slate without any humus; and yet by means of fertilization, a harvest was reaped from this ground, on which, however, not much could be paid to the state in taxes.

The inhabitants of these infertile places, mostly of German descent, spoke of the distance from Mississippi areas as one speaks in western Europe of Asiatic countries.

When I say that the inhabitants of the Mississippi areas are fortunate, I am not speaking of the recent immigrants from Europe. What applies to those is entirely foreign to the natives. I am speaking only of the lot of the latter when I say that all the conditions for successful farming are fulfilled there. Anyone who manages his farm with some degree of skill enjoys an abundance of the best food. No one worries about a roof over his head or protection against the cold of winter. The cheap soil is so excellent that no one with any judgment would dare to complain about laborious cultivation. Cattle, horses, and hogs require neither care nor stables, and they forage for all their feed in the forests and meadows. The climate is mild and pleasant, and there is so much space that for persons without means there are enough attractive tracts on state property where they can live a carefree life without ever purchasing land.

That is the reason a laborer's pay is so high. There are enough people, but all can easily make a living. The pay must be in relation to what

nature herself offers for their services; otherwise they will give preference to nature. The cheapness of food is not due to the lack of a market
for it, but to the extreme ease of producing it.

Just as the father made his domestic arrangements with little effort, it
also costs the son little to do the same without the support of relatives.
An ax and a mattock are sufficient to enable him to establish a homestead in five to six months that will provide ample nourishment for him
and his family. If a person has no means at all, he works for others until
he can acquire a horse, a couple of cows, a couple of sows, and a plow.
This can be done in a single year, since work can be found everywhere at
an annual rate of sixty to seventy dollars.

If a person would consider the good fortune to be acquired by these
means to be insufficient, let me inform him that in the states west of the
Allegheny Mountains one can maintain with three to six thousand
dollars a standard of living that in Germany would surely not be
possible with twelve to twenty thousand. But why all this repetition?
My letters make it unnecessary to give any further details. [C–45]

This is the foundation of the calm conduct of Americans. It is easy
enough to see how such conditions can make the masses of the emigrants into respectable citizens since they offer a remedy even for
serious moral damages that at least prevents their inheritance by children and grandchildren. [C–46]

To be sure, one can raise objections to these observations by saying
that the emigrants, especially the Irish, Scotch, and English, beginning
with the very first settlement, included many persons who in opinions
and inclinations differed greatly from a simple German farmer. But one
must consider that I began with the latter only so that it will be realized
how much in need he is of even external conditions. If the majority of
immigrants were of poor stock, then the present situation of the whole,
the cause of which we are examining, speaks all the more strongly for
the effects of the fortunate environment that I have described.

It is true that aside from the original mixture, the usual instruction in
the lower schools has also spread gradually throughout the entire
population. Extremely easy business dealings, frequent travels and
changes of residence,* and finally participation in state government,
together with an interest in political publications, have brought about
customs and habits, in the interior as well as along the coasts, in the
cities as well as in the country, that Europeans habitually connect with
other than purely rural inclinations and wishes. The education that has
thus developed must, if it is to be judged of a certain level, perhaps be
put in the same class as the semi-education so popular in Europe.

---

*While change of residence is frequently the result of instability and a lack of
perseverance as well as of the attraction of the hunter's life, it can far more often be
attributed to a laudable industry in the founding of new homesteads.

[C– 47] But its influence on aims and actions is so different from the European form that one is completely justified in speaking of special types. The following remarks will deal with this in more detail.

If a person wishes to judge the true character of the education of a man, he will find it only in his aims. As for the rest, appearances are deceiving. Differences in aspirations are closely and inevitably connected with the various stages of education. Here the maxim By their fruits shall ye know them applies. The less a person is imbued with the truth, the less it is a part of his thinking, the less influence it has on his aims. However clearly the words may be impressed on his memory, the truth itself is therefore no more a part of him than if he merely possessed it in a book.

With this as an introduction, let me urgently request the reader to ponder how the so-called educated man in Europe usually differs from the simple farmer.

His memory has been enriched with all kinds of material through schooling or social intercourse. Perhaps he feels sorry for the poor man who still believes the earth to be immovable, who has never heard of Copernicus or Newton. He talks of polar and tropical lands, of the nations of the present and of the past. He knows how to designate the objects of his environment in several languages. He praises the art of poetry, professes a love for music, for painting, and for sculpture. He is physically trained and well versed in everything that is considered important in so-called good society.

Unfortunately, we experience everyday how little such things can be relied upon as a guarantee for the ennoblement of one's inner nature. It remains a part of the shell and does not give to a mind that is torn by violent urges the support [C– 48] that the preservation of a harmonious unity requires. We see it all too clearly when we observe what effect the danger of poverty, or poverty itself, has on the majority of such students of culture when we see how they react to good fortune or to the temptations of ambition and the desire for power. How many come to ruin when faced with even the simplest tests of ordinary life, if greed, vanity, revenge, or physical desires come into conflict with friendship, trustworthiness, or compassion.

As a result of a similar development, the bodily desires will seem to increase by new stimulations. The attachment to people will lead to rapturous aberrations because of awakened ideals. Only the stronger power of a complete image of God in the human mind (which becomes evident only after more profound thinking) can control the individual rays that attract us to objects of the sensuous world. Where this image is lacking there will scarcely be a firm guiding principle that will counteract the sensuous desires, let alone the power of ideals. Thus even the most glorious companions of mankind in this cloudy human field can cause many contrary aberrations. This is particularly true of the sense of honor, insofar as it is based on the striving to attain a higher level of perfection. So-called education will stimulate without guiding, and the striving for perfection will turn into vanity or ambition because of a lack of clarity of mind. A latent sense of freedom will likewise be awakened, but its independent activity can only express itself in a desire for power. The greatest evil of a semi-education becomes evident when it substitutes for the fear of God doubt in the existence of God himself. In such a case there is no hope for a substitute in the inner guidance to become more perfect by striving. [C– 49]

Obviously people of such a nature need a protective environment far more than the simple farmer. Their salvation demands still more urgently a sphere of action that invites them to engage in an occupation.

However, let no one be tempted by the similarity of the word to attribute this character to the education of Americans. It applies only to Europeans and in America perhaps only to the inhabitants of the coastal cities. Although an idyllic innocence seems incompatible with the given bases for the culture in the interior of the United States, it is nevertheless [C– 50] a comforting truth that all that is bad is overwhelmingly overshadowed by good. The critic must be reminded emphatically that practical life has the greatest influence on the culture of Americans. It is a product of their enterprising activity and on the whole serves it; whereas in Europe the reverse is true. There, culture is almost totally a product of instruction in schools, or at least through books, and because of its separation from external life must cause manifold contradictions and aberrations on one side as well as on the other (the ideal and the realistic).

Where the population forces the individual to apply all his activity [C– 51] to the demands of the market, he will soon be limited very closely by competition to his own special business, and everything else will become unfamiliar to him. The market is supplied with good wares, but men themselves sink to the level of machines. Whoever is more interested in the value of a human being than in the abundance of objects of luxury must approve of a situation that permits more manifold activity, whether the market gains by it or not. A ruler capable of utilizing the intellectual and physical powers of a great nation arbitrarily for his own purposes could accomplish things on this earth that will never come about as long as every individual is acting in his own way. But the question here is: Are such things to be regarded more highly than that which develops in the person himself through a freer activity? If all external objects are of value only insofar as human nature attributes value to them, it is surely contradictory in matters concerning the welfare of mankind to praise the condition of a nation only because it furnishes good and cheap wares to the market without reference to the condition of the individual. I would not write so much on this subject if travel reports that made deceptive claims to thoroughness had not mentioned it as a disadvantage of the United States that it is so easy to change from one occupation to another. This, they imagine, necessarily results in shoddy work. But this is precisely the great advantage of Americans, that they are not, as the machinelike people of Europe, limited to a single trade; that they may leave it, without danger of starving to death. It is just this freedom of activity that prevents the horrible distortions that result from the monotonous life of the manual worker in Europe. That is an advantage that is common to every American. [C– 52] But some of the inhabitants of the coastal cities know how to take advantage of it as little as any foreigner. I know merchants who after unsuccessful experiences in business subsist in the coastal cities in poverty, although the rest of their fortune would be more than enough to offer them the best situation in the interior.

Just because in Europe the activity of the individual is limited to such a small territory, because what I am reporting here about the conditions of the Americans sounds like a dream, therefore practical life cannot educate especially. Therefore, farmers in Germany, for example, where public schools are as well provided as in America, are in general far behind American farmers.

On the other hand, schooling in Europe may be criticized in that it stimulates the intellectual [C– 53] powers without being able to offer them a sphere of activity. Thus an unfortunate conflict originates between the demands of the mind and the limitation of the world, in which so many people (who would be worthy of a better lot) work themselves to death. It is common in Germany that in the schools historical paintings and the deeds of the greatest men are set up as examples to youth, and soon afterward they are sentenced for their entire lives to situations (called their occupations) that are a mockery of everything that is ideal.

Here there is a twofold tragedy.

On one hand: The instruction is completely inadequate. More inclinations and desires are awakened without developing the judgment needed to direct them. And this can undeniably be done only at an age long before which, at the present time, education must have been completed. The other evil is that although persons who have enjoyed such an education are most of all in need of an attractive occupation to be protected from aberrations in their striving after the ideal, scarcely enough playgrounds can be established in Germany without arousing concern about public order. And yet far more restrictive are the harmful prejudices that, from the time of the migration of the Germanic tribes up to the most recent times, have adversely affected occupations in Europe. This is especially true of the physical work involved in agriculture. Such work is not refined enough for the cultured European. Tradition, controlled by arrogance, asks little about health and mental serenity, or whether nature herself has vested more dignity in one occupation than in another. She would soon answer that work of any kind, insofar as it is done merely for reasons of external gain, enjoys no preference at all over the others.

An American is free of this folly. His situation has raised him above such an attitude and continues to protect him from it. One should remember how well prepared he is to cope with his country, how easy it is for him to win rewards from the rich store that creation offers to skilled activity. In this lies the true reason for his independence. It is this which protects him from any kind of servitude. No hunger controls an occupation here. Poverty makes slaves. The lack of the necessities of life on the one hand and abundance on the other produce submissive servants and arrogant masters. Where family life produces such conditions, one must not be surprised to find political slavery. In order to realize this truth more clearly, let us transport some individuals from European cities, people of so-called culture, to rural America. I wonder how their education will react there? Their awkwardness will soon seek comfort and help in their prejudices. Most of them will disdain the farm work of the Americans as unworthy of an educated person, and will long to return to their clerical work, to their trades, and their offices. Rather than accustom themselves to various activities that promote physical and mental health on their own beautiful property, they will prefer the most menial indoor work because it be done without one's being seen at it, or because they enjoy some sort of respect among the thoughtless crowd. To acquire riches quickly in order to be admired and envied by dwarfed minds in Europe—that is and has been in general the aspiration of emigrants of this type.

I hope that these pages will provide better information about the situation in the United States than is possible to gain by means of mere statistical reports. [C-54]

The conclusion to which I came, then, was that the final cause of the fortunate situation of Americans is to be sought in external nature. [C-55] In the following chapters we shall become acquainted with the most dangerous enemy of this good fortune, the enemy which of all of them most assuredly threatens it with failure. This is no other than overpopulation, an evil that has covered all of Europe with poisonous boils and yet is foolishly acclaimed as the highest goal of all aspirations.

Fifth Chapter

Concerning the security of the political situation of North Americans and the effectiveness of their political power

In the preceding chapters I have shown on what foundation the political condition of Americans rests. But in order to judge the security of this situation as well as the effectiveness of the power inherent in it (the federal power), it is necessary to study the characteristics of the foundation itself more closely than I have done so far.

We have seen that the whole depends on the relation of the farmer to his external situation.* In order to come to a valid conclusion about the nature of this relationship, one must present its two aspects anew. We must first consider what is important in the nature of the farmer concerning this relationship and then examine what is the essential factor in the other aspect, namely the external situation. The content of the fourth chapter will lead us in this respect to the following:

The farmer looks upon the exclusive possession of a definite tract of land as the condition of his existance.

One could now add briefly that such an interest would be based on self-preservation. But that will not aid in this investigation. For this striving is nothing else but a product of all relations that seem to be connected with earthly existence and by no means a real instinct that is a part of human nature. Therefore, in order to measure its strength, one must examine individually the relations based on the peculiarities of human nature.

In the fourth and fifth chapters of the third part of my work on the essential differences between the states will be found statements concerning the influence of permanent homes, of life in the family circle and in rural surroundings, which should be related to the content of the preceding chapter. From this it will be seen, among other things, that the preference for certain places on earth, which is the basis of love for one's country, may not be disregarded here. [C-59]

The physical instincts and the attachment of the individual members of the family to each other are the factors that generally increase and make effective the interest in landed property.

A sense of freedom will be a part of this interest only in a limited

---

*It would add to the completeness of this study to consider at the same time the aims of other citizens besides the farmers, namely the aims of merchants, artisans, and officials. [C-56] None will be found that are different from those among the farmers because their education and manner of living are not entirely different. The desire to rule, ambition, ruthless greed, and on the other hand, unselfish striving for the betterment of mankind will, to be sure, be found relatively less among the farmers, but will not be entirely lacking. What justifies me, however, in leaving to the reader, in general, the observations concerning the effects of such forces in the United States of America is that, for the present, they play only a subordinate role [C-57] and do not even deserve to be considered secondary bases. It would be a great mistake to interpret these words to mean that there is no decided interest in the present political situation among merchants, artisans, and officials. Everyone seeks to adapt his aspirations as well as possible to the present situation, and the more successful he is in this, the happier he will be. In North America merchants do not shape the public order. [C-58] But because of the fact that many have made their interests coincide with it, it had to become dear to them also, even though it might not have anything appealing to them in itself.

sense, and in case it should express itself independently it will nevertheless appear only as a desire for power.

Likewise the striving for perfection will, on the whole, restrict itself to the field of the same interest and will modify the aims resulting from it; but the basic ideals will not have sufficient clarity and strength to produce an independent aim. It will appear in independent form only as vanity or ambition. Except for this aberration, it will produce an effect more or less in connection with the fear of God and thus determine especially (aside from actual affection) the general interest in the lot of humanity.

As far as the other factor of the relation is concerned, it should be considered to what extent the external situation meets the aforementioned interests of the farmer, to what extent it is favorable to his main interest: the desire for the possession of a tract of land. [C-60]

It will seem favorable to him according to his nature, insofar as it is favorable for supplying him with his physical needs, for the comforts of life—his own life as well as the lives of those persons who are dear to him (who appear as his dependents).

These are the main considerations. They are concerned with a comfortable life in a family circle.

Then, in using the word *favorable* it must be considered whether and to what extent a farmer will have to suffer for such a life: (1) from the point of view of the general interest in the lot of mankind (because of compassion); (2) in the sense of freedom; (3) in the sense of honor, in general in the striving for a certain value, which is the basis of this feeling (the striving for perfection); and (4) in his religious conceptions.

One should notice the words *must suffer*. I wish to indicate hereby that the emotions of nos. 1, 2, 3, and 4 can be effective only negatively, without setting up positive aims.

The positive demands are limited to those main considerations, and if, therefore, there is nothing hostile opposed to the negative emotions, the strength of the bond linking the farmer to the external situation must generally depend on what this situation offers for the comfortable existence of the family for the present, and what it promises for the future.

If one now, after such preliminary statements, considers how I have reported the situation of the farmer [C-61] in the United States, the simple conclusion follows that the majority of the inhabitants undertake great exertions only insofar, will make great sacrifices only insofar, as dangers of a disadvantageous change seem to threaten them. In general they will be willing to make only such sacrifices as the preservation of the present situation requires. The entire Union derives its great power from the consideration for the family life that I have described. [C-62]

The majority of the citizens limit their concern to their own families;

therefore it is often difficult for the statesman who would like to work toward higher goals to arouse sufficient interest. [C-63] I say "sufficient," for we must not forget that every citizen has a voice. If anyone wishes to draw conclusions from this that are unfavorable to the spiritual status of the people [C-64], he must first ask himself whether more could be accomplished with the masses of the people in European countries than is actually being done in North America. Then he will at least refrain from casting aspersions.

If one wanted to attack the Americans, or rather, if anyone wanted to wage war with the American farmers, he would find his greatest opponent in the values of a comfortable existence, and the sense of freedom (with few exceptions) merely within the framework of these considerations. Hostility would be felt by the citizens only insofar as they might be disturbed in the details of their lives. In the case of a prohibition, for example, their complaints would usually be limited to the loss of an individual privilege of which they might thereby be deprived. The unpleasant feeling of limited independence would, to be sure, not be lacking entirely, but it would not be separated from the specific case and enter into the ranks as an enemy in itself. [C-65]

Only in those persons whose intellectual power is so highly developed that it feels its mission is to rule does one find a constant resistance to all arbitrariness. The effectiveness of striving for independence is determined exactly by the effectiveness of striving to be dependent solely on intellectual power. If the dominance of intellectual power is weak, if, in other words, it is not sufficiently conscious of its own significance, it if does not respect itself highly enough, then the disrespect expressed by a third person cannot be felt as so disagreeable as long as another phase of human nature is not attacked at the same time. The latter, however, is the case as soon as disrespect changes to contempt, because contempt directly denies all value and thereby necessarily violates the general striving to maintain one's existence and the sense of honor as a whole in its two fundamentals.* In the prohibition or order that has no other purpose [C-66] than to antagonize the will, there is such an attack. Thereby not only the striving for independence is counteracted but also the feeling of intrinsic worth, on which alone we base the claim to coexistence and independence. The strong feeling that results from a similar hostility is then also to be attributed more to the reaction of the sense of honor which has been attacked than to the striving for independence. Through the attack on the reason he demands its consideration by his fellowmen, man only then becomes conscious of this striving as a characteristic belonging to intellectual power without any relation to his fellowmen.

---

*See: *Concerning the Essential Differences Between the States,* part 2, title 2, chapter 3, and title 3, chapter 5.

Since orders or prohibitions [C-67] that are directed against the will merely as such (which, as one says, are supposed to break the will) affect the sense of honor so much, one must not be surprised at a violent reaction if a similar command even demands an action that in itself is contrary to self-respect. The hat placed on a pole by the provincial governor Gessler belongs in this category.[2] Insults of this kind had to enrage the Swiss people more than all the oppression of greed.

After this discussion it can easily be understood that a hierarchy must be far more offensive to the citizens of the United States than rulership. For everyone of them realizes that a ruling government, as such, is indispensable, and also that the most irritating misuse of it consists in the violation of the self-respect of the governed. The benefit of mere rank, on the other hand, seems to them not only very doubtful, but at the same time a degradation of those without rank, which in itself can be counted among such violations.

A [C-68] hierarchy is sufficiently different from the gradation of a ruling power in itself. A rank due to the power of an office is limited closely to the administration of that office. [C-69] Therefore a person possesses rank only insofar as it is an intrinsic part of the individual official administrative acts. People whom legislation regards as being consistantly engaged in administrative acts seem to have a personal rank. [C-70] But that also is nothing more than illusion. The idea of rank is associated with them because the office cannot be conceived of without rank. In the United States there is no rank other than that of the office in the sense in which I have explained it.

Nevertheless the majority of North Americans oppose the idea of rank almost instinctively. For only a specially trained mind will understand ideas that, as it were, unclearly form a foundation, and only it is able to realize their true relation to the political situation as a whole. [C-71] This explains why decisions are sometimes made that favor rank. This would not happen if all the voters understood clearly what is presented to them for consideration. However I do not believe that the Order of Cincinnatus would not be approved.[3] Forty years ago the situation in America was different. At that time there could be no thought of a majority of farmers. The order is undoubtedly also in conflict with the constitution and its purposes as proclaimed from the beginning. [C-72] The explanation of the conferers of rank, that the advantages should be limited to certain points, is completely powerless against the general effect of the honor bestowed. It does not counteract the inner claims, which are based on the acknowledgment of a higher value. Where rank causes a change in one's own opinion, it also produces secret claims that only await a favorable opportunity to become active. Within the framework of a culture such as is spread over the United States, where there is so little rabble, mere rank offers only a slight reward for true service. Intelligent people pay little attention to it.

It therefore grants them far less than it withholds from those without rank. Only unimportant people are won by it; on the other hand, a large number of able ones are repulsed by it.

According to the purpose that I set for myself in this section, I have now (a) designated the aims (interests) to be considered; (b) indicated their direction; furthermore, (c) it is evident how the situation of Americans is related to them; from these followed (d) the limits of the effectiveness of their executive power, and also (e) how the power within these limits can then be easily estimated. For that purpose one must consider that while the increase of fanaticism (by means of which conquerors and theocrats seek to attain their ends) remains foreign to the main interest in itself, there does exist a calm thoughtfulness that is based on the clear conviction of the importance of that interest. Because an American judges the value of his life according to this interest, he will, in an extreme case, risk his life for it and in despair even willingly sacrifice it. Finally (f) as far as the permanence of such a political foundation is concerned we must again consider both factors of the relationship in order to examine the changeability of each factor itself. This last test is of great importance for legislation.

As long as the external situation remains as it is, the change in the relationship will depend solely on the change of the other factor, namely on the change in the nature of the American farmer. But it cannot be said vice versa that as long as the nature of the farmer remains unchanged, the relationship depends on the change of the external situation. We have seen in the former sections that the nature of the farmer [C-73] himself is controlled by the external situation, that no change of his situation is possible without a change in his nature. As soon as the external situation changes, the other factor will also change, and the change of the relationship is then a result of the change of both factors. Therefore the relationship is not restored merely by the reverse change of one factor.

First, a few words about the change in the nature of the American farmer insofar as it can occur without a change in his external situation.

There will be no chance of a detrimental wealth without a change of the external situation. Wealth exists only in juxtaposition to poverty, because only through the need of those who suffer want does abundance attain the great importance that is otherwise attributed to it neither by the owner nor by others who themselves live in a state of plenty. However there are none here who suffer want, and the consequences of riches, together with the consequences of poverty, therefore belong to the phenomena of a changed external situation.

We must think of the level of culture of the American farmer. It is by no means of the type that would protect him from a deterioration of morals. Bad examples presented in publications or in life, fanaticism of any kind, vanity, ambition, and love of power can have the most adverse effects. The external situation does not offer complete safety from them. However it does have so much effect that without a change, only an unfortunate, but not probable, combination of unfavorable events could create any concern. This is all the more comforting since no direct procedures are to be expected. Legislation is in the hands of the people, and individual citizens will not consider themselves so weak as to require tutelary arrangements. I say "direct"; naturally, the influence of excellent statesmen can make use of other considerations of the citizens to found institutions designed to improve the morals of the people. There is, however, no hope at all for a truly national education.

In the states where slavery is permitted, the outlook is worse. The culture of the masters of the slaves cannot satisfactorily cope with the evils resulting from slavery. The dangers that threaten merely from the increase in the number of slaves belong to the study of the external situation. But the remark is apropos here that the adverse influence of slavery on the morals of the slave owners can be counteracted only by national education and special institutions for the supervision of morals, and the citizens of North America will never agree to this. Therefore there remains no other means than to work for the gradual [C-74] abolition of slavery itself. In this respect more cooperation can be expected from the slave owners.

In order to judge at all what may be expected from the legislation of Americans, one must consider the nature of the voters. Such a study will destroy all false hopes. Who, for instance, will expect from the majority that they will recognize the dangers of their situation, which gradually develop for ethical reasons? Who will presuppose such a capacity for self-observation and such perseverance in thinking among the majority of the people? The moral evils that gradually undermine the fortunate situation of the states are not even recognized by their consequences by the masses when it is much too late to remedy them. Therefore Americans also will not realize the destructive results of overpopulation until, some time in the future, they find themselves in the midst of them. Even then the masses will lack the insight to trace the evils back to their true sources. This is at present the case in Europe. The last remark leads me then to the danger that threatens from a change in the external situation and then to the reason I decided to print this travel report.

The situation of the American farmer, which I have described in my report, can hardly be examined closely without keeping in mind, in general, a contrary condition. Even without closer observation, it must very soon strike everyone that among all the advantages, the most important one must always be the great expanse of fertile soil. This conception, however, is obviously based on the idea that the fortunate situation of the individual and of the whole is dependent on a limitation of the population, and that overpopulation could destroy all these glorious advantages. Therefore it leads directly to the point of view that I should like to present to my fellow citizens as the most important in the whole picture.

The unexhausted natural resources of America present, compared to a highly extolled Europe, aspects that can be balanced by no creations of human hands. Only a sediment from rivers, such as Europe has never known, could produce such an extensive cover of fertile soil as is found in North America. In addition there are the magnificent forests. Many cities and artificial roads can be built in a quarter of a century; but the forests that were once the adornment and the wealth of European countries cannot be restored. My letters have shown how little it costs to eradicate the forests and also how foolish it is to term a cover of dense tree growth a disadvantage in a country, as has so often been done in publications and talks about America. If there were a choice between extremes, surely every intelligent man would infinitely prefer a land completely covered with forests to one entirely without trees. To be sure, neither America nor Europe presents such extremes. But at least the suggestion can serve as a basis for comparison. But I do not wish to pursue this trend of thought any further, however easy it would be to establish my point more firmly by references to the individual areas of the old world.

I shall again approach the purpose of this section by repeating that the expanse of fertile soil in relation to the population is the main point in the comparison of the United States with Europe; that one can completely ignore the other advantages, on the one side as well as on the other; and that the external situation of Americans [C-75] depends essentially on a change in this main point. The description of family life alone leads to this result and justifies the assertion made in the preface that most of the evils from which the inhabitants of Europe, and especially of Germany, suffer are due to overpopulation. This, however, is the time to present this statement so clearly that even the slightest doubt of its truth must vanish.—The reader will see how simply the course of research has led me to this view. But I ask your permission to interrupt the discourse with a few remarks that refer to the above-mentioned publication by the American Everett concerning his country and its political situation. [C-76] The author is a member of the diplomatic corps, and his statements may serve as proof that the thinking on the subject he treats is no clearer in America than it is in Europe.

In that publication, Mr. Everett uses the language of someone who feels that he is an expert in his subject matter and looks down pityingly on everyone who does not quite see the truth of his bold statements. [C-77] In order to prove that it is not the external situation, not the country with its appealing possibilities for human activity, that is responsible for the prosperity of the Americans, he poses the question:

Whether perhaps the same fortunate results would have occurred if the legislation had been worse. Answer: Certainly not. Accordingly, the reason for the prosperity is due only to our type of government or to our freedom (volume 2, page 176). What would Mr. Everett say to the following line of reasoning: A child who thrives under care that meets all the demands of its nature by no means owes his well-being to this care. For if poison were mixed with its food, the care would probably be of little help. Its well-being is therefore based entirely on the fact that it is not given poison. Undoubtedly this is Mr. Everett's way of reaching a conclusion. How could the author confuse negative and positive conditions in this manner? Mr. Everett should have made the effort to investigate what influence country life in America could have on the average European, aside from all influences of legislation. Then he would have found that his highly extolled legislation, which he considers the primary cause, was merely the product of a people who were prospering among the blessings of the new land. If the external situation had not transformed the people, if the rabble were just as numerous as in the European states, then the American legislation [C-78] would neither have been passed, nor would it continue to be effective for long in its present form. It is an old truth that the wisest laws can never transform the rabble of the cities into good citizens if they cannot change their external condition. What effect can laws in general have without a fortunate external situation?! But North Americans are the best evidence of what influence the external situation has on human beings who are at a stage of development no higher than that of the masses of Europeans several hundred years ago. They were not helped positively by laws. For beginning with the first colonial era, they never enjoyed greater legal freedom than the inhabitants of England itself. That they could nevertheless develop more freely was solely the result of their external situation and this is also the only reason why, even before their separation from the mother country, there was no rabble in the United States, a great contrast to conditions in England. Whatever it is that induces a beggar to adopt a regular activity, that is the final basis of his prosperity. To be sure, less favorable results could have been attained by restrictive laws. But how can one attribute, with Everett, the prosperity attained to the circumstance that this did not happen? Without doubt the tendency to praise and admire the Americans, and especially the men who contributed much to this good legislation, played an important part in reaching such an erroneous conclusion. But the fame of these men will not be lessened by recognizing this. It is great enough without it to assure them of the gratitude of posterity, and the credit of having created by their laws the attitude of mind that accepted these laws and maintained them they themselves would reject as a strange contradiction. The person who wishes to talk about the welfare of individual human beings as well as about the welfare of a group of human beings must penetrate more deeply into the essence of human nature than was done in the publication by Everett. Everett deals too much with vague ideas that usually produce only erroneous statements. It is due to this fact that in everything that he says in the first and second volumes about the South American countries he can arrive at no more [C-79] definite opinion, and even tends to prophesy for these states a political success similar to that which his country enjoys. Because he places too much weight on that which he calls a type of government, most of the essential things are touched upon, to be sure, but by no means given adequate consideration. If the author realized clearly that the foundation of the states is to be sought in the aims of the people, a brief consideration of the original difference between the Spanish and Portuguese immigrants and the British and German ones, combined with a brief glance at the religious and political influences that existed up to the time of the separation from their mother countries, as well as at the effects of the climate and the natural resources, especially the precious metals, would have kept him from such a prognosis regardless of all his good wishes. It is too evident, in view of such completely different origins and equally dissimilar stimulations to development that the life of individual families—on which alone political success depends after the political power of the mother country is no longer felt—had to develop and must continue to develop very differently from what was possible in the former British colonies.—Everett's reasoning concerning population and overpopulation, which is connected with his assertions about the basis of the political situation, is no more thorough. To him manufactured goods are the basis of true culture. It is unfortunately obvious enough that in using the word *culture* he has nothing in mind but smoothness and show combined with a little sentimentality. This explains why in his book, although it is supposed to deal with politics, he repeatedly and in the pompous tone of a grammarian can talk about polishing and refining the language used in speeches and publications. No one will doubt the value of facile, clear expression. But words are always intended to serve only as the form, the clothing, as it were, of thought; and this must not be forgotten in applying the power granted to mankind in lectures that appeal primarily to the reason of one's fellowman, if one wishes to avoid the criticism of offensive affectation or even insipidity.—Simplicity of customs is, according to Everett, barbarism; manifold needs imply culture (volume 1, pages 201 and 202); the increase in trades demanded by these needs he calls very fortunate, as only thus does it become possible for millions to live together in a limited area. Through supervision and instruction the corruption of morals could easily be prevented. Wherever morals have degenerated, in the large cities and manufacturing centers, the fault is to be sought merely in the laws and the officials. Country life, he says, offered no protection. There were enough degenerate country people, for example, in Russia, in Poland, in Turkey, in the West Indies, and even in the southern parts of the United States.—In all the older and newer schools it has been taught that the independence of the individual is determined directly by his needs, and it is to be hoped that Mr. Everett will accept this view himself. A culture that therefore makes individual citizens very dependent is supposed nevertheless to give only the state freedom. If Mr. Everett were of the opinion that his culture would have to offer the state another advantage at the cost of freedom, he would probably not dare to speak of it as good fortune.— There is no doubt that tropical plants can be grown even in the polar regions through care and cultivation by human beings. But granted that effort and skill could produce the same level of natural development, could one therefore attach little importance to the difference of the climates? Could one do this because even in the best climates other harmful influences can hinder growth, or because the climate can no longer correct the deeply rooted evil? I apply this without hesitation to people who work among the noises and the turmoil of the cities at the mechanical labor of manufacturing and to those who in the quietness of nature occupy themselves with agriculture, horticulture, and stock farming.—But now let us ask Mr. Everett: What manner of laws and officials are supposed to make the difference in the external situation and manner of living of so little importance? Instead of giving any answer, he points to his country and sincerely believes that he has thereby solved the problem.—With such views (which incidentally are too commonly held to require a new publication) concerning the good fortune of the individual and of the whole, it will be less surprising if the author considers the lot of the settlers in the western states deplorable. He has no knowledge of the situation of these settlers and has such erroneous ideas about them as are to be met with only somewhere in Europe. This may be quite astonishing in an American who in his capacity as a writer wants to give information concerning the domestic and political situation of his fellow citizens; but the author's way of seeing things affords a perfect explanation.

For the thinker, further criticism is superfluous. Unfortunately, however, independent thinking is quite uncommon. Even what is written about the state and about human nature must not tax the brain power very much if it is to be accepted. To be sure, it must have a certain coherence, but it must be of the kind that permits some play for the imagination. It is contrary to good manners and propriety to demand a close study of a long series of conclusions. Such pedantic demands are no longer suitable to the present highly cultivated world. Each reader has pondered over so many things that a mere suggestion is sufficient to help him toward a survey of all truths, no matter how many bits of evidence must be integrated to bring about the full significance of the focal points of individual truths. Finally the time will come when even the mathematicians will learn to understand how superfluous their dry method is for the clear understanding of their theorems. Then the highly extolled newer culture will have reached its highest level.

Almost all publications concerning the state begin their presentation with vague ideas. Therefore their opponents always have sufficient opportunity to attack the structure that has been erected, and the battle pro and con is a struggle in the darkness, the end of which generally depends on the endurance of the fighters. No gleam of truth will ever be a decisive factor. This manner of attempting to promote the victory of reason is just as erroneous as it is common among the younger nations. No better way will develop in the near future either, not as long as practical guidance and continuous training in methodical thinking are not considered the essential aim of education. No better way will exist as long as men are not accustomed from youth on to distinguish clearly between probability and actual fact and between the degrees of probability. If the old students of human nature and the state insisted that a person should devote time to the study of mathematics before he listened to their own teachings, the intention was by no means that the theorems of this science were to be considered as the basis of their thinking. The purpose was merely that the student, by means of mathematical observations, become accustomed to methodical thinking, which alone deserves the name of *thinking*. How can one expect someone not even capable of constructive thinking in the area of certainty (necessity) to be capable of it in the area of probability, since it requires an infinitely more sensitive sense of values and far greater circumspection, and certainly also more direction and knowledge of methods. If some who emphasize experience so strongly would understand this, they would beware of objecting so blindly to all contemplative thinking. To be sure, it is true that nothing can be accomplished in the area of probability without receiving impressions of the senses, and to try to construct the world of the senses a priori is extremely foolish. But only a person who has recognized the basic relationships of human nature that make up the area of necessity (certainty) [C-80] is prepared for clearer insight into the world of the senses. Everyone else lacks the eye for it. [C-81] To be sure, he also can see, but with other eyes than the person prepared on the basis of his knowledge of the field to which finally all outward impressions must be related if they are to become the objects of any closer study.

Sixth Chapter

On the effects of overpopulation

In my study of the stability of the domestic and political situation of the Americans, the course of my research has brought me to the dangers that can also threaten them in the future from overpopulation. The conditions in Europe cause me to dwell upon these dangers. For America a detailed discussion is at present of no practical interest; for Europe, however, all the more. Among all the countries, America, or rather the United States, presents a contrast the study of which can best enlighten Europe concerning the effects of its own overpopulation.

In the fourth chapter I spoke about the characteristics of an unspoiled European farmer and showed that the behavior of such a man depends almost entirely on the external situation. I also pointed out that the same is true of the majority of the American farmers and attempted at the same time to present evidence that most Europeans, especially so-called cultured Europeans, are in even more urgent need of a protective external situation than those [C-82] Americans. In order to explain the phenomena of the political situation in the United States I then proceeded immediately to the actual situation of Americans. Our present purpose demands, however, that I emphasize the fact that the same human characteristics are subject to other influences, other incentives, namely those which overpopulation might produce. The question concerning the effects of overpopulation is accordingly resolved into the question concerning the effects on the present external situation and the question concerning the effects upon the people of such a changed situation. Let us consider the following.

Among the harmful results of overpopulation, that of poverty is so inevitable that the two concepts seem to be entirely inseparable. In all places and at all times there is a limit beyond which an increase in population inevitably breeds poverty. Only a fool who dreams of fertility ad infinitum, of superhuman exertions, of an almost absolute value of artificial products, and so forth, can doubt this. But however self-evident this general statement may seem, with regard to a closer designation of this limit, the error prevails too frequently, in oral as well as in written statements, that the study is limited to the soil and the possibility of its utilization without considering the element in human nature that hinders the actual utilization. If one wanted to use direct force in urging the inhabitants of Europe to cultivate the soil, as one does with Negro slaves on the sugar plantations, there would certainly nowhere be a lack of means for producing abundant food. But if one does not agree with this, one should consider what really keeps people from cultivating so many tracts of land.

In times of difficulty and need, a human being worries only about the immediate future. Where the soil does not reward his efforts abundantly, his exertions will be limited to what is necessary to meet only the most urgent needs. If a person can satisfy the demands of the body only by great effort, he will try to limit these demands and prefer to suffer a certain amount of want rather than exert himself unduly. That is perfectly natural, and it would be ridiculous to demand that he should work himself to death in order to avoid future, uncertain suffering. When it is difficult to quiet the pangs of hunger, one does not think of accumulating supplies. If a person can see no good in the present, he will fear the future less. A person works to accumulate wealth only where the external situation promises an adequate reward for his exertion. If this incentive is lacking, there remains only the alternative either to drive the people to work by force, or to expect the transition from scarcity to the most horrible poverty because of unavoidable circumstances such as illness and crop failure. If therefore this step seems shocking to anyone, he must not neglect to consider that blaming the needy for sinking into poverty can only be interpreted as scorn or lack of understanding. Everywhere, therefore, where poverty results because the external situation is too restricted to offer the masses a general incentive to free activity, it must plainly be attributed to overpopulation. [C-83]

Merely this one effect is incontestably so serious that a circumspect public administration has no more important duty than to defend its country and its people against the source of this evil as much as possible. Who is so shortsighted as to fail to realize that at all times the poor have been the greatest enemies of the status quo? Who does not see that a state of want increases the strength of desires, while the simultaneous realization of their helpless condition decreases the mental power to check those desires? How can one be surprised that as a result of these unfortunate aberrations, theft, robbery, murder, revolt, and utter frenzy become rampant? How can one be surprised that people who have long lived in such a sad and distorted state of affairs finally lose all control over their urges and even hate their moments of clear reason as terrifying dreams in which they see their former aberrations not as an improvement of their situation but only as torture? When poverty oppresses the majority of the people, the nobility of humanitarianism is soon destroyed and the most corrupt products of immorality will be termed relief.

But this is only one class of the enemies of domestic and political happiness that are due to overpopulation. Let us now separate them in our thinking and then investigate the effects of the same cause on the rest.

Many whom overpopulation does not actually reduce to poverty experience great worry and a weakening of their confidence in the ability of nature to support them. It thus promotes the growth of individual desires which without this worry could not have had any influence on their better natures. If they have once started on this new path, the next temptation will find less resistance, and gradually their minds must, for their own reassurance, tend toward convincing them that in the restrictive situations of life it is impossible to remain as pure as a child. This kind of citizen, although he cannot be counted among the morally depraved of the former class, is certainly poorly adapted to support the public order since he himself is so much in need of moral support.

Others are induced by the fear of poverty to engage in risky undertakings, the unfortunate outcome of which, together with the consequent despair that they engender, must be attributed solely to a well-founded fear of poverty.

It is overpopulation that causes the passionate grabbing for the lowest offices, and the mere fear of poverty gives rise to a whole horde of acts of servitude that even in the family life serve as an excellent preparation for unquestioning obedience to the demands of political despotism.

Let us also separate this second class from the whole in our minds and see what advantages remain finally for those citizens to whom overpopulation brings neither actual poverty nor fear of want. On the one hand, the same cause that produces (among the poor) the most intense competition by limiting the field of rewarding activity must on the other hand create among the wealthy the most flaccid indolence. Whoever has possessions will soon limit his activities to keeping what he has if the attempts to acquire more involve him in great difficulties and danger. And how can one expect enterprises for the general welfare from those who live in abundance if the prospects for a return of the means expended have become completely unfavorable? A great number of people will find it advisable to engage in no business at all and to live quietly on the wealth that by good fortune is already theirs. Evident to everyone will be the resultant development of all the evils of a debilitating idleness. At best it will be mere idleness, a state in which body and soul degenerate in a general enervation. The worse and the usual result is the tendency to succumb to all kinds of passions. If denied a sphere of activity, the same vitality that inspires a man to the most praiseworthy exertions will indulge itself in an aspect of human nature that is never dormant, in the baser instincts, and awaken a play of forces that wreaks havoc with society and finally can end only with a complete loss of control of the mind over the body. This result seems all the less inevitable if one considers that while overpopulation among the first two classes destroys the balance of human nature by want, it grants immediately to the wealthy the most dangerous power over the needy masses. This same cause produces on the one hand a highly mobile group wavering between impetuosity and cowardice, among whom the outstanding characteristics are greed and a sense of servility. On the other hand, it only encourages the rich to use this power in a destructive manner by limiting the field of praiseworthy activities. Therefore, in a short time not only idleness but also luxury and debauchery, together with a scornful pride that disdains humanity and an arrogant desire to rule, will write the history of this third class.

Thus one sees clearly that wealth is also nowhere more harmful to the people and to their institutions than in the states that suffer from overpopulation. When wealth and poverty as opposite poles, both in full isolated power, affect the population wavering between them, no gratifying signs of happy humanitarianism can be expected. Those, however, who are constantly using the word *work* without delving any deeper into the nature of the states, should ponder deeply the thesis that an activity in which a person is engaged merely because he is forced by dire need is no more beneficial to the nature of the individual or to society than the most sluggish indolence.

This explains why in overpopulated countries, irrespective of the abundance of manpower, the least is accomplished that is deserving of the gratitude of mankind. Everyone lives for the present, motivated by various reasons. Let us compare the accomplishments in the young states of North America with those of recent times in Europe. Here political obstacles will occur to the readers, and it is undeniable that the most various hindrances of this type prevail in Europe. But most of them are due to overpopulation. One should attempt to remove them and consider what improvements can be introduced. If you want to improve the state, you must improve the citizens. If you want to improve the citizens, then remove them and their families from a state of want and place them in a situation where attractions and stimulations will keep them from idleness as well as from avarice. The more this is neglected, the more force and coercion are necessary to preserve the public order, an order that will gradually destroy the freedom of the family and finally will not differ much from the discipline in penal institutions. Thoughtless frivolity is often revealed by the saying "In Europe death by starvation occurs more rarely than in other places." But how can such a consolation bring any comfort in view of the effects of poverty that have been described? It is moral evil that destroys families as well as states. Minds deteriorate even if bodies are barely kept alive. That is why I speak of overpopulation, and not, like others, because of the fear of an actual famine. In Europe such a worry has already decreased because of the greater worries due to the dangers of constant wars. In Germany such a confusion of views and concepts still prevails so that there is rejoicing over the general increase in population in a province while the individual communities do not cease their loud complaints because of the increase of unemployed persons. It is strange that mere enumeration can divert attention so entirely from the characteristics of the things enumerated. For it is the communities only that cause the individual increases in population, and their complaints about increasing poverty challenge each sensible person to inquire, first of all, about the financial status of the new members. But no, compilers of statistics are interested only in mere figures, and even in the case of an increase in the number of beggars they dream of an increase in national power.

From the families of American farmers especially spring forth the strength and vitality that maintain the whole in a flourishing condition. If trade and agriculture remain in the proper relationship, it will be a blessing for the farmer as well as for the merchant. The same is true of industry. Overpopulation would confuse all this. The majority of those persons whose lives are filled with the constant tension of gain and loss, removed from all the influences of rural nature, consider each nobler stimulation of the mind as madness. Such specimens, well known to us in Europe, will crowd out the better merchants, artists, and artisans. Because they consider striving for material possessions much more important than a native nobility of spirit, they try to encourage themselves by the dim prospects of future compensation in luxury and ridiculous ostentation. The same individuals will surround the farmer with their snares and by their superior numbers exert a destructive influence on the state administration and legislation. Their disdain of the simple life and the farmer and their conduct, motivated by greed and love of ostentation, will influence the leaders in society, and because of their words and example the results of a shameless derision of nature will be accepted as the evidence of a superior cultivation of the mind.

Thus the invigorating competition of beneficial activity will be replaced throughout the entire nation by ruthless avarice, which cannot fail to affect the farmer since his changed situation rewards his exertions only poorly, since the prevailing follies, by pressure and disdain, continue to be in a state of feud with these exertions, and since rural isolation is no longer a defense against thieves and robbers.

The thing that finally makes the cup of evil overflow is that along with the changes due to overpopulation, the noise and turmoil of the cities will spread to all families, and nature in all its purity will be banished forever from large portions of great continents. This last criticism is important for the existence of the individual as well as for the whole, to the degree that it is scoffed at by imbecile administrators who consider nothing but figures. Without having the faintest idea that all physical and intellectual powers at the service of the state have their source in family life, they take recourse to measures that, while in their opinion are for the best interests of the state, actually will most surely undermine its foundation. What causes the living together of thousands in a small area to have such a harmful effect on morals other than that the family circles are more subject to the influence of men than to rural nature? The person for whom the soil has no more significance than that it is a means to fill the stomach, and who measures overpopulation only from this point of view, may be well suited to supervise the care of animals that are to be fattened for sale or home use; but may heaven protect the affairs of men from such administrators.

All large cities have at all times been a fertile planting ground for the seeds of moral monstrosities, and Europe has sent too much over to America not to have some effects in evidence here. But there is no trace anywhere of the disasters caused by overpopulation. Whoever in studying the condition of a country looks for decisive factors will find one in North America that thoroughly silences any doubt concerning the domestic prosperity of the inhabitants. The reader will remember that during my whole journey, including all excursions, I saw not a single beggar. The same holds for my return and my trips along the Atlantic coast. Even in Baltimore, Philadelphia, and New York I came across no beggar. [C-84] To be sure, there are poor people who are supported by the richer ones, but far fewer than in Europe.* If one should accidentally meet a beggar in North America, one can be almost certain that he is a recent immigrant from Europe, perhaps from Ireland or from Germany.

Such a phenomenon in a country of 12 million individuals seems like a miracle to Europeans. And this miracle occurs in a country where passports are unknown, where one can travel thousands of miles without once being asked one's name, where, although all of the ordinary police protection common in Germany is entirely lacking, theft, robbery, and swindling are rare. [C-86]

Only the condition of the family life can solve this riddle, the same condition on which alone public order in the individual states as well as in the entire nation is founded. Who can dream here of artificial greatness, or of a mere semblance of power? It is nature herself that, without the aid of any human wisdom, is the direct cause of this condition. It is nature that took to her healing and invigorating bosom the European pupil who was discouraged by the religious and political pressures of the dark past and restored him to cheerful vigor. She purified his heart of immorality. Her rich gifts removed him from that horrible poverty that in Europe changes so many people into beings whom only the most unfortunate class of Hindus resembles. But her foremost concern is directed chiefly toward the preservation of [C-87]

---

*As long as there is no country where the fruits harvest themselves, and where the housework is done by fairies, there will be people everywhere who because of negligence, illness, or the weaknesses of old age are reduced to poverty. In the interior there is scarcely a single poor person among perhaps a thousand individuals; on the Atlantic coast, certainly not more than one in hundred; on the other hand, in Europe there are some places where there is one needy person among four. [C-85]

the birthright of mortal creatures. It is the embryos that she tries to protect. There is less corruption where there is less idleness, where there is more stimulation to innocent activity. Where there is more prosperity in the external life, there is also more happiness, more vitality, more strength. Where striving is toward true objectives, there is less diversion into empty pretense.

As long as there is no threat of overpopulation and no unfortunate training that disdains nature where she offers herself to mankind as a nurse, as long as her direct help is not scorned by the people as being too natural, just so long will there be a nucleus in the country that will be less receptive to the corruption of large cities (the focal points of all passionate indulgence in physical pleasures) as well as to greed, arrogance, ambition, and lust for power.

In America Europe can recognize the results of its own overpopulation. The negative phenomena that are to be attributed to it alone and can be corrected only by a decrease in population provide the answer for anyone who still doubts that Germany also is one of the overpopulated countries. Whoever directs attention to Germany's sandy wastelands, to the barren mountain ridges, will find himself [C-88] opposed by human nature itself; he demands of human nature what it will accomplish only when forced by inescapable power. Whoever speaks of a fatherland must remember that without property there is no home, and without a home no fatherland. He should also consider that exaggeration changes everything into an evil, that absolute limitation to a small part of the earth is contrary to reason and to heaven, that it is folly and a sin for one country to look down in blind prejudice upon all others. He should bear in mind that the fertile hills and valleys of America are assigned to no other creature than to mankind for his use by the same all-powerful Providence that distributed our ancestors over Europe. He should realize that nothing destroys individual families so inevitably as when all children and grandchildren restrict themselves to the home of their fathers. Such a procedure by the descendants can produce only one blessing, namely that of numbers. A whole country by the natural sequence of generations must finally find itself in a condition similar to the property of an individual who has many descendants. [C-89] For Germany this time has long since arrived. Few families are wealthy. A fortune is not wealth when the care of children and grandchildren is dependent on it. The poorest American farmer would not exchange his situation for this. Rich fathers leave this earth with the dismal prospect that their children will not be able to continue their lives on the level to which their rearing in their parental home has accustomed them and justifies them to expect. Opinions have developed that exert such a strict control over external existence with the words *propriety* and *decorum* that the individual can do nothing about it. These opinions have their supporters among the poor and the rich, among the servants, and the masters. They control everything and leave no loophole where the voice of nature would be safe from their ranting. A large number of people suffer more from these unalterable opinions than from actual want. The advice to pay no attention to them is never heeded. They attack concretely. Whatever concerns the body and its surroundings cannot be removed by mere abstractions. Therefore those unfortunate beings who seek escape by suicide from the mental pains of poverty are so greatly to be pitied. They are the unfortunate victims of those oppressive opinions that control all their life situations. Only stupidity can refuse to sympathize with them. By their terrible decision they make it evident enough that the burden that fate placed upon them was too heavy for them to bear. In recent times Germany has seen so many examples of despair that the entire nation should recognize the true cause and its very great significance. Only vociferous superficiality can be satisfied with the judgment of writers who compile the accounts of casualties; it alone can silence the bothersome voice of inner sympathy with empty words of pride and melancholy.

In America all the coercion of obsolete prejudice is absent, and in the interior of the United States suicide because of poverty is unknown. The nature of the person who steals and robs there deviates so much from the norm that the judge who metes out the punishment cannot be strongly moved by sympathy. No more sympathy is felt for such a person than for a beast of prey which we must also pursue for the sake of our own safety. Who can say the same of most of the thieves in Germany? Here our inner feelings are involved in a severe struggle with the knowledge of the demands of the law. To be sure, law must prevail. But the person who can turn a cold shoulder on want that daily causes the most pitiful victims to come in conflict with this law needs nothing but the external situation to become far worse than the thief he sentences.

How many consequences of despair would be prevented if the transition to a life in America would only be made a little easier for the Germans. [C-90] It would offer to the fathers the surest relief from worry; it would assure the most rewarding sphere of influence to the drive to engage in enterprise and praiseworthy activity; and the usual donations to the poor would then be more than sufficient to restore the mentally ill pariahs to happy vitality instead of providing a slight alleviation from physical ills as now. In a single generation the German states would themselves be restored to the health and strength of which they have long been deprived by counteracting those unspeakably harmful effects of overpopulation. At the same time they would see a new colony blossom beyond the ocean that in grateful loyalty would never cease calling down the blessings of heaven upon the mother country and as a second home would receive the late arrivals.— Germany is sensitive to misery and misfortune in distant lands, but it forgets the fate of its own sons.—The consolation of a supposed compensation in an ideal field is of no value. In this earthly life intellectual powers are too closely connected with spatial stimulations. Restriction and death in the one can only result in aberration, paralysis, and destruction in the other.—And finally, I ask the reader, what can one answer to that but, "The country is too far away?"

If France or Italy were as free as the regions along the Mississippi, all warning against emigration would be scoffed at and ridiculed.—If, however, this is really true, if distance is the only factor that prevents the success of the plan, everyone should ask himself whether the evils that result from it will not disappear completely when compared with the infinitely great advantages offered. Finally everything goes back to the outlay involved. For the individual, to be sure, it is considerable. But at the very beginning, organizations could acquire ships and cover the cost of transporting many persons merely with the freight charges on wares. Then it would be shown that it costs less to transport whole families to America than to a remote province in France or Italy. Soon one might come to the conclusion, as has happened in several regions in England, that contributions for the sustenance of the poor, not to speak of the cost of prosecuting and meting out punishment for thefts and robberies, cannot be spent more practically than for transferring the needy to another continent.

It is my chief aim to arouse the interest of Germany [C-91] in this project. Therefore I shall for the present refrain from making more detailed suggestions. I shall indicate briefly one single way of executing such a plan only in order to point out to the insipid jeerers that this is not a question of flighty planning. A company organized in Europe buys tracts of land of an area of five to ten thousand *Morgen*. On these individual tracts towns are founded and populated by colonists who are transported free of charge on the condition that they take over a house in the new town at a moderate price, together with ten to fifteen *Morgen* of land, of which four or five have been cleared, and live there at least six successive years. The security given for this must equal the cost of the journey. The contract becomes void as soon as the colonist violates it. On the other hand, he is free to cancel it by repayment of the traveling expenses. Also the colonists must have enough money so that each can pay for a horse, cows, and sows, together with household utensils and farm implements. The company sees to it that such things can be bought cheaply. If at the same time it makes provisions for a good physician and schools, the town will be sure to prosper, so that all of the land purchased will immediately rise in value three or fourfold (in a favorable case twelve and twentyfold). One should call to mind the value of land near St. Louis. If the new town flourishes, the price of a *Morgen* will easily rise to a hundred dollars. Fifty families make up a nice little town.

These, each estimated at five to six persons, can be transported (perhaps even in foreign ships) to New Orleans for six thousand dollars and for an additional fifteen hundred to two thousand dollars to the Missouri River. If now the landed property of the company near the site of the town to be founded amounted to only five thousand *Morgen*, and if it had cost about seven to eight thousand dollars, then its value would rise upon the arrival of the colonists to at least twenty to twenty-five thousand dollars.—It is entirely wrong to begin with beggars. Every family would have to possess about four hundred dollars of its own. This will also provide some assurance of continuous activity, which cannot be expected from any beggar.

No land on this earth offers more to German emigrants than the western part of the United States. Aside from political reasons, Brazil has not the climate in which Germans can prosper. The new home must have a winter. At present there is a great movement on foot to spread out the population along the Missouri and its tributaries over the Rocky Mountains to the Pacific coast. A waterway through Mexico would make the coast more accessible to Europeans, and it is beyond all human calculation what steamboat service can accomplish in the course of a few decades. The inhabitants of the United States will not present the slightest difficulty to a settlement en masse. [C-92] Here envy, jealousy, and danger to life and property, about which there is so much complaint in Spanish America, are wholly unknown. If millions of Germans should emigrate to the upper Mississippi and Missouri, they would all be welcome. The reason is that the open spaces are so great there, and the opinion of the Americans concerning our good qualifications for adaptability to social conditions is so favorable. As soon as a German has set foot on the soil of the United States it will occur to no American to claim any advantage over him, and in this respect conditions could not be better if the whole country were a German colony. When the number of immigrants reaches sixty thousand, they can organize their own state, the legislation of which they can adapt at will to the customs and usages of their fatherland. This has actually been done by the French in the state of Louisiana and the mouth of the Mississippi.

Germany has only recently expressed its active interest in America through trade and mining companies in which the laudable desire for a more extensive field of activity was obviously the first consideration. I have reason to hope that the subject of this publication will find an all the more general acceptance the closer it is concerned with those aspects of human nature that seem the highest to every level of culture. I may furthermore hope that after England has been admitting its overpopulation publicly for several years, after Parliament itself has begun to promote and support emigration, the opponents of emigration in Germany, who have at all times been glad to adopt the theories of a foreign country, will likewise relax their customary severity and for their part will not oppose a movement toward which the aid of the princes can so easily lead the country in this sacred concern of humanity.

A Postscript for emigrating farmers and for those who contemplate commercial undertakings

A. For Farmers

I have explained repeatedly why I consider emigration for an individual or for a few persons [PS-1] highly dangerous, and I say once more that the greatest danger that threatens is from disease.[1] To be sure in order to live on the Atlantic coast one does need to provide for medical service. However, whoever counts on making a profit by farming or whoever possesses only a small capital should for heaven's sake not stay this side of the Allegheny Mountains. The European who leaves his country already loses by his mere emigration. In addition to that comes the cost of the travel and finally the cost of the new establishment. The American himself can only make up the loss in the case of a change in residence by moving to areas where well-situated, fertile property is still available and can be bought from the state. [PS-2] The situation for the European is far worse. The more quickly he tries to buy from private persons the more he has to fear a disadvantageous contract. The more significant the item is, the more is at stake. And even if the purchase is tolerable, then his inexperience in American agriculture and the whole new life-style present a very dangerous hurdle in the beginning. In short, if the American has a reason to go westward then the European has twice or three times as much of a reason. He is just as much a stranger at the coast as he is in the interior. A few hundred miles are of little concern to one who has traveled across the ocean coming from Germany. And worries about insecurity belong to the realm of dreams. The immigrant can buy property very reasonbly in the western states either directly from the state or from private sources, and he can for this reason not lose very much because the capital is so small. And here is the true place to make a temporary stop in order to make oneself at home in the new country, which would be completely inappropriate in the Atlantic states. By the way, the prospect for the future seems much brighter in the regions along the Mississippi. The Atlantic states have progressed so far that it is impossible for them to keep pace with the West. Whoever settles at present in the Mississippi territory and is not too careless in the selection of the place may expect with great confidence a greater than twelvefold increase in his real estate value within twenty years.*[PS-3] This time is long past for the old states. [PS-4]

---

*It seems assured that the population of the United States will double within twenty

It is unnecessary to remind you that a mere bargain in land should not decide the selection of the place. Only where other conditions are favorable for a happy existence is the price of the property to be considered, and for the European, traveling at his own expense, there is a point where considerations concerning the value disappear completely. It must be rather insignificant for him whether he pays one dollar more or less for an acre. Eighty acres are sufficient for the welfare of a large family, and with the other costs that are unavoidable in the case of emigration and a new establishment a saving of a hundred dollars is too insignificant to consider. Those people who look at countries where emigrants are offered a few hundred acres as a present ought to remember that.

In the assumption therefore that only settlement in the western states promises an absolute success, I can say that the emigration of individuals without leadership and medical protection is to be considered a great risk. For one who has to start out in order not to use up his last bit of money while waiting for a favorable opportunity, however, I have written down the following advice.

The territory of the western states is very expansive, and in making specific references to it the next question is natural; which part would be best to recommend to the German? To this I answer first that the emigrant who intends to make use of the soil should not settle in the southern states, not there where there is no winter. With an urban life-style the change of climates is far less noticeable. But the farmer who suddenly changes from the German farm life to the work of tropical plantations without intermediate stages exposes his physical constitution to the most dangerous disturbances. [PS-5] Settlements at the mouth of the Arkansas are perhaps already too far south. On the upper Arkansas the climate is more agreeable, as is that along the entire Ohio and its tributaries, the Missouri, and the Illinois. Later, after he has gotten accustomed to the seasons in these areas, the German may attempt to move farther south. Even on the Ohio and Missouri he will, in spite of the bright sky in the spring, summer, and fall, look longingly toward winter during the first years. On mountains the air is, to be sure, always pure and the heat is rarely oppressive or depressing. However, whoever moves too far away from navigable rivers will forfeit many of the advantages of his undertakings. Along the great Canadian lakes the winter is said to be too severe. Just because of the long winters many families have moved away from Canada to the Ohio and Missouri. I have heard it said many times that even in the mildest regions of upper

---

years even without immigration from Europe. This alone explains the increase in the value of the property on which every head of the family may depend for the future of his children.

Canada the ground is covered with snow every year for several months, which is very bothersome for cattle raising.

Secondly, one should note that the land is that much more expensive the more one moves from the Mississippi toward the East and toward the old states, for no reason other than the greater population. For in general the fertility decreases with the distance from the Mississippi. The greatest expanses of fertile topsoil are near the biggest rivers. And what areas could be better situated for communication with the world than the banks of the Mississippi? With the constant pressure of the population westward and with the exceedingly easy communication by steamboat, the advantage of Ohio and the state of Kentucky, not to mention others, is not so significant that a newcomer from Europe should overlook the advantages of the countries to the west of the Mississippi, which have only been opened during the last two decades. The uninterrupted immigration from just those states would have to come to his notice very soon.—When I came through the state of Ohio I met several people who were preparing to move to the settlements on Lake Erie. I learned that in this part of the state of Ohio much fertile land still could be bought from the federal government. The climate was described as rather mild, and above all the water transportation was praised. I have not been there, but I cannot believe that the climate there is as good as that on the lower Missouri or on the Ohio, and regarding the waterways, the land along these rivers will not compare unfavorably with the shores of Lake Erie. At any rate along the Mississippi and its tributaries there is a greater choice. The difference in the cost of travel is very minimal. It is to be observed, however, that on Lake Erie many Indians are still living and that in a war with England the main theater of war would be located there in the vicinity of Canada.

Consequently I would recommend to the emigrant the state of Missouri preferably, and I would advise him to travel directly to St. Louis on the Mississippi. [PS-6]

There are two routes. One can travel from Europe either to the Atlantic coast (to Baltimore, Philadelphia, or New York) or via the Gulf of Mexico to New Orleans.

Whoever prefers the first route should observe the following. Coming from the Atlantic coast he has to turn first to the Ohio in order to use the steamboats, which are reasonable, comfortable, and can convey him quickly. He has the choice of reaching the Ohio either at Pittsburgh or in Wheeling. If he lands in Baltimore then the one is as convenient as the other. The difference of 90 English miles by steamboat is inconsequential. The distance from Baltimore to Pittsburgh is figured to be 230 English miles, to Wheeling 260. The route to Wheeling was until recently by far the better. If one lands in Philadelphia one should choose Pittsburgh. The distance is 320 English miles. The freight charges do not amount to more than one and a half to two dollars per hundred weight.* If one lands in New York then one takes the Hudson upriver to Albany, then the great canal to the city of Buffalo on Lake Erie and from Buffalo over the lake to the city of Erie and from there approximately 110 English miles by land to Pittsburgh. This route to the Ohio is, to be sure, very long; however one can cover it in almost the same time and at the same cost as the land route from Philadelphia. It is without doubt more convenient and also more reasonable for the transportation of baggage. As soon as the canal is finished through the state of Ohio to Lake Erie, then one can take the water route from Buffalo and will get to the Ohio River way below Pittsburgh (near Portsmouth). [PS-8]

And now the following should be noted concerning the seasons [PS-9]: (1) That the long New York Canal is usually covered with ice from December to the end of April; (2) That the Ohio above the mouth of the Scioto, where the above-mentioned canal in the state of Ohio begins, has almost every summer, from the middle of the month of July until late in the fall, often to the end of December, too little water for steamers. To travel with other boats would require too much time, approximately forty days to the Mississippi. The ice rarely is an obstacle on the Ohio before the end of December and not longer than to the end of February. Even the lower part of the Ohio, the part below the falls near Louisville, is at times during the fall too low for steamers for several weeks. As big as the river is, there are nevertheless even below Louisville some places where it gets too shallow after a long dry summer. The fall is the best season for land travel in all parts of North America. However, with regard to voyage by water, one has to get information pertaining to the rise and fall of the rivers. In the spring there is no navigable river that lacks water. The Mississippi and the Missouri are always deep enough for the largest steamboats, at least as far as the settlements extend today. [PS-10]

Before one's departure from Germany one should take note of the preceding remarks. [PS-11] Whoever lives near the river Rhine will find boats available all through the year to New York, Philadelphia, and Baltimore from Amsterdam, Rotterdam, and Antwerp. For Northern Germany, Bremen and Hamburg would be best. Concerning the cost, one should inform himself from my letters. Whoever wants to cross the ocean quickly should leave with a New York packet boat from Liverpool or Havre de Grace. They usually cross in twenty to thirty days. From Liverpool the transatlantic fare by cabin costs from 140 to 150 dollars including spirituous drinks and bedding. At Havre one can get the same for 600 francs. [PS-12] However the trip to both of these

---

*When the projected railroad from Baltimore to Ohio is finished it will naturally be used. [PS-7]

harbors is rather expensive for a German, especially if he has much baggage, which, by the way, causes all kinds of difficulties with the customs in England.[PS-13]

May and June are considered excellent calm months on the ocean [PS-14] between Europe and North America. But then to the east of the bank of Newfoundland there are usually westward winds that delay the trip from Europe very much. I would think that the beginning of April would be the best time for one's departure. One would then also be able to get to the Ohio in plenty of time.

In order to get to the state of Missouri by way of New Orleans one would have to leave in December or January so that one would arrive at a time when there is no danger of yellow fever. [PS-15] The voyage there usually lasts from six weeks to two months. From New Orleans steamboats go up the Mississippi almost daily, and to be sure they reach St. Louis in nine or ten days. The cabin price amounts to forty dollars. On deck it would cost only about one-third. But they charge about twice as much for the sea voyage to New Orleans as to Philadelphia, Baltimore, or New York and often even more. In the future this will change. [PS-16] To the present time the competition has been very little. By way of New Orleans the whole trip would cost at least 250 dollars, by way of a seaport at the Atlantic coast not much more than 200 dollars provided that one travels cabin class. Otherwise half of that would suffice or even less. One can without hesitation choose second class on steamboats. (There are only two classes on the steamboats on the Mississippi and its tributaries.) However one has to be careful with the seagoing vessels. Whoever is used to the air of small huts may feel well in the steerage area. And he would also not be oppressed by the subordinate relationship to the captain and to the cabin passengers. If, however, the ship is primarily built for the transport of passengers, then everything depends on the number of the passengers and the honesty of the captain. A ship of 400 tons could quite easily accommodate 160 to 200 people and would have plenty of space in the area below for much freight. The full freight of such a ship (from a Dutch harbor to Baltimore or Philadelphia) rarely brings more than 6,000 dollars. A group of 200 individuals would therefore not have to spend more than this sum. However, instead of uniting and renting the entire ship, most emigrants embark individually, whereby the shipowner often can make an extraordinary profit. That the passengers will then pay twice as much, for instance everybody 150 guilders, and 200 people 30,000 guilders or 12,000 dollars, is not the worst by far. Sometimes 400 to 500, indeed, as incredible as it may seem, 900 people are packed together and each one has to pay as much as if they were all traveling alone in cabin class. Now, however, this nuisance of overloading is prevented by laws according to which only two people can be accepted for every 5 tons, and therefore a ship of 400 tons cannot take more than

160 people. [PS-17] However, in general the contract is entirely dependent on the parties involved. A company of emigrants would do well to enter into such a contract before their arrival at the port. For this reason it is necessary to have one member who is familiar with such business and has been on sea voyages before. Above all, one should take note of the following comment. It is very rare that one can make arrangements for the fare of a few people that are conducive to their well-being in the ship. This can be well arranged for many; however, usually this is overlooked because of a lack of unity and leadership, or the important points of the contract are not expressed clearly enough. If, however, the entire agreement has been arranged in the port so that each passenger can judge before the departure what his future situation will be at sea, then many an inconvenience can be prevented. [PS-18]

Whoever sails for New Orleans should provide himself in Europe with house, field, carpentering, and other implements, and he should take two of each item. Especially let him take: good axes that are approximately five to six pounds in weight, smaller hand axes, broad axes for dressing the timber, wedges for splitting wood, large saws, about six to seven feet in length, for timbering, handsaws, drills and planes, including the wedges, coffee mills, large mills to be attached to a base (to be able to grind grain at home in case there are not any water or horse-operated mills nearby) would save a great deal of trouble; light stoves for wood, also some very long pipe (in order not to need a chimney at the very beginning; it might be worth a great deal over there if one could get under a roof quite quickly, not to mention saving labor with firewood). Mattocks, spades, plowshares and plow chains, heavy chains for dragging timber, copper vessels, iron bedsteads, fire tongs, iron grills, hearth irons for hanging up the cooking pots, spinning wheels, and reels. Such things cost four or five times as much in the interior of America. One should beware of thinking of business speculations when taking one's first trip. What is necessary for such speculation has to be learned in the country itself. The iron tools ought to be covered with linseed oil to protect them against rust, and everything should be packed well.

Whatever a farmer brings along for his own use is free of duty (which in the case of iron implements usually amounts to 20 to 25 percent).* However, with new things one is inclined to have doubts.

Two long shotguns (duck guns) and good rifles should not be forgotten, just as one should bring a pair of riding saddles as well as the bits.

Whoever travels to the Atlantic coast would do best to buy all items there (with the exception of the shotguns), as for instance in the cities of Baltimore, Philadelphia, and New York. The difference in price is so

---

*Quite recently the duty has been raised, which however does not affect my advice given here. [PS-19]

little compared to the difficulties and cost of transport. Saddles are more reasonable in Baltimore and Philadelphia than in Germany or in Holland.—However, everybody should provide himself in Germany with enough underwear for several years as well as with ready-made clothing made of woolen cloth, for tailors' wages are high in all of America. Nevertheless it is advisable to buy at the Atlantic coast rather than in the interior. No one should think that these conditions will change quickly.

Whoever buys along the Atlantic coast has also to pay attention to careful packing and has to direct the transfer so that wherever he travels by water the items will be shipped by the same boat. If one leaves them to be shipped by merchants all the way to the Mississippi then one will often have to wait for half a year for them. Whoever elects this plan anyway should not forget the insurance, which does not cost much. [PS-20]

To make the long trip from the seacoast in the same manner as I have done entails all kinds of difficulties for the newcomer to America. It is best if one uses the mail coaches and the steamboats. Now there are mail coaches from the Atlantic coast straight to St. Louis on the Mississippi (through Ohio, Indiana, and Illinois). On a mail coach one has approximately forty pounds of baggage free; for this reason the excess weight should be sent in advance so that one will find it there where steam navigation begins. They do not charge anything for four to five hundred pounds on the steamboats. In general the freight in America is not very high. A seat in the mail coach from Philadelphia to Pittsburgh costs about twenty dollars, from Baltimore to Wheeling about sixteen dollars (in the year 1824 it cost twenty-two dollars). [PS-21]

As soon as the emigrant has arrived in St. Louis, he should obtain charts of the federal lands from the land office and undertake a few excursions. I would advise him to travel up the Missouri and then board in the country with a clean farmer. Everywhere in the country he can find complete board for a weekly amount of one, one and a half, to two dollars, which includes the board for his horse. He will need a horse. He can buy it better from a farmer than in St. Louis. For thirty to forty dollars a very adequate animal can be found. Living among the farmers the newcomer will have plenty of opportunity to prepare himself for his future living conditions; he may buy a ready-made homestead or may want to establish a new one. But he must not hurry too much. He has to learn to judge for himself and has to use the advice of others with caution; in general he should follow the examples of the people living inland more than their words. At the time of my departure there were homesteads with 120 *Morgen* of very good soil of which twenty to thirty *Morgen* were properly fenced in and had been converted to farmland including orchards, dwelling huts, and barns, offered for 500 dollars.

[PS-22] Whoever erects a brick building, which also may well cost approximately 500 dollars, at such a place will be able to enjoy all comforts and conveniences of country life. It will be unnecessary to warn the newcomer not to settle too far from a navigable river. That would be inexcusable as long as one is so unlimited in one's choice.

Nothing deserves the attention of the settler more than horse breeding. A few good mares, whose care and keep costs practically nothing, will bring more profit than their whole expense will amount to. There is not a shortage of stallions of the most excellent breed. The English have brought them from the Old World from the very beginning. One should keep this line of profitmaking in mind from the beginning when selecting the choice of one's place. Where, for instance, all property is already in the hands of private persons there are usually so many cattle that the feed in the forest is not sufficient. Grapevines, rape oil, and poppy seed oil [PS-23] have, no matter how much their culture may promise, not found the slightest attention either in the state of Missouri or in the bordering countries. As to wine, grapes have always been imported from warmer regions. Also the descendants of the British do not understand viniculture, and those descended from other people have not learned it from their parents. I should think that grapes from the Rhine would do very well on the Missouri, however not in the midst of thick forests. Not far from St. Charles there are extensive areas that ought to be very good for viniculture.

If a significant group emigrates, then the founding of a little town could bring great advantages because the surrounding country would thus immediately gain considerably in value.

Several people could travel together from the Atlantic coast according to the custom of the Americans, which I have described in my letters. Their wagons should, however, not be too heavy. Light but strong freight wagons for two horses are best. Horses at the coast are more expensive than in the interior. I found excellent draft and saddle horses at very reasonable prices in the state of Ohio. The wagons in the seaports are more reasonable. I would suggest that each family should buy a light freight wagon and load it only moderately in order not to need too much horsepower in the beginning. The larger part of the baggage and the goods would have to be sent by freight to Wheeling or Pittsburgh and, after stronger horses are acquired in the state of Ohio, more could be loaded. For such a plan Baltimore and Philadelphia are the places of departure.

The German who understands Latin or French can learn the English language quickly. There are many low Saxon words which in their pronunciation sound exactly as one hears them in various areas of Westphalia and Lower Saxony. The Latin language is for an Englishman the real emergency reservoir from which he daily adopts new words.—Some instruction in Germany should precede this process, however. Few people enjoy instruction on the ocean. Naturally, above all, the terms of the most common situations of life are to be memorized. It would suffice for a society of emigrants if a few of them understood English.

One ought to take money along either in drafts, which can be gotten in all European ports, or in English gold. [PS-24]

B. For Businessmen

Until this time I have talked primarily to the farmers. I have nothing to add for craftsmen, artisans, architects, technicians, chemists, and doctors pertaining to the content of my letters; besides, that which I would like to add concerning business life in the interior of North America also partly concerns merchants.

I have warned the farmers not to proceed too quickly to significant expenditures and in the beginning to be rather the observer, while I tried to call their attention to the fact of how different American agriculture is from European, and particularly from German. To be sure this cannot be said of business. The difference in the procedure of the American businessmen from the German is not such that the immigrating merchant would not soon be able to make his way himself. However, it is always necessary to spend some time in the country itself, and thus this warning also applies to businessmen. What really caused me to repeat it here is the special inclination of businessmen to neglect it in the very beginning. In almost all of Germany it would seem to be a rather tall order to travel deep into the interior of North America for the purpose of business speculation without taking along goods from Europe. Preparatory sacrifices of time and money, whose use cannot be and need not be translated into figures and which cannot be made the subject of proper computations, are not very inviting, not to mention for those who are used in their business life to seeing the fruits of their undertaking in very clear outline form from the very first steps of the execution. What is more natural than the desire to be able to combine with similar preparations at least a business that would cover the cost? And this wish is matched everywhere in Germany by the belief that one can make a big profit with European goods in the interior of America if one imports them directly from Europe and also that very rarely in an importation of goods that is undertaken almost at random from Europe to the interior of North America anything can be lost. How dangerous such opinions are will be self-evident by the description of American business life.

Business dealings in the interior of North America are mainly comparable to the business at fairs. Almost every merchant offers his goods in an open store. Almost no one devotes himself exclusively to the wholesale business in the interior. Everybody considers retail trade a safe basis for his business and all merchants are storekeepers with whom other merchantile transactions are connected.

Only there, where everybody is so mobile and where travel costs so little and has so much attraction during every season, can merchants limit themselves to a similarly convenient manner of marketing. Salesmen with samples and peddlers facilitate shopping very little. On the contrary, most girls and women would not like to lose a reason for riding now and then to the shops in the cities or to the stores in the country (where there is usually a gathering of strangers). One should remember that all white women and girls in the interior of the United States are ladies, and one should not expect to see the ladies living in the country market farm products in the manner of European farmers hiking to the markets. They appear only as buyers, on horseback and in fashionable dresses. The sale of produce as well as that of other goods is the business of men and of servants.

Whoever bears in mind the above-mentioned peculiarity of North American business life will be helped to obtain a clearer concept by the following remarks.

In Europe there is also the general opinion that a merchant in the interior of North America can obtain a significant fortune only by great privations and persistence in all kinds of difficulties and dangers. Because the more intelligent would rarely have occasion to expose themselves to such a situation, it seems comprehensible enough that a European, to be sure, should be able to make his fortune once he has decided to spend a longer sojourn in the American wilderness. This view is totally erroneous. The life of a businessman in the interior of the United States is on the whole far less associated with tediousness, difficulties, and dangers than that of a merchant in France, Germany, and in the rest of Europe. [PS-25] The fact that the American does not need to leave his store to sell his goods already leads to this assumption. As to the wilderness, however, my letters, I hope, will reveal sufficiently, and it will become clear how foolish it is to believe, that the European, merely because he was educated in Europe, can count on an intellectual advantage in the western states. The European businessman, as well as the immigrating farmer, will find himself surrounded everywhere by people who will be able to compete quite well with him and from whom he has to learn all kinds of things from the very beginning.

That nevertheless a respectable fortune can be gained there is merely to be attributed to the large territory where human activity can prosper. I have developed the characteristic traits of this area in the earlier pages and I refer particularly to the Thirty-first Letter. Here I can only repeat that the natural characteristic of the country is the basis of it. The wealth of nature, which surpasses all comprehension, should above all occupy human energies in the Mississippi countries, whereby a detrimental rushing to other occupations must necessarily be prevented. None of these other branches is so extensive that it could not find its complete support in the use of the soil, and this situation could only experience a temporary change in the present century. The attraction to farming and to animal husbandry is too great for another occupation to tie a person down very long when it ceases to be profitable. Businessmen, physicians, artisans, craftsmen, all could adapt themselves without difficulty to farming as soon as the prospects for their various occupations should become dim.—Therefore farming is to be considered the safest basis, and whoever, depending on another occupation, emigrates from faraway countries at random has to remember this just that much more since he could arrive at an unfavorable period for his particular occupation. Let us take the case, for instance, that suddenly many Europeans of one and the same occupation might immigrate. The disproportion that would arise because of this would soon be remedied by switching over to agriculture, but nevertheless this might depress an immigrant who comes unprepared just the same.—Therefore, as I have said before, the attraction to farming is open to all occupations within the proper limits, and the mass of the population is totally directed to making use of the soil. With a small capital very little can be done in business anyway. The wealthier, however, besides their prospect of making profits, will also be attracted by the conveniences of country living, and whoever has recognized this will not willingly sacrifice them for an increase of his income that he will not need for his happiness.

This inclination of the population toward using the soil serves not only to render a negative service to the class of merchants by preventing detrimental competition, but it also gives to the business its real life, which can therefore be explained and comprehended only from the life and activities of the Americans who are occupied with the soil.

Whoever thinks of starting a business establishment in a faraway country should not let himself be guided merely by the temptations of the present time. Europeans who want to open for themselves and for their descendants a permanent sphere of activity in the interior of [PS-26] North America have to pay greater attention to more things than to the conditions of individual speculations. Momentary prospects cannot move a reasonable person to emigration into foreign parts of the world. If I therefore delineate the territory for businessmen in the countries beyond the Alleghenies in greater detail, then it is my chief intention to cause the reader to consider the permanent and temporary peculiarities of this territory.

Undoubtedly the variety of the products of the soil within the Great Republic [PS-27] has the strongest bearing on the sphere of activity of businessmen over there. The United States has such dimensions, extending through the various climates, that if in case of future wars the entire country should be cut off from the ocean for a long time, the mere traffic in the interior would keep businessmen active in the Mississippi countries. However, no one will really believe in wars between the states or in the division of the United States in the near future unless he confuses reality with descriptions of individual party literature.

In Europe one can occasionally read of shipments of goods to faraway markets that the farmers themselves undertake, and there was also some mention made of this in my letters. However, let no one be deceived to conclude that one could get along without the intermediary service of a merchant. Such undertakings occur usually only in places where there are no business people and are usually limited to the trading of grains and meat. Usually the yield from small farms, which occupy by far the greatest space everywhere, is rarely substantial enough so that the planter would not prefer to sell nearby. Wherever the population has grown to a certain level, there also a market will soon develop for the products of the soil, and no one would be more pleased than the farmer who can leave it to the merchant and to speculators to send goods long distances. Only in extraordinary cases of bottlenecks does he find it to his advantage to carry on the marketing himself. The greater the demand for his products the less the farmer lets himself be sidetracked from the business of production. In the middle states where, as in the northern, grain production is the basis of agriculture, most farmers sell their yield in tobacco and cotton nearby, even though they may ship the grain to very distant markets. The trade in wax, tallow, skins, furs, and minerals is always in the hands of merchants. The same is true of brandies [alcoholic beverages], of flour, and many other things. The American sells his products only directly to the consumer if he has an open store at the same time, excluding the usual produce that is brought to weekly markets. Whoever has something to sell, who is not a storekeeper himself, turns as a rule to the storekeeper, who then takes care of the sale for a certain percentage or takes on the wares on his own account. Some farmers, for instance, use the hours of bad weather for making shoes, for building barrels, and for making other implements. All of this is then transmitted to a storekeeper for sale. This seems to them to be the most advantageous and also the most decent way. It is of course easy to understand that it is easy to barter in this manner, whereby the merchant usually wins doubly. I, therefore, once again caution against interpreting the frequent barter trade in the Mississippi countries to mean a lack of cash.

It has further been mentioned in my letters that it was the ambition of every good farmer to take care of the more urgent needs of life in his own household so that as little money as possible need be spent for it. This could mislead some people into believing that one could not earn

much by selling to such farm people. However it is just the opposite. The preoccupation with necessities makes the situation of the farmers here so independent that they think much less about saving the abundance than in Europe, and therefore they spend their cash with a much easier mind for luxury articles, for things of one's fancy, the more unessential they are compared to necessities. The smallest coin on the Mississippi is a silver coin of five and three-forths cents (approximately nine *Kreuzer*). This already indicates that the retail trade cannot be quite so small. One should combine such ideas now with the report that there are no European farm women here and that the women living in the country in North America are just as subject to the changes of fashion (this pertains to dress as well as to domestic appliances) as the city residents; then it will become rather evident that (excluding goods that are meant for one's stomach) the North American trade has an incomparably larger support from the interior consumption compared to the ratio of the population than the trade in any other country of the world.*
[PS-28] It is naturally self-evident that all luxury items in the western states can only be obtained from merchants, as well as most steel and iron goods that farmers need. Compared to the need for them only very few are manufactured in all of the Mississippi countries, and that will continue as long as everybody can acquire a comfortable life by means of tilling the soil. In the old states, where the soil yields less and at the same time is far more expensive, the manufacturers and mills quickly increase because of their sales to the western population.

The lively business of trade as well (as of craftsmen) can be explained, more than by any other reason, by the uninterrupted establishment of new farms and cities, and because this happens nowhere more frequently than in the same Mississippi countries where the attraction to farming prevents an inordinately large increase of business occupations, therefore just in those regions the situation of the merchant must be far more desirable than anywhere else. This applies that much more to those merchants who live near the borders of civilization where the constant immigration is directed. As long as these borders can be expanded the immigrations will continue and with them their peculiar enlivening of trade. In the West the space is largest. Only the shores of the Pacific Ocean will form the boundaries. However, what a substitute the wide ocean itself will then offer, whose shores belonging to the confederation are said to lie in a mild climate full of bays and harbors.

---

*To whom does it not come to mind how little this American luxury of the farmers deserves the screams of protest that some raise against it. It does not undermine the welfare of families. It is merely a harmless play of abundance compared to Europe, in which so frequently the most urgent needs are sacrificed. In this latter, distorted effect, not in that playfulness, lies the destructive character.

(For several years now they have toyed with the idea in the United States of erecting a city at the mouth of the Columbia River without wanting to wait for the natural expansion of the population.)

From this follows with absolute clarity that just as the European who plans to live by using the soil, immigrating merchants also have cause to travel directly to the Mississippi countries. The farmer chooses there a place that, within twenty years, increases twenty times in value without the slightest effort on his part. The same immigrations that effect this produce also ever new, attractive places for merchants—not because of the trade with the Indians but because of the relationships with the immigrants themselves. Most of them have directed their attention to the soil, and, because they are well versed in the useful treatment of it and can without difficulty extract from it great treasures, they also have no hesitation in paying the highest prices for the necessary implements in the stores in their vicinity. Therefore a merchant can easily acquire a large fortune here if he would only make his purchases in the Atlantic seaports of Baltimore, Philadelphia, and New York and resell them in the new settlements. The difference in prices is amazing, although one does not have any duties here and transportation is reasonable and proceeds quickly. Saddles, for instance, which are to be had in those seaports for five dollars, cost twelve to fourteen dollars in St. Louis on the Mississippi and in the cities on the Missouri sixteen to twenty dollars. There is no other explanation for this than that every human endeavor in this area finds high rewards, which again, in the final analysis, has its basis in the abundance of fertile soil and the greatest possible freedom* of all trades from legal restrictions as well as from prejudices of rank, whereby an unnatural influx in certain trades can never be of lasting duration. And thus one can also see how much that opinion is worth, which was mentioned in the beginning, that in order to carry on a profitable trade in America, one would have to import European goods directly from Europe. It does not apply at all to business in the Mississippi countries. In the seaports of the Atlantic coast European goods are not much more expensive than in Europe itself. At any rate the difference is not so great that it could entice a merchant on the other side of the Allegheny Mountains to depart from the customary procedure. This consists in traveling annually once or twice to Philadelphia, New York, and Baltimore [PS-29] to take care of the new purchases and arrange for quick transportation of the purchased goods while a helper continues the business at home. How-

---

*The patent tax that has been introduced in some states can hardly be considered a detrimental limitation. This holds true particularly of the patent tax on the merchants in the state of Missouri. It has the purpose of preventing the roving about of strange peddlers who, as was mentioned before, can scarcely facilitate shopping here.

ever at this time considerable purchases of iron goods are made at the factories in Pittsburgh.

Whoever has founded a business among the new settlements is by no means forced to continue moving with the advancing population. Usually he will have made so many connections that he may leave this migration to the beginners, which allows therefore considerable leeway, which cannot be compared in any way with the old world. Although change takes place rather rapidly, a settled residence has many advantages. In the cities houses can be rented and in the country new ones can be constructed with very little cost which, for the time being, will be quite adequate for their purpose. The fluctuation in the prices at the seaports has (as can be judged by the above) no noticeable influence on the security of the situation of a storekeeper in the interior.

To go further into detail, to give the price of individual goods, is useless. What good does it do, for instance, if I state that a lumbering ax (weighing approximately five pounds) that can be gotten in Germany for one guilder can be had in Balitmore for approximately sixty cents, in St. Louis on the Mississippi for two and a half to three *Kroners*. Too much depends on the form when selling things, besides the inner quality (which American buyers understand very well how to judge), so that one could not proceed to start shipping without any further details. In America one soon learns what is for sale over there, and elsewhere only by a happy coincidence. Above all one has to know what items are made in the family. It would be very wrong, for instance, to bring coarse, woolen cloth to the interior, except that which the finish might recommend, that which could not be done in the households. Furthermore one should remember that one can figure on significant profits only when a formal store is opened and whoever has not prepared himself completely for this should not burden himself with any sizable supply of goods. Some sojourn in the country (in order to orient oneself) is absolutely necessary for every European who wants to make useful plans. Especially the merchant should not think that this sojourn could be replaced with information obtained at the seaports. I was able to tell my friends in the seaports of the Atlantic coast almost as much news about the interior of America on the other side of the Alleghenies as I was able to tell those in Germany. The merchants in the seaports find full occupation in the sea trade, and the Mississippi countries are too far away from the Atlantic coast to travel there for mere curiosity. It cannot be expected that the businessmen of the western states themselves would announce their situation to the world. Whoever wants to become acquainted with them should go to them. He will not be received with jealousy. The sphere of activity over there is so great that no one will be envious of his occupation. The language can be learned very soon on the trip itself. In all cities there, one is able to find the best board and room for four to five dollars a week. In the country it will not even cost half that much; however, as a consequence one also rarely has cause to be satisfied with one's room, even though everything else raises very little objection. I have repeatedly told how reasonably, comfortably, and quickly one can travel in the interior of America. What I have said earlier of the dangers of disease does not concern the businessman. For him much less is to be feared in the entire interior than in Europe in this regard. The coastal towns of Carolina, Georgia, and on the Mexican Gulf are not so important to him, and he can avoid them during the unhealthy season from the beginning of the month of May to the middle of October. The undertaking should begin with a stay of from several weeks up to two months at the seaports of Baltimore, Philadelphia, and New York. There one could try to obtain temporary information concerning the goods that are for sale in the West. The immigrating businessman should make a firm resolution to simply imitate the American in the beginning. He should discard, as much as possible, all preconceived notions that he may have had in Europe, in order to be able to observe without prejudice. He will find there a sphere for his activity for which he does not need such notions. Nothing is more contradictory to his purpose of perceiving reality correctly than the usual idea perceived in Europe that the North Americans are so very backward. Even when the conceit of an ignorant American should tempt a person, the immigrant need not follow it. It hinders calm judgment far too much. Any European who is tolerably informed and who comes to the Ohio, the Mississippi, or to the Missouri not entirely without money and does not disdain a normal occupation will find with some persistence an attractive sphere of activity, and a businessman who does not figure to see his hopes fullfilled in the first year should be advised to remain until he has become more familiar with the new things than is possible on a mere tour. He must have stayed among the Americans for at least six months. He may have reasons that persuade him to return to Europe without having had any commercial profit from his trip. This depends on his particular situation. However, if he attributes the blame to the country he should try to show in his own country through his behavior that it was not he himself who was to be blamed when the new world did not appeal to him.

It is very natural for an emigrant to have an inclination to keep, so to speak, one foot in his home country when he roams through foreign countries. Love for one's country can explain this sufficiently. However, he can afford this only in rare cases without considerable cost. As a rule, the emigrant will do well to renounce his home country for the first ten years and to occupy himself seriously with the thought of making America his home. That will give him that foundation that must be the prerequisite for many advantageous undertakings. Fathers of large families have enough reason in Germany, if only for the one reason of being able to give to their children a secure direction, to invest in the opportunity to look around abroad, and it would certainly be a useful intersession, even without any plans of a future settlement, to influence a member of the family to visit the Mississippi countries and to spend a reasonable time there as a good possibility for the future.

Appendix I

Textual Emendations Made in the Edition of 1834

Preface to the Second Edition

The sale of fifteen hundred copies of the first edition and the Swiss reprint attest to the wide distribution of this book,* and I must not complain that the attention of the public is not to be construed as encouragement to pursue my path.[1] However, beside the many proofs of approval in letters and journals also the other test of my undertaking is not lacking, namely, its effect on such people whose applause one cannot flee enough. How could I have hoped as a public defender of a national issue such as emigration and colonization to remain without opponents in a country where hunger, avarice, and vanity have put so many wheels in motion! The preparation of the work *Europe and Germany* (of which the second volume will appear toward the end of this year) and the large correspondence with those who are interested in my advice did not even afford me sufficient leisure to answer the well-meaning objections and criticisms, not to mention the slander and distortions. I console myself that almost all attacks were sufficiently weak not to deserve an answer. The time is past in which the fate of books was decided through general anathema under the title of a literary journal. Particularly, my book was soon in so many hands that I need not worry about the judgment of a shallow or malicious critic, and the sale of the above-mentioned new work proves to me that my name alone tips the scales against those forces that have appeared against me until now.

With this new edition, it is a question, however, of gathering together all the things that would not be worth the trouble of doing piecemeal. And, therefore, besides the refutation of the well-meant objections, I do not want to leave untouched the apparent animosities. Most of them will be treated at the individually contested points; however, the general attacks such as those that attack openly or covertly the tendency of the book or the credibility of the author can also be answered only in general terms, and for this purpose I know no more suitable place than the present preface.

The first place among such attacks belongs to the article in the *Berliner Jahrbuch für Kritik* (the 1830 issue, p. 907 and following). It may be considered a strong proof of my confidence in my cause and in the public that I have this article reprinted because otherwise it might be known only to very few people. However, I also do not doubt that many readers will be grateful to me when I give them an opportunity to submit their favorable opinion concerning me and my book, compared with the opinion of a professor of history at the University of Halle [H. Leo], and thus so to speak submit it to the test of fire.

Here follows the document, which is complete and faithful to the original, with the exception of the numbers, which, as well as the distinguishing print at several places, are my own.[2]

(1) The reporter considers himself convinced that it must be noticed by every reader of this book who is in the least able to judge written material that there is considerable difference between all the places where the author represents something vivid and those places where he intends to proceed in a argumentative way. For the description of that which he has seen, he shows, to be sure, as much talent as he shows little talent for his philosophical reasoning. No one will be able to read most of the letters without entertainment, pleasure, and enlightenment, while some things of the content as well as

---

*In order to guard against a new reprint, it is to be delivered to all emigration societies for half of the price, which has been set at one and a half *Thaler* Prussian currency by the Weber Bookstore. This is to apply, however, to orders of not less than twenty copies and only against cash payment.

almost the entire treatment that is appended to it concerning the nature of the North American States is only partially subordinate or in part, at least, must be called distorted. We shall pass over all those vivid descriptions of life and nature since samples of those have been picked out by other journals, particularly by the *Ausland*,[3] in considerable degree and have been presented to the German public and since the author has been given everywhere the praise to which he has been entitled; on the other hand, we shall be permitted to consider the tendency of the journal under discussion in general:

(2) It cannot be denied that the social conditions and the living conditions as they are demonstrated by the free North America have something very enticing for certain classes and for individuals who are after certain ambitions and that they must exert a certain charm, particularly where land and life have been treated so vividly by Mr. Duden. Therefore, one can always consider the formation of new states as well as the predominant view in the United States as highly subordinate, for it is just these people of subordinate classes or subordinate ambitions who can be most affected so that they would forget Europe's spiritual wealth and Europe's political grandeur. North America can, to be sure, be characterized by the fact that there the subordinate directions no longer feel as such, so that the differences between higher and lower exist, just because of it also the real preferential treatment of higher moral circles disappears. In place of a mutually determining and maintaining difference of class and education, there the difference of ruling over more or less sensuous means, in other words the difference merely of ownership and of industry, appears, whereby necessarily an equally superficial view of all conditions of life is determined.

(3) This superficial and defiant view of political and social relations is, to be sure, even in Europe characteristic of all classes and individuals who might feel quite at home in North America; only here fortunately it is also the case that these people as well as almost anywhere, as one is accustomed to saying, must have the fist in the pocket, because one would break it open if it were seen. To be sure, one can become so enthralled with this opinion that without having suspected the depth of spiritual life in German literature, not to mention having fathomed its depth, one would exclaim: it is ridiculous self-praise when the Germans maintain that among them there is more spiritual life than in North America. The Americans may forgive the Germans this conceit with respect to this area. I, however, consider myself obligated to name the matter by its rightful name. Only in Germany can such thoughts be uttered without being ridiculed. They are mentioned in connection with equally ridiculous reasons, such as: "The Americans have no history, material life makes too many demands on their energies, and so forth. If it were necessary to refute such statements, it would suffice to point out the old Asiatic and Egyptian colonies along the Mediterranean (which, after all, with what spiritual life? we would ask the author) and especially the glorious development of the Greeks in Italy (were the Krotoneans, the Sybarites, and the Tarentine people[4] ever equal to the Spartans and the Athenians?), who, because of the conditions of navigation prevalent at that time isolated themselves from their mother countries much more than the Europeans did in America. One should call to mind that the Romans, as well as the Greeks, in spite of their glorious history, later degenerated intellectually to such an extent that all lamentation about their disgraceful defeat by the crudest northern hordes must be silenced. And besides, is the former history of Europe less the heritage of the Europeans in America than of those who remained behind in the old home?"

(4) As if anybody would have thought to claim that a people with great historical memories could not degenerate! But rather such a nation could indeed degenerate, for a people that has not yet risen to the height of great historical memories has also not come to a point of its own spiritual character. And this is indeed what the author says in several places, namely, that the North Americans according to their spiritual ways are still very much influenced by the English and that the English education influenced theirs; but we

would like to add here that since as a whole in North America necessary but lower ways of life are dominant, also the branches of science and art alone, which correspond to these ways of life, can be of magnificent effect in North America. The historical memories of Europe are, however, in no other sense those of the North Americans, any more than the historical memories of Greece and Rome are those of all of Europe. That this is really so is proved by the author in another place in a later letter on page 175: "The only thing that I missed here was the proximity of German families who were my friends. The Germans and the North Americans do not differ at all in what is usually called nature and temperament. Also, domestic customs of the natives cannot offend the German immigrant. They are largely adapted to the situation, and one can easily become accustomed to them. Even the language barrier soon disappears. But the bond of common memories will always be missing. However well a German may adjust to the manner of life and the situation of Americans, the charm that social relationships derive from the past is felt all the less the longer the immigrant has lived in his native country."

(5) What a charm the fairy tales of our childhood exercise, which are rooted in the innermost life of the people and in part in the historically rooted memories of earlier times. What charm our folk legends exercise, which we have absorbed with our mothers' milk and which our fantasy combines with hills and rivers, with lakes, and with a crossroads and which have become familiar to us in our homeland from childhood on; what charms are exercised by memories of our imperial cities, our dominant dynasties, the classes to which we belong, the religious parties with which we were educated—what charm does this entire historical heritage exercise on us, on our wishes and ideas concerning the coloring of our feelings, concerning the education of our character, and to all of this we should lightly say farewell for the sake of the fleshpots and the cornfields of North America?—Also disregarding the pain that we would experience to have to listen to people who are completely absorbed by the agricultural, industrial, and mercantile when they assume the competency to talk about the loftiest topics and that spiritual modesty that can be found anywhere and everywhere in our fatherland where superficial liberalism has not yet completely wiped out everything, how could we do without that—also disregarding the pain with which noble people would be faced when emigrating to North America should one not think that there are still bonds that link one with the German soil and that are stronger than the enticements of easy gain of life's existence and of bourgeois value. "The European preconceptions with regard to the rank of professions and of physical activities" are the foundations of all that we consider political excellence no matter how the liberal screamers and writers would rave against them.

(6) The true key to the whole mood of the author seems to be found on page 179. There it reads as follows: "If a small city were founded with the intention of serving the American Germans as a center of culture, one would see a rejuvenated Germania arise and the European Germans would then have a second country here, such as the British have. If only a live interest for such a project would develop in Germany! No plan of the present day can be more promising to the individual and to the whole than such a plan for the founding of a city as the center of German culture in western North America, and especially in the areas west of the Mississippi." Such wishes have frequently been expressed in recent times, particularly to the effect that it would be desirable that Germans emigrating to North America would not lose themselves in the mass of Anglo-Americans, but might form a new German people. Let us say a few more words concerning the necessary consequences of realizing this wish.

(7) When people who are not forced by necessity leave their homeland, then, with few exceptions, only two motives are at the root of their action. Either the conditions of real circumstances in their homeland are not adequate to what they consider reasonable, or the circumstances of their homeland do not offer the free play to their need for the employment that they seek. The latter are people who in general are oriented toward appearance, the former however have become addicted to the service of abstract ideas,

because only this will lead to a collapse of reality. In the case of the founding of all colonies that were not instituted by the governments themselves with definite goals and for a limited purpose and kept strictly in this narrowly focused frame, we see how certain ideas that were inherent in conditions in the homeland become caricatures in their abstract isolation because of their one-sided application, just because they could develop only one-sidedly. These caricatures have at all times also had a decided tendency to be materialistic, sensual, and superficial, as history has demonstrated from time immemorial.

(8) It was not in the ancient cities of Greece, but in the colonial states where democracy and aristocracy degenerated most glaringly into ochlocracy and oligarchy. In the colonial states of the Middle Ages, in Jerusalem and on Cyprus, in the Christian colonial states founded in the Pyrenees on Saracen soil, feudalism became a caricature, and thus the democratic emphasis, which in spite of all denials of some church historians was also present during the Reformation after it had been pushed back everywhere in Europe when it began to stir to moderate limits, has become a characteristic element in America.

(9) At all time, however, the colonies exerted their significant reciprocal effect on the mother countries. In them, so to speak, the spirit of the motherland moves outside, and in this capacity it again affects the motherland by creating an imbalance and changing conditions there. As long as Germany has no independent colonies of her own, she experiences the retroaction of the European colonies only indirectly and not in the same degree as for instance Great Britain does from North America, where the author himself admits that to create a German populace in a colonial land without keeping it under the firmest constrictions of the motherland would mean therefore to create a power that could only exert a disorganizing influence on the condition of Germany. And why that?—Those to whom Germany means so little that they leave it could not possibly be of so much value to the Germans remaining behind that they would care whether the emigrants got lost among other nations or not. The population is, however, not by any means large enough, not to mention too large. So long as a person can comfortably expand and isolate himself merely through his work, his atomic sense will not leave him. Relations of dependency, whose ruling principle is true piety, cannot develop again until space becomes so crammed and life for whole classes becomes so crowded that the latter will recognize with gratitude the helping hands extended to them, and yet we are still a long way away from that point. Now we are only at the point where people demand impetuously that something be done to remedy their plight.

H. Leo[5]

After the first general impression has been overcome, I request my fellow brothers to follow me in a consideration of greater detail.

Already the beginning is of the kind that all attempts to find some reasonable sense in it fail. A mind must be able to combine superior ability to comprehend the human machinery (for it is certainly clear from paragraph 2 that it is not only a question of rural nature) with the most striking inability to think about it. To what reasonable person must it still be made comprehensible that similar things to what I have related about North America and even the information of a certain Leo cannot be understood by themselves? That prior to that the proper setting has to be prepared and, to be sure, through long philosophical reasoning with avoidance of all of Leo's confusion. But the critic whose clumsy style is apparently caused by awkward thinking seems, it is clear, to have advanced to the thesis on his own that the mind of a person is a camera obscura in which the life and action of nations are portrayed by themselves. In truth, since his conviction of spiritual life beside ours must be based primarily on his own conception, then in the case of the arbitrary expression of Leo's conviction, which from the beginning considers anybody who judges differently incapable of judgment, nothing is left except the alternative that the mind of the critic is indeed similar to a camera obscura or that he wanted to direct his comment in the manner of a carnival quack or a judge at a inquisition.

Yet let us read on. Immediately after this beginning Mr. Leo says (2) that North America to be sure has its attractions, but only for people of subordinate standing, education, and ambition. What would be more natural with such words than to look at the personality of the critic? Who is this Mr. Leo? Of what station is he? And what is he really striving to accomplish? I humbly confess that I have no reason to be proud of my profession. But it is not at all clear to me why I should rank it below that of the professor. And as to his aspiration, I ask once more, what is it Mr. Leo is striving to do? What is my ambition? Heaven knows what Mr. Leo thinks of it. At any rate it is a foregone conclusion for him that I am after external and sensual objectives (2 and 7). How full of contradictions this world is. Just the tendency that Mr. Leo seems to feel is so very much directed toward material things has earned me back home the reproach that I do not stress them sufficiently and pursue fantastic ideas. However, what must help the reader arrive at an answer as to the difference between me and the critic is after all the question of how this Mr. Leo, who so disdainfully looks down on all earnings, makes a living. I wonder whether by chance he holds his professorship without pay and whether he does not accept pay for his writings. No matter what answers I may get, I enjoy the peace of mind of being able to face my judge without hesitation when it comes to a strict investigation of my actions as to whether lower considerations had any part in them.

Paragraphs 3, 4, and 5 follow in a lovely sequence. Let the reader read them with circumspection and try to find that depth in Mr. Leo that he so completely misses in me. It is part of the most common phenomena that a poor wretch offers his dullness for depth by proclaiming depth. But if the intellectual in Mr. Leo could not even be so much incited by a call to a professorship at a university to recognize the silliness in a trick scarcely forgivable to one of the weakest students, then one may indeed doubt that there is anything at all in him that could be excited. His efforts to shroud his dull view even more with smoke through wordiness remind us only too much of children and ostriches who believe they can make themselves invisible to others by closing their own eyes or by hiding their faces. The contents of paragraphs 3 and 4 concern really the author and teacher of history. One, or rather I (for I would like to agree to anything with which I am in disagreement with Mr. Leo and would appear without the following publication if only my adversary had not used trickery when he first appeared, as if he supported his claims by other authorities rather than the naked authority of Leo), so I cannot hide my amazement when reading comments on Greek colonies, as can be seen in paragraph 3, written by a public teacher of history and published in a literary journal of our century. Truly, the content of my travel report cited in the critique seemed to me to be done in such a manner that I could not have expected an attack upon any part. In the beginning I thought new manuscripts must have been found, and so I inquired among the philologists. Then I looked around for handbooks, but in the older as well as in the newer I found only one and the same answer. In Eschenburg's *Handbook of Ancient Classical Literature*[6] one reads for instance on pages 59–60 as follows:

"The region of land occupied by them was called Greater Greece. It was separated from Sicily only by a narrow strait and because of it there developed among both countries many associations of the languages, the sciences, mores, and laws. Since these countries enjoyed a long undisturbed peace, the Romans not waging war on them until relatively late, and their association with the Greeks proper continued, the arts and sciences enjoyed a very happy continuation among them. Here we note only the school of Pythagoras flourishing in Greece, therefore called the Italian school, and the Eleatic sect derived from it and founded by Xenophanes.[7] Also Greater Greece and particularly Sicily were the home of excellent men who are still famous for their talents, sciences, and writings, such as Archimedes, Diodorus, the poets Theocritus, Moschus, and Bion, the orators Lisias and Gorgias, as well as others."[8]

In the *Handbook of the History of Antiquity* by Heeren[9] it is written: "It was just the colonies founded by the Greeks to the west of the motherland along the Mediterranean that surpassed the others in power as well as in wise laws." And what does Heeren mean by the others? He means, as he clearly tells us, those on the coast of Asia Minor where Greek culture developed its first and most beautiful buds and from which also the Greeks in their motherland obtained the direction of their aesthetic education, namely the fatherland of Homer, of Alcaeus, and of Sappho. Then in the same handbook there follow several closely printed pages pertaining to the individual western colonies, such as (1) on Tarentum where the most flourishing period was between 500 and 400 B.C.; (2) on Kroton; (3) on Sybaris; (4) on Thurii; (5) on Locri Epizephyrii; (6) on Rhegium; (7) on Cumae, which in turn founded Naples in Italy and Messina in Sicily.[10]

Whoever works through this completely and with care and finds in each work pertaining to the Greeks, the English as well as the French, the Italian, and so forth, similar remarks to those by Heeren and Schlosser[11] will surely join me in my amazement and will ask with me whether one can be a teacher of history today without knowing something of the famous legislator of Locri whose laws are said to have existed unchanged for two hundred years. Together with me he will ask whether one can be a teacher of history without knowing of the same Zaleucus who, according to Strabo, was the first to separate the judicial power from the legislative. What, has Mr. Leo never heard of Charondas? never of Archytas? never of the three hundred thousand warriors who Sybaris drew up against Kroton? nothing of the seven Krotonians who all won the prize at the same time in the Olympic games? And if the gentleman critic puts so little weight on all that as he does on Pythagoras and his students, does he not know that among the colonists of new Sybaris there was the father of history himself? Surely, Mr. Leo would not doubt the flourishing of an American colony if he, who boasts of a distant relationship with that father of history, would be among the colonists, and yet he questions the flourishing of the colonies in Italy where Herodotus spent many years of his life and even concluded his life as a peaceable citizen?[12]

To be sure, these are signs of ignorance that might be excused by loss of memory. But how can the passage occurring under no. 4 be excused where it is written: "The historical memories of Europe are in no other sense those of the North Americans, any more than the memories of Greece and Rome are those of all of Europe"? Are perhaps the whites in North America not a part of the modern European development? Or do the words *modern European development* have no meaning for Mr. Leo? Does the whole historical light of Mr. Leo not reach to the sentence that modern European development sprang forth from a Germanic and Roman element as from new buds, and that the history and development of the Greeks and Romans appeared in addition as completely separate by themselves? Can there be a more telling proof for the assertion that in Europe people write textbooks on history who do not at all care about the true composition of historical data? The cockeyed view of the critic is so bad that he even uses one passage of my travel report that speaks of reminiscenses of my own life to support his absurdities.

After these examples of historic depth the critic again occupies himself with my personality without having researched it in the least except as he believes to see it in my book and gushes forth recitals of influences that are usually felt least by those who babble loudest about them. If one hears Mr. Leo talk about the forces of nationality one could believe that he was talking about an adversary who carelessly despised everything that cannot be devoured with a greedy mouth, in whose veins not a trace of German blood runs. Therefore it can surely not surprise anybody if I ask with amazement what passage in my book would give cause for this. Whoever appears as a public speaker in similar affairs must be prepared for a severe examination of his actions, his character, and his life, besides receiving criticism of his words; and to be sure that much more the more information about it concerning the value of his advice is to be expected. It was my purpose to guide every reader with the first preface to my travel report and with several passages in the report toward this direction. However, Mr. Leo considers this superfluous. He believes he recognizes from an author's words all that motivates and drives him. I confess that I did not limit myself to his writings when I examined the personality of Mr. Leo—which the reviewer as a discussant of the same subject has to put up with just as I—but rather I inquired about his standing and aspirations in the case of the questions suggested above as well as regarding his nationality and his life-style. And in doing this, again there was no evidence that could deter me from a comparison with Mr. Leo with respect to Germanness and way of thinking.

It makes a strange impression to hear some warm praise of the modesty in a document of unsurpassed presumption, to hear it from a man who forces himself on a Europe praised by him for its humility, where hardly any province, city, social class, or corporation would elect him as their spokesman for social or state affairs, and then croaks of liberal screamers and writers. It is well known that wherever political parties are, selfishness leans upon one of the parties. The names of liberals and antiliberals are also highly indefinite among the Germans, and on both sides the worst individuals can be found to whom politics merely serves as a pretense. I am just as little inclined to subscribe to everything that is usually termed liberal as to the sentences regarding the divinity of autocratic power. But no matter in which party I may be counted, none of the sincere of either party would condemn me for the reasons for which this strange critic slanders me.

I would consider him who would have to refute that nonsense that Mr. Leo has already produced on paper as even less favored by fate than Mr. Leo himself. To write thick books of history without revealing truths takes a better imagination than that of Mr. Leo. For this reason one cannot doubt that some truth does appear in his works. But one should guard against deriving it from the author. How much untruth would have to be transferred from one brain to whole volumes that can present so much that is confused, false, and distorted on a few pages, a brain that deduces the difference between the Greek colonies and their mother states from the circumstances that the first were colonies, but the others were not (8); since after all every student comprehends what part colonization has also had in the development of the mother states, it will not be necessary to elaborate further on it.

If finally (6) the critic finds the right key to my mood in my wish for a center of German culture in North America and then seeks to put this mood on trial by the alternative that can be read under no. 7 (which in itself may be considered a model of the narrowmindedness that Mr. Leo respects so highly), then I find it far more convenient to find his mood and his ill humor. Without any middle clauses I need only point to the content of no. 9. Herein lies the explanation to Leo's being, as far as writing and words can give an explanation about our inner being, so that every syllable of commentary is superfluous. Whoever dares to talk in such a manner about the distress of the Germans and can say aloud that the distress is not yet great enough and that we should get to the point of licking, like dogs, the hands of him who throws crumbs to us, he will reap the full disgust from the lowliest as well as from the highest who has but a trace of Germanic blood in him for such unspeakable behavior, no matter whether he swears to his feelings for the most sacred interest of Germany in a thousand folios. Whoever publicly confesses that the present emergency is desirable for European humanity also puts himself in the alternate situation that he should count himself among the number of select to whom it is proper from God and by virtue of law to take advantage of others, or he would have to admit that he is living with the others in the wholesome distress that forced him to deny all nobler feelings because of the bread that he expected from a compassionate master to satisfy his hunger.

As proof that my irritated sensibility did not have any part in my answer, I remind the reader that I kept silent for over a year. My book is addressed to the sensible people of all classes, and among them there are many who care little about the pedantic behavior of so-called scholars and consequently also do not suspect what sins against nature and reason, what silly quarrels and passionate denials of Christian charity, occur for the sake of mere words and letters. Primarily for their sake I was not permitted to leave Leo's anathema entirely to its own nothingness. If nevertheless my speech on it seems to betray to someone a special inner emotion, then I beseech him to look back to the details of the criticism and to ask himself whether it would be possible to submit it to a new reading even after a lapse of months and years without experiencing a certain indignation? My emotion does not exceed this indignation that all will feel whom my book does not displease. There is such a gulf between Mr. Leo and me that his praise would upset me more than his rebuke. And between what I call spiritual and antispiritual, high and low, noble and servile, pure and dirty, cloudy and clear, deep and shallow, depraved and unspoiled, distorted and natural and what Mr. Leo calls it, there is such a difference that if at an eventual mustering of humanity he should be ranked among the healthy and reasonable, I would patiently join the sick and foolish without awaiting my judgment. It is a consolation for me that in that case I may not find myself without some pleasant company, vouched for by the practical effect of my book as well as the comments of the best journals and those of a man whose authority pretty much invalidates that of Mr. Leo. Shortly before his death the famous Niebuhr, after examining a part of the work *Europe and Germany,* wrote the following.[13]

I thank you, sir, for the kind transmission of the synopsis of the work that you have planned. Already in the general part whose plan you have specifically given I saw several points touched on in which we agree while differing from the predominant opinion. Those, however, which will be treated in the subsequent parts excite my expectations in an even higher degree since your views emanate from the bright and uninhibited observation, the love for the truth and independence of the spirit concerning the vivid matter at hand that makes your report on America superb, yes indeed classic, and the advice pertaining to it as inspired by your practical mind. If only those settlement plans that we discussed frequently would reach execution and your thoughts be taken to heart by those who are in a position to do something for it.
With highest respects, I remain, dear sir, your most devoted, Niebuhr
8 December 1830

That was an attack on the trend. Now to the attacks on the credibility of whomever else had to appear, because not everyone who counteracts emigration and colonization has the courage to admit it openly. In this class a clumsy piece of work, which cannot be held up high enough to an unsuspecting public as a sad sign of the degradation of our literary journals leading to shameless calumny and insolent falsifications of writing, deserves the first place. I know the weight of my words before the law and the judge and say it forcibly in order to keep the attention of the reader in suspense for the case per se.
A so-called collective-critique of several books referring to emigration to North America appears in the *Jenaische Literatur-Zeitung* (and to be sure in the supplement to the March issue of 1833). It begins under the heading "Newest Colonization Works" with a travel report. Without in the least referring to any claim or final conclusion of the book, which has been discussed in all parts of Germany and received with much acclaim for the past five years, the critic from *Jena* labels it curtly as completely superficial, fantastic, and exaggerated. I do not feel like playing the philanthropist with such a sneerer and cannot force myself to overlook compassionately the faults which he reveals in his ridiculous insolence. On the contrary I consider it highly propitious to the good cause not only to reveal without forbearance the way in which he himself staggers about in his exaggeration and superficiality but also to show his crude ignorance, his silly contradictions, and, what is far worse, the apparent falsification of the evidence used against me.
The complete comment regarding me and my book does not total one quarto page, but it would be hard to commit a greater sin against reason and honesty in so little a space. To every review of a book belongs without doubt the work as such, without

presenting to the readers any mixture of extraneous material. Instead the critic begins vice versa with a general accusation that I have the intention of luring emigrants to the state of Missouri, and he then presents the contents of the book as it fits this accusation with these few words: "Mr. Duden depicts for us the state of Missouri as a true paradise where all possible kinds of fruit grow wild, and similar fantastic splendors."

The clumsy piece of work can be upset by the simple explanation that the creator, who accuses me of fantasy and exaggeration, criticizes a phantom created by him rather than my book and that particularly the phrase *of all possible kinds of fruit in the woods along the Missouri* is a ridiculous exaggeration on the part of the critic, which his brain adds to my description and which he subsequently attacks as having originated with me. However, he must not get off this easy, he who sins more from malice than from folly. I want to pursue the fellow step by step in order to show the public that the way in which he takes the field against the phantom confused with my report is still stranger than his conception of the report itself.

One should not look at all for some method in his scribble. Having stated that I describe the state of Missouri as a paradise where all species of fruit grow wild, he begins the real attack on my book or on his fantastic conception of it with the phrase, "that all this is not so can be seen, and so forth," and nevertheless he had previously attacked my description of the Missouri climate by putting it on the same level as that of Brazil. This sortie, however, should not be overlooked because of its irregularity, and if his readers do not take it so exactly or want to doubt the prudent seriousness of the fighter, then I ask them to look at the later page (at the discussion on the Giessen Emigration Society) where the Arkansas territory bordering on the state of Missouri is placed with emphasis in the deepest south of the Union. I wonder how this geographer may judge the climates? That he does not know anything of what the physicists consider basic is shown by his comparison of the Missouri climate, which almost every winter covers the river with firm ice, with that of Brazil, in whose tremendous area no trace of a German winter can be found, as is shown by the older as well as by the more recent reports, the latest of which is by the traveler Dr. F. X. Ackermann (Heidelberg, published by Groos, 1834),[14] there is no trace of a German-type winter on the seacoast nor in the highlands, which rise several thousand feet above sea level. The critic seems to define the climates according to the summer heat, not suspecting how hot summer is in the Polar regions and that one suffers more from the heat in Petersburg in Russia than along the Rhine River. The Arkansas territory, which extends only over three and one-half degrees of latitude, is just as far removed from the deepest south of the Union, in other words, from Florida, as the southern half of Germany is from southern Italy. The states of Mississippi, Louisiana, Alabama, and Florida lie considerably farther south than the critic's deepest south; and partially more south lie the states of Georgia and South Carolina. The northern third of Arkansas lies in the same latitude as the state of Tennessee, to which the amazing geographer urgently invites the German emigrants (in supplement 26) (1) in order to keep them from Brazil on the Missouri, which is a few degrees farther north, (2) so that they would try their hand at Merino sheep raising, and (3) so that they could give him (the critic) a report about the success of the experiment. Truly it is no small task to go through such silliness with patience and read how the same babbler does not talk about a tropical climate either in the state of Tennessee or in Kentucky, nor in the state of Ohio, all of which do not lie farther north than the areas on the left bank of the Missouri, indeed he does not even mention the state of Illinois, which is separated from the state of Missouri by the Mississippi River. Yet without the slightest scruple he repeats that Duden's Eden is similar to Brazil. Until now I have only had to deal with an outpost skirmish. The nice fighter begins the real war, as stated before, with the remark "we can see that all of this is not true by looking at, and so forth," and so I will cite everything in detail that he sees.

First he refers to a written report of the brothers Tscharner[15] from Chur who settled in the western part of North America, in which it is written:

"In the city of St. Louis we found several Swiss and Germans, but of all these people we did not hear much that was pleasant concerning the state of Missouri. They said that it was too hard and too expensive to clear the woods and in addition the soil was not everywhere as fertile as Duden had said."

Secondly he refers to the testimony of the physician Kaspar Köpfli from Sursee who had settled in Illinois. In his little book, *Bright and Dark Sides of New Switzerland,* Sursee, 1833, page 57, he talks of colorful notions that have been conveyed by me regarding the country there.[16]

Thirdly he refers to the report of Mr. P. von Zoya[17] from the state of Illinois "that all members of his company had preferred this state, because it required too much work on the Missouri to clear out the dense forests."

It is this and nothing more with which the critic believes he can completely invalidate my book. For immediately after these and no other statements of witnesses he exclaims:

"So we see from these reliable reports that Mr. Duden's colorful notions are more idealistic than founded on truth."

And merely as a superfluous remark he seems to add:

"The most correct judgment of the state of Missouri, which is completely unsuited for Germans, can be found in Brauns's *On the Ideas of Emigration to America,* Göttingen, page 217, where its bright and dark sides are pointed out with an impartiality, but about which we are not able to report here because of lack of space.[18]

After this proof so beautifully delivered concerning the correctness of my descriptions, a compassionate explanation follows stating why I had not been able to furnish anything of worth for emigrants: that I had lived as a physician on the Missouri, just as I was now residing in Bonn as a physician, with a female cook (*maid,* to use the language of the critic) who kept house (which is appended as if it were a natural consequence) and that I had described everything absolutely superficially.

However, before the conclusion the warrior so sure of his victory seems to have been touched by a little scruple, which he attempts to overcome with a harangue that is to be listed as the fourth element of proof. It reads:

"Why did, in order to cite one more, the state of Missouri so charmingly described by him (Duden), which is several thousand English square miles* bigger than Ohio, Indiana, and Illinois, have only 140,070 souls in 1830 while Ohio had 937,650, Indiana 341,582, and Illinois 157,575?[20] The reason is that Missouri does not possess all the facets attributed to it by its worshipers, but stands far behind those states to the west, which were created simultaneously (!!!) as to quality."

The warning exclamation forms the conclusion:

"We therefore give the well-meaning (!!!) advice not to let oneself be enticed to Missouri by Duden's book any more than to Brazil by Schäffer's."[21]

With this one would have the entire attack before one's eyes if the confused scribbler did not present passages in his critique of the two reports by Köpfli that also belong here. I want to list them as the fifth and sixth pieces of evidence against me.

(5) In the review of the travel report of the Köpfli family and Suppiger (Sursee, 1833, Schneider Bookstore),[22] one reads:

(a) with reference to the route and the cost of emigration:

"The fourteen people would have saved more than three hundred dollars if they had traveled via New Orleans to St. Louis rather than via New York. One could therefore see how carelessly those act who nevertheless choose the latter route."

In support of this statement the critic refers to page 226, where Salomon Köpfli (the son of the physician) says:

---

*Let the reader not be too impressed by these thousands of square miles, but let him remember that every thousand is less than fifty German square miles.[19]

"How much more convenient and cheaper the trip must be via New Orleans will be understood by everybody, however we had to consider Duden's advice," to which the critic comments:

"What a shame that Duden's advice caused them more than double in time and cost."

(b) With reference to what the emigrants found in St. Louis, we read:

"Here now in Duden's Eden, where the Swiss society had arrived after so much cost and so many detours, they found it so uncomfortable that we soon afterward find them settled twenty-seven miles away in Illinois."

(6) In the review of *Bright and Dark Sides of New Switzerland* already mentioned, finally the following critical puff appears:

"On page 55 the author speaks of some of his efforts, his beautiful aspirations that now have tumbled down, and therefore warns by no means to yield to any extravagant fantastic idea of the United States, for which particularly Duden is to be blamed."

So this is the complete corpus delicti, and now I ask the reader to accompany me on an examination of it.

All that the critic musters against my descriptions from persons who themselves had been on the spot consists merely of statements that clearing the forest was too hard and costly, that the soil was not everywhere as fertile as I say, and the reproach of my fantastic ideas that Mr. Köpfli is supposed to have made.

For the time being I abstract from the little word *supposed,* and by taking the pieces of evidence so far as the critic gives them, I raise the question whether they in themselves seem to be sufficient for a reasonable person to make the statement that my report was absolutely superficial, untrue, and extremely exaggerated. Where, I ask further, is it written there that the soil along the Missouri is everywhere very fertile? Did I not repeatedly speak of the degrees of fertility, mention the poor stretches, and touch on the characteristics of the best soil? And even with the reference to the clearing of the forest, did I not discuss in detail in the Fourteenth, Eighteenth, and Thirty-first letters to what the difficulties can be reduced? Did I not furnish the safest measure in stating the cost for which each *Morgen* (of 160 square rods or 43,560 London square feet) could be cleared? Did I not tell that it costs at the most fifteen Rhenish guilders? And that for that sum the land would be completely ready for the plow, and that no settler could make use of more than ten to twenty *Morgen* of tilled land during the first few years, that the cattle could feed in the woods, and so forth? Where have these decisive points ever been contested by the critic or his witnesses, not to mention been refuted? Or do the words *hard and costly* not indicate clearly enough from what kind of emigrants these complaints emanate? That they come from people who have set out without the means that were judged indispensable according to the Thirty-first Letter and, in spite of my warnings, wanted to undertake the clearing of their first field personally? And, although I had to advise in general against emigration across the ocean for people without means, did I not myself remark that the natural prairies, to be sure, were important for the poorer settlers, and at the very place where I remarked that the state of Missouri was not lacking in them? Where has the least of these important details been observed by the most superficial of all critics? Instead, he rather giddily indulges in slandering generalities and seizes with particular joy the phrase *fantastic ideas* without, however, producing one single other proof that the Köpfli family did not buy land on the right bank of the Mississippi and in the state of Missouri, but rather eight, I repeat, eight hours from it in the state of Illinois. And it is just this example that the unconscionable reviewer draws from a little book that affirms my descriptions from the beginning to the end as being absolutely true. On page 208 and following the Messrs. Köpfli cite exactly the motives for their choice; and that, instead of dissatisfaction with the state of Missouri, the advantageous offers of their seller had drawn them to Illinois is additionally most clearly evident from other places, which, however, the critic is careful to avoid. For right after the motives described (page 215), one reads:

"The longer we live in this strange land the better we learn to understand Duden's book," and so forth.

Shortly before (page 201) one could read in a letter still dated from the state of Missouri:

"That I must confess, that all investigations and everything I have seen with my own eyes agree with Duden's information, and so on."

Further:

"Everywhere where we asked an immigrant how he was and whether he wished he were home, we received the answer: I am satisfied, now I am well off; during the first two years I sometimes had to toil and moil, but now I am accustomed to the country, its customs, and its language, and I have long forgotten my old home country.—One usually hears such remarks. But it is no wonder, for the most common man lives here too well!"

The reader will be amazed that one could dare to cite such a book against mine, since it talks of mine only with praise, without the slightest reproach. However, the critic puts the crowning statement to this impudence by referring to my advice not to travel via New Orleans. Mr. Kaspar Köpfli entered into a correspondence with me before his departure from Europe, and although I appealed in my answers expressly to his own judgment whether he would choose the state of Missouri or Illinois after he had made excursions from St. Louis, I nevertheless referred him concerning the route to be taken to pages 249 and 260 of my book (pages 332 and 347 of the first [German] edition), where it says that during the summer months from May to October one would have to avoid New Orleans because of the yellow fever. And since Mr. Köpfli wanted to depart in the spring (as, indeed, he did depart according to his printed report, at the end of April 1831), he turned toward New York. The remark on pages 225 and 226 made by Köpfli and used against me by the critic refers to this and it follows here in its entirety:

"The immigrants from Germany begin to take their way via New Orleans. Thus at the same time as we, on 16 April 1831, the ship *Boston* filled with immigrants set sail from Havre for New Orleans. Since that time we have spoken with some of those immigrants, who very much praise their route (even during the dangerous season). They encountered no storms and arrived in New Orleans in fifty-eight days after fine weather, and all were well. They had paid 130 francs a person for steerage, and children under six years were counted three for each full fare.—How much more comfortable and reasonable this voyage must be can be seen by everybody, however Duden's advice had to be considered here."

Apparently in this passage only the comfort and reasonableness are stressed, nevertheless, the danger is remembered, and it probably never occurred to the author to reproach me. The critic, however, looks at it quite differently; and without in the least knowing what was, and still is, important about that advice, he exclaims, as stated: "Too bad, we note, that Duden's advice caused them the loss of more than double in time and cost." What should I say against such a scribbler? What would the same have said if the Rhine-Bavarian Society, which against my advice traveled in the summer via New Orleans to the Missouri and lost several members because of yellow fever, had complained that what happened was the consequence of my advice?

However, let us abstract for a while from the evil intention of the critic and look beyond the arguments per se at the praise attached to them by the writer Brauns of Deensen: "We find the most correct and quite impartial judgment of the state of Missouri, which is completely unsuited for Germans, and so forth." Does not the genuine inclination to keep the criticism up, if at all possible, correspond to just that wretchedness of those arguments and to the uncontested fact that Brauns never lived in the state of Missouri but rather several hundred miles from it, that he uses the words *we find* in connection with the mention appearing later (issue 26 in the discussion of another book) of his own view of an area in Pennsylvania, which leads us to the assumption that the critic had still other personal reasons for his assertion? None of the witnesses quoted who had been on the Missouri talks about the climate, and yet the critic talks most decisively about it. What question is therefore more natural than to ask on what he is basing his claims? And when toward the end he gives the Germans this well-meaning advice: "We therefore advise not to let yourself be enticed to Missouri by Duden's book as little as to Brazil by Schäffer's," what question is then more natural than: "Who is this *we*?" Has this *we*, the one who can convince us so poorly with strange authorities, ever been personally at the locations in question? And if he has, why should we believe him more than anyone else? Why does he not at least name himself, so that one could examine how much his authority really means, he who cannot contest Duden's book either from its own content or with any testimony of a third who does not only report hearsay? In vain! In response to such objections the critic offers at the end of his writings and reports extending over a big fascicle (in which he has included a few evidently poor ones without malice) in a sneering tone only the letters *Br. Ds.*

Indeed, the reader unfamiliar with the lies and deception, the silliness and charlatanery in literature, would not imagine any such thing as that in matters on which the well-being and the fate of so many families depended, in matters that everybody involved wants to examine if possible themselves and not blindly believe only on the basis of the most celebrated name, that one would publicly dare attempt in our day to substitute for the complete lack of reasons and evidence the use of the mere column of the *Jenaische Literatur-Zeitung* and to change the modest *I* into the blown-up *we*. Such a reader must form for himself a strange picture of the minds for whom such literary papers are primarily printed, of minds for whom a bald *we* on whose existence and meaning no one can obtain closer information, or whoever gets it can but laugh; a *we* that is supposed to have a magic power to disseminate without any delay thick as well as thin volumes filled with facts and conclusions like empty fog.

In the case of those people who are under the spell of this magic, even the most effective arguments will be of just as little help to me as if I were to hold up to the master and his black arts the well-known works of D. B. Warden and Timothy Flint,[23] in which for each major place of my book, and especially for my description of the climate along the Missouri, the strongest support can be found. However, one means is left to me, nevertheless, that is hardly going to fail with the most transcendental respect for the records of our book courts. To be sure, the master has let himself be carried away by his self-confidence of being able to dole out glory or disgrace according to his whim to authors on colonization to defy the oldest power in the realm of scholars, the gentleman of logic, in such a manner that even cuts off the appearance of a conciliatory interpretation. Let us listen. The powerful criticism is also spread concerning the work of the American traveler Dr. Gerke (which appeared in 1833 at Hamburg from Perthes and Besser)[24] and says, among other warm eulogies pertaining to that book, that it has adequately answered all questions relevant for an emigrant. Now, however, I invite the reader to convince himself quickly that it was just Mr. Gerke who in his appraisal of many works on North America, incorporated in the above-mentioned work, declared mine to be the best of all that have appeared so far. What may have escaped the unfortunate critic completely, Gerke expressly protests against drawing the conclusion of collusion because of the agreement of my book with his. He stated that he had not read my book until he had finished his, and our agreement was based on the fact that we both had seen and judged correctly.—From this one can also judge how much Mr. Gerke—with whom I sincerely enjoy working toward a mutual goal—will feel honored by the praise of our mutual critic.

According to the old rule, I have saved the best for the last. Evidence enough is available of the confusion, shallowness, ignorance, and contradictions of the critic. Thus I could pass over the question raised at the end of the review and the foolish answer, according to which Missouri, which did not become part of the Union until 1803, is supposed to have entered life simultaneously with Illinois, Indiana, and Ohio, which had been ceded from France already in 1763,[25] even without reminding the reader that just the slight difference between the population of Illinois and that of Missouri speaks against this silly conclusion. However, in the introduction of my defense there is talk of falsification, and this might be the best time to meet the suspicion that I may have used stronger words, to be sure, than may be fair. Well, I shall not hesitate any longer and shall proceed to reveal one page of the so-called review, which must resolve any doubt concerning the nature of its source.

Already, when mentioning the publication printed under the title *Travel Report of the Köpfli and Suppiger Families,* I showed that these families in no way complained about me. When I read the *Jena* trash I did not yet know of the other publication of Köpfli entitled *Bright and Dark Sides,* and so on, and the words of the critic pertaining to it.

"On page 55 the author speaks of some of his beautiful expectations, which by now had crashed down, and warns of 'exaggerated, fantastic notions for which Duden is primarily to be blamed,' " did not make a weak impression on me. I would not expect such a thing from the Messrs. Köpfli. I immediately sent for the little book, opened it to the designated page, and found in confirmation of my suspicion more than I suspected. In the first place, I found that the talk of collapsed hopes did not originate with the American Köpfli, to whom the critic attributes them, but with a Köpfli who remained in Switzerland. Secondly, not one syllable was directed against North America, not to mention against my book, but it referred solely to warnings against plans that entailed the accord of many people. Thirdly, that the person who, according to the critic, is responsible for the complaint said exactly the opposite. For immediately on the subsequent page, 57, one can read quite clearly that I am not to be blamed for the somewhat colorful notions that one is wont to get through my book. Just what I complained about is also lamented by father and son Köpfli, namely, that the reports on North America are poorly understood, and for that reason he admonished not to find more good in them than there really is and also not to overlook the adverse. Nevertheless, the shameless reviewer asserts, depending on the assumption that one would not read the original in Germany, that Köpfli blamed me, even when he expressly says the opposite.*

What should I call such a method? Is it anything but a wicked falsification for wicked purposes? The courts will examine it more closely. You, however, who decry the Americans because of selfish tricks look to the branch in your country that wants to maintain the first place in worldly affairs in the category of "Sciences and Humanities" and observe with what machinations they strive to kill the truth in it. As silly and full of contradictions as the review is, it is nevertheless sufficiently consistent in its plan to rob me of all credibility. And whoever could allow himself a falsification of evidences will not hesitate to insinuate that my trip never had the purpose that my book states, that I went to the Missouri because of my own livelihood as a physician, and since I did not manage to succeed there I returned to Germany. To be sure, it is better to live as a physician among the Indians than in Germany as a hungry reviewer. However, I can cry out to the hungry scribbler who would like to attribute his own false motives for my actions to his annoyance that the kind deity has spared me so far from his need; and, if He should ever tempt me with it, I would surely rather die than spend my life in such a miserable way as he does. In all areas of human endeavor one hears in Europe complaints about disturbances that are caused by envy and greed. Teachers, civil servants, and physicians complain that they have become disgusted with their professions because of them. But to these complaints a much worse is added, namely, that it is almost impossible to call their attention to ideas that concern the welfare of many people without being attacked by a mob that considers the field of printing its own domain. Verily, if there were another way of disseminating ideas, not a single line should be printed in order to avoid ever colliding with such rabble.

---

*Concerning the advantages that according to the second publication by Köpfli Illinois is supposed to have over Missouri see below (in the note to the Postscript).

It may be considered likely that it is not unrelated to the objective of the murky trash to degrade my book in order to pander the works of Brauns, which are mentioned so often in it without hereby affecting Mr. Brauns himself. The name of Brauns of Deensen (in the Duchy of Brunswick) is also hidden in the abbreviation *Br. Ds.* However, how many other names exist to which the abbreviation would fit equally well? The quality of a North American traveler who knows the districts of Venango, Crawford, and Warren in Pennsylvania again fits Mr. Brauns, but to how many others inside and outside of Europe does it not fit just as it does to him? Even the frequent combination of this quality with that of a reviewer not common in Germany until now does not guarantee anything because the true originator of the libelous pamphlet could have feigned both qualities by hiring a third person for the purpose of disguising and introducing his lies and intrigues into the literary journal. It can be assumed from my explanation that I know full well what I am saying here and that I am accusing the editors of the literary journal of complicity. In the beginning I was inclined to absolve them at least of any evil intention. But after I have twice challenged them to name the critic I see the matter differently. My first request was prompted by the comparison with Sir von Schäffer, because I did not yet know the forgery. The editors' office answered that they were not allowed to reveal the name except in the case of obvious mistakes and injustices on the part of the critic and in case the latter had jeopardized the honor of the institute. Thereupon I notified the office of the forgery with the comment that they surely would consider it an injustice and a jeopardy to the honor of their institute. I am convinced that the second letter was also received and must now conclude from their refusal to reply that it is an insolent defense of the slanderer or assume that the editorial office fears to make its position even worse by revealing his name. The latter would, to be sure, fit the situation that the critic was the same person as the author of a work praised in the review. Mr. Brauns attributed so much weight to the praise in literary journals that he has incorporated in his work, entitled *The Liberal System,*[26] and so forth, the following passages.

On pages 8 and 9 one reads:

"First of all I express my sincerest thanks for the highly complimentary assessment of that part, and so forth, to Professor Berghaus of Berlin,[27] who has become very dear and valuable to me because of his several complimentary reviews of my earlier works."

"Even by far exceeding my most ardent wishes another review distinguished by a model of thoroughness and soundness appearing in the *Blätter für literarische Unterhaltung,* 1832, pages 118–24, sought to call the attention of the educated public to that part, an effort that in the esteemed judgment of my highly respected publisher did not remain without success. And yet the great pleasure of meeting this worthy reviewer most laudably distinguished by a mature, educated mind, a rare kind-heartedness, high talents, and thorough knowledge has not yet been afforded me. In spite of all investigations the name of this brilliant man who by far outshines so many thousands of reviewers of our century has as yet remained undiscovered by me. I wish this highly esteemed stranger, who has founded in my heart an indelible monument of respect, would reveal his dear name to me and thus satisfy one of the most ardent wishes of my heart, for 'man's tender blossom grows only where gratitude and kind-heartedness exist.' "

On page 10 one reads:

"Beside these reviews, which have appeared with reference to the first part, I list on this occasion the following reviews and critical notes pertaining to my earlier written works that have come to my attention: (1) *On the Ideas of Emigration to America,* Göttingen, 1827 . . . *Blätter für liter. Unterhaltung,* issue of December 1828. I do not know the brilliant and talented author of this most thorough and sound review. How he would please me by revealing his name! . . . (2) *General Political Annals,* by C. von Rotteck, issue of March 1831.[28] The worthy author of this equally excellent and highly complimentary review signs himself with the pseudonym *Julius Velox.* By revealing his true name the highly respected author would oblige me deeply."

On page 12 one reads:

"I herewith render my sincere and honest thanks to those great and worthy men who have contributed to the dissemination of my works by writing complimentary and thorough reviews."

However, from this it does not follow that Mr. Brauns has written these reviews himself, just as it does not mean that he is a party to his own praise in the slanderous article. Mr. Brauns as a writer on North America and emigration prefers to list great literary bibliographies, which, as is generally known, I do not do. In his so-called *Liberal Systems* (Potsdam, 1831, and the 33d Vogler Buchhandlung) he mentions the most insignificant older and newer writing, as for instance the brochure by Butte, *Reminder to My Fellow Countrymen Who May Be Tempted to Emigrate from Europe* (Cologne, 1816); the work by Hazzi on emigration (Dortmund, 1812).[29] Furthermore, he draws on the works by Lips, von Fürstenwärther, Bromme, von Bülow, von Morris, Bir[k]beck, Hecke, Gall, Schmidt, Prince Bernhard von Weimar, and innumerable others.[30] However, in not a single syllable does he mention my travel report, which had been circulated at that time over all of Germany, had been cited in all good journals, and had been reprinted in Switzerland. From this, to be sure, one ought to surmise a special dislike of me and my book; but that is far from complicity in that calumny and falsification. I know neither anything good nor anything bad of Mr. Brauns, except that he has written bad books on America. In order not to be accused of partiality in any respect I will abstract from it, too, and will state that quite recently a reviewer of the *Göttinger Gelehrten Anzeigen* called Brauns's books excellent and the author a worthy man. I cannot exceed the limit of mere enumeration of evidences incontestable as such. I have to leave it up to the judge to decide what they prove individually or collectively for or against certain persons. It suffices to have shown before the public in my defense that the miserable work of *Jena,* whoever is its author, is a scandalous product of lies and calumny.* If this were not so, if the slightest trace of genuine doubt in the well-being of German colonists in the state of Missouri would have been revealed, then I would immediately submit the most convincing proof for it here, which I shall save now for later use in an appendix for objections that may be more deserving. At that time I may be permitted to take an argument just from this insulting work that even with the most malicious will nothing can be produced against the state of Missouri, if the critic would not reveal such an outstanding incompetence beside his ill will. But thus I merely have to add that with a little more intelligence he could have saved his distortions and

---

*In order to counteract any distortion of the facts I shall have it reprinted here verbatim:

"We cannot give our approval to the trend predominant in this book 'to recommend Missouri to the Germans as the most suitable state for colonization,' just as we could not give it to the work published a few years earlier by Sir D. Schäffer, which had a similar purpose, to recommend to Germans a southern area for colonization, namely, Brazil, that at that time was highly praised, but has now been recognized for its true worth or, more correctly, its faults and thus has been almost completely forgotten. Where the climate is so opposite to that of Germany as in Brazil and Missouri, it is impossible that German settlements could prosper. On the other hand, here Mr. Duden depicts Missouri as a true paradise where all sorts of fruits grow wild in the woods and other such crazy stuff. That all this is not so, we can see from the writings of the brothers Tscharner, who emigrated from Chur in Switzerland, settled in the West of the Union, and reported in the journal *Der Nordamerikaner* of 13 July 1833, which was published in St. Gallen, where one reads: 'In St. Louis, the capital of Missouri, we met several Swiss and Germans, but from all these people we did not hear much that was pleasant about the state of Missouri; it was reported that it was difficult and too expensive to clear the forest, and in addition the soil was not everywhere as good as Duden had described it.' A similar judgment on Missouri is also made by the medical doctor Kaspar Köpfli, who emigrated to New Switzerland in Madison County of the state of Illinois, in his very readable book, *Bright and Dark Sides of New Switzerland in Illinois,* written in March of 1833, Sursee, 1833, page 57: 'In order to obtain these—namely, more reasonable, appropriate concepts about America by which emigrants would anticipate and

falsifications, since one can easily understand that there is not a land in the world that would satisfy all who for one reason or another set out from Europe, as well as that most dissatisfied people would rather blame the land and me than themselves. To be sure, there are many people who do not think so far, and in our cultivated Germany it is only necessary for a complaining letter to arrive from any American city to have a throng of voices exclaim, "There we have the genuine truth." Without examining from whom the letter is, what it really contains, definite details or general anathema, it is accepted as a work that overrules the earlier ones like a newspaper does its preceding issues. Let no one scoff at the gullibility of the Indians and Negroes; we have stronger evidence for that in Europe among people who can read, write, calculate, and understand foreign languages. If mere traveling to distant countries would be enough to give the competence of deciding about countries, people, and human endeavor, then surely the first voice would be due the sailors. Nevertheless in the case of those journeying from Germany to America one forgets very much what they take along from their home country as their qualifications, so that the naked date of their message from an American city seems to be absolutely sufficient. Whether the city is located a few hundred miles from the area about which the message reports is of such little importance as if the correspondent had been personally in that area. Even more rarely a scruple is raised as to how the emotional state, demands of the world and men in general, or special purposes or interests may affect the descriptions of the foreign region. One even commits the contradiction of on the one hand calling the emigrants enthusiasts who completely failed to appreciate the really good in their old home country and exaggerated the bad things, and yet on the other hand applauding as pure truth what afterward one of the people who are nowhere happy says about America, which outweighs any more favorable report (even if it were to carry the imprint of reason on every page). More general attacks against me have occurred. However, the treatment of the two most noteworthy takes so much space that I must treat the others summarily. As a matter of fact beside some ridiculous zeal they do not offer anything that any reader cannot answer for me. I shall mention only one attack in detail because it happened under the protection of the robe of a priest.

In a paper that appears under the title of the *Hannoverische Magazin* in Hameln (1833 issue, number 46), an anonymous simpleton who declared the whole of North American nature including her people to be deformed called me a wicked swindler, and a

---

prevent many inconveniences, it is above all necessary to banish the somewhat fantastic ideas of the land here that have been conveyed by Duden.' Similarly it is reported by Mr. P. von Zoya of Hickory Grove, Bond County, Illinois, who set sail in October of 1832 with the second group of the Swiss Emigration Society for Missouri and arrived safely with the group in St. Louis in Missouri, whereupon however all members preferred to settle in Illinois 'because in Missouri too much work was required to clear the thick forests' (*Der Nordamerikaner,* 6 July 1833). From these reliable reports we see that Mr. Duden's colorful ideas of Missouri are more idealistic than based on truth. The most correct judgment pertaining to the state of Missouri, which is completely unsuited for Germans, can be found in Brauns's *On the Ideas of Emigration to America,* Göttingen, 1827, pages 217 and following, where its bright and dark sides are emphasized with impartiality, but which we are not able to reproduce here because of lack of space. Dr. Duden, now a physician in Bonn, kept house in Missouri for a couple of years accompanied by a maid and has described everything throughout only superficially. He has completely disregarded the dark side of Missouri, while on the other hand he praised its bright side to the sky. Why did, in order to cite one thing more, the state of Missouri so charmingly described by him which is several thousand English square miles bigger than Ohio, Indiana, and Illinois, have only 140,074 souls in 1830 while Ohio had 937,670, Indiana, 341,582, and Illinois, 157,575? The reason is that Missouri does not have all the facets attributed to it by its fantastic worshipers, but as to quality stands far behind those states of the West created simultaneously. We therefore give the well-meaning advice not to let oneself be enticed to Missouri by Mr. D, any more than to Brazil by D. Schäffer.' "

black-frocked theologian found it consistent with the gospel to introduce slander into the world through his recommendation. The author is said to be a lawyer without talent or practice who nevertheless wanted to support emigration by his talents and after consuming his meager means was seized by a kind of despair in the state of Pennsylvania and turned his rage against the country and me. This sounds reasonable. But it may appear less reasonable that an individual who has to preach brotherly love and peace for the enjoyment of his sinecure and is supposed to warn with apostolic unction of bad repute as well as of robbery and murder could write a complimentary preface to the product of insanity as the parish pastor Schläger has really done.[31] In calling the author a man of high education he furnishes the world with an incontestable measure of his own education. I shall teach the rash shepherd, since the gospel does not suffice, through law to what limits the solicitous zeal for the salvation of his flock is to be kept and that in the future he should not trumpet everything out into the world that a madman has shouted to him. The pastor, without doubt, never read the book against which he lets himself be used as a spokesman. Otherwise it would surely have occurred to him to trouble himself to get information so easily obtainable on the Lower Rhine that the author, even though he does not wear the priestly halo, nevertheless bravely dares to stand beside Mr. Schläger as far as love for humanity, unselfishness, and honesty are concerned.

While I am talking about myself I want to add those things, in God's name, upon which, in the long run, one will have to look in the case of everybody concerning whose intentions and plans one seeks to obtain thorough information. Until now I could not make up my mind to call the attention of the readers to it, since after all they could have little interest in knowing who and what I am. Now, since it is part of an evaluation of a report in which the public is increasingly interested, I may do it without any doubts. I was born at Remscheid in the Duchy of Berg. After my law studies in the years 1806–1810 in Düsseldorf, Heidelberg, and Göttingen I became an auditor at the court of law in Düsseldorf and toward the end of 1811 (with a waiver of the legal age) justice of the peace of the canton Mülheim. In 1813–1814 I participated as a volunteer (lieutenant and adjutant) with the First Batallion of the Second Regiment of Berg (afterward the Twenty-eighth Prussian Infantry Regiment) in the war against the French. After returning to my civilian office, I was appointed senior judge in Mülheim, which, however, I declined. Thereupon I was also charged with the office of justice of the peace of the canton of Richrath, and thus I administered two offices of justice of the peace for three years. In 1820 a Royal Cabinet Order appointed me (state's) procurator at the Court of Inquest in Mülheim; and after this office was closed I served as state's procurator (second assistant of the chief procurator) in Cologne, until in the fall of 1823 I requested a temporary leave because of the condition of my health and subsequently my definite release because of my travel plan (of which the first attempt had failed because of the death of a friend in the West Indies who had intended to join me for this purpose). The duration of the leave, which was later on extended, I spent in Bonn with medical studies, to which I had earlier already devoted much time. After the formal royal discharge, which occurred approximately nine months after submission of my application, I left the European continent and went to North America. The cost of this journey as well as the entire stay at the coast and in the interior of the Western continent was defrayed solely from my own money without ever accepting the slightest compensation for the medical help that I afforded my neighbors on the Missouri. Rather, in addition, I gave away my whole supply of medicine and drugs. After my return I lived in Paris for half a year and the remainder of the time in Germany, partly in the house of my parents in Remscheid, partly in Bonn, where I am still living, and to be sure solely from the income of the parental inheritance which is sufficient for my modest needs.—The Preface to the First Edition and the work *Europe and Germany,* and so on, give information concerning the real reasons for my leaving the career of a civil servant who had become an integral part of his office and taking steps that to him would be considered adventurous. Because, however, one rarely expresses oneself clearly enough in front of people of that nomenclature, I shall emphasize here especially for them the points by which one can arrive at so-called adventurousness in the simplest way in the world. Surely, thoughts concerning the fate of one's fellowmen also belong to the administration of a court of law unless it has to be considered nothing but a mere sinecure? Also a criminal justice officer might hardly be reproached for a speculative aberration if he occasionally yielded to contemplations while endeavoring to protect the order of the state from attacks through inquests and punishment; the incentive to such attacks is constantly growing because of poverty and destitution as well as because of the changing and increasing needs that come with development. And yet should it be an extravagance if somebody who sees himself educated solely for the defense of the order of the state in general notices while contemplating the purpose of his efforts that the main road to the goal is completely misunderstood? Is it supposed to be an extravagance when an officer of criminal justice gets tired of preventing people through torture from committing criminal acts while nothing is undertaken against the increasing incentive to it caused by poverty and destitution? Is it supposed to be adventurousness to exclude oneself from the one side for the protection of private property and persons for which enough new helpers offer themselves daily anyway in order to try another direction, which until now has been completely neglected by the modern nations, but had always been considered the first by the older? What will the coming generation say that would protect such arguments in the present from the suspicion of fantasy! It has been difficult for me to express these thoughts. However, by inviting anybody now who is interested to inquire minutely into whether I have ever in my whole life given cause even a single time to be suspected of dishonesty or of selfishness, and—since it is important for the mentality of the sons to know that of the fathers—by inviting him at the same time to investigate the reputation of my father who at his early death did not leave the widow with a dearer bequest than the admonition not to spare anything in the education of his children, I also demand of all who juxtapose my *Report on North America* with forbidding descriptions a similar statement that might lead to a disclosure concerning the motives of their actions. I believe that I have at least the right to expect from the German public a reward for my efforts and that it may afford me protection against the calumnies and slander and that those who sincerely praise my striving would express their disgust orally or in writing depending on the opportunity, especially against that scum whose venom is sent into the world under the captions of humanity and the welfare of the people, who may do it because of low greed for money or because of ridiculous arrogance—like the Germanic Thersites[32] who compares me with the Pied Piper of Hamelin because I am presenting to the German strength a region in which no miserable college freshman can play the great judge while he lets himself be fed and taken care of by the same common welfare to whom he pretends to be indispensable.

At the end of these complaints one more comment, that my work for the better use of the earth upon which alone the salvation of Europe and Germany is to be hoped has not in the least been disapproved until now by any of the princes on whom one likes to put the final blame for all hardships. All that has happened in opposition to it has emanated from the people themselves. I have therefore that much more reason to ask my fellowmen to look less to the political obstacles of an ordered emigration than to watch that rabble beside them that jumps on any good sowing like vermin of the darkness, and when examining all that is printed, written, and spoken that comes under the heading of this book not to rely on anything but their own good judgment. For him who is incapable of judging for himself it is really bad in the present-day world, but in matters pertaining to emigration and colonization truth is being clouded by all bad sources simultaneously, and whatever cannot be accomplished by deceit and malice will be finished by the spectacles of miseducation and folly (which may well be well-meaning).

Preface to the First Edition

P– 1 (Sentence changed). (d) what could be expected in regard to social intercourse . . .

P– 2. Word *only* deleted.

P– 3 (sentence changed). . . . other things, which, to be sure, have value . . .

P– 4 (addition). In the year 1829. According to a wish frequently expressed, a map of the state of Missouri is attached to this second edition. It was drawn according to the maps of Lucas in Baltimore (with consideration of Tanner's map) and will, although it can make as little claim of any special accuracy as the originals, nevertheless serve as a means of orientation. The general praise of North American maps on page 175 rarely fits the small ones, as the comparison of two adjoining maps by the same author shows, in other words, the map by Lucas of the state of Missouri and that of Illinois, which differs greatly even in the bends of the Mississippi, among other things.[33]

Contents

Con– 1 (addition, above). Preface to the second edition for the purpose of dealing with several general attacks on the author, pages 262– 280.
Preface to the First edition, pages 5– 11.

Con– 2 (addition). Addendum for emigrating farmers, pages 245– 53 and for those who are contemplating commercial ventures, pages 253–261; including extensive notes pertaining to emigrations that took place after the return of the author and pertaining to reports of some emigrants particularly with reference to their objections to the advice to settle on the Mississippi or the Missouri and the jealousy between individual North American states and districts.

First Letter

1– 1 (sentences changed). I shall write you in Europe. I found here an American ship that will set sail with the first favorable wind for Baltimore.

1– 2 (sentence changed). The opinion of N. concerning my undertaking does not surprise me.

1– 3 (sentence changed). . . . I consider it expedient to express mine before I begin my investigations.

1– 4. Words *of this land* deleted.

Second Letter

2– 1. Written 30 June 1824 . . .

2– 2. *frequent* changed to *many.*

2– 3. *Punta del Gada* changed to *Ponta Delgada.*

2– 4 (addition). , corn,

2– 5 (addition). diluted sulfuric acid (between eight to sixteen drops of concentrated acid in half a pint of water) and

2– 6. Word *more* deleted.

2– 7 (sentences changed). . . . to become sailors because of other considerations than those resulting merely from the nature of the illness.

2– 8 (sentence changed). Otherwise, however, this sailor cure is permissible only with completely healthy children.

2– 9 (footnote). Let the reader here combine the above with my remarks in the work *Europe and Germany* [I], pages 35, 36, and 464. Because I myself suffer so much from seasickness I shall probably take my second trip to the interior of North America from a port of southwest Europe, from Bordeaux, or even from a Portuguese or Spanish harbor through the Gulf of Mexico (via New Orleans). To be sure, leaving Portugal one can be in Madeira in a few days, and from there to the Gulf of Mexico one has regular easterly winds even in winter that propel the ship without swaying and shaking. Between central and northern Europe and North America the sea is always sufficiently choppy to cause attacks of seasickness. I would not venture out on it again without having purified my digestive organs with emetics and purgatives. I would also strive to counteract vertigo and pressure on the brain by strong bloodletting well ahead of time and would observe the scantiest diet during the first weeks. However, I do not want to recommend this method to everybody. With some it might earn me the reproach that the method of prevention is worse than the sickness. Because the retention of bile and food in the upper intestines increases the malady the prescription of so-called cooling laxatives (such as Epsom salts and cream of tartar or tamarind) is suggested for all afflicted with seasickness. The favorite drink of molasses (usually syrup) and water, which sailors like, is also to be recommended to all who enjoy it.

Third Letter

3– 1 (addition). are striped all around,

3– 2 (footnote). It is also called this on German ships, although the term *log* in English means in general a piece of wood.

Fourth Letter

4– 1 (sentence changed). . . . or clay), the hollow base of the plumb line . . .

4– 2 (footnote). Now (in the year 1834) the voyage is considerably cheaper. See below for details.

Fifth Letter

5– 1. *three hundred* changed to *two hundred.*

5– 2. *forty* changed to *sixty.*

5– 3. Word *fruit* deleted.

5– 4 (addition). (according to others, Patapsko).

Sixth Letter

6– 1 (footnote). In 1833 the population of Baltimore is said to have been approximately 85,000, and in comparison with European cities it should be noted that neither rabble nor beggers were to be found. As early as 1831 eighteen steamboats sailed daily to and from neighboring cities. To be sure, a city like Philadelphia, which is about 120 English miles away, is still considered to be in the neighborhood because one can reach it within twelve hours. It is not unusual here to pay 3,000 dollars (7,500 Dutch guilders) for a bare building lot. Earlier one even had to pay 8,000 dollars.

6– 2 (addition). , an imitation of the column on Place Vendôme in Paris, which itself is a copy of the Trajan's column in Rome

6– 3 (paragraph continued). But even the least service of a servant costs this much. One has to pay for having somebody carry one's belongings from the steamboat to the inn no matter how close the inn is or whether the luggage is light or heavy.

6– 4 (addition). (so-called boarding houses)

6– 5 (footnote). This has not changed by now (1834). Therefore one should not be misled by the talk of American seamen concerning the expensive life in American cities. To be sure, earlier one's subsistence there amounted to twice or three times as much.

6– 6 (footnote changed). The duty on wine was very much reduced later.

6– 7 (sentence changed). A foreigner must not accept banknotes from strangers.

6– 8 (footnote). We know from newspaper reports that the present (in 1834) head of the executive branch (Jackson) was against the continuance of the Bank of the United States. Its charter ends in 1836. If the president should veto the bill advocating renewal then the bank most likely will cease operation. It is reported that as a consequence of measures taken by Jackson against the bank over sixty smaller banks have stopped payment already. Emigrants therefore would be well advised for the time being not to accept any American Bank notes and to insist on cash in all transactions. Below, more concerning transportation of cash.

6– 9 (footnote). Any enclosure is called a fence. This type of zigzag fence, however, is called worm fence or Virginia fence. In the northern coastal states one sees more frequently the straight fences known in Europe.

6– 10 (addition). peppermintlike

6– 11 (footnote). Now (1834) about 5,000.

6– 12 (addition). , named after the Swede Kalm[34]

6– 13 (addition).—short branches of those ranges whose special designations contribute to the confusion mentioned above.

6– 14 (footnote). This does not apply, it is to be noted, in the case of the road between Philadelphia and Pittsburgh but rather to the road between Baltimore and Wheeling, which passes through more scenic regions and in general is far better. Now (1834), to be sure, Philadelphia has a canal to the Ohio.

6– 15 (footnote). The floorboards are always joined together as the floors of granaries in Germany, and all are literally dried by an open fire after they have been dried in the open air, which is called seasoning.

6– 16 (sentences changed). . . . . his room and board and where also the keys hang for the individual guest rooms.

6– 17 (addition). It is also praiseworthy that in first-rate inns there is a stability of prices that permits the guests to figure their expenses in advance and that nowhere are tips known.

6– 18 (footnote). It is reported that between three and four thousand two- and three-team wagons have been counted in one year on the old road to the Ohio, from Philadelphia to Pittsburgh.

6– 19 (footnote). It is really the black spruce (*Pinus Canadensis*) from which beer is brewed by boiling down the branches and then sweetening the liquor with molasses (syrup).

6– 20 (paragraph continued). There is also a university here, but it is one of those small ones that would be denied that designation in Europe.

Seventh Letter

7– 1. 1,200 changed to 1,100.

7– 2 (footnote). In 1833 the great national road, which will someday run to the Pacific Ocean, had progressed to Vandalia in the state of Illinois. For this reason traveling by land to the Missouri is now far more convenient than when we did it.

7– 3 (paragraph added). I do not deny that the English pronunciation of the word *Ohio,* which sounds like *Ohio* [spelled phonetically in German] displeases me very much. And I am even more displeased if one imitates it in German, as almost all Germans do in America. The name is Indian, and the Indians speak Ohio. The French took their pronunciation from the Indians. The English, however, saw the word written before they heard it pronounced, and thus it happened, in accordance with their grammar, that the sound *i* developed rather than *e.* To be sure, to be consistent in the case of the word *St. Louis,* I would then also have to not emphasize the *Lou.*

Eighth Letter

8– 1 (sentence changed). . . . but little rye and no barley, which accounts for the fact that the beer was expensive.

8– 2 (sentence changed). It is a thankless task . . .

8– 3 (sentence changed). Here in Tarlton we again had to repair our wagon.

Ninth Letter

9– 1. Chillicothe in the State of Ohio, 30 September

9– 2 (footnote). The Ohio– Erie Canal, which has been completely operative since 1833 and passes very close to Chillicothe, should boost the development of this city considerably.

Tenth Letter

10– 1. Cincinnati in the State of Ohio, 7 October 1824

10– 2 (sentence changed). However, in spite of most favorable descriptions, I nevertheless did not hope to be able to travel . . .

10– 3 (footnote). In 1830 over 24,000 and in 1833 approximately 30,000.

10– 4 (sentence changed). . . . fifteen hundred to two thousand feet wide here.

10– 5 (addition). (a first and a second bottow [*sic*])

10– 6 (sentence changed). The upper terrace is sixty to eighty feet . . .

10– 7 (addition). , a medical school

10– 8 (footnote). Later I saw a living one in the zoo of the Jardin des Plautes in Paris with a sign: The terrible bear of northern America.

10–9 (sentence changed). . . . the small town of Newport; and opposite Newport, in other words, on the other side of the Licking River, which empties here, is the small town of Covington.

Eleventh Letter

11–1. Louisville, in the State of Kentucky, 11 October 1824

11–2 (footnote). Mr. Köpfli, on the other hand, asserts in his travel report (printed 1833 in Sursee in Switzerland)[35] that he drank some pretty good wine from Vevay at twenty-five cents (about thirty-six *Krone*) a bottle in Cincinnati.

11–3 (sentence changed). The land, which has its name from the Kentucky River which empties about eighty miles above Louisville (near Port William) into the Ohio, was for a long time . . .

11–4 (footnote). In 1833 one counted twice as many.

11–5 (sentence changed). There most of it is reported to still belong to the Union.

Twelfth Letter

12–1 (addition). (as did the first inhabitants of the United States, the French).

12–2 (sentence changed). . . . clothe the region in magical beauty . . .

12–3 (footnote). He is reported to have drowned in the Wabash.

12–4 (footnote). On the lower Mississippi there is also a town of this name.

12–5. Word *low* deleted.

12–6 (addition). to ninety

12–7 (sentences changed). . . . merely a military post. In 1780 it was encircled with walls and towers, of which only the ruins remain.

12–8 (addition). Now only a small part of the great territory is called Louisiana, in other words, the state at the mouth of the Mississippi in which New Orleans is located.

12–9 (sentences changed). My future letters shall touch on the real purpose of my journey more closely. I do not like to give . . .

12–10 (sentences changed). . . . and settled at the little town of Vandalia, the seat of the government. The little town was just founded at that time and named according to the wish of Mr. Ernst. Perhaps remembrances from his student days contributed, since earlier at our universities a group of north German students adopted that name for their fraternity. The undertaking of Mr. Ernst failed. He himself died of a virulent fever.

Thirteenth Letter

13–1 (footnote). The highest rate for an ordinary letter is twenty-five cents (thirty-six *Kreuzer*) even if the distance should exceed a thousand miles (naturally it is understood to be within the confines of the United States). Only it must not consist of two or three separate pieces; otherwise it will cost twice or several times as much. For a distance of 400 miles or less the rate is one-fourth less; for 150 miles and less, half that much; up to a distance of 30 miles the rate is only six cents. Newspapers cost one cent apiece if they are not sent more than one hundred miles across the borders of their state; otherwise, one and a half cents.

13–2 (addition). running through the mouth of the Kansas River.

13–3 (addition). , the 36°, however, for the short stretch between the Mississippi and the St. Francis River.

13–4. *Otoes* changed to *Panis* [*Pawnees*].

13–5 (addition). (descendants of the Missouris).

13–6 (sentence changed). . . . there are still almost no settlements.

13–7 (footnote). Now (in the year 1834) the settlements of the Germans, with few exceptions, are restricted to the left bank of the Missouri, although St. Louis was more easily accessible from the right [southern] side of the river and was therefore more inviting. See below for greater detail.

13–8 (sentence changed). . . . The catfish (sheatfish, *Silurus galanis*), often weighing . . .

13–9 (footnote). When buying land, the European must naturally not forget to investigate whether and to what degree the land is exposed to floods (which may be a much worse fault than a lack of water, which can be remedied by digging a well). Indications are not always immediately apparent. Trees and plants reveal this evidence only where frequent flooding occurs. In the case of large streams the height of the land is to be compared with the height of the spring flood, which, on the Ohio and Missouri, is almost twice as high as it is on the Rhine. Small rivers and creeks flood, however, with most heavy rains, therefore at all seasons, for which reason great care is necessary when purchasing bottomland.—Recently the word *bottom* was translated as marshy land. However, just as one cannot call the plains of the German rivers marshy land (sea land), one cannot call those of American rivers that, especially if they, as those of the Ohio and the Missouri, are located so far from the ocean.

13–10 (addition). The farther toward the West the wider the elevated space between and the more the prairies gain in width.

13–11 (addition). ; although famous physicians do recommend the use of lime water against calculus.

13–12 (footnote). In coastal cities they are sold in stores and markets.

13–13 (footnote continued). —General Washington is said to have found a sycamore of thirty feet in diameter on an island in the Ohio River.

13–14. Parenthetical phrase deleted.

13–15 (addition). (one should really say from the United States)

13–16 (sentence changed). . . . with large rivers, all this the buyer can have together without taking the price into consideration.

13–17 (sentence changed). The prices rose too high and the result was that later they fell too low.

13–18 (footnote). The public lands of these regions are congressional lands, in other words, they belong to the United States and not to the individual states. Some of the old states along the Atlantic coast own, to be sure, considerable tracts; here, however, the states own only those lands that the U.S. government has transferred to them by special titles. When a tract of public land has been surveyed it is then auctioned off to the highest bidder, but only once. Land not sold on this occasion can then be purchased for $1.25 per acre. Initially the owner is given a receipt by the land office acknowledging payment, which is sufficient legal proof of ownership until the president of the

United States can furnish a bill of sale (patent) signed by him personally, printed on parchment, and provided with the seal of the United States, for which one often has to wait a whole year without, however, endangering ownership of the property, which was acquired upon payment. This explains how wrong the opinion is that all land was originally for $1.25.

13– 19 (sentence changed). This would not be true if it were not for the fact that both flowed from far northern regions, and the Missouri in addition originated on a plateau that had an elevation of several thousand feet above sea level.

13– 20 (footnote). The reports of the years 1828 to 1834 praise one winter and then complain about the next. Thus the winter of 1832– 1833 was reported to have been very mild, and the winter of 1833– 1834 very harsh. The Americans assured me that formerly every winter had been as mild as the one of 1824– 1825. Only in the last eight years have the winters become more severe.—Outside the tropics one winter is probably never identical to another, and thus occasionally even on the lower Missouri a kind of weather may occur that may appear contradictory to my findings, especially to those [Germans] not long in residence there. But when the correspondent for the magazine *Ausland* reported in the March issue of 1834 that he was suspicious of my findings in the Missouri valley, so too must I be suspicious of his entire travel. First, because a resident of Illinois need not travel to the mouth of the Missouri to examine the Missouri climate; and second, because with the climatic similarity of both states hardly anybody in Illinois who believes in the good climate in Missouri would change his mind because of a short trip across the nearby state line. If my suspicion is unfounded, then the correspondent himself is to be blamed. Whoever reports on a region that so many Germans are eager to know about should not hide behind anonymity. He must make himself known so that the authenticity of his observations may be corroborated. See below for more details concerning this reported article.

13– 21 (footnote). One may conclude from this that with the climate in Germany it would be difficult to extract much sugar from maples, especially since the sweetness of the sap is dependent on the weather. At times it is potable as sugar water as it comes out of the tree. In Bohemia experiments on a large scale with American sugar maple have been made for some time, but I have not heard anything reliable pertaining to the results.

13– 22 (addition). muscovados,

13– 23 (addition). At first I thought that this operation would ruin the forests, but I have become convinced that a tree with a diameter of one and a half to two feet can supply five pounds of sugar annually without suffering the least damage.

13– 24. *one to two* changed to *two to three*.

13– 25 (paragraph added). My opinion has been reinforced that the correspondent [in *Ausland*] cited above derived his observations from books and letters rather than from a personal journey to the Mississippi. The work by Flint of which he writes appeared in its first edition in Cincinnati in 1828[36] and became known to me only after my travel report had been printed. I have called attention to it in the work *Europe and Germany*. However, if the correspondent insinuates that my travel report is to be counted among the reports for emigrants that have become superfluous, then he does not explain why it has received such a good reception in Europe. I could remind him of Goethe's poem in which a reviewer is compared with a guest who after eating his fill turned to his neighbor at the table in order to criticize the meal. It is the purpose of my book to present North America to the European as no North American who is not acquainted with Europe could do it. And if I consider it a preparation for judging American life in general, then I also have to consider it a preparation for comprehending and respecting the descriptions made by Americans themselves. The acclaim of the public testifies that this objective was not completely missed. If the correspondent of the *Ausland* fails to register approval, then he will nevertheless not deny that my descriptions of the Mississippi valley were the first to call the attention of the emigrating Germans to those regions where even the North Americans are moving. And if he does not accept that, then I feel obligated to state frankly that my report could only emanate from the execution of a plan that until then had been judged fantastic and eccentric both in Europe and in North America. Only a considerable acquaintance with the life of the upper classes and especially with the philosophies that guide it will make it possible to judge its relationship to the life of the colonists (the new settlers) in the interior of North America. But in order to become acquainted with the life of these colonists, one has to experience it for years, and the fact that rarely has anybody decided to do whatever would have made it possible to succeed in that is the reason that there was really no abundance of faithful and thorough descriptions of that situation.

Fourteenth Letter

14–1 (footnote). For several years a reduction in price had been expected, but up to this time (1834) in vain. Bills were introduced in Congress to lower the cost to twenty-five cents per acre or to grant all public land within their borders to the individual states. However, in 1832 prevailing laws were so altered as to allow one to purchase tracts of only forty acres if that was all one could afford; while all others had to continue to buy nothing less than lots of 80 acres. See below for more details. To obtain large tracts of land from Congress at cheaper rates is difficult and time-consuming. There are, however, individuals who offer many thousands of acres for sale at lower prices. In these cases, however, the quality (of the location or fertility of the land) is poorer, or, even worse, the title is not free and clear. He who purchases from the federal government can select the good land, thus including or rejecting the poor land from his purchase.

14–2. Words *for my purposes* deleted.

14–3 (footnote). With reference to land, various terms are used: now *farm*, and then again, *plantation;* and it would be wrong to assume that the latter term would be applied only to places where cotton and sugar are grown.

14–4 (footnote). At such springs one generally sees a drinking utensil, in other words, a dipper made of a stemmed gourd, hanging on a nearby bush. These gourds are expressly grown for this purpose, just as other gourds are grown as large containers for dry goods.

14–5 (paragraph continued). Usually these houses consist of one single room with two doors, which face each other. Whoever needs more space builds two rooms side by side and connects them with a covered walk. Board partitions also exist. However, he who thinks to spare himself the trouble of constructing several buildings would soon change his mind because of the weight of the timber that would be required for such a large construction.

14– 6 (footnote). This too has been declared false, and someone has asserted that it would cost double or triple the amount. I cannot do more than pledge my name and honor that my entire account is true. He who holds it in error without having traveled there to corroborate my findings would be advised to investigate my qualifications and my will to tell the truth compared to that of the shallow reviewer of the *Jenaische Literatur-Zeitung* who reported that I lived as a physician on the Missouri River and was now residing in Bonn as a physician. If it is a question of credibility, then one must investigate the entire career of the speaker, and once again I invite anyone who is interested to inquire along the lower Rhine where I have spent twelve years as a jurist, especially in the towns of Mülheim, Cologne, Bonn, and Düsseldorf, whether I would be considered capable, from selfish motives or for personal gain, to risk the welfare of my fellowman as some of my anonymous and pseudonymous critics who write to appease their hunger have done only too often.

14– 7 (footnote). Land covered with brush is more difficult to clear, to be sure, but the difference in the cost is rarely more than two or three dollars per acre. Besides, during the first few years a settler who does not have many people to assist him hardly needs more than ten to twenty acres of tillable land. One only has to cut the brush (particularly the hazel) above the roots and then rip open the ground with a team of oxen. A large number of immigrants arriving in areas where the population is still small may well force up the price for such labor. To prevent this I would recommend that initially only a few acres be cleared. No adequately well-off colonist would feel pinched to pay a few dollars more for this and later on he will surely be able to find help for lower wages, especially if family members do not wish to engage in such work, which is too strenuous to Europeans in the beginning.

14– 8 (addition). and even penetrates the outer skin.

14– 9 (footnote continued). This malady called milk sickness is said to have destroyed several herds of cattle along the Missouri in 1833.

14– 10 (sentence changed). . . . derive a good income from growing, if not merely from gathering, the ginseng roots growing wild, which are so treasured in China, not to mention . . .

14– 11 (footnote continued). Nevertheless nobody should let himself be prevented from first providing a secure agricultural basis.

14– 12 (paragraph continued). A plant also grows here that is similar to corn and whose fruit panicles when bound together are used as brooms. It is called broom-corn. Its fruit kernels look and taste like buckwheat but are not used for anything except for sowing for the brooms. Another plant resembling corn furnishes the so-called chocolate-corn, kernels the same size as the former and also growing in panicles (not in ears). When cooked with milk they produce a drink that is similar to chocolate, although more in color than in taste.

14– 13. *banks* changed to *left bank.*

14– 14 (sentence changed). . . . (watermelons, which the French call *pasteques* and which are well known in Germany, are called here muskmelons), . . .

14– 15 (footnote). It is called picayune (pikiuhn!) (in other words, *pecunia*), or a bit.

14– 16 (footnote). This must indeed seem strange to many a reader. Everybody knows what type of dwelling could be built for six hundred dollars in Germany, especially in the Rhine region. How can it be more favorable in a country where wages are so high? Last February (1834) a German from Missouri (who wants to take his wife and children to Missouri) visited me. He told me of a formal offer, which he intended to accept, for the construction of a six-room brick house for the above sum (on his farm at Lewis Ferry near St. Charles). All carpentry and wallpapering were included. He added that making and laying bricks at four dollars a thousand was the going rate there. However, one really must see the skill of the American builders in order to understand this.— Construction is much more expensive in coastal cities because of the high cost of building lots, living expenses, and building materials.

14– 17 (footnote). In all American taverns French brandy is available that, to be sure, is unadulterated but is usually of too dark a color. A drink served with sugar and water costs usually twelve and a half cents. In summer ice is added, especially in the coastal cities where it is even considered a regular addition to beer. Furthermore, in coastal cities one finds fountains with artificial mineral water installed in streets where the businessman in a hurry can obtain a pleasant refreshment for a few cents.

14– 18 (addition). , where saddles are cheaper than in Germany

14– 19 (addition). door

Fifteenth Letter

15– 1 (footnote). *Creek* in the interior of North America means a brook.

15– 2 (addition). ; tales of bigger ones seem to me to be fantastic.

15– 3 (footnote). *Moccasin* is also the name of a kind of Indian shoe often quite beautifully decorated with bristles of hedgehogs and coral.

Sixteenth Letter

16– 1. *Disregarding* changed to *In spite of.*

16– 2 (addition). *(Didelphis opossum)*

16– 3 (addition). , and if it gets into one's eye it endangers one's vision.

16– 4. *two* changed to *one.*

Seventeenth Letter

17– 1. Words *of all kinds* deleted.

17– 2. *These birds* changed to *They.*

17– 3 (paragraph continued). But they are also supposed to feed on the fruit of the cocklebur *(Xanthum strumarum),* a noxious plant much hated by farmers. These fruits have husks that cling to clothing far more tightly than our burs. In general there are so many plants with burlike fruit in the North American woods that the domestic animals often return covered with them. The most common food of that type of parrot* is probably the seed of the plane tree, where they are most often seen.

---

*Even in the most southern parts of the United States no other species is reported to exist, just as is the case with monkeys.

17– 4 (footnote). In 1830 the high yield of the mines on the Fever River brought this price down by one and one-half to two dollars.

Eighteenth Letter

18– 1 (footnote continued). —This was still the price in 1833.

18– 2 (footnote). Generally it is said that there are never more than thirty rainy days a year.

18– 3 (footnote). If one thinks I exaggerated here then one can consult the works of the botanist [F. A.] Micheaux, who stated that Europe had only thirty-seven varieties of trees growing to a height in excess of thirty feet, compared to one hundred and thirty-six in North America.

18– 4 (sentence changed). . . . are called butternut, shellbark, pignut, and bitternut.

18– 5 (addition). (overcup white or bur oak)

18– 6 (addition). black or

18– 7 (addition). *sive falcata*

18– 8 (sentence changed). . . . aromatic wood *(Laurus benzoin,* spicewood), various kinds of sumac . . .

18– 9 (footnote). The correspondent of the journal *Ausland,* previously mentioned (page 287), has also objected to my description of my farm. He stated that there was no view and that there was no sign of arbored walks (it probably should have read shady paths, since nowhere did I speak of arbors?), and so forth. It cannot be surprising that the correspondent does not agree with me as to what should be considered beautiful in America, if one considers the judgments pertaining to European regions. The fact that he expects paintings of a country that has, so to speak, just sprung forth from the creative hand of nature, to which belong cities, villages, and fields, and men's creations in general, must give rise to suspicions as to his ability to judge beauties of nature. I admit that besides my interest in these regions there was always the thought of what might become of them if man does not destroy nature. But my regret at not being able to see right now the charming variety that one sees from the hills along the upper and middle Rhine usually very quickly disappeared when I remembered the misery that reigns in the interior of the picturesque groups of German villages. Whoever loves cliffs can also find them along the Missouri. However, if most of them are hidden by gigantic trees, then let us remember that the bare cliffs painted along the Rhine River afford pleasure only to those passing by and hardly to those who have to live among them. Yet, in order to show the public a little more of what that criticism of my farm is worth, I shall refer to the remarks other travelers have made, namely to the works on North America by Dr. Gerke,[37] which appeared in 1833 in Hamburg with Perthes and Besser, in which the location was called paradisiacal. I also refer to the comments in letters of von Martels of Osnabrück,[38] who cannot praise its charms enough and keeps urging me to prepare ten more acres of woods so that they can be rented out as fields. Here I have to add as a supplement to the Thirty-first Letter that my concern that a renter might ruin the appearance of the trees to which I had become accustomed through mistreatment caused me to demand rental conditions that put off some people. And this is the reason that after the dissolution of the first rental contract no new renter has appeared.

If the increased value of the land influences me to overcome this concern, then I can easily remedy the objectionable appearance of the land not being cared for. Anybody who notices at all that until now I have not spent much money on my property has failed to understand the reason a dwelling hut and fencing had been built. I do not know whether German settlers make serious or joking remarks about them. I do, however, know quite well and I constantly learn that these settlers are too grateful to me for my travel report to find pleasure in the skirmishes of the correspondent of the *Ausland* and that they consider his talk of bitter hours completely empty phrases. I could name many German inhabitants who would contradict the authority of the unnamed superficial visitor to the Missouri valley. In order, however, to provide those who might be interested with a shorter way of examining the truth, I refer them to two persons who have recently returned from Missouri, to Mr. Heinrich von Martels of Osnabrück and to Mr. C. E. [E. K.] Angelrodt of Mühlhausen in Thuringia.[39] These gentlemen, or their relatives, in case they themselves should be on the other side of the ocean again, will bear witness that not one single German of good reputation on the Missouri has complaints about deceptions for which I am to blame.

Nineteenth Letter

19– 1. Word *direct* deleted.

19– 2 (addition). very

19– 3 (sentence changed). . . . south side of the Missouri the Shawnee had a so-called city.

19– 4. *settlement* changed to *huts.*

19– 5 (addition). 1812–

19– 6 (sentence changed). . . . stirred up and assisted by another power . . .

19– 7 (sentence changed). . . . easily allows them to be checked.*

19– 8 (addition). reflection and of

19– 9. Word *true* deleted.

19– 10. *children* changed to *babies.*

19– 11 (sentence changed). . . . the assumption that they did not grow up in the garden of innocence.

19– 12. *atrocities* changed to *traits.*

19– 13. Preceding sentence deleted.

19– 14. *roaming* changed to *unsettled.*

19– 15. *repelling* changed to *the most repulsive.*

19– 16 (sentence changed). And from this originate . . .

19– 17 (sentence changed). . . . to the Indians; even though not in an ambition that finds satisfaction in methodical murder of defenseless and help- less people.

19– 18. Word *John* deleted.

19– 19. *declare* changed to *depict.*

19– 20. *suffered* changed to *had to suffer.*

19– 21 (sentence changed). The usual reports of shocking incidents carry little weight . . .

---

*The short Indian war of 1832 took place to the north of the northern border of the state of Missouri and in the northern part of Illinois, over three hundred miles from St. Louis.[40]

19–22. Words *on this earth* deleted.

19–23 (addition). and remains

19–24. *mere* changed to *hasty.*

19–25 (sentence changed). . . . cultivation of the soil; because this is considered the essential condition of culture here in America as well as in Europe.

19–26 (sentence changed). . . . fraudulent greed, everyone has been . . .

19–27 (addition). and British

19–28 (sentence changed). . . . to describe in detail the life and existence of the Indians . . .

Twentieth Letter

20–1 (footnote). Its skins are used to make hats; they are, however, far inferior to the beaver pelts. A genuine beaver hat costs nine dollars and more; however, such merchandise is not seen in Germany.—By the way, the raccoon is a timid, small animal and does not look at all like a bear.

20–2 (footnote). Some American Germans have distorted their names in a strange manner to ensure the correct pronunciation; thus, for instance, in a city in Pennsylvania, I saw the name *Achenbach* changed into *Aughinbaugh.*

20–3 (footnote). Whoever confuses the essential with the unessential will encounter many contradictions; thus it would strike him, for instance, that he hears, on the one hand, a number of Christian names that occur only among Jews in Europe, such as Cain, Jonathan, Enoch, and so forth; and then, surnames that are changed into Christian names that do not appear in the Christian calendar, such as: Washington, Franklin, Harvey, Wilson, and so forth. Even the title *esquire* (skwi͞ər), which is approximately equivalent to our *Wohlgeboren,* appears as a Christian name. Otherwise (when used alone) it designates (at least among the colonists on the Missouri) the local justice of the peace, who is never called *judge* in documents, as the judges in higher courts, but *justice of the peace.*

20–4 (footnote). To be sure, men here give more of an appearance of profiteering than in Europe, but it is strange how one can be deceived by seeing herein a virtue of the Europeans and misjudge completely, firstly, what better opportunity is afforded hereby; secondly, that in Europe there are far more people who live at the expense of others and who, in their struggle to earn a livelihood, cover themselves with a cloak of piety, of patriotism, and of honor; and thirdly, that the great number of European beggars, thieves, and good-for-nothings is lacking here; thus, here the entire population is openly and without disguise concerned with useful occupation in earning their livelihood. Similar to this deception, which attributes the worst shortcomings of Europe to nobler interests, is above all the argument that American cities are too monotonous because they lack narrow and crooked alleys, delapidated houses, and cesspools.

To be sure, the more recent Europeans show wherever they appear that they have not yet outgrown the stage in their development in which money and material goods have an overwhelming influence. But how may those who do not write one line without payment and do not administer an office without salary, neither the office of teacher nor of judge nor of priest, dare conjure up this unclean spirit?

20– 5 (addition). In the year 1833 I read the following notice in an American newspaper (in the Baltimore *Commercial Chronicle and Daily Marylander*): In the city of St. Louis in the state of Missouri two Germans by the name of Philipp Hermann and Jacob Hubbart are said to have arrived and to have taken an apartment together. The former, who had brought with him about $1,800 in order to buy land, is said to have disappeared, and after some time he was found dead in a well with a stone around his neck. The postmortem on the body and further investigation revealed that he had been poisoned by hydrocyanic acid and that the murderer was no other than Hubbart, who had exchanged his first apartment for a new one in another part of the city and was in possession of that money.

Oh, if an American would hit upon the idea of making a list of crimes that are committed again and again in his country by European immigrants! That would be a just punishment for the German public, which enjoys so much the silliest slander of Americans that its best journals are filled with these. In the *Morgenblatt* this taste is put to the strongest test with a series of pictures of North American life. They are presumed to be published by a woman.[41] But why this deception? If they were really from the pen of a woman, I would like to ask the question: What would appear more repulsive, a nation with all its swindling avarice or a lady who could thus talk about it? I am of the opinion (which I partly owe to my legal offices) that the chronicle of every European small town surpasses all vices of which the North Americans as a whole are accused; and at the worst the North Americans could look therein for a strong defense against the correspondent of the *Morgenblatt*. Who does not know how one is surrounded by beggars and crooks in Europe if one appears anywhere as a well-to-do stranger? Nowhere in all of America are beggars to be found except those who have recently arrived from Europe. I would think that such a phenomenon, never contested by any traveler, would speak sufficiently for the argument that there too fraud could not be as bad as in Europe. In spite of this simple logic, one counts so much on the thoughtless gullibility of the Germans in presenting to them as truths descriptions that reveal everywhere traces of fiction, which are publicized either without naming the authors or with a name that everybody must recognize to be fictitious. It is a shame that an effort to ameliorate the general misery by the most effective means is counteracted most vigorously by cultured people and that one uses the advantage of working with the best literary magazines for the purpose of paralyzing the most sincere reports concerning the countries that invite colonization under the pretext of illuminating the darker side.

I believe that I will be rendering a service to the emigrants in their relationships with North Americans if I protest publicly against drawing conclusions from such assertions pertaining to public opinion in Germany.

20– 6 (footnote). I regret to have to say here that in the above, some men see a defense of slavery, although I would have expected them to have keener eyes.

20– 7 (footnote continued). In the constitution of the state of New York there is, however, one paragraph that, under certain conditions, allows the free people of color the right to elect officials.

20– 8 (addition). , even in churches they have seats separate from the whites
20– 9 (addition). prior to their complete corruption
20– 10 (footnote). The Germans who have settled in Illinois since my return

will have to confirm this as Dr. Gerke has already done in his book (which appeared in 1833 in Hamburg with Perthes and Besser). He remarks in it that Illinois was excellent for fathers with strong sons. Whoever, however, wanted to have his fields taken care of by strangers, would do better to turn to the state of Missouri, where slaves may be kept.

20–11 (addition). That is different in the Atlantic states (at least in the middle and northern). Many free Negroes and mulattoes are found there who offer themselves for all kinds of services and thus depress the demands of the white servants to some extent.—

20–12 (paragraph continued). Before one knows about the responsibilities of slaves, whom one cannot exchange as easily as servants in Europe, one should just rent them in order to prevent getting into an unfavorable relationship with the servants because of unfair treatment of them.

20–13. *younger* changed to *another.*

Twenty-first Letter

No changes

Twenty-second Letter

22–1 (footnote changed). I remind you here of the reports on the South Sea islands, where there are likewise said to be wonderful songbirds with the most splendid feathers.—The purple thrush is also called *Cardinalis Virginiana* and commonly called *redbird* or *Virginia nightingale.* The beak, however, resembles more that of a finch than a thrush. And farther south there is still another bird of purple color of the same size called the tanager.

22–2 (Latin changed). *(Turdus Orpheus, vel polyglottus)*

22–3 (addition). , has a broad spadelike beak, to enable him to catch flying insects, and gray feathers, and is of the size of a cuckoo, and, like the latter,

22–4 (footnote). It is said that the Indians call it *wishtonwish.* According to others, this name is applied to the prairie dog, a kind of woodchuck *(Arctomys ludoviciana)*, which lives in colonies and has a loud bark.

Twenty-third Letter

23–1 (footnote). However, this also took place in the year 1811, which the French still call the year of the waters *(l'année des eaux).*

23–2 (footnote). A similarly false impression can also be gained by a one-sided acceptance of the most faithful description. Formerly I expected this only of youthful exuberance and of people who grew up without education. But now (1834) I learn more and more that among publishers and editors of literary journals as well there is no lack of people who, no matter how clearly one would attempt to express oneself, are capable of comprehending only a part and consequently cannot arrive at a conclusion for which a synthesis of a certain number of concepts is necessary; for, while one attempts to make them acceptable to the latter they forget the former.

Twenty-fourth Letter

No changes

Twenty-fifth Letter

25– 1 (footnote). Some people maintain that the Wapiti, which, like the Canadian deer, is called red deer, is one and the same. He is said to be larger and has around his rear a yellow half-moon approximately six inches wide, which in turn is surrounded by a black line. I do not recall ever seeing such a characteristic sign on a Canadian deer. The Virginia deer is distinguished from the Canadian, besides his color, by a rather long tail and by the fact that he is significantly smaller.—The elk is also confused with the *moose-deer*, particularly by the French. The former is said to have round horns like the deer and belongs to the species of deer; the moose-deer on the other hand has flat shovel-like antlers and is not found south of the forty-fourth degree, which however may not be true of the cold highlands near the Rocky Mountains.—A farmer on the Missouri owned tamed elks that could be hitched up.

Twenty-sixth Letter

No changes

Twenty-seventh Letter

27– 1 (footnote). The village of Kahokia lies also on this river and is said to have had, under French rule, a population of 7,000 people.

27– 2 (sentence change). . . . (called *American bottom*), between three and eight miles wide and eighty miles long . . .

27– 3 (sentence changed). . . . the Mississippi), a row of towerlike cliffs opposite of which, on the western bank, Portage des Sioux is situated.

27– 4 (sentence changed). . . . Lewis and Clarke, Pike, Nutall, and School-craft [42] . . .

Twenty-eighth Letter

28– 1 (footnote). For this reason I have advised the immigrants when they set out from Europe in spring or summer not to travel by way of New Orleans. However, several have done it in spite of this and have had to pay for it with their lives. Is it possible that I could be reproached just because of this advice? Let whoever has not yet read the Preface to the Second Edition look at it so that he may be convinced what kind of people are occasionally working with German literary magazines.

28– 2 (addition). of yellow fever.

28– 3 (paragraph continued). It need hardly be mentioned that it should be well thinned (approximately eight to sixteen drops of concentrated acid in a half-pint of water) and that one should drink it from glass or porcelain containers (by no means from metallic containers) and that one should be careful not to get this solution in one's eyes or on one's clothing.

28– 4 (sentence changed). . . . which no inhabitant of the woods of the state of Missouri escapes entirely.

28– 5 (footnote). The noise that some make with reference to the American fever air deserves no attention. In all wooded valleys of Germany, intermittent fever (cold fever) is found just as frequently as in North America. Let me point out the area between Bonn and Cologne; where in Rösdorf [*sic*], in Alfter, in Dottendorf, and on the right bank of the Rhine, in Spich, Bergheim, and Troisdorf, there is almost always intermittent fever to be found. In the beginning the evil was worse everywhere in Europe, as well as in America, wherever swamps had been dried out or forests had been cleared. A swamp of slight dimensions near dwellings should, immediately after the water has been drained, be covered up to a height of a few inches by earth that has been taken from far below the surface and must contain no decayed vegetable matter, for instance, loam, and all danger of poisonous miasma would disappear. However, is there a place where this ever happens? One, instead, enlarges the surface of the harmful substance hoping to destroy it through the dangerous evaporation. Thus in the year 1833, in Bonn (which is very much interested in attracting visitors and could easily do so), a sewer was openly led around half the city instead of below the surface and toward the Rhine River, even though everybody must realize that a liquid with a strong odor in a bottle filled to the narrow mouth, no matter how big the bottle, would scarcely infect the air of a room, while on the other hand a teacup that has been spilled in a bowl would drive away even the least perceptive person. How, however, one can believe in draining a sewer that has constantly been supplied with new additions of rotten material and has brought all the rainwater to a foul fermentation is even more amazing. Certainly, one should never boast of one's culture where preventive measures against foul air are considered a waste. For this reason, ancient nations began the construction of their cities with the most durable foundations below the surface of the earth.

Twenty-ninth Letter

29– 1. *fellow inhabitants* changed to *neighbors*.

29– 2 (sentence changed). . . . is said to have adopted the Napoleonic Code with few modifications.

29– 3 (footnote). No one can serve longer than twice as president (that is, longer than eight years).

29– 4 (paragraph continued). It is further to be noted that the federal representatives are nominated directly by the citizens while the federal senators, on the other hand, are nominated by the legislative body (that is, the legislative officials) of the individual states.

29– 5 (paragraph continued). The word *Bund* (federation) suits really very poorly for the whole, just as poorly as the word *state* suits for one of the twenty-four compartments. For the sovereignty that is a part of the concept of the state really applies only to the totality; a relationship from which one can separate oneself only by force and war cannot be called a federation. The so-called states cannot revoke their relationship to the so-called federation any more than an individual family can separate itself from the state in which it lives. A few American theoreticians, to be sure, maintain that the opposite is true; however, this is absolutely against the clear wording of the laws.* It is equally difficult to arrive at a suitable meaning from the Constitution for the

---

*In South Carolina, recently, this theory was to be applied in practice. But the great majority of Congress condemned it.[43]

term *president of the United States*. To be sure, he does not preside anywhere, neither in the House of Representatives nor in that of the senators (in the latter, the vice-president presides). Since his main functions are to execute the laws and resolutions of Congress, the word *governor* would at any rate be more appropriate. However, he also has a significant part in the legislative and decisionmaking power, since all decisions of Congress (except those pertaining to adjournment) have to be submitted to him for approval and his veto can only be overcome by a new vote (and not by a simple majority) but by a two-thirds majority of the votes in each house.*

29–6 (footnote). In the Preface [to the Second Edition] there is a remark pertaining to a professor at a German university who responded to this thesis that the history of modern Europeans no more concerns the North Americans than the history of ancient Romans and Greeks concerned modern Europe.

29–7. Preceding sentence deleted.

29–8 (footnote). Only the names developed at that time. Concerning the confusion of names that developed later and according to which many persons were called *anti-Federalists* who were formerly called *Federalists* and vice-versa, no explanation is found even in Rochefoucauld Liancourt,[44] who has written half a volume concerning the political parties. He actually says, at the end, that even he does not see the light. Hopefully, the second part of my work *Europe and Germany* will furnish this.

29–9 (footnote). I would like to insert here the word *outside,* so that the idea of the differences in age and education and the mood depending thereon, for or against innovations, would not be disturbing.

29–10 (sentence changed). . . . . every citizen, expressly admonishes them to calmness.

29–11. *local* changed to *North American.*

29–12 (footnote). In Europe one wants to replace this interest with political forms, and there are still scholarly and ignorant heads that dream that they can change the condition of the European into that of the North American through legal institutions. To be sure, there are also in North America many theoreticians who attribute all progress there to political wisdom and, because a certain form is necessary, draw conclusions from the latter to the former without hesitation.—It might, by the way, be noticed by many that the political architects of North America with a conservative inclination have not taken better advantage of the higher age, which generally rejects innovations. In almost all states, it is sufficient to obtain a reputation of preserving and improving the Constitution and the laws by belonging to the youthful group. One can become a representative at the age of twenty-one, and at the age of twenty-five one can become a senator in Maryland, in Pennsylvania, in Alabama, in Indiana, and in Illinois. In Missouri, the ages of twenty-four and thirty-three respectively are required; in Delaware, twenty-four and twenty-seven; in Louisiana, twenty-one and twenty-seven; in Mississippi, twenty-two and twenty-six; in Ohio, twenty-five and thirty; and the same age is also required by the federal

---

*Also, the banking question, which was mentioned on page 29, will have to be decided by such a vote; and according to all appearances, it seems that there will be more than half of the senators in favor of the proposal of the president; not to mention, the House of Representatives, which is favoring him.

government. Kentucky requires twenty-four and thirty-five; Tennessee, however, requires only twenty-one for both offices. The present dissension between Congress and the chief executive (Jackson) may even strengthen this shortcoming, since in spite of the small differences in age, the House of Representatives is showing itself more inclined to innovations than the Senate;—although perhaps it can be attributed more to the fact that the federal congressmen are nominated by the citizens (and, to be sure, for two years), while the federal senators are nominated by the legislative officials of the individual states (and, to be sure, for six years). However, I would like for every critic to consider how, as long as the newer society affords so little influence to the older members of the family in everyday life, great influence could be obtained for older citizens in public life. One should certainly not hope to substitute by constructs what the citizens themselves will have to bring about. In the second volume of the work *Europe and Germany* I have treated this in greater detail.

29– 13 (addition). So just as the Europeans, the Americans usually look for an external reason for a disagreement whose inner reason they do not understand.

29– 14 (sentence changed). The interests of the parties are so far from being uniform that often in the families of the most decided Federalists the young people, in their natural inclination to innovations, are attracted toward the Democrats.

29– 15 (sentence changed). (at New Orleans on 5 January 1815).

29– 16 (footnote). To be sure, already on 24 December, a peace treaty at Ghent was drafted. However, the ratification was lacking and it was stipulated in the treaty that it would not be binding until four months after its ratification. I wonder how it would have been if the British, instead of suffering a defeat, had gotten possession of New Orleans?

29– 17 (footnote). Since the publication of these letters, the concern (or hope) that the Union and thus the entire American splendor will cease has developed anew stimulated by two events. The first, the tariff fight and the obstinacy of North Carolina, seems to have passed successfully.[45] The other is the trouble pertaining to the Bank (of the United States); and the American as well as European statesmen fear the worst. However, I can only repeat that, compared to that in Europe, family life in North America is too independent to be disturbed by storms in public life. If suddenly all authority would cease, then, to be sure, the safety of individuals and of their property would be badly off in Europe; however, that is not so on the other side of the ocean. There, at the worst, disturbances would occur only in the big coastal cities, but the farmers, and those are the ones with whom we are really concerned, would suffer such little disruption of their family life that they would soon restore order by means of new political unions and resolutions. Thus I have depicted the extreme to which it could develop because of the quarrels of the officials, of the representatives, of the senators, and the president.—As far as the fight concerning the bank is concerned, the measures of the president might be a worse evil than that which he wants to combat. In a country where wealth does not have poverty as its opposite, no conspiracy of the rich is to be feared. To be sure, if there were no rich in the United States, the resistance against other powers, as for instance, the reputation of the military or the officials, would be weaker. However, as long as there is no guarantee against the misuse of the latter powers, in human nature or anywhere else, little would be gained; and a war against the influence of wealth in the United States that is not led merely against the minds and hearts of the rich (by favoring higher insight and higher interests) has such an appearance of radicalism that even the French and English radicals would have to shrink back before it, [these very fellows] who find an apology for the need that in Europe is the opposite of abundance. By the way, it is difficult to reconcile the document of 10 April 1816, by which the Bank of the United States was founded, with the seizure of public deposits instituted by the president. However, since, according to the Constitution, the Senate has to judge the behavior of the president only when the House of Representatives files a complaint, then even with the well-known censure resolution the Senate seems also to have overstepped its authority.—At this occasion, I should like to call attention to a translation of the North American Constitution by Mr. J. H. Engelhard (which appeared in 1834 with Sauerländer in Frankfurt am Main).[46] Whoever has even only superficially perused it will be armed against many a false report and slanted opinion concerning the United States.

Thirtieth Letter

30–1 (footnote). [Timothy] Flint also put too much weight on this freezing over without indicating the actual level of the thermometer. The correspondent mentioned on page 287, to be sure, refers to Flint, but not with respect to the climate. I therefore add that Flint not only agrees with my description of the winter in the state of Missouri, but expressly states that the climate of Illinois is the same as that of Missouri. —Toward the Rocky Mountains, the elevation of the ground gradually increases so that near Council Bluff already (at a latitude of 41°31′ and a longitude of 19°45′) the climate approximates that of Canada.

30–2 (footnote). Just last year, in 1833, an air disturbance [tornado] tore down several stone houses in the city of St. Louis and also a part of a newly constructed church; a few years earlier (I believe, in 1830), a little city in the state of Tennessee (if I am not mistaken, Shelbyville), including the courthouse and the church, was so quickly destroyed that many people perished.[47]

30–3 (sentence changed). New Madrid at the southern border of the state of Missouri and the surrounding region . . .

30–4 (sentence changed). . . . extending approximately four to five hundred miles toward the west . . .

30–5 (footnote). Flint, too, does not seem to contradict this. He, just as I, has not been personally beyond the western border of the state of Missouri. I have mentioned earlier that, in the case of the state of Missouri, he speaks of a lack of timber without having any grounds for it.

30–6 (sentence changed). . . . receive heat from the sun about two hours longer . . .

30–7 (footnote). In order to appreciate the effect of direct sun rays properly, one should hold a thermometer at different times of day and seasons alternately in the shade and the sun. In the beginning of May, already one will find in Germany in the morning, at about seven o'clock, a difference of 4 to 6 degrees Reaumur and at noon, one of 12 to 15 degrees.

30– 8 (addition). and iron

30– 9. *cooled* changed to *cooling.*

30– 10 (footnote). We are not discussing here the meadows in the state of Illinois, which are generally considered better.

30– 11 (addition). the president of the United States or by

30– 12 (footnote continued). Only these settlers must not forget to acquire some woodland and provide for new timber in the future by seedlings which grow very well in most meadows. Whoever, however, has so much money that he need not be concerned with spending one hundred dollars more or less should not be deterred by the European fear of clearing a forest. Since my return several well-to-do Germans have purchased property on the prairies of the state of Missouri as well as those of Illinois. Although their choice may have been very good, it is nevertheless an error to attribute to it the problems of clearing a forest.

30– 13 (sentence changed). The procedure, which is directed by two surveyor-generals who are appointed for the entire United States, is as follows.

30– 14 (footnote). It has already been discussed on page 288 that a law permits the sale of forty acres in case of need. The buyer of these forty acres must expressly swear that he will cultivate them himself.—By the way, let no one pay attention to the ridiculous opinion of some critics of America as if that regularity (as for instance, that of the streets in a city) would be obvious in the country. The size of the lots prevents this even on very level, bare ground, not to mention on hilly or wooded ground.

30– 15 (two paragraphs added). The surveys are furnished in duplicate: one copy for the local land office, the other for the general land office, which forms a division of the Department of the Treasury and is under a separate head, the commissioner of the General Land Office in the capital city, Washington.

Navigable rivers, lead mines, and salt springs are excluded from sale; the rivers as general avenues which are exempt from any taxes, the lead mines and salt springs to be leased by the government.

Thirty-first Letter

31– 1 (footnote). Here I remind you of the note on page 291. Because the property contains only four *Morgen* for cultivation and the remainder is still covered with timber, some renters were not attracted by it. In addition, I included in the first rental contract various conditions pertaining to the conservation of trees, which may also be of little attraction. I have persisted in this in spite of the warning of my authorized representative because I am more interested in the appearance that the place gives in a natural state than in the small rent, and thus it has not produced rent for several years (1834). Since this has come to the attention of some, I expressly wish to point out how many Americans leave their lands completely unused in the hope that they will be compensated by the increased value that will result with a rise in population. And we must add that my investment (which has fulfilled its intended purpose) is so insignificant as not to result in a considerable loss by a complete return of the soil to its original state, while, on the other hand, there was enough danger from careless management which would predispose me not to send a hasty remittance of the sum necessary for better management.

31–2 (footnote). Therefore, I am always concerned that an emigrant from a city to the interior of North America would not find what he is seeking. Whoever wants to live as a farmer in North America, let him first become acquainted with the situation of European farmers in order to be able to judge the difference. Most European city-dwellers emigrate with fantastic expectations and dream of an idyllic world that depends on something more than beautiful nature.

31–3 (addition). , and the climate

31–4 (footnote). In the case of such remarks, should it be possible that I can be accused of inciting people to rash emigration, that even people who consider themselves called on to speak to the public, who work on literary journals, can do it? They are the same who accuse me of attempting to tempt people to come to the state of Missouri, although I have praised from the very beginning to the end (for instance, here and in the fourth chapter below) the Mississippi territory in general and have stressed in particular the advantages of the states of Ohio and Kentucky; but I support my recommendation of the state of Missouri, however, mainly because of the low price of land. If I also express a wish for a German community life, this shall never mislead me to jeopardize for it the individual and the family interests of the emigrant. I am not possessed by the crazy vision that sees a beautiful community life while families perish in misery; and I will, for the time being, labor only for a happier future, so I endeavor to persuade the Germans to use the unoccupied regions of the earth better than in the past. It is irrelevant to me whether emigrants prosper in one or the other region of America as long as they do prosper. However, how can I hope that there where so much selfishness rules that one has even lost faith in other motives, how can I hope that anybody would hold this attitude as a basis for criticizing my writings?

31–5 (footnote continued). Several emigrants (among others, the Messrs. von Martels) regret not having followed this advice, and I therefore have to reiterate it most urgently once again in this new edition. On the other hand, I can well advise ladies and unmarried men to take along faithful female servants, but only for duties within the house.—Concerning the reduced travel expense, see below.

31–6. Words *in Germany* deleted.

31–7 (footnote). One cannot imagine to what extent the American surpasses the European in the felling and splitting of trees. A common laborer between eighteen and twenty years old does not require an hour to fell an oak with a diameter of three and a half to four feet, and, at first glance, he can tell by looking at it whether it can be split easily. To be sure, he is not concerned with whether the wide notch decreases the length by a few inches more or less, which needs to be considered in Europe. Also, the axes of the Americans are far superior to those used in Germany, to be sure, not only because of their shape but because of the material. The American ax has a square shape and weighs approximately four and a half to five and a half pounds. The axes that are elongated from the cutting edge to the back are called *French axes* by the Americans, and they are not at all well thought of.

31–8 (footnote). People know how to circumvent the laws against this, and in a few cities, for instance, in Philadelphia, societies that have been founded for the support of the immigrants are too weak.

31–9(footnote continued). Together with the seed this quantity weighs more than four times as much. The seeds are extracted by combs attached to a roll operated by water or horsepower, for which one would have to deduct here in Missouri one-third of the cotton. Machines of the smallest type are said to be able to produce approximately four hundred pounds of pure cotton daily (which at this time costs about twelve cents a pound). The seeds that contain a useful oil are, however, rarely used for this purpose, but are thrown away, and at a place where no pigs can get to them, for they are said to be very harmful to them.

31–10 (footnote continued).—One of my neighbors raises five hundred pounds of dry leaves of the common Missouri tobacco to the acre *(Morgen* of 160 square rods) without the use of any fertilizer.

31–11. *old* changed to *eastern.*

31–12. *eight* changed to *almost seven.*

31–13. *two-hundred-thirty-mile-long* changed to *the several-hundred-mile-long.*

31–14 (footnote). It is now (1834) completed and from Portsmouth to the city of Cleveland on Lake Erie it is three hundred and six English miles long.

31–15 (footnote). It has been completed for quite some time now (1834) and is called the Louisville-Portland Canal.

31–16 (footnote continued). and that they will not bring any fever to the land, which the canals do only too frequently.—In the spring of last year, 1833, the railroad had been completed for approximately sixty to seventy miles and people began to take round-trip pleasure excursions on the same day from Baltimore to the southern mountains (the mountains on the other side of Fredericktown), which is approximately fifty English miles away. That the railroad was not completed any farther was caused by a suit with the Ohio-Chesapeake Bay Canal Company, which was decided against this company.— In the meantime, Philadelphia has realized its direct connection with the Ohio by the great Pennsylvania Canal mentioned on page 283 and the railroads. In the year 1827 one scarcely dreamed of it: the rivalry with Baltimore has expedited this. The canal begins at the city of Columbia on the Susquehanna and proceeds for 172 miles to Holidayburg, which lies 910 feet above sea level. From there, a railroad that is 37 miles long runs over the 2,291-foot-high crest of the Alleghenies to Johnstown at 1,154 feet of elevation, where the canal begins again and continues to Pittsburgh. One computes the distance from Columbia to Pittsburgh to be 313 miles. Now, however, Columbia is still eighty miles from Philadelphia and, as far as I know, is not connected with it by a canal, but by a railroad.—Also since my return, a canal from Dayton in the state of Ohio has been completed to Cincinnati which connects the valleys of the two Miamis with the latter city. I know that it was intended to build this canal from Dayton to Lake Erie, that is, to the Maumee (also called Miami of the Lakes), which flows into Lake Erie, but I do not know how far it has been completed.

31–17 (number changed). $15,341,171   00

31–18 (footnote). The later history of the tariff disagreement has sufficiently confirmed this. The North Americans are becoming increasingly tired of the limitations imposed on the life of the individual by financiers. (Note to the second edition.)

31–19 (footnote). How accurate this was we know from the latest reports, according to which the debt was reduced to a few million by 1833.

31–20 (sentence changed). The military schools at West Point on the Hudson and at Monroe near Norfolk have an excellent reputation.[48]

31–21 (addition). (It is noteworthy that all this has developed far more favorably later.)

Thirty-second Letter

32–1. *1819* changed to *1820*.

32–2 (footnote). In 1833 it was more than double.

32–3. Parentheses deleted.

32–4 (footnote). Varied lengths of the Ohio are reported. According to the shortest estimate, it is not quite one thousand miles, and the stretch of the Mississippi from the mouth of the Ohio to St. Louis not quite two hundred miles.

32–5 (footnote). How much this has already been changed can be seen below in the Postscript.

Thirty-third Letter

33–1 (footnote). In 1833, the fare downstream was only twenty dollars, upstream only twenty-five dollars, and the freight of one hundred pounds upstream 62.5 cents and downstream 37.5 cents.

33–2. *nine* changed to *eight*.

33–3 (footnote). That this advice is not directed to all settlers is explained in the Postscript.

33–4 (footnote). In the travel report of Köpfli, mentioned in the Preface [to the Second Edition] it says on page 191 that I would be even more amazed if I could see Cincinnati now (1831). Since my return it is said to have doubled. In 1830 alone, over 1,500 new buildings are said to have been built. The customary daily wages of the craftsmen are two dollars.

33–5 (sentences changed). . . . was an evil person and that private revenge had motivated him to a deliberate collision because he had taken our ship for the steamboat *Messenger*. A court investigation has been requested.

Thirty-fourth Letter

34–1 (footnote). This danger has been averted in time by the great Pennsylvania Canal. A canal from Pittsburgh to Lake Erie was planned also; whether the project has been carried out, I do not know. In general, Pennsylvania, to which Pittsburgh belongs, is distinguished by canal projects. Its area amounts to approximately one-fifth of Germany and contains now already (1834) a network of small and large canals that extends for more than seven hundred English miles.

34–2 (footnote). The steam frigate that was built by the late Fulton in 1814 in New York and had a length of 145 feet and a width of 55 feet and a steam power of 120 horses is said to have been destroyed last year (1833) by fire.

34–3 (footnote). It will not be necessary to go into special details since now (in 1834) almost twice that many are there. One should not forget in considering the complaints concerning the many accidents involving American steamboats that a great number of them are involved. However, it cannot be denied that the North Americans risk even their lives by a greater activity than do the European recluses.

Thirty-fifth Letter

35– 1. *Harwey* changed to *Harvey.*

35– 2 (sentence changed). The distance by water to Baltimore is 115 to 120 English miles, and that to New York just about the same.

35– 3 (footnote). The distances are given with certain differences. Thus, according to Mitchell,[49] the distance from New York to Philadelphia via Trenton, Princeton, Kingston, and New Brunswick is given as ninety-eight miles; via Bordentown, only eighty-nine; according to Tanner, on the other hand, the former is one hundred and the latter, ninety-one miles. Now (1834) the isthmus between the Chesapeake Bay and the Delaware River is intersected by a canal that passes Delaware City and St. George; there is also a railroad going across for sixteen miles from Newcastle to Frenchton.

35– 4. Preceding phrase deleted.

35– 5 (footnote continued). —In 1833, the trip between both cities cost two and a half dollars and took scarcely ten hours. From New York to Albany on the Hudson, 150 English miles, is said to cost only half a dollar.

35– 6 (addition). (which is here over a mile wide and on which the city lies in the bend of a crescent like Cologne on the Rhine)

35– 7 (footnote). It is said to have amounted to not quite 110,000 in 1820 and, by 1830, already 170,000. All newspapers have reported on the endowment by Girard, which is so large that all city expenditures can be covered by its interest, for which reason, in the future, all communal taxes will stop (taxes about which, now and then, there are some complaints, even in North America).[50]

35– 8 (footnote). This bank has its original location in Philadelphia and only offices at other places.

35– 9 (footnote). The banks of the Hudson toward Albany are praised for being very picturesque, for which reason the spas of Saratoga are very much visited by people from the South. In the area of West Point (where the military academy is, which was mentioned on page 304), the secondary ranges of the Allegheny Mountains described on pages 32 and 33 reach the Hudson. A part of them, which is called *Catskill,* is said to rise with its peak, Round Top, 3,500 feet above the river. At the eastern side of the Hudson are mountains that separate the state of New York from the states of Connecticut and Massachusetts; furthermore, there are the Green Mountains, which run through the middle of the state of Vermont to Canada; and then the White Mountains, which run through the middle of New Hampshire and, at the forty-fourth degree of latitude, have a 7,000-foot-high peak that is called Mount Washington. One usually calls these mountains east of the Hudson by the general name of *Alleghenies,* and I referred to them thus also on page 34. But, if Warden (in the second and ninth chapter of volume 1, pages 24 and 372) designates them as an apparent continuation of his Blue Mountains (that is, the Southern and Northern mountains), I could not agree with him together with other authorities who believe that the Southern Mountains as well as the Northern Mountains run along the west side of the Hudson.

35– 10 (footnote). In 1820, it is said to have amounted to approximately 120,000; by 1830, already over 200,000.

Thirty-sixth Letter

36– 1 (addition). , or one and a half German

Concerning the Nature of the North American United States

C– 1 (Preceding three paragraphs changed). In order to assure that my view will bear the necessary weight, I will have to abandon the formerly used informal form of the report and approach the stricter method of the mathematician, which when it becomes a serious question of proof and counterproof, is the only appropriate method. It would certainly be much more convenient for me to indicate only briefly what was really at stake, and say, for instance, the existence of the entire Union, as well as that of the individual states, depended entirely on the conduct of the citizens; because there existed no power except theirs, but the legislative power and through it, all power emanating equally from all individual citizens; and since already more than two-thirds are farmers, it is primarily a question of their conduct. The conduct of the farmers again would depend on their external situation, and finally the external situation would depend on the relation of the population to the amount of land. To be sure, this train of thought will be evident in my presentation. But such a bare indication will satisfy only the person who is already familiar with the results. And since for this purpose neither occasional notes nor general hints, nor a loose combination of fragments of information is satisfactory, I must urge the reader to follow patiently the thread of the methodical presentations that began with the second chapter (possibly using the abstract of that sketch), and in order to be able to appreciate the impact of the final result properly, to pay close attention to the context.

C– 2 (sentence changed). In order, however, not to fail in the examination of the family life of the American and yet achieve one's objective quickly, I pose the following two questions.

C– 3 (sentence changed). . . . the large field of my task of dividing into areas, without which it would hardly be possible to avoid the most adverse confusion.

C– 4 (sentence changed). Moreover, I consider the words used definite enough so that no further explanation will be needed and remind the reader of the Twentieth Letter.

C– 5. Preceding two sentences combined.

C– 6. Preceding phrase deleted.

C– 7. Words *written and oral* deleted.

C– 8. Word *political* deleted.

C– 9 (sentences changed). . . . the sense of freedom is not only undeveloped, but has even been nipped in the bud; that is, they have even forfeited some of what was theirs by birth alone, and what stirs so unmistakably if one acts only in order to arouse his will to enmity.

C– 10 (sentences changed). . . . than actually existed, because we liked to attribute the real difference (because of overzealousness or arrogance) to an ennobling rather than a worsening of human nature.

C– 11 (sentence changed). . . . any more frequently than in our hemisphere.

C– 12 (sentences changed). . . . their fortunate external situation; for its justification the following sentences may serve for the time being. It requires only . . .

C– 13. Words *the effects of* deleted.

C– 14 (sentence changed). . . . on norms of the mind, that is, not subject to the change in the environment . . .

C– 15. Remainder of sentence deleted.

C– 16 (sentence changed). If the political situation in North America . . .

C– 17 (sentence changed). Firstly, power, laws, and order derive equally in all the citizens; . . .

C– 18 (sentence changed). . . . external conditions, then no reasonable person can imagine the opposite to be true of the Americans.

C– 19. Preceding six words deleted.

C– 20. Word *intellectual* deleted.

C– 21 (addition). , the mere semblance of it, are in one country as rare as in the other.

C– 22 (sentence changed). That the cultivation of the mind produces an elevating influence there, only those fools can doubt who look for real life in schoolish quarrels.

C– 23 (footnote). What distinguishes the North American most from the European is the urge to colonize. This, however, is not completely due to instinct, but rather to the reasoning of statesmen, scholars, and priests, which in America has always been opposed.

C– 24 (sentence changed). Their efforts were undeniably of great importance.

C– 25. Words *of the Americans* deleted.

C– 26. This and following paragraph combined.

C– 27 (sentence changed). And if we found this situation so different . . .

C– 28. *could* changed to *must.*

C– 29. This and following paragraph combined.

C– 30. Question mark deleted.

C– 31 (sentence changed and added on to previous paragraph). And if one places the statement beside the restatement that the families . . .

C– 32 (sentence changed). . . . to the former, which can only justify a more exact consideration more and more.

C– 33 (sentence changed). It is these families who live from the soil of the new country who really matter.

C– 34 (remainder of chapter changed). It will be superfluous to refer back to the earlier chapters, in which both the idea that the European students had emigrated from specific European classes as well as the idea that dreams of a magical power of high intellectual qualities existed, were rejected. Thus nothing more is to be said concerning the perimeters of the investigation, but rather all our attention is to be directed toward its inner nature.

C– 35 (sentence changed). . . . our next task is to examine the influence . . .

C– 36. *full* changed to *precise.*

C– 37 (sentences changed). . . . between the states, in which in general the deeper reason for my statements concerning the political condition of the North American is to be sought. Therefore, to the point.

C– 38. This and following sentence combined with word *and*.

C– 39. *isolate* changed to *imagine*.

C– 40 (sentence changed). Let us not disdain to consider most carefully from which aspects the desires and actions of such a man may be determined.

C–41. *church religion* changed to *religious things*.

C–42 (paragraphs combined). . . . to maintain its leading role. That is, in persons of a similar type . . .

C– 43 (preceding two sentences changed into new paragraph). In order not to get lost in generalities, I invite the reader to recall North America and to consider what that country might offer to our simple farmer who meets the same condition of good conduct.

C– 44 (sentence changed). I admit freely that I am always afraid that I may be thought guilty of exaggeration as soon as I talk about these offers in Europe; because indeed I have things to report that in the Eastern Hemisphere have always been a part of the fairy-tale world.

C– 45 (paragraph added). Must I follow up this picture of reality with the assurance that the immigrant British and German farmers are doing well there and are concerned with nothing more than protecting themselves from political disturbances?

C– 46 (paragraph changed). However, no matter how understandable it may be that a similar situation may make every industrious emigrant into a respectable citizen and that it may offer a remedy even for serious moral damages or at least prevent their inheritance by children and grandchildren,* then one can raise objections to my deductions by saying that the number of emigrants, especially the Irish, Scotch, and English, . . .

C– 47 (footnote). That a higher education is here as rare as in Europe, I have said earlier. I would like to add here expressly that the ways to it stray away from practical life here just as easily as in Europe, in general divert from a life more influenced by immediate impressions of nature and get entangled in sterile reflections.

C– 48. Remainder of sentence deleted.

C– 49 (sentence changed). There is no hope for a substitute in guidance to become more perfect by striving.

C– 50 (sentence changed). . . . with the given bases for the American culture, it is nevertheless . . .

C– 51. *activity* changed to *strength*.

C– 52. Preceding sentence deleted.

C– 53. Word *intellectual* deleted.

C– 54. This and following paragraph combined.

C– 55. *nature* changed to *conditions*.

C– 56 (sentence changed). It seems that for the sake of exactness of the study that the aims of other citizens besides farmers, namely the aims of merchants, artisans, and officials, should be considered.

C– 57 (sentence changed). What justifies me, however, to report on those

---

*It occurs to me here that I have not yet mentioned the strange thing, that there are here in North America far fewer physical infirmities. One hardly ever sees deformed or hunchbacked people, and the children of Europeans with the coarsest or most distorted faces have regular features, which in no way betray any brutality.

classes, is the fact that they, according to their numbers and their attitudes toward real property owners, play only a subordinate role . . .

C–58 (sentence changed). In North America neither merchants nor public officials shape the public order.

C–59. This and following three paragraphs combined.

C–60. This and following four paragraphs combined.

C–61. Words *the farmer* deleted.

C–62. This and following paragraph combined.

C–63 (sentence changed). . . . therefore it is often very difficult to arouse sufficient sympathy for nobler interests.

C–64 (sentence changed). . . . unfavorable to the spiritual values of the transatlantic people . . .

C–65. This and following paragraph combined.

C–66 (sentence changed). In prohibitions or commands that have no other purpose . . .

C–67. Words *or prohibitions* deleted.

C–68 (addition). mere

C–69 (sentence changed). A rank due to the power of an office does not extend beyond the administration of that office.

C–70 (sentence changed). People who according to laws are constantly engaged in administrative acts seem to have a personal rank.

C–71 (sentences changed). . . . instinctively, without recognizing its true relation to the political situation of the whole.

C–72 (addition). , although, since it was founded solely for service during the Revolutionary War, it will soon die out.

C–73 (sentence changed). As we have seen in the former sections the nature of the farmer . . .

C–74. *gradual* changed to *future.*

C–75. *Americans* changed to *transatlantic fortune.*

C–76 (sentence changed). . . . the above-mentioned publication of the American Everett (p. 304).

C–77 (sentence changed). . . . and looks down with proud regret on all who think differently.

C–78. *legislation* changed to *laws.*

C–79. Word *more* deleted.

C–80 (sentence changed). . . . of necessity, (that which is certain, absolute), . . .

C–81 (sentence changed). Only in this way can we recognize the basic condition of human nature, and this recognition is the indispensable condition to a clearer view in this world of senses and experiences.

C–82. *those* changed to *the.*

C–83 (footnote). To make the distortion irreparable, in Europe those people who do not produce one single straw, who do not lift one finger to work in the area on whose fruits human existence depends, oppose most vigorously the applicability of this principle pertaining to poverty in Europe. We observe that almost every starving German farmer achieves prosperity as soon as he gets to the interior of North America, and in spite of this the exterior situation is not supposed to be blamed for his earlier misery. Is it not an amazing consequence of learned folly that he refuses in North America to attribute the success of humanity to the exterior situation, while on the other hand in Europe he does attribute starvation? I do not misjudge the course of modern progress and know quite well that even though all services of priests, teachers, and officials emanate from sinecures and salaries, they do not become worthless or dispensable because of this. However, whoever endeavors to work as a journalist or writer for the welfare of humanity without confining himself to the limits prescribed by his profession, let him consider that he must subject himself for this reason to a test of his will and ability from which no professional examination excuses him; and since his determination and his view depend so much on individual conditions, let him further consider how poorly it becomes him, who is fed and clothed by the classes working for their physical needs, to declaim denials of their troubles, cares, and worries. Is it not ridiculous if he, who is aware that he would starve as soon as his sinecure or salary ceased, declaims incessantly and loudly about aversion to work and laziness and calls it patriotism to lash out against it, with hollow phrases, that not everything is running on the old track where he feels so exceedingly happy, and considers the needs of others nothing but whims. I have read that a certain somebody, whose body is not deprived of the least for which many wail, declared compassion for the poor to be silly sentimentality and loudly proclaimed he had been assured that the poor could stand deprivation easier than one believed, and besides, man was, after all, not on this earth to pamper his body. As long as such things happen in journals in Germany, things are not likely to get better, and people will continue to recommend that criminals be banished to unoccupied lands and will not mind paying the transportation costs, but they will decry attempts to help needy people to get there before they become criminals, as foolishness and extravagance. Avarice goes arm in arm with stupidity. Just as there has been in Europe for centuries a class that speculated during crop failures and wars with the plight of its fellow citizens, so today many people try to use the distress of others to increase their own wealth. These are the ones who would curse a situation in their country in which the wages for physical labor could approach the North American level, in other words, in which the lot of those who are solely dependent on hard physical labor would truly have to improve. These are the practical friends of overpopulation whose applause is taken by the theoretical (as well as their own) for pure patriotism.

Note of the second edition.

C– 84 (sentence changed). Even Baltimore, Philadelphia, and New York are free of beggars.

C– 85 (footnote continued). In New York, however, in the year 1832, there were four poor people among one hundred. That no internal reasons were responsible for this is proved by the circumstance that at that time in the poor house there, among the approximately 2,200 individuals, almost half of them were Europeans. One should also deduct the number of colored people. In Philadelphia, for instance, in 1830, among the 16,000 colored there were almost one tenth of them poor.

C– 86 (footnote). On page 102 the statement appears that among four thefts hardly one is committed by a native American. In order to be more exact I would have to say: by a native white American. For the number of colored thieves in relation to the whites corresponds even in the northern states, where there are in general few colored people (one figures nowhere more than one for every thirty whites), here one to seven, there one to two. In Maryland, where one counts one colored to every six white persons, the ratio of colored thieves to white was recently two to three.—Among thirty white thieves not more than one female is found; on the other hand with the colored one finds one among ten. In the police prison of Philadelphia in 1826 there were about 1,200 colored among the 1,800 individuals; and in the "house of refuge" (a corrections institution for young criminals) in New York in 1831 half of the inmates consisted of Europeans (born in Europe).

C–87 (addition). what must be

C–88 (sentence changed). Whoever directs attention to Germany's sandy wastelands, moors, and barren mountain ridges, will find himself . . .

C–89. *descendants* changed to *heirs*.

C–90. *the Germans* changed to *us*.

C–91. *Germany* changed to *Germans*.

C–92 (sentence changed). Concerning a settlement en masse one need not fear the slightest difficulty either from the policy of the United States or from her individual inhabitants.

A Postscript for emigrating farmers and for those who contemplate commercial undertakings

PS–1 (footnote). These words have been interpreted to mean that one need only emigrate in large groups in order to avoid all danger. This, however, would mean following actual requirements for a happy success very poorly. These are:
(1) The monetary means that have been described in detail in the Thirty-first Letter;
(2) Good leadership;
(3) Medical protection; and
(4) The proximity of friendly families from the same country.
However, large societies fulfill only the two latter conditions, and their advantage concerning the former consists in general in pernicious illusions.

Such an illusion is the belief that the loss of individual strength in money can be compensated by the number of people. To be sure a group of well-to-do families can proceed according to the plan mentioned on page 241. However a group of poor families cannot raise its resources so much with a mere purchase of land that the cost of the establishment can be gained before the establishment itself. No reasonable person will be inclined to advance these costs, if one would not afford him more influence than any other member as a means of security of his money, that is, to further the well-being of the colony. Accordingly the regulations of the societies that are composed of well-to-do, as well as poor, people, in which without regard to the contributions, one voice is to be as valid as that of another, must be judged. Projects based on equality fail in America as well as in France. Well-to-do people are to be advised against such associations because they endanger their fortune and the poor person is to be advised against it because he has to fear that in the case of a dissolution of the society he is left to his own devices. Whoever wants to help a poor family should enter into an association with it ahead of time in Europe and advance to the family the necessary money. If he does not want to do that then he should rather travel without the family, in order not to have to face the alternative of sacrificing his fortune or exposing his associates to misery.

Concerning the requirement of good leadership it appears even more precarious, because large societies cannot be directed as comfortably as small groups. The larger the number of persons the more circumspection is necessary to prevent disturbances and accidents. In my correspondence with emigration societies I have not tired of calling attention to this fact. To travel across the ocean together is the least difficult. To remain together on the other side, however, requires that the whole thing be organized like a group of soldiers moving out to war, and just as one has to watch out that the group does not perish before it ever reaches the battleground, there are similar worries for a group of emigrants on a foreign continent. Here, too, those precautions must not be lacking that permit small groups to separate from the whole, or according to which the whole can be divided into groups that may be able to exist independently of each other. And concerning the transportation as well as the provisions in the interior of North America, it is necessary for the leadership of a society of two hundred persons to have more circumspection than would be required in Europe to lead thousands. Especially must the advance agents prevent the convoy from getting to a location where there are contagious diseases, as happened in 1832 to German emigrants who came to St. Louis on the Mississippi into houses that were occupied by people infected with cholera. If each group has a light freight wagon, their tents, their beds, and some cooking utensils, then it can stay outside of cities and villages and can thus be spared completely such diseases, as were those German emigrants who had already settled in the country.

Finally, I have also warned the societies not to buy large tracts of land so that at a later division some families by necessity get a poor lot. One should look for the best soil in small pieces and leave the poorer soil for the time being to the Congress so that no one would have to pay too dearly for the proximity of fellow countrymen. To be sure, no emigrant from Europe should isolate himself from everybody or even settle near Indians. But no one who is reasonable would want to sacrifice that which is necessary for a comfortable existence and inherent in a pleasant rustic settlement simply in order to have Germans around him rather than Americans. The plan on page 241 does not fit for every emigration society.

Well-to-do emigrants who want to take care of their own move do well to limit themselves to a group of six to twelve families (approximately twenty-five to fifty people) and should act according to page 260 of my work *Europe and Germany*. If, nevertheless, a family wants to start out on its own, then it must not forget the question of who is to be the leader in case the father dies. I can add to this that with the German population, which is by now quite advanced in the lower Missouri, one can find advice and support that one could not expect earlier. One should therefore, however, not believe that one could arrive there naked and be received by fairy queens.

I wish I were able to give here a complete listing of the German pioneers who have arrived in Illinois and Missouri since my return, but I have to limit myself to the following names because of the delay of notes. I hope that the letters that were announced by Mr. Heinrich von Martels will furnish more of them.

To the south of St. Louis on the Meramec and north in the vicinity of St. Charles many German farmers and craftsmen have settled. Approximately fifteen English miles above St. Charles on the right bank of the Missouri at Lewis Ferry (in Bonne-Homme-Bottom) lives Mr. E. C. Angelrodt from Mühlhausen in Thuringia together with Mr. F. C. von Dachroeden and Mr. J. F. Janssen. Then follows the farm of the brothers Kaiser from Wetzlar; farther up are the farms of Messrs. Warrenberg, Eggers, Wöniger from Bremen with three other young men from the same place (I do not know whether they are on the right or on the left side of the river); then on the left side you come upon the property of Mr. Palk, an Englishman, who was in Berlin for a long time, and farther on the property of Mr. Gray, an Englishman who also had lived in Germany for a long time; then to the Messrs. von Martels from Hanover, then to the brothers Hospez from Witzenhausen in the province of Hanover, then to the property of Mr. Hospez from Kassel, to the two farms of the brothers Mallinkrodt from Dortmund, to the farm of Messrs. Rathje from Stade, then to the property of Messrs. Blümner from Neustadt/Dosse, then to the farm of the two Messrs. Huttawas (architects) from Berlin, to the farm of Mr. Walk from Sweden, to the farm of Mr. Rasmus from Bracke near Bremen, then to the two Messrs. von Spankenen from Eupen, then to the Messrs. Kunze and Anger from Nordhausen, to the farms of six Messrs. Schrader from Münden and Duderstadt. On the prairies the following have settled along Deer Creek, four miles from Femme Osage: Mr. Goltermann from Magdeburg, Mr. von Aak from Switzerland, and the two Messrs. Schulz from Kassel. Mr. Schmitz from Düsseldorf has settled on the right side of the river near Newport.[51] A few miles below his property someone has begun establishing a city called Washington.[52] On the left bank of the river in the valley of the little stream, mentioned before by the name of Femme Osage, approximately twenty families of farmers from Osnabrück have settled.[53]

This number is said to have doubled already by the spring of last year, 1833. Since that time several hundred well-to-do German families have set out for this location, and one may hope that the area on the lower Missouri will soon be entirely German. Without doubt the colonists will take care of a permanent commission that will be charged with instructing the newly arrived people so that not one or the other would be too much overburdened.

Concerning the above-mentioned people it has been repeatedly reported to me that all of them consider themselves fortunate to have followed their resolutions and are very grateful for my travel report. However, I also learned that in St. Louis other emigrants have appeared who run down North America and my book, but only people who according to this book should not have emigrated. Most of them, to be sure, are said to have barely been able to pay for the transatlantic crossing and the others had either completely or almost completely spent their money in the city for fear of slight discomfort or inconvenience or because of ridiculous prejudices and fantastic ideas concerning rural life until they were completely ruined by the cholera or were driven away. Should I have not had my report printed because of such readers? Or how should I have written it differently in order to gain a hold on prudence where there is no prudence possible? It is very probable that the European Germans will soon have a base of support in North America that can serve for all of her sons as a secure support to establish a situation free from care, for which the prospect in Europe is more and more disappearing. How will these selfsame critics speak then who are still defaming my views?

PS–2 (addition). (confederation).

PS–3 (footnote). This passage has been contested in a book concerning which I would like to comment further. I mean the book that appeared in 1833 in Hanover, published by Hahn and entitled *Short Description of the United States of North America, According to their Statistical, Political, and Commercial Conditions, as well as in View of the Morals and Living Conditions, as well as Detailed Precautionary Rules for Emigrants According to his own Observations and Experience by August Witte.* Mr. Witte does not belong to those who write against their own convictions concerning America. That he wishes to advise his fellow countrymen as faithfully as well as I is everywhere apparent in his book. It is also not without value. But self-defense requires that I uncover its faults. Even though where I have been expressly named my book is approved, I nevertheless have to consider it as a whole directed against me. The preface already indicates this because in it all previous writings without exception are condemned; pages 68 and 89 alone, and particularly page 96, remove any doubt. On page 96 it reads as follows: "The farmer will be able to gradually increase his wealth only by following the directions that have been given in the preceding and practicing industry and economy; it would be foolish however if he would expect as a result of the reports of some romantic representations that his property would increase in value twelvefold within twenty years, and so forth, and so forth." Mr. Witte without doubt believes to have proved several significant errors on my part; however, I trust that he will not hold a possible displeasure against me in case I can prove as a means of justification several significant errors on his part.

In the preface it reads: "Even far more than a correct, complete, and unbiased description of the United States in general, practical advice is lacking for emigrants that is based on experience." Who does not recognize in this by looking at the title the announcement of a book that is supposed to make all earlier ones unnecessary and furnishes in 118 small octave pages everything concerning which others had written several volumes? However one can surrender to such hope only to the end of the same preface, where it is clearly stated that the promised completeness could not be expected in statistical data or such based on natural history and also not in the information concerning the Constitution and the laws, as well as concerning the administration, justice, and so forth, because others had given enough information about these things. Is this not quite a limitation on that complaint concerning the lack of a complete and correct description of the United States in general? And how does one evaluate such a limitation if it not only conflicts with the title but also with the introduction? Does one not call it a contradiction or inconsistency? The author explains, however, in the very same preface that contradictions and inconsistencies are the genuine test of books, to which he is also subjecting his. Now, however, concerning the description itself.

It is clear to everyone that the description of the physical quality of the land should belong to a description of the United States no matter how brief it may be. Well, let us read the first chapter and regard what is offered under the category of "General Overview and Climate" and let us ask whether one would learn something fundamental or something new concerning North America.

To be sure, one does derive from this what the passage of the preface wants to convey, namely that the author does not intend to furnish any detailed natural history information.

In the second chapter (page 7 and following) the opinion is expressed that the flourishing condition of the Union is not to be attributed to the Constitution alone, without offering any reason at all or without even mentioning the reasons that others have attempted to give. One can further read that the Constitution would soon have to undergo several significant modifications. Thus, for instance, it is not appropriate that the people nominate servants of the state. The people certainly could not judge the qualifications for these offices, and it is for this reason that tailors and shoemakers are appointed to be justices of the peace. However, the author later says that until the present no significant disadvantages have arisen from this since the people as a rule were electing honest people who made the administration of the offices bestowed on them a matter of honor; as in general, to an American the respect of the public was valued above everything. (If the author had not discovered any contradiction herein, however, then those who occupy themselves professionally with legislation will see it.) In the same chapter one reads also that the Americans possessed, to be sure, nationality, which rooted itself, because it was tantamount to the affection for their country; that with them the new impressions could easily wipe out the old ones, because, to be sure, all immigrants with few exceptions had been people from the lower classes whose pride had been flattered tremendously to be given some weight here as citizens of the state. (I wonder where the author might have gotten his history of the British emigration?) Nevertheless, nationality will not be able to retard the collapse of the Union for long. The rich owners of plantations in the southern states wish to have a monarch in order to be able to trade court appointments and decorations for the Republican freedom. I wonder where Mr. Witte got this idea? Had he himself been in the South? The news is really too significant to be left without any proof.

In the third chapter (page 13 and following) the author maintains that the customs of the Americans appeared to an educated European quite rude in many respects. He offers as proof that the people sit here with crossed legs or with legs pulled up under them. If one reads this after the complaints concerning the indecent positions one would almost believe that he is talking of women, who after all compete in posture as well as in behavior in general with the most careful European ladies. Furthermore he offers as proof that people who lay claim to a good education here even chew tobacco. So, the author does not know that with the Spaniards this custom has always been practiced among the educated people and because of the manifold contacts with the North Americans could easily have been taken over by them. He calls it disgusting without thinking how others would judge smoking and taking snuff. Following this, one reads that although the American is far behind the European in exterior polish he surpasses him in morality. The author attempts to justify this judgment by the standard that his moral yardstick furnishes him. As such he considers the avoidance of three evils that he designates as the three chief vices of humanity: drunkenness, passion for gambling, and lust. Fraud, defamation, conceit, and others are not considered. Conceit has, according to the author, nothing to do with morality and belongs in the fourth chapter of his little book (page 19 and following), in which he tells (probably also as news?) that the education of an American is more practical than that of a European; and he repeats the old assertion that the encouragement that the external situation furnishes the American youth for founding a household of his own weakened the dependence and the affection between parents and children, which, if it were really true, would not prove anything more for the Europeans than that among them the children are forced to a dependency on their parents. What is furthermore said concerning the canals, the railroads, and the highways has also been said before, particularly in my travel report.

In the fifth chapter (page 28 and following) one reads that if the trade balance with Europe would no longer be at a disadvantage for the Union its land would have to become one of the richest on earth. This qualification shows how faithfully the author follows the old doctrine of a balance. He neither considers that when the American land increases in value through cultivation, through buildings and other works of man (not to mention the great output of gold), particularly however through the increase of population, then the difference in the balance of about 10 million dollars is without significance; nor does he contemplate that North America would obtain in order to pay for these articles that it receives from Europe (to cover the negative balance) gold and silver from other foreign countries. The author thinks neither of the trade with the West Indies and South America nor of that with Africa, with the Levant, with East India and China. This chapter closes with the exaggerated claim that until recently it has been extremely dangerous to travel in American steamboats because the sailors are so careless and daring; during the first six months of the year 1832 not less than twenty-three steamboats are said to have shipwrecked on the Ohio and Mississippi. No doubt everything has been included in these statistics that has been torn from its mooring place during the big spring flood of the same year.

In the sixth chapter (page 38 and following) bloody religious wars are prognostigated for North America with the statement: "Thus world affairs repeat themselves in an eternal cycle; that which in one country leads to too much of a restriction of religious freedom leads in another to complete permissiveness."

In the seventh chapter (page 45 and following) the military is reviewed and is considered by the author, as an expert, as in general poor, the regular troops as well as the militia, which, according to the opinion of the author, was not worth anything and owed its victory at New Orleans only to the unreasonable disposition of the English commander-in-chief (Packenham [sic]).[54]

With the eighth chapter (page 53 and following) that part begins that concerns the emigrants more closely. My criticism to this point was only to prepare for the consideration of what might be expected in this most important matter in regard to the author who opposed, with an almost passionate ardor, my judgment, which had been calmly motivated, concerning the various areas that would be suitable for German colonists. To this groundwork belongs this one point, which I have not touched on at all yet because the author had given me no material for it. Mr. Witte has incontestably intended to tell the truth and, as far as his writing could not be contradicted by conclusions, as far as facts are concerned, and it is therefore a question of having seen and experienced something in America, I may only consider the question whether he had seen and experienced it correctly; and here again it is of prime importance how far he has been able to see and experience correctly. Mr. Witte had been personally in North America and the title of his book is based on this. Now, however, North America is very big and along the Atlantic Coast one does not learn more of the Mississippi and the Missouri than one would learn in France and Germany of Turkey and Russia. Above all, therefore, as a part of his reasoning and his challenge to believe him and not me wherever he speaks of the state of Missouri, it would have been necessary to explain whether and how long he had been in this state. This however is the thing that one misses completely. The author speaks, to be sure, of a sojourn of several years in America and of his travels; but nowhere does he mention where he had been. The only specific reference is that he had stayed in the state of Ohio below the fortieth degree of latitude, therefore four to five hundred English miles from the Mississippi. And nevertheless his statements are in general as if they were supposed to be valid for the entire Union. Let us therefore examine, for instance, whether that which is written in the eighth chapter concerning the hunt and the singing birds has been said merely with reference to the state of Ohio. For both fit very poorly for the state of Missouri. In 1833 it was reported to me that turkeys (which according to Mr. Witte are getting rarer and rarer) are still appearing in the fields in large flocks as they had before.—It is a paradox of natural history to the author that there are no real partridges in the United States, that it was a kind of quail that is just called by that name. Whoever visits the collections of natural science in the big European cities (particularly the Royal Garden in Paris) will find an opportunity to decide whether Mr. Witte or Cuvier and Blumenbach are right.[55]—Also the false antithesis of the bad song and the pretty feathers is repeated here.—The author says that one should not have an exaggerated idea of the fertility of the soil, as a few travelers seem to want to give the impression. Here he, however, himself testifies to a yield of fifty to sixty bushels of corn per acre,—yes, indeed to ninety to one hundred in individual cases. I am glad that I do not have to consider myself among the travelers who exaggerate since I have never reported more regarding the state of Missouri. However, right after this, there follows this remark, which directly contradicts my book: that is, that the price of grain in the western states (therefore also along the Missouri) is in no relation to the wages of labor; and that therefore less care is spent on the tilling of the fields. In these few words there is a strange commingling of truth and error. According to them one should believe that the western population could better spend its strength in other occupations than in agriculture and that it would be more advantageous to them if the grain could be bought from the East than if they raised it themselves. Surely Mr. Witte had not intended to say this, since he well knows that it is just the other way around and that year after year one brings by way of the Ohio a lot of grain to the Atlantic states. I have also reported how high the wages are in North America and further I have said on page 115 that in the western states no significant agriculture can be carried out without slaves by people who do not want to work themselves or cannot. Whoever sees herein a confirmation of the assertion of Mr. Witte, I must remind him of the explanation (given at the same time) which attributes the high wages for servants to the difficulty of finding servants, not to the lack of people but rather to the abundance of fertile soil which invites everyone to have an independent income. Concerning the high wages in the West no complaint is raised (at least by the natives), but rather there are complaints concerning the lack of people who have an inclination to let themselves be hired; and this is based on the surplus of fertile soil. Whoever wants to bring his own bodily strength into play cannot use it more advantageously than in agriculture. And just as such a person is able to find white servants sooner and can urge them more easily to follow his interests than he can those who seem to be too haughty for physical labor, he will never have cause to complain concerning the disproportion between yield and cost. It is true that the price of grain in the West is considerably lower than in the East and also that the wages for service are, if not higher than in the East, nevertheless nowhere lower. And it is not less true, thirdly, that in the West the fields are not as carefully tilled as in the East. However the connection that Mr. Witte makes concerning the premises is completely opposite to the truth. He has disregarded two other circumstances, although they have been touched on in the same pages, namely the different fertility and the different prices of the soil. Along the Ohio and the Missouri the work of one day can yield more grain than in Pennsylvania, Maryland, Connecticut, and so forth, in two days. Therefore, in the West the price of the grain may be lower and the wages for service may be higher than in the East; the relationship of both to each other remains therefore favorable. And it is also erroneous to state that because of the unfavorable relationship between prices of grain and the daily wages less care is applied to the fields because this unfavorable relationship itself is lacking. Besides, however, there is a basis for a confusion of concepts. Mr. Witte's words sound as if one in general would not spend much work on the fields in the West. However, the real difference between the West and the East consists in the fact that in the East where the soil is more expensive one strives to harvest more from a limited space; along the Ohio and Missouri, on the other hand, the same work is spread over a larger space and, for instance, instead of plowing one *Morgen* several times, several *Morgen* are plowed only once, which apparently is partly attributable to the natural fertility of the soil and the farmer is even more tempted because of the abundance of such soil.—The author also does not know anything of the regular protection of cornfields against squirrels, because he has not met them in the state of Ohio.

In the ninth chapter (page 66 and following) he writes: " The Americans leave their property so easily because no pleasant memories hold them to it, such memories being incompatible with the toils and difficulties under which it had been acquired." Here one can counter the author again with what he says himself right afterward. On the same page 67 he speaks, to be sure, of the great charm that clearing the wilderness has for an American. The American thus finds pleasure in his work, which is so hard on him that it embitters his memories!!! If the author had recognized the colonization urge (which is now also getting stronger in Europe because it is connected with a certain stage of development more closely than with an inviting exterior situation) as the true cause he would have spared himself this contradiction. The memories of childhood attach a person to the parental home in North America just as much as anywhere else, and one may probably say that there are far more families in which memories could develop over there than in Europe. Or could they develop better in countries where the greatest part of the population has to change residences as tenant farmers and renters so frequently as with us. On page 68 the author forgets his earlier argument so completely that he sketches a description of the situation of the so-called new settlers in which even the sharpest eye can scarcely discover a trace of that great charm. Just because the advice that follows for emigrating farmers is primarily based on it, and what appears further in this advice against me is in the relation of a specialization to generalities, I will summarize it in my criticism.

I am sorry also to find Mr. Witte of the opinion that I put particular weight on whether Germans find good homesteads in one or the other part of the great Union. It disagrees with my printed remarks as much as with the ones written in letters to some emigrants. I have recommended to several very urgently the states of Ohio and Kentucky, as particularly the Messrs. von Martels, who are now living in Missouri, can testify. Why I advised in my Postscript to travel to St. Louis has been sufficiently justified; there is only a single motive that I have not mentioned, because I believed that it was self-evident, namely my more exact acquaintance with the situation of one settler on the Missouri. If I were to give to an emigrant whose financial situation does not permit lengthy traveling and who can stand even less several attempts at settling when he asks the question "Where?" a definite answer, then I had to, as everybody would understand, let this familiarity be decisive. From this fact alone I could draw a rather strong excuse in case I have not recognized sufficiently well the advantages of the other areas of the Union.

I may attach to this introduction the following explanation: That I have never regretted this advice up to the most recent time, and how little the opinion of Mr. Witte may affect this, I hope to show very easily.

Above all I ask the reader whether the state of Missouri is suitable for German settlers and do not confuse it with the question whether they should buy congressional land. I speak of the great mass of good congressional land in the state of Missouri because in general it holds the prices of land lower than in other states. I expressly recommend to German emigrants that they buy homesteads that have already been established. And since for the time being sufficient opportunities offer themselves along the Missouri I could brush away the warnings pertaining to the difficulties and deprivations that are connected with founding such new homesteads with the little remark that one would not have to accept this advice. (If suddenly very many people would immigrate, then in the state of Ohio also ready accommodations would be lacking). I could also briefly remark in reference to the disgust with slaveholding, which strangely enough those people display most violently who reproach the United States that there no white person would lower himself to service or other lowly or dirty work, as if anybody would have to do this motivated by a naked feeling of duty, that one is just as little forced to do this on the Missouri as one is in Ohio. However, with me it is a question of the defense of certain points to which the emigrants look, and among them belongs certainly the place in my book to which I attach this big note. Mr. Witte explains, to be sure, my assertion that one might figure in the state of Missouri to raise the value of one's property twelvefold within twenty years as fictitious, and I just want to show now what material for my own defense is furnished by the remarks of the attacker. Mr. Witte, on page 68, himself accepts that I have meant multiplying the legal value of one and a quarter dollars by twelve, and thus he protects me from a malicious interpretation of my words, which might have been somewhat ambiguous. According to this the acre would have to rise in value within twenty years to fifteen dollars and thus increase by thirteen to fourteen dollars. Well, what does Mr. Witte report concerning the price of land in the state of Ohio? On page 92 one reads that the price of the best land is twenty dollars. So I merely have to add that twenty years ago it did not cost even six dollars, and the entire argument of Mr. Witte is in vain. Even in the populated parts of the Miami area it did not cost any more in 1815, as Warden (vol. 2, p. 271) acknowledges. In the year 1787 Symmes bought three hundred thousand acres for two-thirds of a dollar an acre from the government and later sold it again, generally for two dollars. As one can understand, Mr. Witte, as well as I, speaks of the quality of the land without any local advantages. These increase the price tremendously. Thus Warden says that near the main villages of the Miami region the price ranged, already in 1815, from twenty to forty dollars, while in the more distant areas it was still four to eight dollars; with so-called improvements (by which one understands primarily the clearing to make tillable land, fences, orchards, and farm buildings) it is approximately 25 to 100 percent higher. Within three miles from Cincinnati a *Morgen* costs already fifty to one hundred and fifty dollars. One meets a similar increase of prices in the vicinity of all (real) cities in the state of Ohio, although Cincinnati is ahead of all. And yet Mr. Witte, on page 96, wants to pretend that the increase by thirteen to fourteen dollars was a mere stroke of luck in a region like Missouri where there is still ample free play for the establishment of cities and villages. Even though my sentence pertaining to the state of Ohio did not seem applicable, with reference to which it does not fit now any better than earlier when the regions were freer of cities and villages, it is nevertheless the greatest rashness to discard it completely and to muster at the end the reasons that involve the author in the deepest contradictions. Page 96 reads, to be sure: "How could one reasonably imagine that land would increase in price significantly as long as there are still millions of acres of the best soil available at one dollar and a quarter?" Now I shall first ask "Where are they to be had?" Uncontestably in the state of Missouri. On page 86, number 2, the author however states that in the state of Missouri the land along navigable rivers and along roads was owned by private persons who were not at all inclined to sell below the price. I cite the latter place only in order to underscore the contradictions and not in order to acknowledge them or to contest them. For the very same purpose I point back to page 68, where one reads that people move from the eastern states to the western because in those areas good and well-situated parcels of land are already high in price; and on page 82, where the clear words are printed that in the Atlantic states the soil is either too barren or too expensive, so that the emigrant would not have to travel any farther westward than to the Ohio. How would it be if I were to place the same argument against this remark, which the author uses against my advice to go farther westward? When I said: "Can one reasonably imagine that in one part of the Union the land had become so expensive while still millions of acres were available for one dollar and a quarter?" How? If I said: "Is it feasible that in the state of Ohio the best land without consideration of the locality would cost twenty dollars while so many millions of *Morgen* of the best land are available for purchase from Congress?" For the same reasons that in the Atlantic states the soil is more expensive than in the state of Ohio, the soil is this state is more expensive than on the Missouri; and for the same reasons it will be more expensive in the future in the state of Missouri than ever farther West. The mass of congressional land is nowhere unconditionally (even on the Missouri) above the price. Near the city of St. Louis the acre costs several hundred dollars while a few miles from there it can be had at one and a quarter to eight dollars.

I believe that I could conclude my criticism (which, as I have said, I have undertaken only in defense) and counter the reports concerning the unhealthy condition of the state of Missouri, concerning the wild animals and the vermin, concerning the difficult marketing of farm products, concerning the bad nature of slaves, the menace of the nearby Indians with nothing else but that the author had everything from hearsay alone and, in a country where the land-owner of the eastern part helps to despise the western until he sells his land and can move there himself, has not guarded himself carefully enough against wrong reports.

PS—4. Preceding sentence deleted.

PS—5 (footnote). Invitations to Florida and Alabama have misled several Germans in spite of these cautions. A few have died of bilious fever, others have saved themselves by going to northern states.—In the Preface it has already been mentioned that a collabarator on the *Jenaische Literatur-Zeitung* has equated the state of Missouri with Brazil and is locating the Arkansas territory in the deepest South in the Union.

PS—6 (footnote). A few people have declared this place to be the center of the entire book and have accused me of wanting to entice people to come to the state of Missouri. People of this kind I should answer with the old saying: "Whoever thinks evil does evil." I can very well differentiate those who without mistrusting my feeling differ from my opinion, as has among others Mr. P. Schori, who in his book *The newest from the state of Ohio* (published with Dalp in Bern, Chur, and Leipzig in 1834), pages 39 and 40,[56] comments in the following way: "You have great and detailed general reports on North America, on geography and natural conditions, on the manner of living, manners and customs of the inhabitants, church and school instruction, and so forth, and in this regard nothing else is left to me than to refer you to Gottfried Duden's report. Löwig also gives a great deal of information.[57] I was not disappointed by these writings for they contained the pure truth even though I do not agree with Duden's view about buying congressional land (and that may be the most important thing for the state of Missouri), as of course the views cannot be the same with everybody: this however does not affect the veracity of those reports." Such considerate distinctions cannot be expected from the mass, neither from the literary mass nor from the other. I am always disposed to communicate with people who are capable and inclined to communicate, and therefore I add here that the difficulties connected with the first settlement in virgin forest and the deprivations that one has to suffer are by no means as severe for an American who is familiar with the circumstances (as I have experienced it myself) as Mr. Schori imagines. It is as a rule better, however, for a European without that guidance and help, which I consider a prerequisite for emigration, to buy an already established homestead than to attempt to establish one himself. My report does not contest this view, but on the contrary calls attention to the acquisition of such ready-made homesteads (in the

Twelfth Letter and in the Postscript for emigrating farmers). Mr. Schori
assumes that I advise unequivocally the buying of congressional land, and
consequently he is mistaken. He is also mistaken in the assumption that one
could not buy homesteads in the state of Missouri that spare the buyer the
situation of being a so-called new settler. Above all I had to consider the
monetary means of the emigrants and had to state what fits the person who
posesses the sum that I designated as the minimum. He who does not possess
more and yet wants to live from agriculture I cannot advise any better even
today than to emigrate to Missouri. One has to choose in the whole world and
in all situations between two evils, and it is merely a question of selecting the
lesser of the evils. For emigrants who do not have to be concerned about a few
thousand dollars the appended advice (which was written expressly for less
wealthy people) permits, to be sure, some modifications. And thus I have
recently recommended to the Messrs. von Martels, in case they want to settle
along the Missouri, to acquire a second place instead of the place on the Ohio
that is for the time being more convenient; however, the later influx of
educated German families on the Missouri has made this superfluous; and the
Messrs. von Martels want to limit themselves to their beautiful acquisition
there. If with individual emigrants the choice of a place in the large Mississippi
territory depends on the amount they can spend and the manner of their
settlement, then the state of Ohio does not fit as well for an emigration en
masse, which I had to consider in my report and indeed did think; and after a
few years the author of that pamphlet, who in the meantime will have become
more familiar with colonization, will, I have no doubt, advise his own relatives
to go to the more expansive areas that I necessarily wanted to point out to a
numerous people such as the Germans in order to be able to speak of a possible
alleviation of the needs back home by means of emigration.

By the way, one should not believe that the arguments concerning the
advantages of the different parts of North America rage only among the
German emigrants. It merely moved to them from the North Americans. It
existed there for quite some time, and it may be useful to give a few details
concerning the original causes for this. It is clear that very often the interest in
money and monetary assets is the only reason. It would indeed be asking a
great deal that somebody should despise his own property on which his very
existence depends. Indeed there are still other reasons and, to be sure, those
which are free of all suspicion of personal gain. How easily does one not
become attached to a definite place of residence so that one no longer sees its
true or its imagined advantages and is more or less blinded to the advantages of
other places? And how natural is it that there where one has built one's own hut
one would also like to see those of one's friends and in general of good people?
In North America from the Atlantic Coast to the western side of the Mississippi one meets a mutual praising and criticizing, exaggeration and denigra-
tion of the various states and districts; and a political crank could find herein
sufficient danger of the collapse of the confederation in the near future. The
citizens of Virginia, for instance, minimize Pennsylvania, and those of Pennsylvania minimize Virginia. Just as much as the Northern Atlantic states agree in
their criticism of the southern states and vice versa, thus all Atlantic states agree
in the criticism of the West. And to make this game complete, there is a similar
quarrel between the western states and districts themselves. Particularly in the

state of Ohio, the state of Indiana is decried and even more the state of Illinois and the state of Missouri. The things that Mr. Schori and Mr. Witte mentioned concerning these states find their source solely in the fact that both these gentlemen were not cautious enough. It is easily understood that in their defense against this, the states of Illinois and Missouri make common cause. However, disregarding this attack, they are quarreling among each other no less fiercely. That the Germans who settle definitely in the West therefore participate in this quarrel gradually more and more is to be expected, and that is the very reason a very careful evaluation is necessary concerning their reports. One should not be angry with them without further examination because, as mentioned before, it can be a very good and honest opinion. But, part of the advice for the new emigrants from Germany is to call attention to this fact. I can not repeat it often enough and it concerns me above all that the German emigrants will prosper, and therefore I am just as happy to hear of the well-being of German settlers in Illinois as of those on the Missouri. However, in a true report concerning both states I was not permitted to suppress the individual view according to which in general the latter deserves to be given preference. I have offered a motive for the view and have put the reader in a position to examine its individual support in itself as well as the reaction to its personal situation and mood. It was not by any means detracting from the state of Illinois; indeed, I had to admit that the state could expect a brilliant future from its great fertility, its location, and its water routes. And if the conclusion should be drawn from one part of my travel report that I also consider this whole state unhealthy, then I am ready to contradict this immediately. Without doubt there are a number of places in it that are inviting for settlements, and an emigrant who does not need servants may well select his place there near a navigable river or near a traveled turnpike (but not in the wet bottomlands).

And now the following to apply these remarks to the report that was mentioned in the Preface [to the Second Edition] as the Köpfli report. I need not repeat that the reproach does not appear in it that the shameless falsifier makes with respect to me. In case the Messrs. Köpfli and Suppiger consider me to favor the state of Missouri, then nevertheless they do not distrust my good will in the least, since they expressly free me from all guilt where my descriptions when understood erroneously have produced fantastic ideas. These gentlemen therefore should not consider it a mere mistrust of their opinions that I do not take their judgment concerning the state of Missouri as biased just because of the successes of their settlement in Illinois and their relationship to the new country (which govern each more or less)—primarily however because of the reaction to the senseless disparagement of the state of Illinois concerning which Mr. Salomon Köpfli complains on page 59; consequently I do not declare myself less unbiased (since I am here in Europe and cannot be more strongly attached to a state because of a few hundred acres than to another state). To be sure, we agree in the description of those Mississippi countries so very much that a reasonable European would not be able to find from our differences anything terrible concerning the emigration, and none of us has heard the saying "Hither or nowhere!" How could I justify the general statement concerning the western states made on page 185? To me it is a question of weighing the greater and the lesser of those great goods that are promised colonizing activity by almost the complete Mississippi territory; and alone from this it can be interpreted if in a few points in which my report contradicts that of the gentlemen in question I endeavor to pull the scales down on my side. The fact that the one loves the dark forests, the other the open prairies can have an effect on a third party only insofar as he loves either this or that surrounding. However, aside from that I maintain that to Mr. Köpfli the clearing of the woods seems far more difficult than it actually is, just as I also maintain that he misjudges the relationship of the planters to the slaves. The fact that Mr. Köpfli has not confirmed my statement concerning the water that tastes of iron vitriol I attribute to the fact that he has not been in all areas along the road from Vincennes to St. Louis. I found it to be so for a whole day's trip; however, I do not doubt that it is better along Silver Creek where Mr. Köpfli lives, since I did not have to complain about it during the last day of my travel. If, however, it is printed on page 7 in the pamphlet *Bright and Dark Sides,* and so forth, that one should not look for real fruit trees (growing natively) either in the forests of Illinois or in those of Missouri, then this is apparently a rash statement. I remind him only of the pecan nut tree, whose fruit is incontestably finer than that of the king nut tree of the Eastern Hemisphere and is said to grow as frequently along the Illinois River as I have seen it along the Missouri; of the fruits of the mulberry trees, which Mr. Köpfli will not find less delicious. There are also, at least along the Missouri, several kinds of plums and among them a bright red one of the size of a large walnut that tastes very good; furthermore, I do not understand why the persimmon tree and the papaw tree should not be called fruit trees since their fruit, if it does not surpass the best European fruit, certainly equals it in taste. To be sure the judgment depends very much on the individuals but not so much that the difference between Mr. Köpfli and myself can be noted.—Finally I remind him of the grapes, of which I have found some rather lovely ones. If these plants are not along Silver Creek, then surely they cannot be missing from all of Illinois. There is nothing else left to me but to pledge again my honor and my name for the full truth of my descriptions, whereby, however, I again agree now as before with the warning of Mr. Salomon Köpfli not to overlook the unpleasant alongside the really good or to exaggerate the good fantastically and to deceive a person fantastically concerning the dark sides.

PS–7. Preceding footnote deleted.

PS–8 (footnote). This advice requires the following modifications regarding the road and canal projects that have been executed at this time (1834). Whoever lands in Philadelphia can use the new railroad canal connection to Pittsburgh mentioned on page 303. Whoever arrives in Baltimore can, if he wants to travel by land, at first use the railroad mentioned on the same page and then take the excellent turnpike on the other side of Wheeling, which continues through the states of Ohio, Indiana, and Illinois almost to the Missouri, without having to be concerned about the dry or wet seasons. And finally, whoever gets to Lake Erie by way of New York should now not travel to the city of Erie, but rather to the city of Cleveland where the big Ohio state canal ends.

PS–9 (sentence changed). Hereby, nevertheless, the following should be noted:

PS–10 (footnote). I have read a contradictory assertion, which belongs to the many erroneous things that are printed daily pertaining to North America.

PS–11. Preceding sentence deleted.

PS– 12 (footnote). The Köpfli family, however, was charged 750 francs in 1831.

PS– 13 (addition). and France.

PS– 14 (sentence changed and entire paragraph placed ahead of preceding paragraph). In addition (relative to the first route) concerning the time of the trip it is to be noted that May and June are considered excellently calm months on the ocean . . .

PS– 15 (footnote). If one wants to travel to the Missouri before winter then one can leave Europe in September. Without any special accidents one would then arrive in New Orleans before the end of the river navigation. Should this not happen, then the time could be well used until navigation is opened again if one would travel as far up the Mississippi as ice is not an obstacle, for instance to Natchez, and there board with a farmer in order to become acquainted with American rural life. Worries of violent attacks on life and property should not prevent this, since nothing of this sort occurs among the whites there.

PS– 16 (footnote). Conditions have already changed so very much that in 1833 one was able to travel from Bremen to New Orleans for 150 *Thaler* Prussian currency as a cabin passenger.

PS– 17 (footnote). A ton is according to weight 2,000 pounds, according to space, 40 cubic feet.

PS– 18 (footnote). Note for the second edition. Because of harassments about which many complain who have emigrated via France and Holland, I would like to suggest to the Germans from the south as well as from the north to turn to Bremen. If for the transport of persons as well as their effects covered freight wagons are rented, then the cost cannot be any greater than traveling via Holland or France and one is not exposed to the difficulties with passports and security bonds that the French as well as the Dutch make. It is clearly understood that one should write to Bremen ahead of time in order not to be forced to have to wait for a sailing opportunity too long, and for those who lack acquaintances there I would like to recommend the Messrs. Westhoff and Meier. The prices of the seats on the ships departing from Bremen are lower than in Holland and France and in general lower than at the time of my trip. The charge for a place in a cabin is eighty *Thaler* in gold; I had to pay eighty dollars. The voyage in steerage including board for persons over twelve years of age is forty *Thaler* in gold or eighty guilders Rhenish, for children between the ages of eight and twelve a fourth less, for children between four and eight years one-half less, for children between one and four years of age three-fourths less, for children under one year of age five *Thaler* or ten guilders. However, for every four adults only one child is permitted at this price. In case the ratio of the children to the adults is greater, one will have to pay more for the children. In a few North American ports a small fee is charged the immigrants, which however is designated for the support of the immigrants even in case of accidents.

PS– 19 (footnote changed). In the year 1833 as a result of the protest in [South] Carolina a new tariff was instituted according to which the entrance duties are to cease gradually.

PS– 20 (footnote). Note for the second edition. Some emigrants have regretted not taking more baggage along in accordance with my advice; this was partly because they thought that their travel would be hindered by it and partly because the prices are supposed to have fallen in America since my return, partly because European items were inferior to American in quality. I have to say the following to this. The prices are still consistently more than twice as high as in the cities of Philadelphia, Baltimore, and New York. The person whose capital is limited may therefore put up with the bother and buy all metal implements, excluding the cast-iron items, in those cities after he has quickly acquired the necessary knowledge prior to this from a farmer of the neighborhood and has learned to make the proper choices. Also, let him not fail to buy a few good saddles on the Atlantic coast. Whoever, however, travels by way of New Orleans and cannot buy in the Atlantic cities should not spend a great deal of money on cutting implements until he has become acquainted with the North American implements. I do not know how the prices are in New Orleans, but they are probably considerably higher than in those Atlantic cities, even though not as high as on the Missouri. In St. Louis, to be sure, occasionally good things can be bought at auctions that are arranged by merchants at lower prices. However, the emigrant cannot depend on that just as little as he cannot depend on such opportunities in Europe.—Whoever travels by way of England may inquire there which house, field, and craftsmen's tools are frequently shipped to the United States, and he might provide himself with one or the other there.—In 1833 in St. Louis the same ax that one could buy in Philadelphia for approximately sixty cents (one and a half guilders) costs one and a half dollars; the same holds for saws, chains, shovels, hoes, and several other things. Of the large saws (trees saws) one should buy only those made of rolled steel. A mattock belongs to the most common house and field implements and is used for pulling up stumps; it has a thick long leaf that is very sharp in front and has on the backside an ax; planters call this a grubbing hoe, merchants call it a mattock. Furthermore, one needs an iron for ripping shingles, which is called a froe. The tree saw is called a crosscut saw, the iron wedge is called an adz, the carpenter's drill an auger (to make holes of one-half to two inches), the broad ax for dressing timber a broadax. These items are absolutely essential for erecting a homestead.—If I have not done it before, then I also recommend umbrellas, dust coats, caps and coats of thick beaver cloth, and for those who travel by way of New Orleans I recommend that they take along a half-covered buggy and some light four-wheel freight wagons. It is not necessary to be concerned about the width of the wagon, which usually is sixty English inches; however, one could have a device built in for an optional widening or narrowing.

PS–21 (sentence changed). . . . to Pittsburgh costs about sixteen dollars.

PS–22 (footnote). With the industry of the Americans as described concerning the establishment of new plantations or farms there is still today (in the year 1834), in spite of the many immigrations, no lack of opportunity to make reasonable purchases.—In an article by a correspondent of the *Vossische Zeitung* in Berlin it was stated recently (in June 1834), pertaining to the state of Missouri, that there, according to the local laws, no foreigner was permitted to possess property. If there was no change in the constitution of that state within the most recent times (which does not seem likely to me) then this assertion is erroneous. Not only are there no laws in the constitution of the state of Missouri that exclude foreigners, but article 10 is decidedly in their favor, as anybody can convince himself by reading the translation of Engelhard.—At this very moment a letter reached me from the same correspondent who had disseminated that news item which contains the sentence: "For, according to the laws of the state of Missouri, no foreigner may sell property or may bequeath it, and so forth." The correspondent had originally written "possess real estate" and only after this word had been crossed out he substituted the others for it. Therefore, one is permitted to purchase and own just as before. Nevertheless, I consider the new version in violation of the constitution, and if I wanted to assert my sale's contract, which was given me by the state when I bought the property and which expressly states that the land is not only my property but also safeguards it to me and to my heirs and assigns forever, then the highest court that is competent for criticism of states' laws that violate federal laws must speak in my favor.—The same letter (of 20 April 1834) states with new assurances that German settlers are prospering, that steamboat navigation on the Missouri is now quite lively and that at times three steamboats pass by in one day, and that I would be amazed at the rapid progress of the settlements on the Missouri if I were to see them with my own eyes.

PS– 23 (addition). , drugs, as well as rhubarb and opium,

PS– 24 (footnote). Whoever, however, takes silver along or more gold than can be easily saved by the person himself in case of shipwreck must not forget insurance. And the same holds true for traveling in steamboats in America itself. Recently, through neglect of this precaution several emigrants have lost their entire fortune. They carried the same in cash on themselves in a steamboat that wrecked on the Mississippi. The rate of interest is considerably higher in the interior of North America than in Europe. Ten percent is about the usual. However, nobody should be misled to take along money that has been securely invested. The main thing is also in America to take care of one's capital and to this belongs the knowledge of American laws as well as the local knowledge (information concerning the pledges), which is hard to obtain in advance. It may not be superfluous to remark that in number 218 of the new *Speier Zeitung* for the year 1832 advice for emigrants appeared under my name that I must deny completely, and in the same paper (number 231, of the year 1833) I reported it as completely false. In order to prevent a similar erroneous conception of my remarks I recommend to the emigrant to write down all questions with respect to his undertaking and to look for the answers for them in this book. With further considerations concerning his plan more and more questions will surface, and by obtaining a written answer to them he can provide himself with a secure basis in his mind, which must proceed any kind of action.

PS– 25 (footnote). This assertion is repudiated in the work by Mr. Witte, which was mentioned before, although his other comments concerning the life of American businessmen agree in general with mine. I have stated just as expressly as Mr. Witte that the European has to become acquainted with this life first before he can take advantage of it; however, if he does not consider it very enviable then he is not fully acquainted with the difficulties of German merchants.

PS– 26. Words *the interior of* deleted.

PS– 27. Words *within the Great Republic* deleted.

PS–28 (sentence changed). . . . from the interior consumption than the trade in any other country of the world.

PS–29 (sentence changed). This consists in traveling annually once or twice to Baltimore, Philadelphia, or New York . . .

Appendix II

Editors' Annotations

Editors' Introduction

1. The annotations that follow were contributed by all of the individuals whose names appear on the title page and in the Acknowledgments. Portions of the Editors' Introduction first appeared in a study of the St. Louis German element. See George H. Kellner, "The German Element on the Urban Frontier: St. Louis, 1830–1860" (Ph.D. diss., University of Missouri–Columbia, 1973), pp. 1–46.

2. Marcus L. Hansen, *The Atlantic Migration, 1607–1860* (Cambridge, Mass., 1940), pp. 148–49.

3. Wilhelm Engelmann, ed., *Bibliographica Geographica* (Leipzig, 1858), pp. 184–93.

4. Franz Löher, *Geschichte und Zustände der Deutschen in Amerika* (Cincinnati, 1847), p. 277; K. E. Levi, "Geographic Origins of German Immigration to Wisconsin," *Collections of the State Historical Society of Wisconsin* 14 (1898): 373. For specific accounts promoting German emigration to various midwestern states, see T. Bromme, *Michigan* (Baltimore, 1834), *Illinois* (Bamberg, 1835), and *Minnesota als eine Heimat für Auswanderer* (n.p., n.d.); H. C. Gerke, *Der Nordamerikanische Rathgeber nebst den in den Jahren 1831 und 1832 in der Union gemachten Reisebeobachtungen und Taschen-buch [sic] für Beleuchtung des Duden'schen Berichts über die westlichen Staaten Nordamerika's*, reprinted in *Deutsche-Amerikanische Geschichtsblätter* 16 (1916): 280–333; [Joseph Suppiger], *Reisebericht der Familie Köpfli & Suppiger nach St. Louis am Mississippi und Gründung von New-Switzerland im Staate Illinois*, ed. Kaspar Köpfli (Sursee, 1833); Gustav Richter, *Der Nordamerikanische Freistaat Wisconsin* (Wesel, 1849); Theodor Wettstein, *Der Nordamerikanische Freistaat Wisconsin* (Elberfeld, 1851); Caul de Haas, *Wisconsin: Winke für Auswanderer* (Barmen, 1846); Friedrich Koch, *Die deutschen Colonien in der Nähe des Saginaw Flusses* (n.p., 1851); Ferdinand Römer, *Texas* (Bonn, 1849).

5. The complete titles and publication data of Gottfried Duden's works are: *Bericht über eine Reise nach den westlichen Staaten Nordamerika's und einen mehrjä hrigen Aufenthalt am Missouri (in den Jahren 1824, '25, '26, und 1827), in Bezug auf Auswanderung und Uebervölkerung* (Elberfeld, 1829), 2d ed. (Bonn, 1834), and two special editions sponsored by the Swiss Emigration Society (St. Gallen, 1832, 1835); *Kampf gegen einen literärischen Löwen und andere Unholde, oder: die Vorrede zur zweiten Auflage des Berichtes über eine Reise nach den westlichen Staaten Nordamerika's* (Bonn, 1834), a pamphlet reprinting the Preface to the Second Edition of *Bericht über eine Reise; Ueber die wesentlichen Verschiedenheiten der Staaten und die Strebungen der menschlichen Natur* (Cologne, 1822), 2d ed. (Bonn, 1835); *Europa und Deutschland von Nordamerika aus betrachtet, oder: Die Europäische Entwicklung im 19ten Jahrhundert in Bezug auf die Lage der Deutschen, nach einer Prüfung im Innern Nordamerika*, 2 vols. (Bonn, 1833–1835); *Die nordamerikanische Demokratie und das v. Tocqueville'sche Werk Darüber als Zeichen des Zustandes der theoretischen Politik. Nebst einer Selbst-anklage Wegen seines amerikanischen Reiseberichts zur Warnung vor fernerm leichtsinnigen Auswandern* (Bonn, 1837); *Der Preussische Entwurf einer neuen Strafgesetzgebung und sein Verhalten zum Rheinlande* (Bonn, 1843).

6. U.S., Bureau of the Census, *Population of the United States in 1860: Compiled from the Original Returns of the Eighth Census* (Washington, D.C., 1864), pp. xxix, xxxii.

7. O. G. Libby, "Early German Settlers on the Lower Missouri," *Mississippi Valley Historical Review* 1 (1914): 271–72; Hansen, *The Atlantic Migration*, p. 149.

8. Alice H. Finckh, ed. and trans., "Gottfried Duden Views Missouri, 1824–1827," *Missouri Historical Review* 43 (July 1949): 334–43; 44 (October 1949): 21–30.

9. William Bek, ed. and trans., "Gottfried Duden's 'Report', 1824–1827," *Missouri Historical Review* 12 (October 1917): 1–21; (January 1918): 81–89; (April 1918): 163–79; (July 1918): 258–70; 13 (October 1918): 44–56; (January 1919): 157–81; (April 1919): 251–81. Bek also wrote a series of articles on Germans who followed Duden to Missouri. See William Bek, "The Followers of Duden," *Missouri Historical Review* 14 (October 1919): 29–73; (January 1920): 217–32; (April–July 1920): 436–58; 15 (April 1921): 519–44; (July 1921): 660–99; 16 (October 1921): 119–45; (January 1922): 289–307; (April 1922): 343–83; (July 1922): 522–50; 17 (October 1922): 28–56; (April 1923): 331–47; (July 1923): 479–504; 18 (October 1924): 114–29; (January 1925): 338–52. See also Bek's study of "George Engelmann, 'Man of Science,' " *Missouri Historical Review* 23 (January 1929): 167–206; (April 1929): 427–46; (July 1929): 517–35; 24 (October 1929): 66–86; and his work on "Nicholas Hesse, German Visitor to Missouri, 1835–1837," *Missouri Historical Review* 41 (October 1946): 19–44; (January 1947): 164–83; (April 1947): 285–304; (July 1947): 373–90; 42 (October 1947): 34–49; (January 1948): 140–52; (April 1948): 241–48.

10. Karl Hartnack, "Ein Beitrag zur Geschichte der Bergischen Auswanderung nach Nordamerika," *Zeitschrift der Bergischen Geschichtsvereins* 59 (1930): 174; Duden, *Bericht über eine Reise* (1834 edition), p. xxxvi (see also the Preface to the Second Edition in Appendix I); Langes to editor, 7 July 1971, Remscheid, Germany, and in possession of The State Historical Society of Missouri. According to Langes, city archivist for Remscheid, two sons named Gottfried and Leonhard were born in 1785 to Katharina and Leonhard Duden. Although it is known that Gottfried and Leonhard were brothers, no manuscripts survive to link them as twins. Leonhard followed his father's profession and operated the family's apothecary business until 1846 when he sold it to Friedrich W. Augustin of Remscheid.

11. W. Engels, "Aus der Geschichte der Remscheider Adlerapotheke," undated pamphlet, Remscheid city archives. Xerox copy in possession of The State Historical Society of Missouri.

12. Hartnack, "Geschichte der Bergischen Auswanderung," p. 175; Duden, *Bericht über eine Reise* (1834 edition), pp. xxxvi–xxxviii (see also Appendix I).

13. Ibid.

14. Friedrich Lütge, *Deutsche Sozial—und Wirtschafts—Geschichte* (Berlin, 1952), pp. 226–34, 336, 357; Herman Dieterici, "Ueber die Vermehrung der Bevölkerung in Europa seit dem Ende oder der Mitte des siebenzehnten Jahrhunderts," *Philologische und historische Abhandlung der königlichen Akademie der Wissenschaften zu Berlin aus dem Jahre 1850* (Berlin, 1850), p. 84; Theodore Hamerow, *Restoration, Revolution, Reaction: Economics and Politics in Germany, 1815–1871* (Princeton, 1958), pp. 19–20.

15. Mack Walker, *Germany and the Emigration, 1816–1885* (Cambridge, Mass., 1964), pp. 1–41.

16. Ibid., pp. 24, 29–30.

17. Friedrich List, *Schriften, Reden, Briefe,* 10 vols. (Berlin, 1928–1935), 1:100–106.

18. Hans C. von Gagern, *Ueber die Auswanderung der Deutschen* (Frankfurt am Main, 1817), pp. 3–8.

19. Moritz von Fürstenwärther and Hans C. von Gagern, *Der Deutsche in Nord-Amerika* (Stuttgart, 1818). Fürstenwärther reported on the tragic situation of Germans in the United States. Duden was familiar with this account and with the ideas on emigration advanced by Gagern. Although the relationship between Duden and Gagern was never one of deep friendship, Duden's later schemes for planned colonization and the establishment of emigration societies and his general caution about emigration approximate those of Gagern. The major difference between the two was

Duden's decidedly favorable description of America and his conclusion that the German nation was on the brink of collapse. See Duden, *Tocqueville'sche Werk,* p. 61.

20. Walker, *Germany and the Emigration,* pp. 104–5.

21. Duden, *Bericht über eine Reise* (1834 edition), p. xxxviii (see also Appendix I).

22. Duden, *Ueber die wesentlichen Verschiedenheiten der Staaten.* The editors relied solely on the 1835 edition of this work since they could not obtain a copy of the original 1822 edition from the German archives. It seems unlikely that more than a handful of copies were ever printed, because Duden wrote in the introduction to the 1835 edition that the first edition had been poorly printed and distributed.

23. Ibid.

24. Bek, "Duden's Report" (October 1917): 6–7, refers to him as Louis Eversmann.

25. Eversmann purchased an adjoining piece of land of approximately 130 acres. When Duden returned to Germany in 1827, he gave Eversmann power of attorney to deal with matters pertaining to his property. Duden's exact acreage, according to an 1839 Warren County tax statement was 308.88 acres. By 1848, Eversmann owned 460 acres of land and 6 slaves. See Tax Receipt, Warren County, Mo., 1839; Tax Receipt, Warren County, Mo., 1848; and Statement of Power of Attorney, 6 March 1827, Warren County, Mo., Eversmann Papers, State Historical Society of Missouri Manuscripts Collection, Columbia.

26. Duden, *Europa und Deutschland,* 2:468n. Bek, "Duden's Report" (October 1917): 4, argues that Duden returned to Germany because his neighbors gave him little or no intellectual inspiration. This argument fails to acknowledge Duden's activities and his writings on emigration and overpopulation prior to his emigration to America to inspect conditions for possible German settlement. No evidence exists to indicate that Duden ever thought of permanent residency in the United States. The only conceivable source for Bek's argument might be Duden's remark that he missed the "companionship of Germans" while in Missouri.

27. Hansen, *The Atlantic Migration,* pp. 106–19; Walker, *Germany and the Emigration,* pp. 9–19, 34–38; Maldwyn A. Jones, *American Immigration* (Chicago, 1960), p. 101.

28. Fürstenwärther and Gagern, *Der Deutsche in Nord-Amerika;* Ludwig Gall, *Meine Auswanderung nach den Vereinigten Staaten von Nord-Amerika,* 2 vols. (Trier, 1822). Like Duden, Gall was a Rhinelander, a member of the Prussian bureaucracy, and deeply moved by the emigration of 1816–1817. Gall's account, however, was one of the most contemptuous to appear at the time. It was particularly damaging to America because it appeared at a time when no other new or extensive description existed.

29. Two works guilty of such misunderstanding and misinformation, and known to Duden, were C. G. D. Stein, *Handbuch der Geographie und Statistik von Nord-Amerika* (Leipzig, 1826), and C. Sidons, *Die Vereinigten Staaten von Nord-Amerika nach ihren politischen, religiösen, und gesellschaftlichen Verhältnissen betrachtet* (Stuttgart, 1827), Sidons was a pen name used by Karl Postl. For more information on Sidons, see the Thirteenth Letter.

30. Duden, *Europa und Deutschland,* 1:1–9, 17–18.

31. Hector St. John de Crèvecoeur, *Letters from an American Farmer* (New York, 1963), pp. 62–63.

32. Hansen, *The Atlantic Migration,* p. 95; Walker, *Germany and the Emigration,* pp. 126–29.

33. Walter O. Forster, *Zion on the Mississippi: The Settlement of the Saxon Lutherans in Missouri, 1839–1841* (St. Louis, 1953), pp. 88–89, 97–98.

34. Gustav Körner, *Beleuchtung des Duden'schen Berichts über die westlichen Staaten Nordamerika's,* in *Deutsch-Amerikanische Geschichtsblätter* 16 (1916): 280; Löher, *Geschichte und Zustande,* p. 277; T. S. Baker, "America as the Political Utopia of Young Germany," *Americana-Germania* 1 (1897): 66; Friedrich Arends, *Schilderung des Missis-*

ippithales [*sic*], *oder des Westens der Vereinigten Staaten von Nordamerika* (Emden, 1838), p. iii; Heinrich Börnstein, *Fünfundsiebzig Jahre in der Alten und Neuen Welt. Memorien eines Unbedeutenden,* 2 vols. (Leipzig, 1884), 2: 17; *Anzeiger des Westens* (St. Louis), 29 January 1836; Hermann Steines Diary, 26 May 1834, in Bek, "Followers of Duden" (April–July 1920): 439. According to Steines, Duden "lured [to Missouri] hordes of the sons of Germany."

35. Hermann Haupt, "Die geplante Gründung einer deutsch-amerikanischen Republic," *Deutsche Revue* 32 (1907): 117–18.

36. Bek, "Followers of Duden" (April 1924): 422n.

37. Duden, *Bericht über eine Reise* (1834 edition), pp. xix, xxiii, xxxiii, 380n (see also Appendix I); [Suppiger], *Reisebericht.*

38. Theodor Hilgard, Sr., "Geschichte der Auswanderung einer deutschen Familie nach dem Westen der Vereinigten Staaten von Nordamerika im Jahre 1835," *Das Westland: Nordamerikanische Zeitschrift für Deutsche* 1 (1837): 113–30. This magazine was edited by the highly respected German physician Georg Engelmann and by Captain C. Neyfeld of St. Louis and was published by Joseph Engelmann in Heidelberg, Germany. Only three issues appeared, all in 1837.

39. Theodor Hilgard, Sr., *Meine Erinnerungen* (Heidelberg, 1858), pp. 276–79.

40. Grabs to Philipp Barez, August 1831, partially reprinted in Duden, *Europa und Deutschland,* 1:238.

41. [Suppiger], *Reisebericht,* p. 201.

42. Friedrich Münch and Paul Follenius, untitled pamphlet setting forth suggestions for German emigrants belonging to the Giessen Emigration Society (Giessen, 1833), Missouri Historical Society, St. Louis; *Aufforderung und Erklärung in Betreff einer Auswanderung im Grossen aus Teutschland* [*sic*] *in die nordamerikanischen Freistaaten,* 2d ed. (Giessen, 1833); John A. Hawgood, *The Tragedy of German-America* (New York, 1940), pp. 109–36.

43. Irmgard Erhorn, *Die deutsche Einwanderung der Dreissiger und Achtundvierziger in die Vereinigten Staaten und ihre Stellung zur nordamerikanischen Politik* (Hamburg, 1937), pp. 31–32; see also Kellner, "The German Element on the Urban Frontier," pp. 85–87.

44. William Bek, *The German Settlement Society of Philadelphia and Its Colony, Hermann, Missouri* (Philadelphia, 1907).

45. Hans Kohn, *The Mind of Germany* (New York, 1960), pp. 49, 51.

46. Paul C. Weber, *America in Imaginative German Literature in the First Half of the Nineteenth Century* (New York, 1926), p. 119; Baker, "America as the Political Utopia of Young Germany," pp. 66–67.

47. G. A. Mulfinger, "Lenau in America," *Americana-Germania* 1 (1897): 22–23, 25.

48. Marlon D. Learned, "Ferdinand Freiligrath in America," *Americana-Germania* 1 (1897): 60–61.

49. Baker, "America as the Political Utopia of Young Germany," p. 67; Arends, *Schilderung des Missisippithales* [*sic*], pp. 479–80.

50. Körner, *Beleuchtung des Duden'schen Berichts,* p. 300.

51. *Das Hannoverische Magazin* 46 (1833): 17–25.

52. Duden, *Bericht über eine Reise* (1834 edition), pp. xvi–xvii (see also Appendix I).

53. *Didaskalia, odor Blätter für Geist, Gemüth* [*sic*] *und Publizität,* see especially numbers 27, 28, and 29 for 1836.

54. *Berliner Jahrbuch für Kritik* (Berlin, 1830), pp. 907–12; portions of H. Leo's criticism may be found in reprinted form in the Preface to the Second Edition, in Appendix I.

55. J. H. Rausse, *Reisescenen aus zwei Welten nebst einer Behandlung der Zustände in den West-Staaten der Union* (Gustrow, 1836), p. 187.

56. Duden, *Bericht über eine Reise* (1834 edition), p. i (see also Appendix I).

57. Ibid., pp. i–xl; Duden, *Europa und Deutschland,* and *Tocqueville'sche Werk,* pp. 84–104.

58. Duden, *Bericht über eine Reise* (1834 edition), p. xvi (see also Appendix I).

59. Ibid., pp. xxiv, lvii–lviii.

60. Duden, *Tocqueville'sche Werk,* p. 100.

61. Ibid., pp. 92, 93, 96.

62. Duden, *Europa und Deutschland,* 1:191, 2:339, 476.

63. Included in Duden's *Tocqueville'sche Werk* and titled, *Dudens Selbst-Anklage wegen seines Amerikanischen Reiseberichts zur Warnung vor fernerm leichtsinnigan Auswandern.* On p. 97 of this work Duden mentions the possibility of his journeying to America a second time, but no record exists to indicate that he did so.

64. Alice H. Finckh, "Gottfried Duden, an Altruist," *American-German Review* 14 (October 1947): 10.

65. Although the exact date of Duden's termination with emigration promotions is not known, his last known published work appeared in 1843 and focused on Prussia's implementation of a new penal code for the Rhineland. See footnote 5 above for exact title and publication data.

66. Finckh, "Gottfried Duden," p. 10.

Preface

1. Although this particular passage is unclear as to Duden's exact reference to public debate regarding emigration, he presumably was addressing himself to the German emigration fever that gripped the country immediately after the Napoleonic War.

The Treaty of Paris sanctioned emigration out of states that had changed rulers but remained silent on emigration to foreign countries. Because of it, a disparate set of local and state policies emerged. State officials, inclined to favor a cameralist approach that saw population in terms of state wealth, labored to prohibit emigration, while local officials, desiring to be rid of the poor and indigent, encouraged it. State officials interpreted the mass exodus as having been induced by swindlers and demagogues trying to damage Germany. Local officials drew a direct and accurate connection between economic want and emigration. The debate on the reasons and policies for emigration led certain states and towns to establish courts of inquest and to file official reports on emigration, and everywhere interested people collected massive amounts of newspaper clippings on the exodus. Duden himself had served on the Mülheim Court of Inquest, and what he witnessed moved him deeply and partly explains his interest in the German emigration to America.

For further information on Duden's experiences at Mülheim, on the 1816–1817 exodus, and on the emigration policies and debates, see Duden, *Bericht über eine Reise* (1834 edition), p. xxxviii (see also Appendix I); Walker, *Germany and the Emigration,* pp. 1–41; Ewald Schnitzer, *Der Nationalgedanke und die deustche Auswanderung nach den Vereinigten Staaten von Nordamerika in der ersten Hälfte des 19. Jahrhundert* (Leipzig, 1935), pp. 20–23; Eugene von Philippovich, ed., *Auswanderung und Auswanderungpolitik in Deutschland* (Leipzig, 1892), pp. 110–15.

2. Duden, *Ueber die wesentlichen Verschiedenheiten der Staaten.* Duden's arguments here are a crude summation of his investigations, begun in 1814 when he returned from the Napoleonic War and resumed his legal duties. Many of

Duden's conclusions on the need for Germans to emigrate in this and in his other works stem directly from this study.

3. In the seventeenth and eighteenth centuries European states fashioned policies designed to increase population with the belief that increased population increased state wealth. Although accurate figures are not available for Europe or Germany before the nineteenth century, reliable estimates suggest that the policies of the states proved successful. Europe's total population increased from an estimated 100 million in 1650 to 187 million by 1800, and by 1850 Europe had approximately 266 million inhabitants. See Antonio Llano, "Population and Wages," *American Journal of Sociology* 5 (1900): 200–208; A. M. Carr-Saunders, *World Population: Past Growth and Present Trends,* 2d ed. (London, 1966), pp. 17–31; W. H. Bruford, *Germany in the Eighteenth Century* (London, 1959), pp. 157–60.

4. This argument originated in Duden's *Ueber die wesentlichen Verschiedenheiten der Staaten,* where he also expressed his conviction that massive reform efforts would be detrimental to both the state and the individual, and distasteful to him.

5. See section II of Editors' Introduction for specific references to Duden's education, legal career, and his seemingly effortless economic and social mobility within the Prussian bureaucracy.

6. Approximately twenty thousand Germans emigrated to the United States in 1816–1817 alone, and other thousands found their way to Brazil, Poland, and the Transcaucasian lands of the Russian Empire before many became disenchanted with emigration to foreign lands in the 1820s. Walker, *Germany and the Emigration,* pp. 8–16, 31–41; Hansen, *The Atlantic Migration,* pp. 106–19.

7. Although Duden never cites more than a few titles throughout this work, his writings suggest that he was familiar with the following works prior to his departure for America: Friedrich Schmidt, *Versuch über den politischen Zustand der Vereinigten Staaten von Nordamerika* (Stuttgart, 1822); Fürstenwärther and Gagern, *Der Deutsche in Nordamerika;* Gagern, *Ueber die Auswanderung der Deutschen;* Gall, *Meine Auswanderung;* L. Buhle, *Reisen durch die Vereinigten Staaten von Nord Amerika,* 2 vols. (Nürnberg, 1808); Ferdinand Ernst, *Bemerkungen auf einer Reise durch das Innere der Vereinigten Staaten von Nord-Amerika im Jahre 1819* (Hildesheim, 1820); J. V. Hecke, *Reise durch die Vereinigten Staaten in den Jahren* 1818–1819 (Berlin, 1821).

8. Duden's emphasis on agriculture as an occupation for emigrants was not unusual for his time. The material available to him on American conditions and on the reactions of returning Germans to living conditions along the eastern coast only deepened his convictions. His emphasis on agriculture also reflects Duden's total commitment to an agrarian romanticism that held that agricultural life provided vital rejuvenating qualities. The establishment of agrarian communities in the New World became Duden's chief focus in advising prospective emigrants.

9. Duden clearly tried to separate himself from those who had expected America to be a utopia and who had seen it differently after their emigration there. For a better understanding of this German literature of disillusionment with America before 1820, see Joseph Scheben, *Untersuchung zur Methode und Technik der deutschamerikanischen Auswanderungsforschung* (Bonn, 1939), pp.

127ff; Fürstenwärther and Gagern, *Der Deutsche in Amerika,* which vividly describes the lamentable situation of Germans in America in 1817; Gall, *Meine Auswanderung*; Hansen, *The Atlantic Migration*, pp. 107–19.

10. Between 1815 and 1820 Pennsylvania Germans published circulars describing the enormous economic prospects of their new home, and these were widely distributed along the Rhine and Main rivers. Rhine boatmen and ship agents acting in behalf of shipping companies, too, promoted emigration to the New World, describing life there in idyllic terms. Hansen, *The Atlantic Migration,* p. 82; Walker, *Germany and the Emigration,* p. 7.

11. The enemies of emigration were for the most part state officials who had enacted legislation prohibiting emigration during the eighteenth century and once again in the 1820s. Prussian Minister Johann von Justi perhaps expressed it well when he said, "No nation can have too many inhabitants." Hansen, *The Atlantic Migration,* p. 19; Walker, *Germany and the Emigration,* pp. 29–30; Schnitzer, *Nationalgedanke und die deutsche Auswanderung,* p. 22.

12. Schmidt, *Versuch über den politischen Zustand.* Such misconceptions about the United States were still present as late as the 1830s when American government, geography, and life were sometimes presented in a distorted and inaccurate manner. Hansen, *The Atlantic Migration,* p. 146.

13. While some historians have called Duden "doctor" because of his medical knowledge, the editors have failed to uncover any evidence that Duden ever obtained a medical degree. What is known, however, is that Duden indeed studied medicine for a few semesters and that his father operated an apothecary in Remscheid, a business his brother continued until 1846. Most likely Duden gained some practical experience and knowledge on the treatment of illness and disease by assisting his father, which may have led to his later medical studies at the University of Bonn. W. Engels, "Aus der Geschichte der Remscheider Adlerapotheke," undated pamphlet, Remscheid city archives. Xerox copy in possession of State Historical Society of Missouri.

14. William Godwin (1756–1836), a prolific writer of essays and pamphlets in history, social philosophy, fiction, and verse. His *An Enquiry concerning Political Justice and its influences on general virtue and happiness* (London, 1793; 1797; 1798) was regarded by the British authorities as dangerously liberal in thought because of its belief in the perfectability of mankind.

Thomas R. Malthus (1766–1834), English political economist whose *An Essay on the Principle of Population* (London, 1798) was as much an attack on Godwin's ideas as it was a popular formulation of a theory of overpopulation based on the observations of others.

Godwin responded with his own essay, *Of Population. An Enquiry concerning the Power of Increase in the Number of Mankind, being an Answer to Mr. Malthus's Essay on the subject* (London, 1820). Although the two men never did reconcile their difference, the controversy focused attention on the subject of overpopulation throughout Europe, and spontaneous warnings in almost every language soon appeared. For further discussion of the overpopulation controversy, see Kenneth Smith, *The Malthusian Controversy* (London, 1951), and the excellent account of E. P. Hutchinson, *The Population Debate: The Development of Conflicting Theories up to 1900* (Boston, 1967).

15. Alexander Hill Everett (1790–1847), Boston-born editor and diplomat. Some of Everett's publications included *Europe: Or a General Survey of the*

Present Situation of the Principal Powers (Boston, 1822), *America: Or a General Survey of the Political Situation of the Several Powers of the Western Continent, with . . .* (Philadelphia, 1827), and *New Ideas on Population, with Remarks on the Theories of Malthus and Godwin* (Boston, 1823; 1826). The latter work argues that an increase in population does not automatically lead to greater misery, distress, and scarcity as Malthus had postulated. Everett believed an increase in population in areas with sufficient unoccupied land would lead to higher levels of civilization, science, and the division of labor, which in turn would produce a greater abundance of the necessities and comforts of life. Significant for Duden's arguments was Everett's stress on agriculture, which he called the natural employment of man, and his belief that scarcity or abundance has a direct relationship to a country's political and physical situation.

Whether Duden arrived at his conclusions independently of Everett is difficult to determine, but the arguments of both are strikingly similar. Duden was familiar with the German version of Everett's work, *Amerika, oder allgemeiner Ueberblick der politischen Lage der verschiedenen Staaten der westlichen Festlande,* trans. Hoffmann and Campe (Hamburg, 1828). Duden refers to Everett frequently in his treatment of the political situation of North America, which appears at the end of the letters.

First Letter

1. Duden's selection of Rotterdam as his port of departure was in keeping with the practice of other German travelers of the time and was natural after the opening of steamship service from Cologne to Rotterdam in 1816. Hansen, *The Atlantic Migration,* p. 82.

2. Although Duden never identifies "N," he might be referring to Barthold Niebuhr, a Danish-born historian who taught first at the University of Berlin and then at the University of Bonn from 1822 until his death in 1831. Duden often discussed German colonization with Niebuhr.

Second Letter

1. The word *our* refers to Duden himself and to a young German agriculturalist named Ludwig Eversmann who was Duden's traveling companion. Friedrich Münch has stated that Duden also was accompanied by an "elderly female cook." Münch's information may be reliable, since he corresponded with Duden before his departure for America and settled in the area of Missouri formerly occupied by Duden. Although Duden later refers to his female cook, the editors have found no evidence that she actually sailed across the Atlantic with him. See note 6, Sixth Letter, for a biographical sketch of Eversmann. Friedrich Münch, "Für die Geschichte der deutschen Auswanderung," *Deutsche-Amerikanische Monatshefte* 1 (June 1864): 481.

2. Hellevoetsluis, on the southern coast of the island Voorne, Netherlands, which is separated from the mainland by the Waal and Mass rivers.

3. Presumably the captain considered sailing across the Sargasso Sea, avoiding both the North Atlantic Current and the Canaries Current of the Gulf Stream.

4. Duden here meant Angra do Heroísmo and Ponta Delgada. Fayal is not a

city but one of the islands. Perhaps Duden meant the city of Horta, the main town of Fayal.

5. Because of the high risks involved in transatlantic crossings in the early nineteenth century, many marine insurance underwriters wrote contracts prohibiting captains from entering unscheduled ports. For wording and conditions of such contracts, see Harrold E. Gillingham, *Marine Insurance in Philadelphia, 1721–1800* (Philadelphia, 1933), pp. 8– 10, 108, 111.

6. Captain James Cook on his second voyage recorded shoals off the Azores, and a few years later F. H. Alexander von Humboldt mentioned earlier volcanic eruptions there. J. C. Beaglehole, ed., *Journals of Captain James Cook on his Voyages of Discovery: The Voyage of the 'Resolution' and 'Adventure,' 1772–1775*, 2 vols. (Cambridge, Eng., 1955– 1961), 2:680; von Humboldt, *Personal Narrative of Travels to the Equinoctial Regions of the New Continent, during the Years 1799–1804*, trans. and ed. Helen Maria Williams, 7 vols. (AMS Press; reprint, New York, 1966), 1:96.

7. Duden suffered much seasickness on this journey. The illness was also bypassed in other contemporary medical journals, and those who covered it had little to say on the matter in the 1820s. Usher Parsons, *Sailor's Physician* (Providence, R.I., 1824), pp. 71– 72; John Dawson, "Brief Essay on the Marine Disease Usually Termed Sea-Sickness," *Boston Medical and Surgical Journal* 46 (March 1852): 129.

8. Duden was correct in attributing part of the cause to the rolling of the ship, but contemporary physicians disregarded pressure on the brain as a cause and instead advanced the idea that the deprivation of blood from the brain caused vomiting and dizziness. Parsons, *Sailor's Physician*, p. 71; Dawson, "Essay on Sea-Sickness," pp. 130– 31; F. Willia Fischer, "The Nature and Treatment of Sea Sickness," *Boston Medical and Surgical Journal* 36 (July 1847): 514– 15.

9. Baron Friedrich Heinrich Alexander von Humboldt (1769– 1859), German naturalist, traveler, and statesman who published several treatises of his travels between 1799 and 1804.

10. On treating seasickness, medical advice differed widely, agreeing only on the benefits of fresh air. Some suggested the use of ether and spiced foods if eaten cold, others suggested ginger plaster, coffee, tea, opium, and acetate of ammonia. Parsons, *Sailor's Physician*, p. 71; Dawson, "Essay on Sea-Sickness," pp. 133– 34; Fischer, "Sea Sickness," p. 517.

11. Duden here is in agreement with current medical advice, but some of his contemporaries were still prescribing aromatic and spirituous drinks. Dawson, "Essay on Sea-Sickness," pp. 133– 34; Fischer, "Sea Sickness," p. 517.

12. René A. F. de Reaumur (1683– 1757), inventor of an ethyl alcohol thermometer around 1730; 0 degrees marks the freezing point and 80 degrees the boiling point of water. Here, approximately 12 degrees Fahrenheit.

Third Letter

1. According to Captain Cook such waterspouts were not uncommon, being produced by whirlwinds and measuring from fifty to sixty feet at their base. Beaglehole, *Journals of Captain Cook*, 2:140– 42n.

2. In the late eighteenth and early nineteenth centuries it was common to rely on thermometer readings for locating the Gulf Stream. Subsequent studies demonstrated that this technique was unreliable due to the presence of cold pools within the Stream. Duden's temperature readings are identical to those given by von Humboldt. Henry Chapin and F. G. Walton Smith, *The Ocean River* (New York, 1952), pp. 124–26; Henry Stommel, *The Gulf Stream* (New York, 1961), p. 6; von Humboldt, *Narrative of Travels,* ed. Williams, 1:51–52.

3. Duden's treatment of the Gulf Stream closely approximates that of von Humboldt, and it is crudely similar to our present-day understanding. Von Humboldt, *Narrative of Travels,* ed. Williams, 1:47–70; Chapin and Smith, *The Gulf Stream,* pp. 96–172.

4. Properly known as storm petrels. Naturalists on Cook's second voyage identified storm petrels, long-winged petrels, Antarctic petrels, and blue petrels. Beaglehole, *Journals of Captain Cook,* 2:40–41, 42n, 64, 68n, 76. These birds are called "Mother Carey's chicken" by sailors, which possibly derives from "mater cara," "dear mother." The Virgin Mary is the patroness of seamen.

5. Properly known as Portuguese man-of-war and not to be confused with the man-of-war birds.

6. Probably Johann Reinhold Forster (1729–1798), Prussian-born Scottish-Prussian minister turned naturalist who, along with his son J. Georg A. Forster, accompanied Captain Cook on his second voyage of discovery between 1772 and 1775. Of Johann Forster, Beaglehole has written that for ocean voyaging "no man was ever by physical or mental constitution less fitted." Nevertheless, both Forsters wrote accounts of their travels. Georg Forster, *A Voyage Round the World in 'H.M.S. Resolution'* (London, 1777), and Johann Forster, *Observations made during a Voyage Round the World, on Physical Geography, Natural History, and Ethic Philosophy* (London, 1778). Beaglehole, *Journals of Captain Cook,* 2:xlix and passim.

7. Duden's description of the difficulties in locating exact longitude in the early 1820s was not unusual, and the instruments available were often unreliable. Not until the British admirality pushed for more accurate navigational instruments were the compass and chronometer perfected, in 1840 and 1834 respectively. Chapin and Smith, *The Atlantic River,* pp. 113, 116, 118; Hansen, *The Atlantic Migration,* pp. 173–75.

Fourth Letter

1. Cape Henry marks the southern and Fishermans Island the northern entry point of Chesapeake Bay.

2. Duden was mistaken here. England was the only country that had attempted to regulate transatlantic passenger service prior to 1819, when America passed its first federal statute. The English law of 1809 specified, in addition to the number of passengers and provisions, that each ship must have a surgeon on board. The American law of 2 March 1819 had no such provision but limited the number of passengers to two for every five tons of register, required that each passenger be supplied with sixty gallons of water, one hundred pounds of salted pork, one gallon of vinegar, and one hundred pounds of ship bread, and that each ship captain keep and file a report on the number of passengers carried. Possibly, each ship captain automatically

stocked medicines for his crew and when he engaged in transporting passengers simply increased his supply. Hansen, *The Atlantic Migration,* pp. 102, 253; U.S., Congress, Senate, *Reports of the Immigration Commission,* 41 vols. (Washington, D.C., 1911), 39: 6, 342–46, 395–96.

3. Keeping water fresh aboard ship was always a problem, and the poor quality of drinking water was always one of the immigrants' chief complaints. One German traveler heading for America in the early 1830s wrote, "Our drinking water stinks like liquid manure." Wulfing Diary, 27 October 1835, in Eugene Tavenner, ed., and Carl Hirsch, trans., *The Letters of Gustav Wulfing* (Fulton, Mo.,1941), p. 14.

4. American ship captains were universally recognized as superior to others and as more conscientious in their dealings with passengers. Many of them owned or were at least part owners of the ships they sailed. Duden's praise for his captain and crew, and for the services they provided, was usually repeated only by those who traveled in cabins. Generally, despite legislation prohibiting it, each ship carried as many passengers in its steerage compartment as it could hold, resulting in almost intolerable conditions aboard ship. See Hansen, *The Atlantic Migration,* pp. 117, 184, 253, 255–56, 300; Frances Wright, *Views of Society and Manners in America,* ed. Paul R. Baker (Cambridge, Mass., 1963), pp. 6–7.

Fifth Letter

1. The British capture of Washington, D.C., during the War of 1812 led the War Department and Congress to expend funds for coastal fortification. Authorized by congressional legislation of 29 April 1816, the Corps of Engineers spent over 3 million dollars for coastal defense between 1817 and 1824. After 1824, however, "fortress walls rose slowly," and many of the projected forts were still incomplete by the time of the Civil War. Emanuel R. Lewis, *Seacoast Fortifications of the United States* (Washington, D.C., 1970), pp. 26, 28; C. J. Bernardo and Eugene H. Bacon, *American Military Policy: Its Development since 1775,* 2d ed. (Harrisburg, Pa., 1961), pp. 145, 167; Russell F. Weigley, *History of the United States Army* (New York, 1967), pp. 163–64.

2. Because of the extremely high mortality rate on transatlantic ships immediately after the War of 1812, many American ports of entry established regulations governing passenger disembarkation, quarantine stations, and health requirements. Hansen, *The Atlantic Migration,* p. 258; for Maryland laws for 1814, 1815, 1833, and 1835 relating to immigration, see Senate, *Reports of the Immigration Commission,* 39: 681–85.

3. The fort, a star-patterned fortification of earth and masonry, is located on a peninsula dividing the Patapsco River and guarding the approaches to Baltimore's inner harbor. Weigley, *History of U.S. Army,* p. 98; Lewis, *Seacoast Fortifications,* p. 24.

4. Maj. Gen. Robert Ross (1766–1814), commander of the British troops, rode to the top of a knoll overlooking Baltimore during the first skirmishes of battle. Two American members of the 5th Regiment of the Maryland militia, Daniel Wells and Henry McComas, shot him there. Weigley, *History of U.S. Army,* p. 132; Francis F. Bierne, *The War of 1812* (New York, 1949), p. 314.

5. According to the official U.S. census returns, Baltimore's population was

62,738 in 1820 and 80,620 in 1830. Richard C. Wade, *Slavery in the Cities* (New York, 1964), p. 325.

Sixth Letter

1. The monument to the citizens of Baltimore is a clustered column resting on a huge stone on which are inscribed the names of those who lost their lives.

2. Perhaps Duden meant Charles Willson Peale (1741–1827), portrait painter and naturalist who established a museum of natural history in Philadelphia known as the Philadelphia Museum. One of his sons, Titian Ramsay Peale (1799–1885), was also a naturalist and assistant manager of the Philadelphia Museum. Conceivably, some of the museum's artifacts may have been exhibited in Baltimore. Horace W. Sellres, "Charles Willson Peale," and William H. Downes, "Titian Ramsay Peale," in Dumas Malone and Allen Johnson, eds., *Dictionary of American Biography* (New York, 1934), 14:344–46, 351–52.

3. In 1820, Baltimore had the largest black population of any southern city with a total of 14,683, of whom 10,326 were free and 4,357 slaves. Baltimore retained her number one ranking in 1830 with a total of 18,910 blacks, but New Orleans was close behind. Wade, *Slavery in the Cities,* pp. 325–27.

4. Duden uses *Gallawagen,* the German name for a coach used by the heads of state. The modern spelling is *Galawagen.*

5. Duden exchanged his currency at the Baltimore branch of the Second Bank of the United States, which had been in serious financial trouble a few years earlier. At the time of Duden's visit, Nicholas Biddle headed the entire Second Bank system and was working to establish a sound banking policy. Although some state banks still overextended themselves by issuing notes without sufficient specie, the practice was no longer so widespread and the rate of discounting notes seldom dropped below 1 percent. Bray Hammond, *Banks and Politics in America from the Revolution to the Civil War* (Princeton, 1957), pp. 260–325.

6. Duden's traveling companion was Ludwig Eversmann (1799–1858), one of ten children, six sons and four daughters, born to Alexander Eversmann (1759–1837) and Marianne Löbbecke Eversmann (1765–1809). Between 1814 and 1824, Ludwig Eversmann worked on a variety of agricultural estates. This work included stints as supervisor of the estates Edelsburg and Frönsberg, which belonged to his uncles Karl Heinrich Löbbecke and Wilhelm Löbbecke respectively. In 1821 young Ludwig had grown tired of working for his uncles and sought employment with Baron Karl vom Stein. Since Stein did not immediately have employment for him, Ludwig returned to Edelsburg until 1824, when he traveled to Bonn for a family reunion. In Bonn, Ludwig met Gottfried Duden, who had been acquainted with Karl Eversmann, brother of Ludwig and a fellow jurist. Ludwig, who had earlier considered emigrating to Pennsylvania for the purpose of setting up his own farm, liked Duden, and the two agreed to emigrate together to America.

When Duden and Eversmann landed in America they headed for Missouri and there bought adjoining parcels of land in Montgomery, now Warren, County. Through sound investment of periodic sums of money advanced him by his relatives, Ludwig Eversmann had accumulated 465.13 acres of land and owned 6 slaves by 1843. When Duden returned to Germany he gave Eversmann power of attorney to deal with matters pertaining to his lands. Eversmann subsequently acted as agent for its sale to George Münch in 1857. See Eversmann Papers, 1819– 1859; "Biographical Sketch of Ludwig Eversmann," typescript, State Historical Society of Missouri.

7. The Cumberland Road, more commonly known as the National Road, was built by the federal government despite presidential vetoes, constitutional complications, and sectional jealousies. The road started at Cumberland, Maryland, the terminus of the Frederick Pike originating in Baltimore, and extended to Wheeling, Virginia, by 1818, to Columbus, Ohio, by 1833, and to Vandalia, Illinois, by the middle of the century. Built at an average cost of $13,000 per mile, its stone base and gravel dressing and its stone and wooden bridges made it the best road in the country at the time. Philip D. Jordan, *The National Road* (Indianapolis, 1948); George R. Taylor, *The Transportation Revolution, 1815– 1860* (New York, 1951), pp. 17, 19, 22, 30.

8. See the Fourteenth Letter.

9. These towns are currently known as Ellicott City, Poplar Springs, and New Market, all in Maryland.

10. William Darby, *The emigrant's guide to the western and southern states and territories comprising a geographical and statistical description of the states* (New York, 1818).

11. Duden undoubtedly meant to reverse the two definitions and use the words *in the broader sense* to refer to the Appalachian Mountains rather than the Allegheny Mountains.

12. These mountains may then have been known by either name, but they are generally called Appalachian today; extending from the Canadian province of Newfoundland southwest to central Alabama in the United States, the range includes the White Mountains in New Hampshire, the Green Mountains in Vermont, the Catskills in New York, the Alleghenies in Pennsylvania, the Blue Ridge Mountains in Virginia and North Carolina, and the Cumberland Mountains in Tennessee.

Duden's serious attempt to unravel the confusion regarding these mountains was only partially successful and demonstrates the prevailing notions about geographical place names. Because such misimpressions were important in sustaining the Europeans' inaccurate knowledge of American geography, the editors have thought it important to preserve Duden's text. Notes have been added only to clarify items when absolutely necessary.

13. Constantin François de C., comte de Volney (1757– 1820) had several editions printed of his original French work on America. The English translation by C. B. Brown was titled *View of the Climate and Soil of the United States: to which are annexed some accounts of Florida, the French colony on the Scioto, certain Canadian colonies, and the savages or natives,* 2 vols. (Philadelphia and London, 1804). A German version was also issued as *C. F. Vollneys* [*sic*] *Reisen durch die Vereinigten Staaten von Nordamerika. Mit einer Charte und Kupfer,* 2 vols. (Hamburg and Mainz, 1804).

14. These are currently known as the Ouachita Mountains, separated from their northern neighbors, the Boston Mountains and the Ozark Plateau, by the Arkansas River.

5. The mill rose nine stories above the water level and was by far the most imposing building in Cincinnati at the time. It was consumed by a spectacular fire in 1832. See Wade, *The Urban Frontier,* p. 58; Wade incorrectly lists the date of the fire as 1823.

Eleventh Letter

1. In this and the next two sentences, Duden spells Lawrenceburg as "Lawrencebourgh" and "Lawrenceburgh."
2. Approximately 9 to 15 degrees Fahrenheit.
3. Frederickborough has not survived.
4. Port William is currently Carrollton.
5. In 1825 the Kentucky legislature incorporated the Louisville and Port-land Canal Company and authorized it to issue $600,000 in stocks. The United States government also contributed $235,000 for construction of the canal. Work began in 1826, and the first steamboats passed through in December 1830. See James Hall, *The West: Its Commerce and Navigation* (Cincinnati, 1848), pp. 78, 81; Wade, *The Urban Frontier,* pp. 192, 199–200, 218; Taylor, *The Transportation Revolution,* pp. 47, 67–68; Isabel McLennan McMeekin, *Louisville: The Gateway City* (New York, 1946), pp. 84–85.

Twelfth Letter

1. Duden probably underestimates the population here, especially since Indiana had 343,031 inhabitants in 1830.
2. George Rapp (1757–1847) and a group of associates traveled to the United States in 1803 to investigate possible settlement locations for their religiously separatistic followers. After searching for several months, they purchased several thousand acres of unimproved land on the Connonquessing River in Pennsylvania and called their community Harmony. In 1804 over eight hundred of Rapp's followers crossed the Atlantic; about six hundred settled in Harmony with Rapp, the remainder followed P. F. C. Haller to Lycoming County, Pennsylvania.

Although the Rappites prospered in Harmony, increasing population and rising prices for land induced them to search for a new settlement location. Consequently, George Rapp sold Harmony in 1815 and established a new settlement in Indiana known as New Harmony. In 1824 Rapp and his followers decided to sell their community, and in 1825 Robert Owen purchased it. The Rappites returned to Pennsylvania and there established their third settlement, this time along the Ohio River and in the present town of Economy.

Though George Rapp died in 1847, the Rappites' prosperity and success at communal living continued well into the late nineteenth century, with many of the members becoming extremely wealthy communal capitalists. The Harmony Society officially closed its doors as a communal institution in 1916.

For further information on one of the most successful and longest-lasting communal experiments in America, see J. A. Bole, *The Harmony Society* (Philadelphia, 1904); Karl J. R. Arndt, *George Rapp's Harmony Society, 1785–1847,* rev. ed. (Cranbury, N.J., 1972); George B. Lockwood, *The New Harmony Communities* (Marion, Ind., 1902).

3. In the next few pages Duden interchangeably uses the words *plains, prairies, savannas,* and *meadows.* The editors have determined the most appropriate English word by the context of the narrative. Duden seems to have been mistaken here in his mileage estimates. A square German mile is only 1.32 times as large as a square English mile.

4. Morris Birkbeck (1764– 1825), a substantial English farmer, emigrated to the United States in 1817, purchased about sixteen thousand acres of prairie land west of the Wabash River in Illinois, and founded the town of Albion. His capital exhausted, Birkbeck produced two extremely popular volumes of promotional literature in hopes of attracting English settlers, *Notes on a Journey in America, from the Coast of Virginia to the Territory of Illinois* (Dublin, 1818), and the more significant volume *Letters from Illinois* (Philadelphia, 1818). See George Flower, *History of the English Settlement in Edwards County, Illinois* (Chicago, 1882); C. W. Alvord, *Governor Edward Coles* (Springfield, Ill., 1920); and J. W. Iglehart, "The Coming of the English to Indiana in 1817 and their Hoosier Neighbors," *Indiana Magazine of History* 15 (1919): 93– 117.

5. Schmidt, *Versuch über den politischen Zustand.* Schmidt's account of conditions in America was one of the most caustic to appear in the 1820s. This is Duden's second negative reference to it, the first appeared in his Preface.

6. For a map of St. Louis showing the fortifications of 1780, see Reps, *The Making of Urban America,* pp. 76– 77.

7. Duden has recorded some minor errors here in regard to the transfer of Louisiana. By the secret Treaty of Fontainebleau in 1762, France ceded Louisiana to Spain; and in 1800 at the Treaty of San Ildefonso, Spain ceded it back to France. In 1803 by the Treaty of Cession, the United States purchased it for $15 million, although the formal termination of Spanish rule in Louisiana was not effected until March 1804. For further details on both the French and Spanish activities in Louisiana, and more specifically in Missouri, see William E. Foley, *A History of Missouri: Volume I, 1673 to 1820* (Columbia, Mo., 1971), pp. 1– 96.

8. John G. E. Heckewelder (1743– 1823) wrote at least two accounts of his missionary activities among the Indians of the Ohio valley. Presumably Duden was referring to Heckewelder's *A Narrative of the Mission of the United Brethren among the Delaware and Mohigan Indians, from its commencement in the year 1740 to the close of the year 1809* (Philadelphia, 1820).

9. The population of St. Louis in 1820 was close to 5,000 inhabitants, and in 1830 it stood at 4,977 inhabitants. St. Louis's population remained stationary until the mid-1830s when German and Irish immigrants began to settle there, accounting for 52.1 percent of her total population in 1850. See Kellner, "The German Element on the Urban Frontier," pp. 85– 167.

10. Ferdinand Ernst came to the United States in 1819 as the head of a settlement society composed of approximately thirty families. Ernst paid the entire bill for the Atlantic crossing and eventual settlement near Vandalia, Illinois. Fever killed many of the settlers, and Ernst was forced to give up his colonizing scheme. See Ernst, *Bemerkungen auf einer Reise,* and Newton Bateman and Paul Selby, *Historical Encyclopedia of Illinois and History of Fayette County,* 3 vols. (Chicago, 1910), 2:621– 22.

Thirteenth Letter

1. Duden was mistaken in his reference to the Missouri being almost exterminated by the Sioux. Before 1800 the Missouri had experienced their greatest defeat at the hands of the Sac and Fox. This defeat caused them to become disorganized. The ravages of warfare, smallpox, and the breakdown of tribal customs caused the virtual disappearance of the Missouri; in 1804 only thirty families of the tribe reportedly existed. See Robert T. Bray, "The Missouri Tribe in Archaeology and History," *Missouri Historical Review* 55 (April 1961): 218–19.

2. For more information on the species of fish in Missouri, see William L. Pflieger, *The Fishes of Missouri* (Jefferson City, Mo., 1975).

3. Franklin was laid out in 1816. By 1820 the community contained about one thousand residents. Duden referred to Old Franklin in this letter. In 1828 the threat of flooding prompted the residents to move to the present site of New Franklin, about two miles from the original townsite. Columbia, laid out in 1820, was still a very small community.

4. This is Duden's third negative reference to Schmidt and his account of America. Clearly Duden wished to discredit him as a reliable observer and to correct some of the German people's misconceptions about America's interior. See Schmidt, *Versuch über den politischen Zustand.*

5. A medical term referring to a concretion formed in the body, usually in the bladder or kidney; commonly called a kidney stone.

6. Generally used to describe any of a variety of trees or shrubs with unusually hard or heavy wood.

7. F. A. Micheaux (1770–1855) was a French silviculturist, botanist, and traveler. Originally published in Paris in 1804, this work was translated into English and published in London as *Travels to the West of the Alleghany [sic] Mountains, in the States of Ohio, Kentucky, and Tennessee.* Micheaux's work is included in Thwaites, *Early Western Travels,* 3:105–306.

8. The stream was Lake Creek. For further information and a description of Duden's homestead, see the Eighteenth Letter.

9. Although Duden used the English name, the stream bears the French name of Femme Osage. The area of Montgomery County in which Duden settled became part of Warren County on 5 January 1833.

10. A rute was an old measure, approximately ten to fourteen feet depending on locality. It roughly equaled a rod.

11. Friedrich Münch reported that Duden and Eversmann met a German by the name of Küchental in St. Louis who advised them to travel to the Femme Osage area if they intended to purchase public land. Supposedly they became lost during the trip and, as night approached, stumbled upon the house of a Pennsylvania German named Jacob Haun. Münch further stated that Haun helped them select their land and rented a portion of his home to them until their dwellings could be constructed. See Friedrich Münch, "Für die Geschichte der deutschen Auswanderung," *Deutsch-Amerikanische Monatshefte* 1 (June 1864): 481–84.

12. While Duden's brief description of public land sales reflected the general governmental policy, in reality a variety of practices and policies prevailed. For a useful summary of legislation, administrative directives, and court deci-

sions regarding lands before 1860, see W. W. Lester, *Decisions of the Interior Department in Public Land Cases, and Laws Passed by the Congress of the United States: Together with the Regulations of the General Land Office* (Philadelphia, 1860).

13. The editors have been unable to document that Duden stayed with more than one farmer. However, his traveling companion, Ludwig Eversmann, recorded paying board and lodging fees to several individuals between 1824 and 1826. The most frequently listed names were Jacob, Mathias, and Nathaniel Haun; Jim Linde; Daniel Lynn; and a Mr. Dorothe. See "Book of Expenditures, 1824–1826," Eversmann Papers. Duden originally intended to stay with farmers only during the winter of 1824–1825, but he did not move into his dwelling until the spring of 1826. For further information, see the Eighteenth Letter.

14. Whenever Duden referred to a farm of more than a few acres, he often used the German word *Pflanzung,* meaning plantation. Wherever applicable, the editors have substituted the appropriate English equivalent.

15. C. Sidons was one of the pseudonyms used by Karl Postl, an Austrian priest who left Prague in 1823 and made his way to New Orleans. Between 1823 and 1826 he traveled extensively in Louisiana and up the Mississippi and Ohio rivers, finally settling for a while in Pennsylvania. Although there are some ambiguities in Postl's life and career, his extensive writings as Charles Sealsfield gained a wide readership and his observations on American life are now generally considered to have been perceptive and accurate, although somewhat colored by his own political views. During the midnineteenth century he became known as "the greatest American author" for his ethnographical novels, but the secret of his identity was not revealed during his lifetime. Since his death in Switzerland in 1864, Postl's life and works have continued to interest scholars. The book Duden cited was *Die Vereinigten Staaten von Nord-Amerika nach ihren politischen, religiösen und gesellschaftlichen Verhältnissen betrachtet* (Stuttgart and Tübingen, 1827) or *The United States of North America as They are in Their Political, Religious and Social Relations* (London, 1827).

Fourteenth Letter

1. The editors have been unable to uncover the identity of this individual. Possibly, Duden's friend might have been Benjamin Kurtz or his uncle John Daniel Kurtz. In 1833 both advised Martin Stephan and his Saxon Lutherans to read Duden's account for detailed information on Missouri settlement. For further details, see Walter O. Forster, *Zion on the Mississippi: The Settlement of the Saxon Lutherans in Missouri, 1839–1841* (St. Louis, 1953), pp. 86–89.

2. See the Sixth Letter.

3. Volney, *View of the Climate and Soil of the United States.*

4. Commonly called the European whortleberry; also any of several other species of blueberries.

5. A German linear measure equal to about .12 to .10 of an inch.

6. William Hancock, a native of Kentucky, reportedly came to Missouri and Montgomery (now Warren) County around 1798. He settled on land that became known as Hancock Bottom. Hancock was the first to farm in the

Missouri River bottom of Warren County. See *History of St. Charles, Montgomery and Warren Counties, Missouri* (St. Louis, 1885), p. 1030; William Bryan and Robert Rose, *A History of the Pioneer Families of Missouri* (St. Louis, 1876), p. 214.

7. In 1839 Duden's 310 acres were assessed at $900, on which Ludwig Eversmann, who held power of attorney, paid $1.12 in taxes. In 1855 the same piece of land was taxed for $2.50 plus an additional $1.60 for the Lake Creek School Fund. Eversmann's own real estate and personal property grew yearly, so that by 1848 his estate was taxed at $14.02, plus an additional $2.88 for the Lake Creek School Fund. His taxable property and assessed value were as follows:

7 horses, 4 cows, 1 yoke ox	$ 200
6 slaves	1,100
71.78 acres of land	180
140.00 acres of land	300
59.5 acres of land	150
121.85 acres of land	250
73.00 acres of land	150
money on loan	800
total assessed value	$3,130

For both Duden's and Eversmann's taxes and personal property evaluations, see Tax Receipts, Property Evaluation Lists, and Lake Creek School Fund Receipts, Warren County, Mo., for the years 1826–1855, in Eversmann Papers.

Fifteenth Letter

1. Duden's precise meaning in this sentence is not clear. If he meant to apply the term *drainage basin* to Lake Creek, then only a few scattered clusters of dwellings existed. However, if he intended to apply it to the entire region of his acquaintance, then the number of settlements was fairly reliable.

2. Possibly Jacob Haun or one of his sons.

3. Duden refers here to the timber rattlesnake.

4. Duden refers here probably to the Western pygmy rattlesnake (*Sistrurus miliarius streckeri*).

5. This was a common misuse of terms. Even such noted naturalists as John and William Bartram used *alligator* interchangeably with *crocodile*. See Helen G. Cruickshank, ed., *John and William Bartram's America: Selections from the Writings of the Philadelphia Naturalist* (New York, 1957).

6. In his *Versuch über den politischen Zustand,* Schmidt argues that ticks caused a variety of fever-related illnesses that sometimes resulted in death.

7. Duden probably referred to chiggers.

8. Johann Friedrich Blumenbach (1752–1840) was a well-known professor of natural history at Göttingen University's Institute of Physiology. He published a variety of works on anatomy, anthropology, physiology, and natural history in Latin, French, and German. The *Handbuch der Naturgeschichte* first appeared in Göttingen in the early 1780s and, in 1830, it underwent its 12th edition. Of many other editions, an English translation of the 10th German

edition was published in London in 1825 as *A Manual of the Elements of Natural History.*

Sixteenth Letter

1. Duden is mistaken here on both instances. Daniel Boone died on 26 September 1820, five years earlier than Duden indicates. Although Boone became seriously ill at the home of his son-in-law, Flanders Callaway, he returned to the home of his son, Nathan Boone, and died there three days later. For further information on Daniel Boone and his children's activities in Missouri prior to 1820, see John Bakeless, *Daniel Boone* (New York, 1939), pp. 351–416.

The area in which Duden purchased land and took up temporary residence was predominantly settled by the Boone clan and their Kentucky friends. Presumably, since Duden did not travel farther west than Montgomery County, Duden acquired much of his information about homesteading, pioneer life, and related subjects from these transplanted Kentucky pioneers. This may in part account for Duden's frequent references to the almost complete self-sufficiency of pioneer farming, the ease with which the whole process could be accomplished, and the joys of living in a virtual paradisiacal wilderness.

2. Although Daniel Boone discovered the salt spring, his sons erected a salt works and shipped the salt to New Orleans. Ibid., p. 392.

Seventeenth Letter

1. Duden probably refers to the lake formed by Lake Creek near its mouth.

2. Duden here refers to the Carolina paroquet. In the late 1850s flocks of these birds began to disappear. Known as parrot or parakeet, the birds were particularly disliked by Missouri farmers, since the large flocks destroyed corn crops. See Otto Widmann, *A Preliminary Catalog of the Birds of Missouri* (St. Louis, 1907), pp. 113–16.

3. For a reliable general account of lead-mining activities in early Missouri, see Ruby J. Swartzlow, "The Early History of Lead Mining in Missouri," *Missouri Historical Review* 28 (April 1934): 184–94; (July 1934): 287–95; 29 (October 1934): 27–34; (January 1935): 109–14; (April 1935): 195–205.

4. The area, some thirty-eight miles northwest of Ste. Genevieve, was known as Mine à Breton. Around 1773, hunter Francis Breton discovered lead ore there. Moses Austin, who previously had operated lead mines in Virginia, came to the area in 1797, secured a land grant from the Spanish government, and within a short time revolutionized mining in the area. See Swartzlow, "Early History of Lead Mining in Missouri," *Missouri Historical Review* 29 (October 1934): 32; Foley, *A History of Missouri,* pp. 10, 59–60; James A. Gardner, "The Business Career of Moses Austin in Missouri, 1798–1821," *Missouri Historical Review* 50 (April 1956): 235–47.

5. Variations in spelling probably due to owners' usage.

Eighteenth Letter

1. Sidons, *Die Vereinigten Staaten von Nord-Amerika.*

2. According to Friedrich Münch, Duden spent the rest of his stay in Missouri in the smaller structure, which both Münch and Duden called a hut. Duden's larger house was never completed. See Münch, "Fur die Geschichte der deutschen Auswanderung," pp. 481–84.

3. Hired help and a slave built all of Duden's buildings, cleared and cultivated his land, cooked for him, and attended to the general duties associated with farming. Many Germans who read Duden's account invariably overlooked his financial resources, periodic sums of money sent from Germany, and his use of a slave and hired help.

4. The editors were unable to identify this indentured family.

5. See the Thirty-first Letter.

6. Prince Paul Wilhelm von Württenberg, 1797–1860, was the son of the king's brother, Duke Eugen Friedrich of Württenberg.

7. Lake Creek School, a one-room schoolhouse.

8. Warden, *A Statistical, Political and Historical Account.*

9. Cornelius Tacitus (55–ca. 117), the great Roman writer, is chiefly remembered for his histories of the Roman emperors from the death of Augustus to that of Domitian. His treatise on the Germanic tribes remains the major extant Roman account of the tribes of Central Europe. Tacitus's unhappiness with Roman society led him to romanticize the Germanic peoples and their environment, describing them as simple, virtuous, and rugged, and the Germanic family as a model of simplicity and virtue.

10. Commonly known as the tumblebug.

Nineteenth Letter

1. For accounts of Indians in Missouri, see Carl H. and Eleanor F. Chapman, *Indians and Archaeology of Missouri* (Columbia, Mo., 1964), pp. 113–17; Duane Meyer, *The Heritage of Missouri—A History,* rev. ed. (Hazelwood, Mo., 1970), pp. 126–36. A recent historian of Missouri in the national period agrees with Duden's assessment that the Indian population was so sparse and so passive toward the newcomers that they presented no significant barrier for settlement. Throughout the 1820s, Missourians pressured the federal government to negotiate a series of removal treaties. From 1823 to 1832, all the Indian claims to land in Missouri were extinguished in exchange for new lands in a designated Indian Territory in Kansas. For further information, see Perry McCandless, *A History of Missouri: Volume II, 1820 to 1860* (Columbia, Mo., 1972), pp. 51, 55.

2. The War of 1812 produced a series of skirmishes between white settlers and Indians in Missouri, mostly in northern Missouri. The incident described here by Duden did occur. Robert Ramsey, who had settled in the area before 1802, already walking with a wooden leg, was badly wounded, three of his children were tomahawked to death, and two others were barely able to escape. Bakeless, *Daniel Boone,* pp. 388–90. For a fine general treatment that assesses the hostilities between the whites and Indians in Missouri as serious during the War of 1812, see Foley, *A History of Missouri,* pp. 146–65.

3. Actually, a series of isolated attacks broke out throughout the 1820s and 1830s when the Missouri Indian tribes were removed from their lands. For further information, see McCandless, *A History of Missouri,* pp. 55–57;

Dorothy J. Caldwell, "The Big Neck Affair: Tragedy and Farce on the Missouri Frontier," *Missouri Historical Review* 64 (July 1970): 391–412.

4. Duden's citation has some errors. It should read Bernard Romans, *A concise natural history of East and West Florida* (New York, 1775). Romans (ca. 1720–1784) was a sea captain more noted for his navigation guides to the Gulf of Mexico and the Caribbean than for his natural history of the Floridas.

5. For a more philosophical treatment of the subject than appears within this letter, see Duden, *Europa und Deutschland,* 1:320–40.

6. In another work Duden compared the Indians to the early Germanic tribes on the basis of the following similarities: love of drink, love of play, wagering of most valued possession, and war and hunting as the major preoccupations of both. Ibid., p. 327.

7. Jonathan Carver, *Travels in the interior parts of North America, in the years 1766, 1767, and 1768* (London, 1778). Duden probably used the German translation, *Reisen durch die inneren Gegenden von Nord-Amerika in den Jahren 1766, 1767, und 1768* (Hamburg, 1780).

Volney, *View of the Climate and Soil;* Romans, *A concise natural history.*

John Oldmixon, *The British Empire in America, containing the history of the discovery, settlement, progress and state of the British Colonies on the continent and islands of America* (London, 1741). Two known German translations were published, one as *Das gross-britannische Scepter in der Neuen Welt; oder politische und geographische Beschreibung aller engländischen Plantagien, so wohl auf dem vesten Lande als denen in Amerika gelegenen Inseln* (Hamburg, 1715), and the other as *Gross-brittanische Amerika nach seiner Erfindung, Bevölkerung und allerneuesten Zustand* (Hamburg, 1710).

Jean François de Galaup, comte de La Peyrouse [Leperouse], *A Voyage Round the World, Performed in the Years 1785, 1786, 1787, and 1788,* was originally published in Paris in 1797, and subsequently the work was issued in London in 1798, in Edinburgh in 1798, and in Boston in 1801.

8. For some reason Duden never updated this portion of his treatment of Indians in subsequent editions or in his other works. Customarily, Duden took great delight in reporting new events, policies, and conditions in America. Perhaps, Duden might have been too embarrassed to alter his statement that the American government's Indian policies were based on "principles for which no civilized people on this earth need be ashamed," particularly after the wholesale Indian-removal legislation of the late 1820s and 1830s.

9. During the Napoleonic War several regiments of troops with oriental-like features crossed Germany on their way to Paris. Most notable among them were Russian-recruited Kalmucks, cossack and Crimean Tartars, and several regiments of Egyptian Mamluks in service to Napoleon.

Twentieth Letter

1. In the regions cited here, South German dialects are spoken that are different from Duden's Rhenish or the Low German dialects. Less educated people tended to speak their native dialects rather than the standard High German, and consequently they often experienced communication problems and appeared provincial or uncultured.

2. For additional information on the Pennsylvania Germans and their reli-

gion, see Wayland F. Dunaway, *A History of Pennsylvania* (New York, 1935), pp. 340–49.

3. Duden here refers to Bülow, *Der Freistaat von Nordamerika.*

4. For some reason, Duden omits the state of Maine.

5. Warden, *Statistical, Political and Historical Account.*

6. No satisfactory explanation exists for the origin of the term *Yankee.* After the Battle of Lexington during the Revolutionary War, New Englanders used the term. They created a mythical Massachusetts (not Rhode Island) Indian tribe, the Yankos, that earlier New Englanders supposedly had defeated in battle. It was claimed that the Yankos gave the tribe's name to its conquerors. The word meant invincible. In retaliation, Virginians, angered because the New Englanders had not assisted them in fighting the Cherokees, used the Cherokee word *eankke* (coward, slave) to label those "Yankees," whom they believed had shirked their duty. Duden, therefore, was correct in his understanding, although he spelled *eankke* as *cankhe.* See Mitford M. Mathews, ed., *A Dictionary of Americanisms* (Chicago, 1951), p. 1896.

7. Duden here probably refers to Thomas Anburey's *Travels through the Interior Parts of America* (London, 1789) or Anburey's *Anburey's Reisen im inneran Amerika* (Berlin, 1792). The first work was available in French or English by 1793.

8. Preelection concern over Jackson and his radicalism did exist; see John William Ward, *Andrew Jackson: Symbol for an Age* (New York, 1955).

9. German mercenaries were used by the English during the Revolutionary War. See Christopher Ward, *The War of the Revolution,* ed. John R. Alden (New York, 1952), vol. 1.

10. Sidons, *Die Vereinigten von Nord-Amerika.*

11. For those who desire to pursue the history of the slavery debate there are a number of works to consult. Among these works are Kenneth M. Stampp, *The Peculiar Institution: Slavery in the Ante-Bellum South* (New York, 1956); Winthrop P. Jordan, *White over Black: American Attitudes toward the Negro, 1550–1812* (Chapel Hill, N. C., 1968); Robert W. Fogel and Stanley L. Engerman, *Time on the Cross: The Economics of American Negro Slavery* (Chicago, 1974); Donald L. Robinson, *Slavery in the Structure of American Politics, 1765–1820* (New York, 1970); U. B. Phillips, *American Negro Slavery* (New York, 1918); and Eugene D. Genovese, *The World the Slaveholders Made* (New York, 1969). For slavery in Missouri, see Harrison A. Trexler, *Slavery in Missouri, 1804–1865* (Baltimore, 1914).

Historically, Missouri Germans usually have been considered antislavery. Even though Duden's period in Missouri was brief, this continuation of the Twentieth Letter illustrates that he was a mild apologist for slavery and that he countenanced to some degree the views of the defenders of the system. A more intense defense was offered by Thomas R. Dew, *Review of the Debate* [of the Abolition of Slavery] *in the Virginia Legislature of 1831 and 1832* (Washington, 1833).

12. The American Colonization Society acquired Liberia, and in February 1820, eighty-eight freed slaves left the United States aboard the *Elizabeth* to settle on the land situated on the west coast of Africa. From 1821 through 1867 the society sent six thousand free blacks to Liberia. Freetown, a British West

Africa seaport in the republic of Sierra Leone (directly north of Liberia), was founded in 1788 by British philanthropists as a settlement for freed American slaves.

13. In 1808 Congress did not prohibit exportation of slaves from Africa. It did prohibit their importation from Africa into the United States. Some illegal slavery did, of course, go on. See Philip Curtin, *The Atlantic Slave Trade: A Census* (Madison, Wis., 1969).

14. No satisfactory secondary treatment of the law of slavery exists. A good survey is Stampp's *Peculiar Institution.* Some states in the 1830s accorded lighter punishment for the homicides of slaves than for the homicides of free men. See George M. Stroud, *A Sketch of the Laws Relating to Slavery in the Several States of the United States of America* (Philadelphia, 1827), and Jacob B. Wheeler, *A Practical Treatise on the Law of Slavery* (New York, 1837). Emancipation of aged and sick slaves was prohibited unless a security bond or some other procedure guaranteed that they would receive proper care.

15. For numerous instances of black-white intermarriage, see James H. Johnston, *Miscegenation in the South* (Chicago, 1939).

16. Duden undoubtedly refers to the Santo Domingan slave revolt led by Pierre Dominique Toussaint L'Ouverture in 1801. Santo Domingo (now the Dominican Republic) achieved independence from Spanish rule in 1821. At the time of Duden's writing, the country was under the control of Saint Dominique (present-day Haiti).

17. Information about the free black's status may be found in Ira Berlin, *Slaves Without Masters: The Free Negro in the Antebellum South* (New York, 1975).

18. A number of citations concerning violence and poisoning are found in H. T. Catteral, *Judicial Cases Concerning American Slavery and the Negro* (New York, 1968).

19. An examination of newspapers of the period and pertinent county histories failed to disclose any information about this particular incident.

Twenty-first Letter

1. Whether the honeybee was native to America or transported to the continent remains a matter of controversy. See Daniel L. McKinley, "The White Man's Fly on the Frontier," *Missouri Historical Review* 58 (July 1964): 442–43.

Twenty-second Letter

1. For additional information, scientific names, and the number of species of owls, doves, woodpeckers, and other birds, see Widmann, *Birds of Missouri.*

2. A mixture of water with sand, once ingested, would cause the hummingbird to die.

Twenty-third Letter

1. Duden refers to one of Alexander von Humboldt's many writings.

2. In June 1824 flooding on the Missouri ruined a potentially good corn

crop and for a time delayed postal delivery. See Louis G. Johnson, "Floods and Flood Control in the Missouri River Basin" (Ph.D. diss., University of Missouri–Columbia, 1959), p. 26.

3. Duden's comment about "bad air" reflects the incorrect belief that the air carried malaria. Today we know the mosquito is the carrier.

4. *Rhus radicans,* as Duden states, is not sumac, but it is poison ivy. Seven varieties of sumac exist in Missouri; none of them is poisonous. Duden's confusion on this was not unusual. As late as 1870 George Vasey made the same mistake. See Julian A. Steyermark, *Flora of Missouri* (Ames, Iowa, 1963), pp. 999, 1003, and Charles V. Riley and George Vasey, eds., "Poison Ivy," *The American Entomologist and Botanist* 2 (July–August 1870): 285.

Twenty-fourth Letter

1. The inner bark of the elm can be eaten as food.

2. No species of spruce (*Picea*) occurred naturally in Missouri during Duden's time. He probably mistook the eastern red cedar (*Juniperous Virginiana*) for spruce.

3. Duden refers to the bur oak in this instance.

4. Duden would have been able to locate all the trees and bushes mentioned except the "four kinds of walnut trees." While six species of walnut are recognized in the United States, only two are found in Missouri—black walnut, *Juglans nigra,* and butternut, *Juglans cinerea.* Duden may have observed variations in the black walnut. See Steyermark, *Flora of Missouri,* and Elbert L. Little, *Check List of Native and Naturalized Trees of the United States* (Washington, D.C., 1953).

Twenty-fifth Letter

1. The rattlesnake Duden refers to is the timber rattlesnake (*Cvotalus horridus horridus*). See Paul Anderson, *The Reptiles of Missouri* (Columbia, Mo., 1965), p. 286.

2. For biographical information on William H. Ashley, see Harvey L. Carter, "William H. Ashley," in LeRoy R. Hafen, ed., *The Mountain Men and the Fur Trade of the Far West* (Glendale, Calif., 1969), 7:23–34. Jedediah Smith actually located the South Pass, which would have allowed the type of travel Duden forecasted.

Twenty-sixth Letter

1. For a general description of iron and iron mining, see James Norris, *Frontier Iron: The Maramec Iron Works, 1826–1827* (Madison, Wis., 1964), pp. 5–7.

2. See *History of Franklin, Jefferson, Washington, Crawford & Gasconade Counties, Missouri* (Chicago, 1888), pp. 461, 475.

3. Duden probably is mistaken here. Salt was being manufactured in Howard County, considered part of the Boonslick country.

4. For information concerning the Fever River lead mines, see Joseph Schafer, "Sectional and Personal Politics in Early Wisconsin," *Wisconsin Magazine of History* 18 (June 1935): 448–49.

Twenty-seventh Letter

1. Volume 1 of the *Transactions and Collections of the American Antiquarian Society,* additionally titled *Archaeologia Americana* (Worcester, Mass., 1820), contained a long article by Caleb Atwater of Circleville, Ohio, on the mounds in Ohio that later scientific archaeological investigations would attribute to the prehistoric Adena and Hopewell people. John Heckewelder, a missionary to the Delaware Indians in the late eighteenth century, published legends of those Indians concerning the mound builders of the Midwest in the first volume of the *Transactions of the Historical and Literary Committee of the American Philosophical Society* (Philadelphia, 1819). By consulting these sources Duden was utilizing the conclusions of the foremost published authorities of the time that these are the origins of the mound builders in North America. Unfortunately, both Atwater's and Heckewelder's theories that the mound builders were a separate and superior race to the other prehistoric people of North America were based on erroneous conclusions. For a recent publication on the historical and archaeological background of the North American mound builders, see Robert Silverberg, *Mound Builders of Ancient America: The Archaeology of a Myth* (Greenwich, Conn., 1968). Neither Baron Alexander von Humboldt nor Friedrich Schmidt dealt extensively with the archaeology or the theory of the North American mound builders in their publications.

2. In the above paragraphs Duden lumps the mounds and earthworks of the Adena-Hopewell people of Ohio, Indiana, Kentucky, and West Virginia together with those of the later Mississippian people of the southeastern states and the Mississippi valley. See Silverberg, *Mound Builders of Ancient America,* chaps. 6, 7.

3. The Trappists were members of a Roman Catholic monastic order that stressed a secluded life of silence, prayer, and physical labor.

4. The mounds that were located on the site of St. Louis, Missouri, have been destroyed. Present-day archaeologists believe them to have been an extension of the numerous Mississippian Cahokia earthworks in the American bottoms across the river in Illinois. Maj. Stephen H. Long described and mapped the St. Louis mounds in 1819. See T. R. Peale, "Ancient Mounds at St. Louis, Missouri, in 1819," *Smithsonian Institution, Annual Report of the Board of Regents Showing the Operations, Expenditures, and Condition of the Institution for the Year 1861* (Washington, D.C., 1862).

5. Lewis and Clark, Zebulon Pike, and Thomas Nutall examined and discussed mounds only in passing in the narratives of their journeys.

Twenty-eighth Letter

1. For the most part, Duden's observations agree with those in Dr. John Sappington, *The Theory and Treatment of Fevers* (Arrow Rock, Mo., 1844). Bilious remittent fever probably was chronic malaria. Dr. Sappington's intermittent fever or ague was similar to Duden's malaria. Duden's feverish colds probably were the same as Dr. Sappington's influenza and would cover most respiratory diseases. Croup, as referred to by Duden, could also have been diphtheria.

2. Vaccination, practiced by the Chinese for centuries, was introduced to England about 1700.

3. Dr. Sappington mentions the various ways to treat yellow fever in his *Theory and Treatment of Fevers*. No documentation has been located that yellow fever occurred in Missouri at the time of Duden's writing. However, since Sappington mentions it, certainly some cases were known to exist by 1844.

4. Duden mistakenly blamed the swamps for malaria instead of the mosquitoes that used those areas for breeding purposes.

5. Running surface water easily could carry diseases such as typhoid, cholera, and dysentery. But, in sparsely settled areas, diseases transmitted person to person probably would not become overly contaminating.

6. It is doubtful that naphtha contains any curative powers.

7. Although this use of sulfuric acid cannot be documented, a few drops of sulfuric acid could kill bacteria or liberate some sulfur dioxide. See Dr. James E. Cope, M.D., to the editors, 25 August 1975, State Historical Society of Missouri.

8. Vinegar and honey, as well as vinegar and molasses, were considered to have curative powers. Although Duden states that vinegar made from honey was considered a preventive, in all probability most people used a mixture of vinegar and honey.

9. Duden's description of the influenza epidemic is reasonable. However, his comment about painful swelling does not coincide with the usual forms of the ailment.

10. Duden here refers to chigger bites.

11. This statement by Duden "does not bear medical scrutiny." See Cope to editors, 25 August 1975.

12. For a description of medical practices in Missouri for this period, see Roland Lanser, "The Pioneer Physician in Missouri 1820–1850," *Missouri Historical Review* 44 (October 1949): 31–47.

13. The use of often useless patent medicines was very prominent at this time. See James H. Young, *The Toadstool Millionaires: A Special History of Patent Medicines in America before Federal Regulation* (Princeton, 1961).

Twenty-ninth Letter

1. See *Acts of the Second General Assembly of the State of Missouri* . . . (St. Charles, Mo., 1822), pp. 23–25. Section 4 stipulated that any person who failed to show up for work would be fined one dollar, and if the worker failed to sufficiently exert himself he would be fined two dollars.

2. The law at the time Duden wrote implied that a man could substitute his son, ward, apprentice, or slave to do the roadwork. However, a St. Charles ordinance required both whites and slaves to work on the town's streets. See Trexler, *Slavery in Missouri,* pp. 62–63.

3. Duden here probably meant that only citizens could own vessels that could engage in commerce under the American flag.

4. For a description of early judges, see W. Francis English, *The Pioneer Lawyer and Jurist in Missouri* (Columbia, Mo., 1947), pp. 9, 19.

5. Duden overlooked the fact that at that time United States senators were chosen by state legislatures.

6. Duden's note is confused. For example, no distinction is made for a maximum number of representatives, and the minimum basis for representa-

tion was thirty, not fifty, thousand. See *Constitution of the United States of America* (Washington, D.C., 1837), p. 10.

7. In 1856, the New York City police department became the first department to wear uniforms.

8. At the time Duden wrote, Monroe would have been the "previous" president. No documentation has been located to substantiate that Monroe tied his horse in front of the Capitol. However, it is quite plausible that he did so.

9. Duden refers to the presidential elections of 1824 and 1828.

10. Duden's comments beginning here and ending on page 152 illustrate his confusion about the political parties in the United States. He did not understand the term *Federalist,* either as it referred to supporters of the Constitution or as it referred to the party of Alexander Hamilton, John Adams, and others.

11. Duden here mistakenly has the Federalists supporting the Articles of Confederation of 1783.

12. Duden refers to Jackson's action concerning Alexander Arbuthnot, a trader, and Robert C. Ambrister, a former lieutenant in the British Royal Colonial Marines. For more accurate details, see George Dangerfield, *The Awakening of American Nationalism* (New York, 1964), pp. 49–50.

13. Duden here meant that the people wanted to elect the presidential electors.

14. *The Sufferings of Young Werther* by Johann Wolfgang von Goethe, 1774.

Thirtieth Letter

1. In this letter Duden's weather observations, in the main, appear amazingly accurate and reasonable. His discussions of climatology and micrometeorology, as well as his concepts and approaches, were innovative for his time.

2. Duden's overemphasis on wind-shift regularities is one of the weakest portions of this letter, as is his suggestion in his footnote about magnetic effects having a possible tie with the wind shifts.

3. On the Reaumur temperature scale, water freezes at 0 degrees and boils at 80 degrees.

4. Volney, *View of the Soil and Climate,* p. 120.

5. Duden appears overly optimistic about shipping being unobstructed by ice until mid-February. For a different opinion, see Louis C. Hunter, *Steamboats on the Western Rivers* (Cambridge, Mass., 1949), pp. 221, 224.

6. Warden, *Statistical, Political, and Historical Account,* 2:318.

7. Duden here refers to tornadoes.

8. See Volney, *View of the Soil and Climate,* p. 100.

9. For additional information about the New Madrid earthquakes, see James Penick, Jr., *The New Madrid Earthquakes of 1811–1812* (Columbia, Mo., 1976).

10. Duden probably meant earthquakes or glacial formations instead of volcanoes. For a general description of mineral resources, see *History of St. Charles, . . .,* pp. 533–35.

11. Duden's suggestion that forests predominated to about five hundred miles west of the Mississippi River probably is incorrect. A figure of two

hundred to three hundred miles is more realistic. Possibly Duden's comment was influenced by the greater concentration of forested areas extending westward along the Mississippi's major arteries.

12. Duden may have been referring to Alexander von Humboldt's treatise on temperatures, translated by D. Brewster in 1817.

13. Information on Kervan has not been located.

14. Duden's temperatures are in fair agreement with temperatures for the same cities as recorded by more recent and standardized techniques. There is a contradiction concerning the mean annual temperature for Paris as supplied by Duden. He uses "nearly 52° F," then quotes Humbolt's value of "57.18° F," and later he uses 51.15° F. The Humboldt value "57.18° F" appears to be in error, since it will not convert to the given 10.7° C (10.7° C = 51.26° F). Perhaps this error was typographical and the value actually should have been 51.18° F. Nevertheless, Duden's overall commentary on these points remains valid. The latitude of Mannheim is approximately 49°30'.

15. Duden appears to have exaggerated here; but, even today, large numbers of unsheltered livestock are found in Missouri.

16. Thomas Jefferson, *Notes on Virginia* (Philadelphia, 1794), p. 110.

17. William Darby, *The Emigrant's Guide to the Western and Southwestern States and Territories* (New York, 1818), p. 147.

18. The discussion on oceanic influence is quite accurate.

19. Sun climate is the temperature as it soley relates to latitude.

20. Duden's comments in the preceding ten pages represent an "enlightened" grasp of physical climatology for the period. Some of Duden's arguments "did not emerge clearly until many years or decades later." See Grant L. Darkow, professor of atmospheric science, University of Missouri–Columbia, to the editors, 8 January 1976, State Historical Society of Missouri.

21. A toise is an old French linear measure equivalent to 1.949 meters or 6.395 English feet.

Thirty-first Letter

1. For biographical information on Ludwig Eversmann, see note 6, Sixth Letter.

2. Duden here refers to Prince Lee Bu. In 1783 an English ship, the *Antelope,* wrecked near one of the Pelew (Palau) Islands. For four months the captain and crew were treated hospitably by the natives. Prince Lee Bu sailed to England and subsequently died of smallpox. His people also suffered from contact with the colonial expansionists. During the late eighteenth century the islands' population totaled an estimated forty to fifty thousand, but by the 1920s only a few thousand "discouraged" natives remained. See Percy S. Allen, *Stewarts' Handbook of the Pacific Islands* (London, 1923), p. 240.

In 1820 American Protestant missionaries to the Sandwich (Hawaiian) Islands abolished the original form of government and began a systematic program to Christianize the natives.

3. Construction of the Erie Canal began in 1817, and the canal opened in October 1825. Built in sections, it was open to Portsmouth in October 1832. See Richard B. Morris, ed., *Encyclopedia of American History* (New York,

1961), p. 444; Ronald E. Shaw, *Erie Water West: A History of the Erie Canal* (Lexington, Ky., 1966), p. 52.

4. Either Duden's mathematical calculations were incorrect or a printing error was made in some of the following figures. For example, the figure here should have been $24,778,093.81. See "Report from the Secretary of Treasury on the State of the Finances," U.S., 18th Cong., 2d sess., Sen. Doc. 8 (1825): 5.

5. The expenditure figure for military affairs should have been $5,258,294.77, bringing the total expenditures to $15,314,171.00. Apparently, a transposition of numbers occurred. See ibid. However, Duden made a different correction in the 1834 edition. See Appendix I, 31–7.

6. Duden was mistaken here; the figures were for the fiscal year, not just for nine months.

7. The actual debt totaled $83,710,572.60. See "Report from the Secretary of the Treasury on the State of the Finances," U.S., 19th Cong., 1st sess., Sen. Doc. 6 (1825): 38.

8. Duden's figures here are correct except for the second-class frigates with thirty-six cannon; the number should have been three instead of four. See "Documents from the Department of Navy," U.S., 19th Cong., 1st sess., Sen. Doc. 2 (1825): 152, 154–55.

9. Duden's figures were taken from the "Report of the Postmaster General," U.S., 19th Cong., 1st sess., Sen. Doc. 2 (1825): 165–68.

Thirty-second Letter

1. Duden is mistaken here. Missouri was not admitted into the Union until 1821.

Thirty-third Letter

1. See Hunter, *Steamboats,* pp. 420–26, for a treatment of fares, accommodations, classes of passengers, and other topics. Hunter supplies a less flattering commentary about travel conditions for second-class passengers on steamboats.

2. Catorce, in the state of San Luis Potosí, North Central Mexico, is located in a spur of the Sierra Madre Mountains. The area is rich in mining, producing silver, antimony, gold, lead, and copper. See Leon E. Seltzer, *The Columbia-Lippincott Gazetteer of the World* (New York, 1952), p. 350.

3. Duden's use of the term *mountains* for the elevations near St. Louis is overly generous, as they fall short of the actual definition of the word.

4. A description of American Bottom, directly opposite St. Louis, is located in the *St. Louis Missouri Argus,* 24 May 1838.

5. Duden's navigable lengths of streams apparently were taken from gross estimates by river travelers. Most of the streams listed would not be considered navigable today. William Bridgwater and Elizabeth J. Sherwood, eds., *The Columbia Encyclopedia,* 2d ed. (New York, 1952) or Seltzer, ed., *Columbia-Lippincott Gazetteer,* give the following figures for the entire length of streams: the Missouri, 2,565 miles, or navigable upstream to present-day Sioux City, Iowa, 760 river miles; the Osage, 500 miles; the Grand River (of Missouri),

215 miles; the Kansas with Smoky Hill headstream, 730 miles; the Platte (LaPlatte) with North Platte headstream, 990 miles; the Big Sioux (Great Sioux), 420 miles; the James (Jacque), 710 miles; the White, 600 miles; the Cheyenne (Chien), 527 miles; the Little Missouri, 560 miles; the Yellowstone, 671 miles; the Marias (Maria), 210 miles. There are other tributaries of the Missouri (for example, Niobrara and Milk) with lengths greater than some of those listed by Duden.

6. For Robert Owen and New Harmony, see Bridgwater and Sherwood, eds., *The Columbia Encyclopedia,* 2d ed., p. 1464.

7. For information on William Maclure and his association with New Harmony, see Johnson and Malone, eds., *Dictionary of American Biography,* 12:135–36.

8. For another mid-1820 view of Cincinnati, see W. Bullock, *Sketch of a Journey through the Western States* (London, 1827), in Thwaites, ed., *Early Western Travels,* 19:133–36.

9. For information on Gallipolis and Gallia County, Ohio, see John Kilbourn, *Ohio Gazetteer,* 11th ed. (Columbus, Ohio, 1833), pp. 211–13. The "company" Duden refers to in this paragraph was the Scioto Company and its offshoot, the Compagnie de Scioto. For an excellent secondary source, see Billington, *Westward Expansion,* 4th ed., pp. 208–10.

Thirty-fourth Letter

1. Warden's derivation for Monongahela is correct. Duden refers to his *Statistical, Political and Historical Account.*

2. Duden here refers to the Cumberland Road; see the Sixth Letter.

3. For prices of boats, high pressure engines, and other technical details, see Hunter, *Steamboats,* pp. 122–33. Duden's statement that a steamboat cost "something over five thousand dollars" does not correspond with Hunter's estimates. Size, equipment, furnishings and "finishing the vessel, ranged as widely as from $60 to $250 per measured ton for completed boats." In the early 1820s five steamboats constructed on the Upper Ohio River that ranged between 120 and 168 tons cost the owners "from $55 to $100 per measured ton." Hunter also mentions that during 1824 an eighty horsepower engine could be purchased in Pittsburgh for $5,685.

4. Duden is mistaken here. At that time the navy only had Robert Fulton's *Demologos* (or *Fulton*), and it was used in the Brooklyn Navy Yard as a receiving ship until it blew up in 1829. Not until 1842 was a contract let for a steam warship. See David B. Tyler, *Steam Conquers the Atlantic* (New York, 1939), p. 138.

5. Hunter, *Steamboats,* p. 33, credits England with 315 merchant steam vessels in 1830. It is doubtful that England added 165 of these vessels in three years.

Thirty-fifth Letter

1. The editors have been unable to locate information on the ship *Armata* and its captain, Joseph Harvey.

2. Thomas West, Lord De La Warr (Lord Delaware) (1577–1618), was an

English soldier and was appointed the first governor of Virginia in 1610. He wrote *The Relation of the Right Honorable the Lord De-la-Warre, Lord Governour and Captain General of the Colonie planted in Virginia* (London, 1611). In 1618, he suspiciously died at sea near the Azores. The state of Delaware, the river, and the bay were named after him. The Delaware Indians called themselves Lenni-le-nape. See *The Encyclopedia Americana* (New York, 1961), 8:617d; Delaware Tercentenary Commission, *Delaware Tercentenary Almanack & Historical Repository* (n.p., n.d.), p. 13.

3. Duden refers here to Joseph Bonaparte, the older brother of Napoleon. Joseph was able to buy property because of a special legislative act passed in 1817. Duden's comments are correct concerning Bonaparte and his estate. See Clarence Edward Macastney and Gordon Dorrance, *The Bonapartes in America* (Philadelphia, 1939), pp. 79–91.

4. Duden's population total was excessive. In 1830, Philadelphia's population totaled 82,318. See *Fifth Census . . . 1830* (Washington, D.C., 1832), p. 65.

5. Volney, *A View of the Soil and Climate.*

6. For information about New York City's City Hall and the architectural style, see Alan Gowans, *Images of American Living* (New York, 1964), p. 256.

7. In 1820 New York City's population totaled 123,706, while Philadelphia's population totaled 63,802. See *Census for 1820* (Washington, D.C., 1821), pp. 13, 20.

Thirty-sixth Letter

1. Duden may have been surprised that no pilots were navigating to Rotterdam since that city was the center of Dutch trade in the 1820s.

2. Duden here means Lizard Point, a promontory southwest of Cornwall, England.

3. The editors have been unable to locate the island Goree referred to by Duden. The only Goree Island in Seltzer, ed., *Columbia-Lippincott Gazetteer*, is in West Africa. See p. 697.

Concerning the Nature of the North American United States

1. The Hoffman and Campe publication appeared one year after Everett's *America, or a General Survey . . .* had been published in English by the Philadelphia firm of H. C. Carey & I. Lea. For information on Everett, see note 15 to the Preface, and Henry G. Pearson, "Alexander Hill Everett," in Johnson and Malone, eds., *Dictionary of American Biography,* 6:220–21.

2. Duden refers to Gessler, the early fourteenth-century Austrian baliff of the Swiss canton of Uri. The tyrannical Gessler decreed that the Swiss uncover their heads whenever they saw his hat, which symbolized Austrian sovereignty. The legendary William Tell refused to do this. Consequently Gessler forced Tell to shoot an apple with a bow and arrow from his son's head.

3. For information on the Order of Cincinnatus, see Alvin F. Harlow's "Society of the Cincinnati," in James Truslow Adams, ed., *Dictionary of American History* (New York, 1940), 1:375–76.

A Postscript

1. In the following section Duden is summarizing the arguments for emigration that are spread throughout his letters . For this reason, the editors have not attempted to annotate here those things explained in the annotations to the letters.

Appendix I

1. This preface was reprinted in pamphlet form under the title *Kampf gegen einen literärischen Löwen und andere Unholde, oder: die Vorrede zur zweiten Auflage des Berichtes über eine Reise nach den westlichen Staaten Nordamerika's* (Bonn, 1834).

2. The Preface to the Second Edition is set in a variety of type sizes and italics, apparently in order to emphasize Duden's vehemence against his critics. The editors have not attempted to reproduce all of the varieties of type here, since they do not in any way affect the meaning of the Preface.

3. *Ausland,* published in Stuttgart beginning in 1828, eventually totaled sixty-six volumes through 1893, when it merged with the magazine *Globus.*

4. For information concerning the Krotoneans, Sybarites, and Tarentines, see T. J. Dunbabin, *The Western Greeks* (Oxford, Eng., 1948).

5. Probably Heinrich Leo (1799–1878), a German historian whose work was "colored by extreme reaction." See Clarence L. Barnhart, ed., *The New Century Cyclopedia* (New York, 1954), 2:2434. Among Leo's writings was the six-volume *Lehrbuch der universalgeschichte* (Halle, 1840–1851).

6. Johann Joachim Eschenburg, *Handbuch der klassichen Literatur, enthaltend* (Berlin and Szczecin, 1801).

7. Eschenburg mistakenly gives Xenophanes credit for founding the Eleatic school. Parmenides is considered to be the actual founder; nevertheless, Xenophanes did give impetus to the Eleatics by searching for unity in apparent multiplicity.

8. For brief information on the Greeks mentioned in this paragraph and throughout the Preface to the Second Edition, see Bridgwater and Sherwood, eds., *The Columbia Encyclopedia,* and N. G. L. Hammond and H. H. Scullard, eds., *The Oxford Classical Dictionary,* 2d ed. (Oxford, Eng., 1970).

9. Arnold Hermann Ludwig Heeren, *Handbuch der Geschichte der Staaten des Alterthums, mit besonderer Rucksicht auf ihre Verfassungen, ihren Handel und ihre Colonieen* (Göttingen, 1828).

10. For more information on the colonies listed here, see Seltzer, ed., *Columbia-Lippincott Gazeteer.*

11. Duden probably refers to the writings of Friedrich Christopher Schlosser, particularly his *Weltgeschichte für das deutsche Volk.* Schlosser's original universal history was technical in nature. Under his direction his student G. K. Kriegk edited the history into a popular form, which comprised nineteen volumes. See Henry Smith Williams, *The Historians' History of the World* (New York, 1907), 3:637.

12. Duden's suggestion that Herodotus lived in Sybaris appears incorrect, although Herodotus did refer to Sybaris in his writings. See John L. Myres, *Herodotus: Father of History* (London, 1953), pp. 12–15.

13. Duden probably quotes from a letter written by Barthold Georg

Niebuhr, possibly the "N" mentioned in the First Letter. See note 2 to that letter.

14. Franz X. Ackermann, *Das Kaiserreich Brasilien: Beobachtungen und praktische Bemerkungen für deutsche Auswanderer* (Heidelberg, 1834).

15. The Tscharner brothers from Glarus Canton, Switzerland, arrived in Madison County, Illinois, in the spring of 1833. They accompanied Joseph and Johann Suppiger and their families. See *History of Madison County, Illinois* (Edwardsville, Ill., 1882), p. 105.

16. Kaspar Köpfli, *Die Licht & Schattenseite von New Switzerland in Nordamerika* (Sursee, 1833).

17. The editors were unable to locate any information on Mr. P. von Zoya. Among the sources consulted were the 1840 Illinois census and William H. Perrin, ed., *History of Bond and Montgomery Counties, Illinois* (Chicago, 1882).

18. Ernst L. Brauns, *Ideen über die Auswanderung nach Amerika* (Göttingen, 1827).

19. Duden seems to have been mistaken here. A square German mile is only 1.32 times as large as a square English mile.

20. *The Fifth Census . . . 1830* gives the 1830 population for Missouri, Ohio, Indiana, and Illinois as 140,455; 937,903; 343,031; and 157,445, respectively. See pp. 151, 143, 147, 149.

21. Georg Anton Ritter von Schäffer, *Brasilien als unabhängiges Reich, in historischer, mercantischer und politischer Beziehung geschildert* (Altena, 1824).

22. [Joseph Suppiger], *Reisebericht der Familie Köpfli & Suppiger nach St. Louis am Mississippi und Grundung von New-Switzerland im Staate Illinois,* ed. Kaspar Köpfli (Sursee, 1833).

23. Warden, *Statistical, Political and Historical Account;* Timothy Flint, *Recollections of the Last Ten Years Passed in Occasional Residence and Journeying in the Valley of the Mississippi* (Boston, 1826).

24. Gerke, *Der Nordamerikanische Rathgeber.*

25. Duden mistakenly refers to Illinois, Indiana, and Ohio becoming a part of the United States in 1763. Actually, in 1763 ᵭᵭe land that eventually made up these states was ceded by France to Great Britain as a result of the Seven Years' War. See Howard R. Lamar, ed., *The Reader's Encyclopedia of the American West* (New York, 1977), pp. 241, 893.

26. Ernst L. Brauns, *Das liberale System, oder das freie Bürgerthum in seiner höchsten entfaltung; in einen gemälde des Bundesstaats von Nordamerika praktisch dargestellt,* 2 vols. (Potsdam, 1831–1833).

27. Heinrich Berghaus (1797–1884) was a German geographer and cartographer, best known for his *Physikalischer Atlas* (1837–1848).

28. C. von Rotteck probably was Karl Wenzeslaus Rodecker von Rotteck (1775–1840), who wrote or edited a number of books on history, political science, and natural law, including the multi-volumed *Allgemeine geschichte vom anfang der historischen Kenntniss bis auf unsere zeiten: Für denkende geschichtfreunde bearb* (Freiburg, 1833–1834).

29. Wilhelm Butte, *Erinnerungen an meine teutschen Landsleute, welche versucht seyn sollten aus Europa zu wandern* (Cologne, 1816); Joseph ritter von Hazzi, *Über auswandern u. Fremde, Ein Beitrag zur Gesetzebung* (Dortmund, 1812).

30. Michael Alexander Lips, *Statistik von Amerika; oder, Versucheiner*

*historisch-pragmatischen und raisonirenden Darstellung des politischen und bürger-
lichen Zustandes der neuen Staaten-Körper von Amerika* (Frankfurt, 1828). Duden's reference to von Morris may have been to Jedidiah Morse, *The American
gazetteer, exhibiting, in alphabetical order, a much more full and accurate account,
than has been given, of the states, provinces, counties, cities, towns, . . . on the
American continent . . .* (Boston, 1797); or there may have been a printer's error
and Duden was referring here to Morris Birkbeck. Duden's Prince Bernhard
was actually Karl Bernhard (1792–1862), duke of Saxe-Weimar-Eisenach. He
wrote *Reise ar hoheit des herzogs Bernhard zu Sachsen-Wiemar-Eisenach durch
Nord-Amerika in den Jahren 1825 und 1826* (Weimar, 1828). For the other
citations, see the following notes: 4, 19, and 28 to the Editors' Introduction; 7
to the Preface; 21 to Sixth Letter; and 4 to Twelfth Letter.

31. Duden probably refers to Franz Geo. Ed. Schläger. Among Schläger's
publications was *Die Geistlichen Akzidenzen sollten abgeschafft werden! Ein
Wunsch, nebst einer Mittheilung, wie in Hameln das Bericht- und Leichern-Geld in
eine feste Einnahme verwandelt ist* (Hanover, 1834).

32. Thersites was an "ugly, foul-mouthed fellow," killed by Agamemnon in
the *Iliad.* See Hammond and Scullard, eds., *The Oxford Classical Dictionary.*

33. Duden refers to the map of Missouri by Fielding Lucas, Jr. (1781–
1854), printed in Baltimore during 1824 and reproduced on the endpapers of
this volume.

Henry Schenk Tanner (1768–1858) was an engraver and mapmaker who
lived in Philadelphia from about 1811 to 1850. See James F. Carr, *Mantle
Fielding's Dictionary of American Painters, Sculptors, and Engravers* (New York,
1965), pp. 360–61.

34. Peter Kalm (1716–1779), a Swedish scientist who traveled in North
America and studied its natural history, plants, and agriculture. Kalm wrote
Travels in North America, the first account of its type written by a trained
scientist. See Bridgwater and Sherwood, eds., *The Columbia Encyclopedia,* 2d
ed., p. 1033.

35. [Suppiger], *Reisebericht.*

36. Flint, *Recollections of the Last Ten Years.*

37. Duden probably refers here to Gerke's *Der Nordamerikanische
Rathgeber.*

38. Heinrich von Martels with his father and brothers sailed to America in
1832. After settling near Duden's farm, he returned to Germany in 1833. In
1834, a book by him was published entitled *Letters Concerning the Western Part
of North America, together with a Map of the State of Missouri.* William Bek
translated a portion of von Martels's work and included a brief biographical
sketch of him in "The Followers of Duden," *Missouri Historical Review* 17
(April 1923): 339–47.

39. In 1837, Eli (Emil) Angelrodt was one of the incorporators of the St.
Louis German Academy, a short-lived institution of higher education. The
academy folded for a lack of funds. See Bek, "The Followers of Duden,"
Missouri Historical Review 16 (October 1921): 124n.

40. Duden refers to the Black Hawk Indian War. See Cecil D. Eby, *That
Disgraceful Affair* (New York, 1973), and Reuben Gold Thwaites, "The Story
of the Black Hawk War," in *Collections of the State Historical Society of Wisconsin*
(Madison, 1892), 12:217–65.

41. This series of reports from New York, entitled "Pictures from the Social Life of the North Americans," appeared in sixty-six installments in the *Morgenblatt für gebildete Stände* beginning 17 July 1833 with a "Letter of a German Lady from America" in issue no. 179.

42. Henry Rowe Schoolcraft, who wrote *Journal of a Tour into the Interior of Missouri, Arkansaw, and from Potosi, or Mine á Burton, in Missouri Territory, in a southwest direction, toward the Rocky Mountains, performed in the years 1818 and 1819* (London, 1821).

43. Duden refers here to John C. Calhoun's espousal of the nullification theory, which emanated from the outcry by South Carolina cotton planters against the tariff of 1828.

44. Rouchefoucald Liancourt, François Alexandre Frédéric, duke (1747–1827). Duden was probably familiar with a German translation of his work entitled *Reisen in den Jahren 1795, 1796, und 1797 durch alle an der see belegenen Staaten der Nordamerikanischen Republik; imgleichen durch Ober-Canada und das Land der Irokesen. Nebst zurerlassigen nachrichten von Unter-Canada,* 3 vols. (Hamburg, 1799).

45. For a discussion of North Carolina opposition concerning the tariff question, see William K. Boyd, *History of North Carolina, Volume II: The Federal Period, 1783–1860* (New York, 1919), pp. 178–81.

46. Duden refers to Georg Heinrich Engelhard, *Die Verfassungen der vereinigten Staaten Nordamerika's,* 2 vols. (Frankfurt am Main, 1834).

47. A tornado struck St. Louis during the evening of 26 June 1833. A description of the havoc appeared in the *Missouri Intelligencer,* 6 July 1833. Shelbyville was practically demolished by a severe storm in 1830. See Robert M. McBride and Owens Meredith, eds., *Eastin Morris' Tennessee Gazetteer 1834 and Matthew Rhea's Map of the State of Tennessee 1832* (Nashville, 1971), p. 251.

48. The editors have been unable to locate any information about a Monroe at Norfolk. Duden may have witnessed engineers studying at Fort Monroe at Elizabeth County, Virginia, and have mistaken the fort for a school.

49. Duden probably refers to a map by Samuel Augustus Mitchell (1792–1868), who prepared a number of atlases between 1839 and 1866. In 1834, the Philadelphia firm of Mitchell and Hinman published Mitchell's *Reference Map of the U.S.* See Ronald Vere Tooley, comp., *Tooley's Dictionary of Mapmakers* (Tring, Hertfordshire, Eng., 1979), pp. 441–42.

50. Stephen Girard (1750–1831), French-born merchant, financier, and philanthropist, who settled in Philadelphia during 1776. He made his fortune through foreign trade and real-estate investments. When no buyers offered to invest in the stock of the Second Bank of the United States (1816), Girard subscribed personally for the entire amount—$3 million. Girard served the city of Philadelphia in various capacities, and when he died in December 1831 he left $.5 million to the city, plus over $6 million in cash and real estate was placed in trust to the city for the education of poor white orphan boys. See William E. Lingelbach, "Girard, Stephen," in Malone and Johnson, eds., *Dictionary of American Biography,* 7:319–21.

51. Originally named New Port, later written as Newport, and now known as Dundee, a Franklin County river port community situated at the junction of the Buffalo River with the Missouri River.

52. In 1818 William and Lucinda Owens left Kentucky and settled in

Franklin County, Missouri. Owens, the first clerk of the county, settled in Newport and then purchased the land upon which the original town of Washington was founded. He apparently planned to plat the town lots, but he was killed in a duel on 16 November 1834. The town was laid out on the property still owned by Mrs. Owens on 29 May 1839. Washington eventually included within its boundaries another community, Bassora, which had been platted by Polish immigrants in 1836. See Ramsay Place Names File, 1928–1945, University of Missouri Western Historical Manuscripts Collection, Columbia.

53. A number of the people listed here by Duden are mentioned in William Bek's series, "The Followers of Duden," which appeared in the *Missouri Historical Review* (1919–1925). Those mentioned include the von Martels, Hospez, Mallinkrodt, Huttawas, and Schulz brothers; Kunze; Goltermann; Blümner; Spankenen; Angelrodt; and Father Rasmus. See note 9 to the Editors' Introduction for the full citation of Bek's work. While some of these Germans purchased land from individuals, a number also purchased government land. Thus, information about Friedrich Kayser, Augustus Blümner, Frederick Rathje, Ernest Goltermann, Louis Schulz, and Conrad and Louis Hospez appears in the second volume of the *Record of U.S. Land Sales,* Records Management and Archives Service, Office of the Secretary of the State of Missouri, Jefferson City. Also, some of the men are mentioned in a brief section on German immigration in *History of St. Charles, . . .,* pp. 103–7.

54. Sir Edward Pakenham, brother-in-law of the Duke of Wellington, commanded the expeditionary British forces that were beaten decisively on 8 January 1815. Pakenham, as well as the majority of his officers, was killed in the Battle of New Orleans. The news of the Peace Treaty of Ghent, concluded 24 December 1814, had not reached the United States at the time of the battle.

55. Georges Cuvier, baron (1769–1832), French zoologist who established as sciences the fields of paleontology and comparative anatomy. For information on Blumenbach, see note 8 to the Fifteenth Letter.

56. The full title is P. Schori, *Das neueste aus dem Staate Ohio in Nord Amerika. Vollständiges Tagebuch einer Reise aus der Schweiz über Havre und New York, der Niederlassung im Stark Counti, Paris Township, im Staate Ohio. Mit vielen Bemerkungen, Rathen und Wünschen für dahin Auswandernde, und einem Hinblick auf Auswanderungen nach dem Staate Missouri* (Bern, Chur, and Leipzig, 1834).

57. This probably refers to Gustav Löwig's *Die Freistaaten von Nord-Amerika: Beobuchtungen und praktische bemerkungon für auswandernde Deutsche* (Heidelberg and Leipzig, 1833).

Index

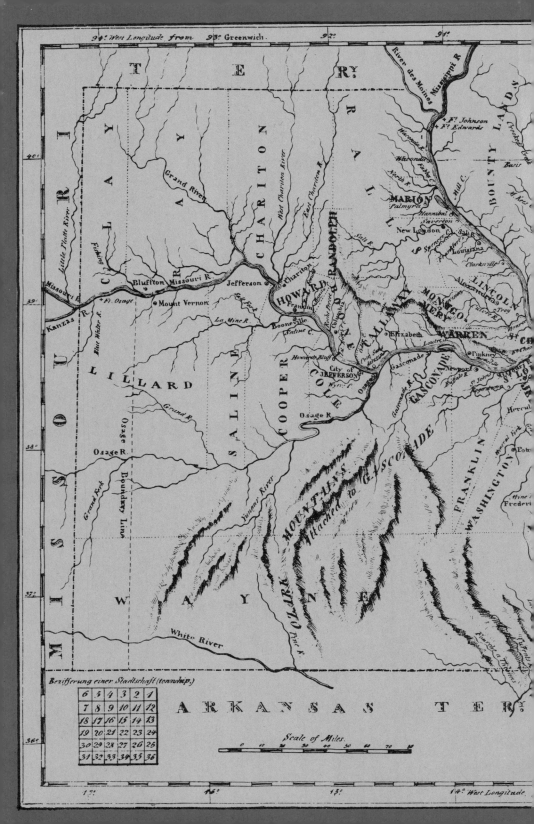